LOOKING AT

MAGAZINE

Edited by Erika Doss

SMITHSONIAN INSTITUTION PRESS
WASHINGTON AND LONDON

Copy editor: Robert A. Poarch
Designer: Amber Frid-Jimenez

Library of Congress Cataloging-in-Publication Data
Looking at *Life* magazine / edited by Erika Doss.
         p.   cm.
   Includes bibliographical references and index.
   ISBN 1-56098-989-0 (alk. paper)
   1. *Life* (Chicago, Ill.).   I. Doss, Erika Lee.   II. *Life*
(Chicago, Ill.).
   PN4900.L55 L55 2001
   051—dc21   2001017006

British Library Cataloguing-in-Publication Data
is available

Manufactured in the United States of America
08 07 06 05 04 03 02 01   5 4 3 2 1

♾ The paper used in this publication meets the minimum requirements of the American National Standard
for Information Sciences—Permanence of Paper for
Printed Library Materials ANSI Z39.48-1984.

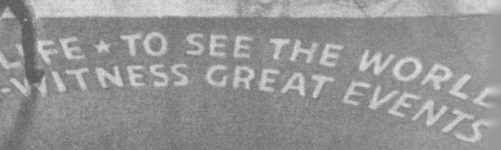

To see life; to see the world; to eyewitness great events; to watch the faces of the poor and the gestures of the proud; to see strange things—machines, armies, multitudes, shadows in the jungle and on the moon; to see man's work—his paintings, towers, and discoveries; to see things thousands of miles away, things hidden behind walls and within rooms, things dangerous to come to; the women that men love and many children; to see and to take pleasure in seeing; to see and be amazed; to see and be instructed; thus to see, and to be shown, is now the will and new expectancy of half mankind.

—Henry Luce, prospectus for *Life,* 1936

CONTENTS

ILLUSTRATIONS

ACKNOWLEDGMENTS

In editing a collection of essays stemming from a national conference, I have many thanks to make to the many individuals and institutions who have helped bring about this project.

This book got its start at the conference "Looking at *Life:* Rethinking America's Favorite Magazine, 1936–1972," held at the University of Colorado, Boulder, September 14–17, 1995. This was the first conference to center specifically on how *Life* magazine, perhaps the single most important general weekly magazine from the late 1930s until its demise in the early 1970s, shaped and influenced ideas about class, ethnicity, gender, and race in America, and throughout the world. A number of terrific scholars participated in our four-day conversation about the magazine, many of whom are included as authors in the following pages, and I thank all of you for your enthusiasm and goodwill. I would also like to thank former *Life* editor Richard Stolley for the important insights he provided during a panel discussion on the magazine, and photographer Gordon Parks for his wonderfully engaging keynote address. Thanks are further extended to Bobbi Baker Burrows and others at *Life* and Time, Inc., for helping make "Looking at *Life*" such as success.

"Looking at *Life*" was accompanied by the exhibition "Country Doctor: *Life* Magazine and Kremmling,

Colorado." Featuring photographs by *Life* photographer W. Eugene Smith of general practitioner Ernest Ceriani in 1948, the exhibit explained how this assignment produced one of the magazine's most memorable photo-essays. Thanks to Paige Turner for organizing this wonderful show. Thanks also to Karen Ripley, Donna Gartenmann, and the Boulder Public Library for hosting the exhibition and a stimulating panel discussion on the "Country Doctor" photo-essay that included members of the Ceriani family and residents of Kremmling.

Hosted by the American Studies Program at the University of Colorado, the "Looking at *Life*" conference was sponsored through generous donations from the Colorado Endowment for the Humanities, the Boulder Arts Commission, and the following University of Colorado offices and organizations: Department of Fine Arts, School of Journalism and Mass Communication, Office of the President, Office of the Chancellor, Office of the Dean of the College of Arts and Sciences, Committee for Research and Creative Work, Graduate Committee on the Arts and Humanities, Implementation of Multicultural Perspectives and Approaches in Research and Teaching, Outreach Council, President's Fund for the Humanities, and the Cultural Events Board of the University of Colorado Student Union.

I would especially like to thank John Buechner, former president of the University of Colorado, and professors Robert Pois, Jim Palmer, and Tom Lyons, and the University of Colorado Eugene M. Kayden Fund for generously helping with funding to make this book possible.

Throughout this project I have benefited from the advice and constructive criticism of many, many people including, especially, Wendy Kozol and Lary May. I would also like to acknowledge the research assistance of Dinah Zeiger, Greg Adams, Joseph Kretteck, Krista White, and Leslie Umberger—thanks to all of you!

Thanks as well to Mark Hirsch at Smithsonian Institution Press for jumping into and staying with this project, and helping to make it a much better product.

Finally, along with all the authors of this volume, we offer this collection in memory of Roland Marchand, a wonderful professor of history at the University of California, Davis, who is sorely missed. Roland's talk at the "Looking at *Life*" conference was among the highlights of our engaging four-day debate about the magazine, and we dedicate this book to him.

ERIKA DOSS

INTRODUCTION

Looking at Life: *Rethinking America's Favorite Magazine, 1936–1972*

In the December 29, 1972, issue of *Life*, the last weekly edition of the magazine, managing editor Ralph Graves printed this letter from eleven-year-old Marta Flanagan of Little Neck, New York: "Dear Sirs: I have adored your magazine for two years. It has always been my favorite magazine. It has articles which interest everybody in the family. Right now I am making a scrapbook of all *Life* Magazine articles which were my favorites. I am making it because then my children will know about my childhood. P.S. I hope *Life* Magazine is still around until I die." Marta Flanagan was not alone in hoping the magazine would endure. In 1970 *Life* was America's "favorite magazine" with over 8 million subscribers. With an estimated "passalong" rate of four to five people per copy, each issue reached as many as 40 million people.[1] Even in late 1972 the magazine was still being perused by millions of people. *Looking at* Life *Magazine* considers how this popular picture magazine caught the public eye, what it meant to its millions of readers, and why, in December 1972, the weekly *Life* came to an end.

In 1936 Henry Robinson Luce, head of the Time, Inc., mass media empire, which already included the weekly news magazine *Time* (started in 1923), the business monthly *Fortune* (first published in 1930), and the radio program and newsreel *The March of Time* (begun in 1931), jotted down his ideas for a new picture magazine:

> To see life; to see the world; to eyewitness great events; to watch the faces of the poor and the gestures of the proud; to see strange things—machines, armies, multitudes, shadows in the jungle and on the moon; to see man's work—his paintings, towers, and discoveries; to see things thousands of miles away, things hidden behind walls and within rooms, things dangerous to come to; the women that men love and many children; to see and to take pleasure in seeing; to see and be amazed; to see and be instructed.
>
> Thus to see, and to be shown, is now the will and new expectancy of half mankind.
>
> To see, and to show, is the mission now undertaken by a new kind of publication, The Show-Book of the World, hereinafter described.

Luce's blueprint for this "new kind" of weekly magazine first took shape as a prospectus sent to investors for the costly venture (estimated startup was around $3 million). He promised to "edit pictures into a coherent story—to make an effective mosaic out of the fragmentary documents which pictures, past and present, are." Moreover, Luce imagined this pictorial project on grandiose terms, writing confidently: "A hundred years from now the historian should be able to rely largely on our Picture Magazine instead of having to fumble through dozens of newspapers and magazines."[2]

Out of that ambitious, even arrogant, editorial vision, *Life* was born on November 23, 1936. Its name came only after a number of others were rejected (including *Candid, Dime, Eye, Nuze-Vuze, Promenade, Rehearsal,* and *The Show-Book of the World*), and Luce paid $92,000 for the rights to a failed humor magazine called *Life*.[3] Thirty-six years later, for 1,864 consecutive issues, Luce's *Life* crafted a "coherent story" and particular historical vision that entertained, informed, and influenced millions. Recognition of the terms and consequences of *Life*'s visuality, of how its look was created (and by whom), and what it meant to those who looked

at it sheds light on the magazine's pictorial mission, and, by extension, on *Life*'s weekly imaging of American society, culture, and politics from the Great Depression to the Vietnam War.

Life's beginnings, along with its wildly popular but financially devastating first years, have become the stuff of mass media legend. From the start, with its first cover featuring a photograph by Margaret Bourke-White of an earthen dam under construction in Fort Peck, Montana (Figure I.1), and its first editorial accompanied by a photo of a newborn child, *Life* was a publishing industry hit. Initially, circulation outran revenue: a first run of 466,000 copies nearly killed it, since advertising rates had been set at 250,000. By the end of the first year of publication, Time, Inc., had lost $3 million on *Life*. But by 1939, with a circulation of more than 2 million (and ad rates substantially raised), *Life* had become one of the most widely consumed magazines in America (and Luce's company began to see its first profits from the picture magazine). In the late 1940s *Life* reached "21 percent

NOVEMBER 23, 1936 10 CENTS

Opposite: **Figure I.1.** *Life,* **Issue No. 1, November 23, 1936. (Courtesy Margaret Bourke-White/TimePix)** *Above:* **Figure I.2.** *Omaha Newsstand* **by John Vachon. (Courtesy Library of Congress)**

of the entire population over ten years old" (around 22.5 million people) and took in 19 percent of every magazine advertising dollar in the country. In 1960, despite the growing competition of television, *Life* sustained a circulation of around six million.[4]

Preceded by the French *Vu,* the German *Berliner Illustrierte Zeitung,* the British *Weekly Illustrated,* and American publications including *National Geographic, Vanity Fair,* and *Mid-Week Pictorial,* and followed by *Look, Ebony, Photo-History, Picture Post, See, Photo, Picture, Focus, Pic,* and *Click, Life* was hardly the first or the only picture magazine in the world—as John Vachon's 1938 photograph of an Omaha newsstand makes clear (Figure I.2). Nor did it always have the highest paid circulation. It was surpassed in the 1940s by competing

weeklies such as *Collier's, Liberty,* and the *Saturday Evening Post;* and it was swept during the postwar era by more specialized magazines like *Reader's Digest* and *TV Guide.* What *Life* did have was iconic presence and cultural prestige. Abstract expressionist artist Jackson Pollock hoarded copies of *Life*'s August 8, 1949, issue, his first appearance in the magazine, "and made sure that everyone saw it."[5]

Getting on the cover of *Life* was considered the pinnacle of postwar success for everyone from the Hollywood stars who craved it to the authors who mocked it. In his screenplay for *A Face in the Crowd* (1957), Budd Schulberg cynically described *Life*'s career-enhancing importance for an obnoxious singer named Lonesome Rhodes: "Lonesome Rhodes could be made into an influence, a wielder of opinion, an institution positively sacred to this country, like the Washington Monument. . . . My study of history has convinced me that in every strong and healthy society from the Egyptians to our own, the mass had to be guided with a strong hand by a responsible elite . . . to begin with, let's try to get him a cover on *Life*. Remind me to call Henry for lunch. . . ."[6]

Life's iconic authority was referenced in any number of postwar movies, and Luce's entire mass media empire was modeled in films such as *Gentleman's Agreement* (1947) and *The Big Clock* (1948). If success is measured in terms of desire, derision, and imitation, *Life* was certainly successful.

Some of the magazine's immediate success hinged on its timing. *Life*'s birth coincided with a number of important technological breakthroughs in the 1930s, including the invention of small, portable, handheld cameras (like the German Leica), new kinds of film stock, and mass color printing. *Life* also took complete advantage of modern pictorial directions in graphics, montage, and layout. The magazine's canny use of the photo-essay and high-quality picture reproduction clearly contributed to its popularity. Even more directly, *Life* catered to what American audiences especially wanted in a modern magazine: lots of pictures. If, as historian Neil Harris suggests, the twentieth century—what Luce called "The American Century"— could be especially characterized as a "visual age," *Life* played a major role in representing and disseminating information and ideas, and shaping their meaning to an ever increasing body of consumers fluent in the language of pictorial communication.[7]

A picture magazine with far-reaching authority, *Life* was also a veritable picture warehouse, its editors amassing hundreds of thousands of photographs annually (printing around 200 an issue) and an archive of around 3.5 million images by 1953.[8] Photographer Edward Steichen culled *Life*'s collection for the pictures displayed in "The Family of Man" exhibition, which opened at the Museum of Modern Art in 1955 and traveled to over thirty-eight countries (including Guatemala, India, and Russia). The paperback from the exhibition is still in print today, having sold over 4 million copies. It was the most popular show of photography in the twentieth century.[9] It could be argued that "The Family of Man" was simply a reified version of *Life:* the pictures that were the heart of the weekly magazine were transformed into art in the context of a museum exhibition. Certainly, the exhibition's astounding popularity stemmed at least in part from the culture of visuality shaped by *Life*.

For all its iconicity and influence, *Life* has been surprisingly unstudied, especially from its context as a popular weekly picture magazine and visual resource. Its history has mostly been in-house, such as Time, Inc.'s, noncritical and generally celebratory coffee-table compilations of *Life*'s "best" pictures and photo-essays. Or the studies selectively focused on the magazine's personalities: Luce, staff members, and its star photographers.[10]

Looking at *Life* made strong impressions, as the authors of *Talking Pictures* (1994) discovered when they asked a variety of people what photographs "spoke" to them. More than a few chose pictures from *Life*. Writer John Updike vividly recalled a picture of a "dancing Wahine" in *Life*'s March 23, 1959, story on Hawaii gaining U.S. statehood. "What I above all remembered," he remarked, "was the ambiguous vehemence of her face and body in their arrested motion." Singer (and painter) Tony Bennett explained that he "never forgot" *Life*'s January 30, 1950, photo-essay on Pablo Picasso: "The reason I've always been affected by it is because everyone puts down modern art. They say, 'These guys can't paint.' But if you show them this picture, they'd see Picasso did this wonderful sketch of a bull in a second. That quick. They couldn't stop him."[11]

Looking at *Life* even changed the lives of some. Anita Roddick, for example, founder of the Body Shop, recalled feeling a profound sense of "responsibility for the humanness of the world and for the future" upon viewing W. Eugene Smith's powerful 1971 photographs of Japanese villagers maimed from mercury poisoning. Like many, photographer Todd Walker credited the

COUNTRY DOCTOR

THROUGH WEEDS GROWING RANK IN AN UNKEMPT DOORYARD, DR. ERNEST CERIANI OF KREMMLING MAKES HIS WAY TO CALL ON A PATIENT

HIS ENDLESS WORK HAS ITS OWN REWARDS

PHOTOGRAPHS FOR LIFE BY W. EUGENE SMITH

The town of Kremmling, Colo., 115 miles west of Denver, contains 1,000 people. The surrounding area of some 400 square miles, filled with ranches which extend high into the Rocky Mountains, contains 1,000 more. These 2,000 souls are constantly falling ill, recovering or dying, having children, being kicked by horses and cutting themselves on broken bottles. A single country doctor, known in the profession as a "g.p.," or general practitioner, takes care of them all. His name is Ernest Guy Ceriani.

Dr. Ceriani begins to work soon after 8 o'clock and often continues far into the night. He serves as physician, surgeon, obstetrician, pediatrician, psychiatrist, dentist, oculist and laboratory technician. Like most rural g.p.s he has no vacations and few days off, although unlike them he

has a small hospital in which to work. Whenever he has a spare hour he spends it uneasily, worrying about a particular patient or regretting that he cannot study all of the medical journals which pour into his office. Although he is only 32 he is already slightly stooped, leaning forward as he hurries from place to place as though heading into a strong wind. His income for covering a dozen fields is less than a city doctor makes by specializing in only one. But Ceriani is compensated by the affection of his patients and neighbors, by the high place he has earned in his community and by the fact that he is his own boss. For him this is enough. The fate of thousands of communities like Kremmling, in dire need of "country doctors," depends on whether the nation's 22,000 medical students, now choosing between specialization and general practice, also think it is enough.

CONTINUED ON NEXT PAGE 115

Figure I.3. "Country Doctor," *Life,* September 20, 1948. (Courtesy W. Eugene Smith/TimePix)

magazine with shaping his career. "I can remember the first day *Life* magazine came out," he said in 1978. "I was working at RKO studios in the paint shop. I went in and everybody was huddled around a table. There were forty people looking at the magazine as somebody turned the pages. It was that much of an innovation. *Life* magazine was part of what further sparked my interest in photography."[12]

Still, *Life* magazine was never America's only common visual denominator, nor its most popular form of mass media. Radio, movies, and television each had much larger and more diverse audience shares. Other mass-circulation weeklies, including *Look* and the *Saturday Evening Post,* as well as more specialized magazines such as *Playboy* (started in 1953) and *Sports Illustrated* (launched by Time, Inc., in 1954), were equally popular in a postwar America where generally higher levels of income and increased opportunities for leisure

Three dead Americans
on the beach at Buna

time allowed middle-class consumers to subscribe to multiple magazines—not just *Life*.

Nor did *Life*'s readers view it with any particular unanimity. This diversity of response became especially clear for me during a discussion of the magazine's September 20, 1948, "Country Doctor" photo-essay (Figure I.3). A perceptive story about Dr. Ernest Ceriani of Kremmling, Colorado, and the pressing needs of postwar health care, the piece featured images by W. Eugene Smith and is considered by some to be the best photo-essay the magazine ever published. In 1995 an exhibition was mounted at the Boulder Public Library of photographs taken by Smith during this *Life* assignment. At a panel discussion following the opening, members of the Ceriani family, residents of Kremmling, historians attending the conference "Looking at *Life*" at the University of Colorado, former *Life* staffers, and others reflected on what Smith's pictures and *Life*'s photo-essay meant to them. Their responses were stunningly diverse. Gary Ceriani recalled the symbolic resonance of *Life*'s article for his father's medical practice and his entire family. Long-time Kremmling residents fondly remembered the article "saying something good about small-town America" and strongly disagreed with scholarly interpretations that cast *Life* and Smith in more critical light.[13] No one looked at *Life*—or at least at this particular photo-essay—with any accord, suggesting that single-minded or monolithic interpretations of the magazine and its meanings are open to challenge.

Dissimilar reactions to the magazine's extensive war coverage offer further indications of its multivalent look and interpretation. In 1995 longtime *Life* subscriber Frederick Ivor-Campbell of Warren, Rhode Island, remarked that his "lifelong abhorrence of cruelty and violence" was "anchored" in his "early exposure" to photographs of the Bataan Death March that he remembered seeing in *Life* fifty years earlier. Gordon Liddy, on the other hand, attributed *Life*'s full-page photo of three dead American soldiers on the beach at Buna, New Guinea (Figure I.4), which was printed in the magazine in September 1943, with hardening the wartime "resolve of the American people."[14]

Reactions were similarly mixed among the 1,300 letters *Life* received following its June 27, 1969, cover article, "The Faces of the American Dead in Vietnam: One Week's Toll," which consisted of row upon row of black-and-white snapshots of the 217 U.S. soldiers who had died "in connection with the conflict in Vietnam" in a single week (see Figure 13.4). Recognizing that the feature signaled *Life*'s growing doubts about Vietnam and American military involvement in the war, Harry Drucker of Hunt, Texas, accused the magazine of "supporting the antiwar demonstrators who are traitors to this country." But Mrs. David Rosenblatt of Hartsdale, New York, wrote that copies of the issue "should be plastered all over this country, on every billboard, telephone pole, store front and even American flagpoles. Wherever people go, particularly congressmen, they should be engulfed with this sea of faces." Tony Cook of San Bernadino, California, said he had been "an adamant hawk" but *Life*'s "article is causing an agonizing 180 degree change of attitude." And Stanley Miller of Miami Beach, Florida, remarked, "Every once in a while there comes a particular photograph that emphasizes an era of man's history. One, a picture of a severely burned Chinese baby during the Japanese raids on Shanghai in 1935 [*sic*]; another, Negro demonstrators being sprayed by water hoses in Birmingham in 1963. The June 27 issue of *Life* has printed 217 such pictures."[15]

Life's hybridity certainly contributed to both its diversity of interpretation and its diverse popularity; indeed, these sorts of multiple responses are directly related to the inherent "flexibility of the magazine format." As art historian Sally Stein notes, mainstream magazines are not read—or looked at—like books, in some "straight, linear process."[16] Rather, we tend to "flip" through popular general magazines, looking at

Figure I.4. "Three Americans,"
***Life*, September 20, 1943.**
(Courtesy George Strock/TimePix)

them in bits and pieces, backward and forward, alternately grabbed and interrupted by their contents. Often we glance at them quickly, in supermarket checkout lines, in bed, on the beach, on the bus; usually, we throw them away when we are done with them and their relevance seems to have passed. This impermanence does not, of course, diminish the import of images seen quickly, because even momentary glimpses can generate lasting memories. Our fragmented readings and responses parallel the ways in which popular magazines are themselves often organized as jumbled assemblages of images, texts, features, and advertisements whose miscellaneous graphics, words, and intended effects are intermingled and often intentionally inseparable.

Life's August 27, 1956, issue was a typical, amorphous 136-page cultural artifact that announced itself with a color cover photograph of Adlai Stevenson and Eleanor Roosevelt at that year's Democratic Party National Convention in Chicago and closed with a back-cover advertisement for Lucky Strike cigarettes (Figure I.5).[17] Inside, the 20-cent magazine featured photo-essays on harness racing and Elvis Presley, pictures from Marilyn Monroe's new movie *Bus Stop,* a long article on global warming and dramatic changes in world weather, a "Publisher's Preview" of *Life*'s forthcoming five-part series on segregation, and editorials on the 1956 election campaign. "*Life* Goes to a Party" focused on the weeklong Dublin Horse Show, while another regular weekly feature, "Speaking of Pictures," captured "the flight of bullets" aimed "head on" at the camera. The magazine's general coverage included an international conference on the Suez Canal, Jackson Pollock's death, rock climbing in Wyoming, fall fashions, and a whistling contest in Richland, Kansas. The issue also contained sixteen letters to the editor and sixty-three full-page advertisements (and many smaller ads) for items ranging from Keepsake diamond rings, Wilson canned hams, Campbell soups, Gleem toothpaste, and Gilbey's vodka to the "big-car beauty" of an Oldsmobile 88.

Considered as a whole, this particular issue is visually dynamic and loud: its slick cover a commanding blend of newsworthy subjects and *Life*'s iconic red-and-white logo; its articles and ads full of arresting images of contemporary personalities and middle-class consumer products; its pages a compelling mix of mostly black-and-white articles and surprisingly vivid color advertisements. This juxtaposition of "instructive" articles and photo-essays in monochrome hues and "pleasurable" advertisements in color gave the magazine a certain rhythm and flow, and guided readers between what to think about (politics, Elvis, the Suez Canal) and what to buy (rings, hams, soups, cars).[18]

It also relieved anxieties regarding *Life*'s overt educational imperative ("to see and be instructed"). The sheer pleasure of the magazine's oversized physical bulk, brilliant red banner, and perky color ads assuaged such concerns and redirected readers toward the immediacy of visual entertainment and the promises of consumerism. It is unclear exactly how much sway advertising agencies actually had in terms of product placement in magazines like *Life.* Still, former *Life* staffer Richard Stolley recalled that Campbell Soup Company ads were "guaranteed" the "key position next

ADLAI'S NEW PARTY

HARRY'S NEW-OLD PLATFORM

How "eating with the eye" seems to make food taste better
...the story behind Campbell Color

Campbell's

Soups • Tomato Juice • Pork & Beans
V-8 Cocktail Vegetable Juices
Franco-American Products
Swanson Products

FRENCH'S MUSTARD
does something wonderful for Hot Dogs!

Double-Creamed for richer flavor

FRENCH'S
MUSTARD

Elvis—a Different Kind of Idol

PRESLEY'S IMPACT PILES UP FANS, FADS—AND FEARS

Opposite: Figure I.5. "Adlai Stevenson and Mrs. Roosevelt," *Life*, August 27, 1956 (Photograph by Cornell Capa). (Courtesy Magnum) *Top:* Figure I.6. "Adlai's New Party," "Harry's New-Old Platform," and advertisement for Campbell's soup, *Life*, August 27, 1956. (Courtesy Campbell Soup Company) *Above:* Figure I.7. Advertisement for French's mustard and "Elvis—A Different Kind of Idol," *Life*, August 27, 1956. (Courtesy French's and Don Wright)

to *Life*'s editorial page," which is substantiated in this particular 1956 issue (Figure I.6).[17] And the magazine's juxtaposition in this same issue of a full-page color ad featuring "juicy hot dogs" (an ad for French's mustard) with a photo of Elvis Presley "beset by teen-age girls" also seems to hint at some sort of editorial intent (Figure I.7).

This intermingling of articles and ads typified *Life*'s look, and much of the rest of modern mass media, where supposedly separate categories of editorial and commercial distinction were, in fact, often indistinguishable. Aimed at fusing art and life, culture and experience, much of twentieth-century American modernism challenged and attempted to transcend those premodern hierarchical modes that emphasized disjunction and separation. *Life* was a major part of an admittedly paradoxical mainstream modernist aesthetic, blending its pictures, editorials, articles, and ads in a decidedly contemporary graphics style that emphasized dynamism and flux and yet also, ironically, aimed at social and cultural cohesion and unity. Particularly in the postwar period, *Life*'s style of "corporate modernism" aimed at a synthesis of seeing with belief, combining visuality with consumerism and nationalism, and attempting to diffuse, or efface, the tensions of class, race, and social conflict in America.[20]

Life's structuring of visual experience was understood by Luce and others at the magazine to be "a new language, difficult, as yet unmastered, but incredibly powerful." This emphasis on the potential mastery of powerful images that might enlighten and "instruct" suggests Luce's overall agenda as captain of American mass media. As he wrote in a first draft of his *Life* prospectus, "We have got to educate people to take pictures seriously, and to respect pictures as they do not now do. . . . While people love pictures, they do not respect them." Luce understood pictures as a "common denominator with low-brows." If appropriately viewed and properly mastered, visual images could shape and direct popular opinion—or the opinions that Luce and fellow *Life* staffers most wanted to be popular. As picture editor Wilson Hicks observed in the early 1950s, *Life*'s pictures conveyed "the body of beliefs and convictions upon which the magazine was founded": "*Life* looked at what people thought and did in a particular way. It stood for certain things, it entered at once the world-wide battle for men's minds. As a result, both word and picture took on extra meaning and vitality. If a picture was alive when it left a photographer's hands because of something he had put into it, it became still more alive for what it was to say as social, political or cultural report and commentary."[21]

The "certain things" that *Life* "stood for" were nationalism, capitalism, and classlessness, a sense of confidence, optimism, and exceptionalism, and the sure belief that the American way was the way of the world. As Luce announced in his February 17, 1941, "American Century" essay, arguably one of the most important declarations of national purpose and identity disseminated in the twentieth century, "We have some things in this country which are infinitely precious and especially American—a love of freedom, a feeling for the equality of opportunity, a tradition of self-reliance and independence and also of co-operation. . . . It now becomes our time to be the powerhouse from which the[se] ideals spread throughout the world."[22] Recognizing the vast appeal of visual culture, most acutely demonstrated by the millions of Americans who, even at the height of the Great Depression, went to the movies each week, Luce and *Life*'s editors seized on pictures as the ideal modern means to influence "men's minds." As James Baughman reflects in this volume (see Chapter 2), the photograph of sexy starlet Cobina Wright on *Life*'s cover during the week the "American Century" essay was published, as well as the pictures in that week's "*Life* Goes to a Party" feature on a Hollywood costume ball, probably captured more of *Life*'s audience than Luce's verbiage about American globalism.

Life's editors tended to view pictures, and the "new language" of photography in particular, in one-dimensional terms. Images were judged as simple (although compelling) and unproblematic didactic tools whose seemingly straightforward communicability might, as Richard Bolton wrote, "serve democracy, helping to construct a modernist *polis* by providing a means of speech accessible to a wide number of participants." By extension, *Life*'s editors understood pictures as an indispensable "means of social control" and recognized the camera's "capabilities for documentation and surveillance" as a primary instrument in their mass media construction of a stable and "regulated" modern middle-class America. "It was the points pictures made," reflected Hicks, "not pictures altogether as pictures, with which they were to put a magazine together."[23]

Pictures, in particular, could make the American "points" that Luce had emphasized in 1941: "freedom,"

Figure I.9. "A *Life* Round Table on Modern Art," *Life,* October 11, 1948. (Courtesy Leonard McCombe/TimePix)

"equality of opportunity," "self-reliance," and "cooperation." Pictures posited the seamless and integrated, independent and yet united American middle class that Luce and *Life*'s editors imagined, solving the problems of inequity, poverty, racism, and alienation by simply imaging a better country and a better world (Figure I.8). The magazine's failure to critically reckon with the complex historical tensions of race, gender, and class in America, or more particularly, with the nation's abiding patterns of systemic or institutional racism and class preference, would have enduring effects. *Life*'s reliance on pictures as simple instruments of liberal reform was fraught with complications, as was the magazine's overall embrace of the integrative mode of mainstream modernism. The fact that such integration was perhaps unattainable—because flux and uncertainty, rather than stability and resolution, were the key components in an open-ended, continuous, and dynamic modern America that focused on *becoming* rather than *being*—made *Life*'s entire pictorial project of modernist unity and assimilation all the more unsteady.

Despite such contradictions, *Life*'s vision of pictorial influence and its own sense of authority most clearly emerged during World War II. After fumbling through its first few years with the pragmatic concerns of cost overruns and advertising rates, the magazine realized that the war provided an ideal opportunity to clarify and expand its mission. Visual censorship marked the first few years of the war: unsure of the outcome and quite sure of the power of pictures in terms of directing popular opinion, the U.S. War Department waited until mid-1943, when Allied victory seemed imminent, to reverse its policy of pictorial suppression. *Life*'s first "real" wartime photograph was the picture Gordon Liddy remembered of American corpses on Buna Beach, an image captured by *Life* photographer George Strock in February 1943 but not published until eight months later.[24]

Life dispatched twenty-one photographers to various combat zones, charging them not only with documenting the war but justifying it in terms of common purpose and just cause. Eager to claim pictures as more than mere news, and to represent themselves as more than mere journalists, most *Life* photographers were drawn to this mandate. Carl Mydans, for one, described his extensive documentation of the war as "an historic record of a period of our times." While other *Life* photographers, including Edward Steichen and W. Eugene Smith, aimed for wartime images with more of a sense of moral outrage about epidemic human violence, they shared a conviction in the deeper symbolic authority of photography—and, importantly, in their own personal command of that symbol making.[25] After the war, they transferred their confident notions of pictorial meaning, mastery, and mission to the American scene, where their photographs came to embody *Life*'s vision of the nation, the world, and, especially, middle-class American society.

In the late 1940s *Life* sponsored a series of four roundtable discussions that engaged distinguished American historians, authors, artists, museum directors, business leaders, union officials, politicians, and others in two-day conversations about such postwar concerns as "The Pursuit of Happiness," "Modern Art," "Housing," and "Movies." Modeled on the Great Books discussions at Columbia University and the University of Chicago in the 1920s, the seminars organized by Walter Paepcke at the Aspen Institute after World War II, and the good-taste ethos of the Book-of-the-Month Club (founded in 1926), *Life*'s roundtables and subsequent magazine articles were similarly predicated on cultural consensus. More specifically, they focused on appropriate modes of culture for middle-class Americans. Aspects of American identity found in the third "inalienable" right of the Declaration of Independence, in modern art, in home ownership, and in leisure were discussed and debated, with each panel of experts concluding that postwar Americans must learn to "contain" these traits and sensibilities "within the boundaries of edification, moral rectitude, and community responsibility."[26] If the postwar nation was to become the global "powerhouse" Luce had prophesied in his "American Century" essay, its citizens needed to be directed and unified in common causes.

Modern abstract art, and in particular the postwar styles pioneered by various American abstract expressionists, was chief among the visual tools on which *Life* relied to shape that citizenry (Figure I.9). The magazine frequently featured narrative styles of American painting prior to and during World War II, including art by regionalists such as Grant Wood and Thomas Hart Benton, and representational works by artists ranging from Georgia O'Keeffe to Horace Pippin. After the war, however, *Life,* like other cultural institutions, tended to view abstract art as the exemplar of the much-touted American virtues of individuality and freedom. *Life*'s praise for abstract art was always pitted, of course, against "the rigidly realistic style that the Soviet government" had "imposed" on its artists; thus was American abstract art celebrated (and neutralized) on sociopolitical grounds, not for its implicit questioning of Cold War culture but for its apparent triumph over communism (supposedly seen in the freedom of its brush strokes and the individualist focus of its subjects). And while *Life* often described abstract art in sardonic terms, referring to Pollock's painting as "dribbling" and as "a source of bafflement and irritation," it consistently hailed it as a "no-holds-barred art of originality, energy, and freedom."[27] Modern abstract art, in other words, was an ideal cultural symbol of the American way of life that *Life* aimed to shape and direct during the postwar era.

Each week, *Life* presented itself to its mainly middle-class readership as the visual theater of postwar national identity. Much of that presentation was directed by Luce himself, who grew up isolated from America until adolescence (his parents were American Presbyterian missionaries in China), and manifested an idealized set of assumptions about national character and purpose. Much of *Life* mirrors Luce's self-confidence and values—values shaped from his religious upbringing, his Yale education, and his upper-middle-class conventions and connections. It also mirrors the "professional-managerial class" of other *Life* staffers, many of whom came from similar cultural and social backgrounds.[28] John Shaw Billings, for example, *Life*'s first managing editor, was a graduate of Harvard, as was Roy Larsen, *Life*'s publisher. Daniel Longwell, *Life*'s first picture editor and second managing editor, was a graduate of Columbia; Archibald MacLeish and Dwight Macdonald, both of whom wrote for *Fortune* and advised Luce and Longwell on *Life*'s initial look, also went to Yale. Together with Luce, these Ivy League–educated white males helped shape *Life*'s vision of a heterogeneous middle-class America, guiding "the mass," as Budd Schulberg satirically put it, "with a strong hand," and molding the magazine into a grand visual experiment where pictures were privileged.

The modern era's widespread sanctioning of visual culture astounded and outraged some. "The hideous wish for pictures," complained author William Dean Howells in 1914, was a potent threat to the supposed superiority of words. *Life*'s earliest critics were similarly fearful; convinced that texts were more "truthful" and "civilized" than pictures, they equated *Life*'s "vogue" for images and its "unprecedented popularity" with the decline of human progress. Accusing *Life* of being a "sensational" step even below tabloids, in 1938 the author of "Picture Magazines and Morons" wrote, for example, that "mankind is well on the way backward to a language of pictures." (He also declared *Look*, which began publication in January 1937, "a fitting title for a magazine aimed at a public afflicted with adult infantilism.") A decade later, Marshall McLuhan denounced *Life* as "nursery entertainment" for "homo boobiens." Its "pictures and ads," he wrote, "produce an aura of sentimental awe for the sub-rational reception of rapid-fire prose, so that the mental situation of the reader is very nearly as low as that of a news-reel audience." Its "penny-arcade vision" and "lethal" manipulation of "critical faculties," he grimly added, was a dangerous affront to "knowledge" and the course of postwar humanity: "Everybody talks about the return of *panem et circenses*. *Life* is just that. Technology and sex and blood. The yellow press has ratted. Instead of prodding the public to the barricades it sends it to the newsstands. By sending *Life* to a party each week the dream-fast readers are given a share in the exotic fooleries of their economic superiors. Thus does *Life* draw the teeth of democratic envy of the rich by representing the rich as unbelievably moronic."[29]

Critics were disgusted with how *Life*, like mass media in general, had seemingly turned its spotlight only on such subjects as crime, sex, and death, and, worse, had trivialized them as visual entertainment. Their evident hostility to the visual image, whether directed at movies (and later, television) or *Life* magazine, was rooted in older, premodern beliefs in the supremacy of the word and the conviction that advanced civilizations were marked by written language and literature. As iconophobia, their animosity stemmed in part from abiding Protestant suspicions of images as idols. Images were considered ephemeral and sentimental and entirely too much about pleasure; hence, looking at pictures—and, especially, the pictures in *Life*—was an irrational act that engaged only dangerously noncritical "faculties."

Such beliefs were grounded in a categorical separation of word and image, the sort of binary opposition that *Life* aimed to erase, or at least merge. It did so by generating a new "visual rhetoric," of which the magazine's photo-essays and its regular features such as "*Life* Goes to a Party" were prime examples. *Life*'s editors clearly recognized the emotional appeal of pictures. Perhaps more important, they understood that a primary characteristic of modernity was its emphasis on immediacy and felt experience. Yet they shared the same concerns as the magazine's critics and worried that the unregulated pursuit of those feelings and experiences could degenerate into social and cultural anarchy. Rather than suppressing images, however, fearing they might erode civilization, *Life*'s staffers aimed to manipulate them to "strengthen its moral core," much as American filmmakers and producers in the 1910s and 1920s strove to manipulate motion pictures to "teach powerful moral lessons."[30]

Life's critics were naive about modern visuality, or perhaps they were simply unwilling to accept how photo-vision had become the primary means by which twentieth-century Americans perceived the world. "Photographic production during the 1920s and 1930s," writes historian Eric Sandeen, "accustomed American readers to interpreting events through images." Even earlier, magazines such as *National Geographic* (started 1888) had encouraged readers to know (and own) the world as a monthly photo album. In the 1910s magazines like the *Ladies' Home Journal* (started 1883) increasingly came to rely on a modern graphics sensibility to deliver messages about gender and commerce. Beginning in 1935, the Farm Security Administration used documentary photographs to persuade Americans of the benefits of the New Deal.[31] By the time *Life* emerged in 1936, national and global "news" was fundamentally visual, a fact that Luce and *Life*'s editors (many of them trained at *Time*, "the weekly news-magazine") were eager to exploit.

There were, of course, multiple tensions in such a project, not the least of which was *Life*'s self-avowed arrogance about controlling the terms of modern visuality and directing the commerce of images. One of the most outrageous instances of this was *Life*'s purchase of Abraham Zapruder's twenty-six–second 8mm film footage of President John F. Kennedy's assassination on November 21, 1963—which "first found public exposure" in *Life* a week later. *Life* paid $150,000 for Zapruder's film. Its printed presence in the magazine gave it a "privileged position" in the long and convoluted history and analysis of JFK's murder; even today, the Zapruder film (recently released for public purchase) retains the sanctity of revelation and visual truth. Yet *Life*'s deliberate out-of-order printing of select frames from the film—done to maximize its most horrific visual moments, one assumes—considerably muddied the interpretations of the specifics of the president's death.[32] For some, the Zapruder film proved Oswald's

guilt as a single gunman; for others, it was incontestable evidence of multiple conspirators. For *Life*, it was a hot visual property.

Richard Stolley (the editor who worked the deal between *Life* and Zapruder) recalled that magazine staffers did little actual market analysis to test their assumptions about audience interests and *Life*'s impact: "We were too arrogant. We felt that we already knew what we were doing."[33] Yet *Life*'s elites were not always so sure of themselves. The magazine's first and last years show it at loose ends, and then finally unraveling, in its attempts to project a unified vision of the American way of life. *Life* was most successful in stabilizing mass media as a vehicle of mass instruction during World War II, and through the 1950s. But construction of a purposeful and united middle-class American nation depended upon shared assumptions regarding the value of such an enterprise not only among the magazine's readers but throughout the rest of the country. When such assumptions faltered, as they increasingly did in the 1960s, *Life* itself faltered.

Perhaps the most obvious tension that thwarted *Life*'s ambitions was the trust the magazine placed in the "legibility of photographs" and images in general. In order to shape how the world and the nation would be seen, and how an American middle class saw the world, the nation, and itself, *Life* tended to rely on a reassuring style of modern documentary photography that emphasized coherence and integration. Kurt Korff, a German refugee who had been an editor at *Berliner Illustrierte Zeitung*, was hired as a special consultant during *Life*'s start-up period in the mid-1930s and guided the magazine toward a "straight" style of photography that was both compelling and controlling.[34] The photographers he recommended, including Alfred Eisenstaedt, Margaret Bourke-White, and Peter Stackpole, were among *Life*'s first image makers, and their narrative styles largely shaped *Life*'s trademark photo-essays for over thirty years. Few of them experimented with avant-garde or oppositional styles of photography that emphasized disjuncture and fragmentation. Rather, they catered to modernist modes of representation that stressed continuity and cohesiveness, sameness and universality, and an engaged humanism—a pictorial look that corresponded to the ideological framework of *Life*'s editors. Most of *Life*'s photographers also tended to "hide" their cameras, mediating the experience of looking at pictures as a naturalized occurrence and consequently helping to define photo-vision as visual truth. *Life*'s pictorial style thus came to be grounded in assumptions of the apparent transparency of images and of their seemingly straightforward sensibility and simple didacticism.

The problem with such assumptions, of course, was how much they were at odds with the idiosyncratic complexity of modern visual culture. Photography, for example, may seem obvious and "real," yet its manipulation of light and chemicals and its language of framing and editing testify to its inherently constructed and multidimensional sensibilities. *Life*'s editors certainly knew this—as their manipulation of the Zapruder film suggests. Their own efforts notwithstanding, they tended to assume that the magazine's photographs could be quickly and easily understood, and that they demonstrated a single point of view. The diverse responses each week in the "Letters to the Editors" column should have persuaded them otherwise. The editors of *Life* recognized the pleasure of pictures—"people love pictures," Luce wrote—and also their instructive potential, but, they ignored their ambiguities and seemed unaware of the individual agency of its own readers.

The entire magazine was riddled with these sorts of contradictions. On the one hand, *Life* was a dynamic modernist hybrid of pictures, articles, and ads; on the other, it was an arrogant mass cultural institution that supposed it could not only direct the terms of modern visuality but also control them, thereby also directing and controlling its model of an American way of life. Failing to reckon with the flux and paradox of modernity and its inherently destabilizing sensibility, *Life* began to come apart even as it was at its strongest. In 1959, for example, the magazine published an ex-

tremely wordy piece titled "The Confused Image America Presents." In it, former *Time* editor Max Ways wrote, "Americans feel misunderstood by the rest of the world, but perhaps the fault is not the world's. Do we ourselves know what we are trying to do? Do we understand what we signify?" As the 1960s loomed, discussions of national "drift" were much in the air, and worries about national purpose and identity preoccupied presidential politics.[35] The fact that *Life*'s extraordinarily long essay was accompanied by only a few cartoons and a handful of tiny photos of world leaders suggests that America's "confused image" was not one that the magazine could visually imagine or easily represent. For once, pictures failed *Life*'s editorial aims.

The argument has been made that static print media could not compete with television. Yet, somehow *Life* remained an extraordinarily popular magazine for more than twenty years after TV was introduced to the middle-class masses in the late 1940s. More accurately, the end of *Life* as a weekly in 1972 rests with the growing fragmentation of mass media into niche markets, and, in particular, the abandonment of broad-based general magazines with mass circulation for narrower, more specialized products oriented to specific audiences.

The *Saturday Evening Post* collapsed in 1969. Following the mistaken economic logic that more subscribers generated more capital—when, in fact, maintaining huge circulations of such a cheap product (in 1972, a half-year subscription to *Life* cost only $3.87) meant a substantial loss of revenue—*Life* recklessly upped its circulation to 8.5 million by buying the *Post*'s subscriber list. *Look* was the next mass-circulation weekly to die, in 1971. In their stead, publishers pursued more tightly focused magazines for more narrowly defined audiences and more specifically targeted ads. Time, Inc., for example, branched out with *Money* (1972), *People* (1974), *Discover* (1980), and *TV-Cable Week* (1983). Ziff-Davis Publishing Company brought forth *Boating, Car and Driver, Popular Electronics,* and *Stereo Review.*[36] *Life*'s failure cannot be entirely pinned on competition from these niche market magazines, however, especially since American appetites for them had actually been whetted in the 1950s—when *Life* was at its strongest.

Perhaps *Life*'s demise may be more fully understood in terms of its own internal contradictions. If the magazine's pictures promised an ideal, autonomous middle-class America (in and of itself a problematic mission), its own institutional framework belied those images and that myth. Staff photographers felt particularly strong about this, many of them tormented by "the machinery controlling image production" of the magazine. Picture editor Wilson Hicks held the authoritative hand in *Life*'s pictorial aesthetic from 1937 to 1950; describing his role in the 1952 book *Words and Pictures: An Introduction to Photojournalism,* Hicks wrote, "Having determined the story he wishes to tell, the editor selects those pictures which relate themselves most readily and effectively to other pictures in developing the story's theme or advancing its action. . . . In addition to answering the question, *'Does the picture say what it is intended to say?'* the editor asks and answers another question, *'Does it say what I want it to say?'*"[37]

More than a few *Life* photographers chafed against this sort of institutional authority. Neither Dorothea Lange nor Ansel Adams, for example, who worked together in 1953 photographing small towns in Utah, were happy with *Life*'s subsequent photo- essay "Three Mormon Towns" (published in 1954). As Adams wrote to Lange: "The Mormon story turned out very sour indeed; a very inadequate presentation which did no good to the Mormons, to photography, and to either of us." W. Eugene Smith, who shot fifty assignments for *Life* from 1946 to 1952, also detested *Life*'s editorial manipulation of his visual material. Writing that he was "disturbed and fed up with assignments such as 'Sadie Hawkins Day' and the 'Butlers Ball,'" Smith eventually

resigned from the magazine. He joined former staff photographers Henri Cartier-Bresson, Robert Capa, and George Rodger, who, bitter about *Life*'s "lack of freedom and initiative," left the magazine to found the picture agency Magnum Photos in 1947.[38]

Life's photographers were not alone among staffers who, especially during the late 1960s and early 1970s, felt that the magazine's overarching institutional attitudes and behaviors were increasingly untenable.[39] When editors Hedley Donovan and Louis Banks endorsed a second term for President Richard Nixon in the pages of *Life* in October 1972, 100 of 145 staffers signed a petition of support for McGovern and insisted that *Life* print their endorsement in its next issue. Their request was denied, further indication of the internal divisiveness that shook *Life*—like other American institutions—during the era. In a sense their request did not need to be printed: it had already been visually endorsed in *Life*'s plentiful full-page color pictures of communal living, rock and roll, Woodstock, LSD trips, Haight Ashbury, the antiwar movement, feminism, and all sorts of other countercultural representations.

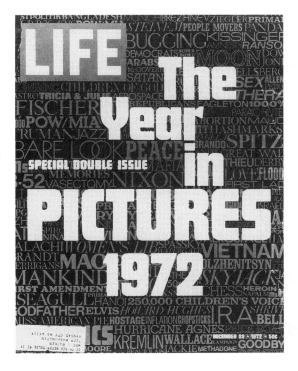

Figure I.10. "The Year in Pictures, 1972," *Life,* **December 29, 1972.**

(Courtesy Eugene Wright)

That *Life*'s management failed to recognize the authority of their own crafting of American visual culture is telling; that they assumed that their editorial positions—their words—were somehow more powerful than *Life*'s pictures reveals just how much they seemed to have abandoned, or simply forgotten, the magazine's inherently visual mission.

In the end, then, it was not just the heavy costs of an overextended circulation, declining income from mass advertising, or competition from television and specialized magazines that killed *Life*. Equally damaging were the magazine's own loss of faith in the power of pictures and its incapacity to recognize that pictures now represented and reaffirmed a decidedly different kind of America than the one originally envisioned by Henry Luce and other *Life* staffers in the mid-1930s. *Life* was always, of course, an elaborate fantasy: there never was an ideal American middle class, despite *Life*'s convincing visualization. But by staying committed to that imaginary vision, *Life* was stymied from committing to anything else or recognizing that the nation, as ever, had abandoned that particular picture and was now engaged in new images of national identity and purpose. Time, Inc., at least, seemed to recognize the futility of continuing with *Life*'s mission. After Luce died in 1967, the company began to seriously reconsider *Life*'s quest, and its value. Finally, in late December 1972, the decision was made to "suspend publication."[40]

As if in admission of its own loss of pictorial confidence, *Life*'s last weekly issue (which was a sellout, like the first issue thirty-six years earlier) featured a cover of just words—*Peace, Olympics, Sex, Jazz, Elvis, Democrats, Women's Lib,* etc.—and the final word, *Goodbye,* in the bottom right-hand corner (Figure I.10). Inside, however, were abundant photographs of Liz Taylor, Liza Minnelli, Bobby Fischer, Mark Spitz, and various other contemporary celebrities and personalities. It was, of course, a foreshadowing of *People,* which Time, Inc., introduced in 1974 as a pictorial product similar in look to *Life* but with no pretensions whatsoever regarding the shaping and direction, let alone the representation, of an ideal middle-class America.

Lately, *Life* has experienced renewed popularity, especially among baby boomers who collect issues of the magazine (priced at anywhere from $5 to $20 each) dating to the week they were born. It has made a cameo appearance in a number of recent movies, from *JFK* (1991) and *Forrest Gump* (1994) to *Toy Story 2* (1999); indeed, the magazine seems to have assumed a certain popular cultural cachet that quickly signals "history," especially post–World War II history, to contemporary movie audiences.

Yet such attentiveness suggests that *Life* is more than just a visual culture photo album of passé fashions and big family cars, of another era's stars, fads, and politics. Whatever nostalgia or fondness that Americans today have for *Life* is perhaps rooted in larger desires for some sort of mass-culture vehicle that speaks to, and for, all Americans—much as eleven-year-old Marta Flanagan praised *Life* for its "articles which interest everybody." Searching for visions of national collectivity, identity, and purpose in the twenty-first century, and looking backward at the previous century for examples and suggestions, we may imagine America's "favorite magazine" as just such a vision. But *Life* was never *everybody's* "favorite," and its inability to reckon with the impossibility of its own American dream or to shape and direct any other, ought to be recognized for the cautionary tale it embodies. As pleasurable as looking at *Life* was— and still is—the magazine was loaded with "contradictory impulses and opposing aims" that necessitate close, critical analysis of the complexity of American desires, past and present.[41]

Life turned sixty in November 1996. The occasion went relatively unnoticed except for a mediocre CBS television special, which, oddly enough, concentrated more on post–World War II American video moments—footage of Neil Armstrong on the moon and POWs returning to America in the mid-1970s, for example—than the magazine's still photography. Or, perhaps it was not so odd after all: Time-Warner, Inc.'s, interest in an all-media empire—especially with the acquisition of the Internet giant America Online—makes television (like the publishing industry it already mightily controls) ripe for takeover. And *Life*'s take on visual culture—to present and represent the "truth" of modern life in the form of documentary-style photography—has become increasingly suspect. We continue to love to look at pictures, but no one seems to trust their veracity much anymore. O. J. Simpson's insistence that that "wasn't really him" wearing Bruno Magli shoes in those photographs did not provoke much of a challenge at his civil trial in 1997.[42] We are drawn to photographs, but few of us can really explain why—what they mean to us, what they represent, how they shape and direct our attitudes and behaviors. We are anxious about issues of representation and looking, about manipulation and propaganda, about being easily led, or fooled, by pictures. As a critical overview of *Life* magazine, this book may help explain this contemporary anxiety about looking and representation, an anxiety driven at least in part by *Life*'s pictorial promises, our eagerness to believe in them, and our profound disappointment when they do not come true.

While *Life* may be most recalled in popular and mass-media memory today for its coverage of World War II and Vietnam, its horrific images of JFK's assassination from the Zapruder film, or its extensive exploration of the space program, this book instead examines how *Life* represented and directed ideas and attitudes about class, ethnicity, gender, and race in America and throughout the world. Essays ranging from *Life*'s coverage of civil rights, sexuality, and the atomic bomb to the magazine's treatment of religion, masculinity, and the counterculture share the common goal of exploring *Life*'s look: its visual style, its popular reception, and its important place in twentieth-century cultural history.

While *Looking at* Life *Magazine* provides a fuller assessment of *Life*'s aesthetics and its influence, it also opens the magazine to other arguments and analyses. Much remains to be considered about the complexities of mass media and visual culture; many important questions remain unformed and unanswered. What, for example, was *Life*'s image overseas: how did postwar Germans, or the Japanese, for example, look at *Life*? How did Cold War Russians respond to their representation in the pages of the magazine? What, to take a different tack, have been the consequences of *Life*'s postwar ideology of classlessness, of its pictures and promises of a uniform American middle class? What have been the consequences of misguided yet abiding assumptions of the seeming simplicity, and easy communicability, of visual culture? These are all issues for further speculation as we look at *Life* and continue to rethink America's favorite magazine.

NOTES

1. Letter to the editor, *Life*, 29 December 1972, 96. On *Life*'s circulation and "passalong" rates—the numbers of people the magazine was passed along to in addition to the initial subscriber—see A. J. van Zuilen, *The Life Cycle of Magazines: A Historical Study of the Decline and Fall of the General Interest Mass Audience Magazine in the United States during the Period 1946–1970* (Uithoorn, Holland: Graduate Press, 1977), especially 247–67.

2. Robert T. Elson, *Time, Inc.: The Intimate History of a Publishing Enterprise, 1923–1941*, vol. 1 (New York: Atheneum, 1968), 278; Loudon

Wainwright, *The Great American Magazine: An Inside History of* Life (New York: Knopf, 1986), 29. Elson noted that Luce, after writing notes about the new magazine for several years, wrote the final prospectus between June 8 and 29, 1936. It is probable that both Archibald MacLeish, who wrote for *Fortune*, and Daniel Longwell, who worked at *Time* (and became *Life*'s first picture editor), also played significant roles in shaping the prospectus; see Wainwright, *The Great American Magazine*, 32–34.

3. Sometimes called *Life, Awful Number* or *Awful Number*, the

humor/literary magazine *Life* was published as a weekly from 1883 to 1931, and as a monthly from 1931 to 1936.

4. On *Life*'s initial success, financial disasters, and circulation see Elson, *Time, Inc.*, 297–98, 329; W. A. Swanberg, *Luce and His Empire* (New York: Scribners, 1972), 144; David Cort, *The Sin of Henry R. Luce* (Secaucus, N.J.: Lyle Stuart, 1974), 108; James L. Baughman, *Henry R. Luce and the Rise of the American News Media* (Boston: Twayne Publishers, 1987), 92–93, 170; and *Photojournalism* (New York: Time-Life Books, 1983), 92–105.

5. For an overview of *Life*'s place in photojournalism, see Wendy Kozol, *Life's America: Family and Nation in Postwar Photojournalism* (Philadelphia: Temple University Press, 1994), 23–50; on circulation figures, see the ad "Ever had a baby?" *Fortune*, January 1940, 135, and van Zuilen, *Life Cycle of Magazines*, 79. On Pollock, see Deborah Solomon, *Jackson Pollock: A Biography* (New York: Simon and Schuster, 1987), 195.

6. Budd Schulberg, *A Face in the Crowd: A Play for the Screen* (New York: Random House, 1957), 76.

7. John Tagg, *The Burden of Representation: Essays on Photographies and Histories* (Minneapolis: University of Minnesota Press, 1988), 13; Neil Harris, introduction to *The Land of Contrasts, 1880–1901* (New York: George Braziller, 1970), 7; Henry Luce, "The American Century," *Life*, 17 February 1941, 61–65.

8. For books on Luce, see note 3 from this chapter and also Robert E. Herzstein, *Henry R. Luce: A Political Portrait of the Man Who Created the American Century* (New York: Scribners, 1994). For books on *Life*'s staff and photographers, see, for example, John Loengard, *Life Photographers: What They Saw* (Boston: Bulfinch, 1998); Wainwright, *The Great American Magazine*; Dora Jane Hamblin, *That Was the* Life (New York: W. W. Norton, 1977); Wilson Hicks, *Words and Pictures: An Introduction to Photojournalism* (New York: Harper and Brothers, 1952); Dmitri Kessel, *On Assignment: Dmitri Kessel,* Life *Photographer* (New York: Abrams, 1985); Vicki Goldberg, *Margaret Bourke-White: A Biography* (New York: Harper and Row, 1986); and Glenn G. Willumson, *W. Eugene Smith and the Photographic Essay* (Cambridge: Cambridge University Press, 1992).

9. Eric J. Sandeen, *Picturing an Exhibition: The Family of Man and 1950s America* (Albuquerque: University of New Mexico Press, 1995), 40–41, 95, and passim.

10. For in-house and commissioned histories of *Life*, see, for example: Robert T. Elson's three-volume set *Time, Inc.: The Intimate History of a Publishing Enterprise*, vol. 1, *1923–1941* (New York: Atheneum, 1968), vol. 2, *1941–1960* (1973), vol. 3, *1960–1980* (1986); *The Best of* Life (New York: Time-Life Books, 1973); *Great Photographic Essays from* Life (Boston: Little, Brown, 1978); Life: *The First 50 Years, 1936–1986* (Boston: Little, Brown, 1986); Life *Decades of the 20th Century* (New York: Time, Inc., 1999). On *Life*'s photo resources see Hicks, *Words and Pictures*, 58.

11. Marvin Heiferman and Carole Mismaric, *Talking Pictures* (San Francisco: Chronicle Books, 1994), 210 and 72.

12. Ibid., 81. Walker quoted in unpublished interview, 1978, courtesy of Melanie Walker.

13. On the exhibition, see Paige Turner, "Country Doctor: W. Eugene Smith and *Life* Magazine in Kremmling, Colorado," brochure written for exhibition of photographs at the Boulder Public Library (September 1–24, 1995); "Country Doctor," *Life*, 20 September 1948, 115–26, reproduced in *Great Photographic Essays from* Life, 64–75. See also Willumson, *W. Eugene Smith and the Photographic Essay*, 31–77, 316–18.

14. Letter to the editor, *Time*, 17 April 1995, 11; Liddy quoted in Heiferman and Mismaric, *Talking Pictures*, 68.

15. Letter to the editor, *Life*, 18 July 1969, 16A. "Faces of the American Dead: One Week's Toll," *Life*, 27 June 1969, 20–31. See also Susan D. Moeller's account of this *Life* feature in *Shooting War: Photography and the American Experience of Combat* (New York: Basic Books, 1989), 397–98, and Fred Ritchin's remarks in *In Our Own Image: The Coming Revolution in Photography* (New York: Aperture, 1990), 118.

16. Sally Stein, "The Graphic Ordering of Desire: Modernization of a Middle-Class Women's Magazine, 1919–1939," in *The Contest of Meaning: Critical Histories of Photography*, ed. Richard Bolton (Cambridge: MIT Press, 1989), 145.

17. *Life*, 27 August 1956.

18. Stein, "The Graphic Ordering of Desire," 160.

19. Richard Stolley, comments made during the conference "Looking at *Life*: Rethinking America's Favorite Magazine, 1936–1972," University of Colorado, Boulder, September 17, 1995.

20. Daniel Joseph Singal, "Towards a Definition of American Modernism," in *Modernist Culture in America*, ed. Daniel Joseph Singal (Belmont, Calif.: Wadsworth Publishing Company, 1991), 1–27; Tagg, *The Burden of Representation*, 14.

21. Luce quoted in Cort, *The Sin of Henry R. Luce*, 48, 133, and Goldberg, *Margaret Bourke-White*, 174; see also John Kobler, *Luce: His Time, Life, and Fortune* (New York: Doubleday, 1968), 105. Hicks, *Words and Pictures*, 85.

22. Luce, "The American Century," 65.

23. Richard Bolton, "The Contest of Meaning: Critical Histories of Photography," in *The Contest of Meaning*, xi; Hicks, *Words and Pictures*, 85.

24. George H. Roeder Jr., *The Censored War: American Visual Experience during World War Two* (New Haven, Conn.: Yale University Press, 1993), 8 and passim; Moeller, *Shooting War*, 206, 210–11.

25. Carl Mydans, *Carl Mydans: Photojournalist* (New York: Abrams, 1985), 31; Sandeen, *Picturing an Exhibition*, 17–18.

26. "A *Life* Round Table on the Pursuit of Happiness," *Life*, 12 July 1948, 95–113; "A *Life* Round Table on Modern Art," *Life*, 11 October 1948, 56–59, 75–79; "A *Life* Round Table on Housing," *Life*, 31 January 1949, 72–86; "A *Life* Round Table on Movies," *Life*, 27 June 1949,

90–110. On the Great Books seminars, the Aspen Institute, and the Book-of-the-Month Club, see James Sloan Allen, *The Romance of Commerce and Culture: Capitalism, Modernism, and the Chicago-Aspen Crusade for Cultural Reform* (Chicago: University of Chicago Press, 1983), 81–85, chaps. 7–8; Janice Radway, *A Feeling for Books: The Book-of-the-Month Club, Literary Taste, and Middle-Class Desire* (Chapel Hill: University of North Carolina Press, 1997); and Joan Shelley Rubin, *The Making of Middle Brow Culture* (Chapel Hill: University of North Carolina Press, 1992). For further discussion of *Life*'s round tables see Sandeen, *Picturing an Exhibition*, 29–30, and Erika Doss, *Benton, Pollock, and the Politics of Modernism: From Regionalism to Abstract Expressionism* (Chicago: University of Chicago Press, 1991), 393–98.

27. Doss, *Benton, Pollock, and the Politics of Modernism*, 398–403; "Jackson Pollock: Is He the Greatest Living Painter in the United States?" *Life*, 8 August 1949, 42–45; "Baffling U.S. Art: What Is It About?" *Life*, 9 November 1959, 69; "The Art of Russia . . . That Nobody Sees," *Life*, 28 March 1960, 60–71. See also Bradford R. Collins, "*Life* Magazine and the Abstract Expressionists, 1948–51: A Historiographic Study of a Late Bohemian Enterprise," *The Art Bulletin* 73, no. 2 (June 1991): 283–308.

28. Richard Ohmann, *Selling Culture: Magazines, Markets, and Class at the Turn of the Century* (New York: Verso, 1996), 188 and passim.

29. William Dean Howells quoted in letter to Frederick A. Duneka, 13 May 1914, *Selected Letters of W. D. Howells*, vol. 6, ed. William M. Gibson and Christoph K. Lohmann (Boston: Twayne, 1983), 55; thanks to Jim Bond for sharing this information with me. "The Current Fad for Picture Mags," *The Literary Digest*, 30 January 1937, 20–22; J. L. Brown, "Picture Magazines and Morons," *American Mercury* 45, no. 180 (December 1938): 404–8; Marshall McLuhan, "The Psychopathology of *Time* and *Life*," *Neurotica* 5 (Autumn 1949): 5–16, reprinted in *Neurotica, 1948–1951* (London: Jay Landesman Ltd., 1981).

30. David Morgan, *Visual Piety: A History and Theory of Popular Religious Images* (Berkeley: University of California Press, 1998), 9 and passim; Lary May, *Screening Out the Past: The Birth of Mass Culture and the Motion Picture Industry* (New York: Oxford University Press, 1980), 42.

31. Sandeen, *Picturing an Exhibition*, 18. On *National Geographic*, see Catherine A. Lutz and Jane L. Collins, *Reading* National Geographic (Chicago: University of Chicago Press, 1993), and Howard S. Abramson, National Geographic: *Behind America's Lens on the World* (New York: Crown Publishers, 1987). On the *Ladies' Home Journal*, see Stein, "The Graphic Ordering of Desire," 149 and passim, and Helen Damon-Moore, *Magazines for the Millions: Gender and Commerce in the* Ladies' Home Journal *and the* Saturday Evening Post, *1880–1910* (Albany: State University of New York Press, 1994). On the Farm Security Administration's photo project, see James Curtis,

Mind's Eye, Mind's Truth: FSA Photography Reconsidered (Philadelphia: Temple University Press, 1989), and Maren Stange, *Symbols of Ideal Life: Social Documentary Photography in America, 1890–1950* (Cambridge, Mass.: Cambridge University Press, 1989), 89–131.

32. Art Simon, *Dangerous Knowledge: The JFK Assassination in Art and Film* (Philadelphia: Temple University Press, 1996), 35–54.

33. Stolley, comments made at "Looking at *Life*: Rethinking America's Favorite Magazine, 1936–1972," University of Colorado, Boulder, September 17, 1995.

34. Sandeen, *Picturing an Exhibition*, 4; Wainwright, *The Great American Magazine*, 15–16.

35. Max Ways, "The Confused Image America Presents," *Life*, 5 October 1959, 156ff; see also Max Ways, *Beyond Struggle* (New York: Harper and Brothers, 1958), and John W. Jeffries, "The 'Quest for National Purpose' of 1960," *American Quarterly* 30, no. 4 (Fall 1978): 451–70.

36. Ohmann, *Selling Culture*, 356–57; David Abrahamson, *Magazine-Made America: The Cultural Transformation of the Postwar Periodical* (Cresskill, N.J.: Hampton Press, 1996), 19–27. See also Elizabeth G. Traube, introduction to *Making and Selling Culture*, ed. Richard Ohmann (Middletown, Conn.: Wesleyan University Press, 1996), xii–xiii.

37. Sandeen, *Picturing an Exhibition*, 22; Hicks, *Words and Pictures*, 60 (italics in original).

38. Ansel Adams quoted in letter to Dorothea Lange, 25 October 1954, as noted in David L. Jacobs, "Three Mormon Towns," *Exposure* 25 (summer 1987): 5–25; W. Eugene Smith quoted in Paul Hill and Thomas Cooper, *Dialogue with Photography* (New York: Farrar, Straus, Giroux, 1979), 258. On Magnum Photos, see Rudolf Janssens and Gertjan Kalff, "Time Incorporated Stink Club: The Influence of *Life* on the Founding of Magnum Photos," in *American Photographs in Europe*, ed. David E. Nye and Mick Gidley (Amsterdam: Vu University Press, 1994), 223–42.

39. Not all *Life* photographers were this disgruntled with the magazine; see my essay on Gordon Parks in this volume, for example. And despite the fact that the weekly *Life* died more than twenty-five years ago, its alumni organization consists of thousands of faithful former employees.

40. *Life* appeared as an annual until 1978, when it resumed publication as a monthly for twenty-two years, eventually selling some 1.6 million copies each month. The monthly *Life* expired in May 2000 and Time Warner, Inc., executive owners of the magazine, announced that it will only be periodically published as a special issue. See Life: *The First 50 Years, 1936–1986*, passim; and Peter Carlson, "Dead Again," *Washington Post*, 1 May 2000, C-1, C-8.

41. Bolton, "The Contest of Meaning," xi.

42. William Booth and Tom Kenworthy, "Simpson Lawyers Dispute Authenticity of Shoe Pictures," *Denver Post*, 24 January 1997, 3A.

PART ONE   TO SEE LIFE

TERRY SMITH

LIFE-STYLE MODERNITY

Making Modern America

During the 1930s, the American Dream came to stand for everyday life as it should be lived. Much has been said about the Dream since. I want to highlight here its form, its capacity to weave its raft of contradictions into the soft urgency of consensus, and the role of Time, Inc., as one of the leading weaving machines of the time. The early issues of *Life* drove the Dream: the hope-against-hope that the competitive energies essential to a capitalist economy could, somehow (and this is the Dream aspect), transmogrify into the human mutuality essential to a democratic society. This "somehow," was, of course, an industrial productivity so great that it became a largesse of goods for all. It was also profoundly ideological, constantly shuttling people between elite exceptionality and everyman ordinariness in ways that made everyone aware that their lives were spent in the middle.

At base, an alliance between the corporations formed after the busting of the family trusts and the professionals creating the emergent welfare state, the Dream was—we might say—the new deal behind the New Deal. Time, Inc., through its publications *Time, Fortune,* and *Life,* was one of the primary agencies in setting the agenda for this risky social contract. Expressed in the nature of these three magazines, Time, Inc., traces what seems to be a simple curve from the elite to the popular. A closer look will show that the process was more one of shuttling between both, as befits the task of weaving contradictions into place. Recognizing this does not, however, diminish the fact that the process was mostly driven by the interests of the corporate elites.

Of all the Time, Inc., publications, *Life* promoted most strongly the magical sociality between products and citizens that dominated this period. This American Dream was not, however, simply an enormously powerful, fictional "desiring-machine." It became a reality by being constantly set against and within reminders of a warring world, especially markers of European difference. The discourse of photography was crucial to this process. Photographic vision inspired the magazine: in this sense, *Life* was a microcosm of the ways in which a photographic aesthetic suffused not only the Dream but the entire imagery of American modernity.[1]

TIME, INC., BEFORE *LIFE*

Time, Inc.'s, commitment to shaping a distinctly American modernity is evident in its evolution from *Time* through *Fortune* to *Life*.[2] This was not a predetermined passage but a reactive one. Like all would-be great capitalist corporations, Time, Inc., was internally driven toward the monopolization of its field and the concentration of its organizational powers, but they did so through provoking change within a market and harnessing the resultant diversity.

Henry Ford's mass production hovered over the beginnings of Time, Inc., in the example of its model, but not its scale of operation. Henry Luce and Britton Haddon, cofounders of *Time* in 1923, began by targeting a market and supplying it with a desired product. In their 1921 prospectus they said:

> *Time* is a weekly news-magazine, aimed to serve the modern necessity of keeping people informed. . . . From virtually every magazine and newspaper of note in the world, *Time* collects all available information on sub-

jects of importance and general interest. The essence of all this information is reduced to approximately 100 short articles none of which are over 400 words in length. Each of these articles will be found in its logical place in the magazine, according to a *fixed method of arrangement* which constitute a complete *organization* of all the news.[3]

Time's first issue, on March 3, 1923, then, was a metamagazine that recycled digested news. The key business intuition was that of applying mass-production procedures to the distribution of information, but not to a mass market. Luce and Hadden serviced their own generation, the quarter million college graduates, primarily from the East Coast and the Northern industrial centers, "an elite group which he hoped would include the most important people and young men and women on the way up."[4] *Time* writers developed a distinctive prose style, mixing hard-fact, modernizing business talk with modernist literature, often bordering on undergraduate excess. Their articles featured a dynamic syntax, a mobile social tone, and traces of self-mockery, all cast within a profound conviction of their moral seriousness and global significance.

During the 1920s, Time, Inc., was devoted to the fabulation of the world of U.S. business. In a speech in March 1929, while beginning to think about *Fortune*, Luce said, "Business is, essentially, our civilization; for it is the essential characteristic of our times. That which controls our lives and which is necessary for us to control is the science and technology and the development of credit and the circumnavigability of the globe—in short, modern business. Long since has business ceased to be a low and private and regrettably necessary affair to be escaped when possible. Business is our life."[5] Luce went on to argue that "the significant change is the incipient public curiosity as to the model and objectives and processes and personalities of industry and commerce and finance."

This connection is typical of the desire for exchange between the elite and the popular, which marks Luce's entire outlook. The relationship between these terms change, however, and are never intended to be equal. At this point, they remain heavily weighted in favor of the elite. In his February 1929 prospectus for *Fortune*, Luce said:

> We propose to become a national institution, perhaps the greatest of all institutions which are concerned with criticism and interpretation. The field which lies open is as immense and as rich as was ever offered to journalistic enterprise. We have wars to record, strategy to admire, biographies to write. The 20th Century trend in merchandising, the growth of the chain store system, is no less significant in the century's development than the decline of the theory of state's rights. Industry is a world in itself, for which we must be critics, historians, biographers, and secretaries.[6]

Fortune was launched, after the New York stock market crashed, in February 1930. By taking this bold step, Time, Inc., moved a step beyond *Time*'s line production of news: it sold modernized "business"—that is, the new corporations as distinct from the old entrepreneurs—a new set of representations of itself. It attempted to ground these people in the business culture that they were creating, but not completely, and not in full self-awareness. And it did so while tracking the formation of this culture and noting the signs of its emergent aesthetic. Only partly modernist in style, however, *Fortune* accurately re-presented the taste of its clients, exemplifying what I have called an "aesthetic of the ensemble," even in its presentation of art.[7]

A clear example of this is an April 1943 advertisement in *Fortune* for the Gulf Refining Company, which summarizes the new corporate ensemble in broad strokes.[8] "Men who live for tomorrow" are visionaries who see past their factories of today toward a world that balances the harmonies of the premodern small town and the near-future metropolis. The past is not only present but a desired half of the future. The city is not futuristic but a cleaned-up version of New York or Chicago, the other half of what is desired. And desires

become possible under the benign gaze of the executive, whose benevolent dictatorship works through the light touch of the telephone.

LIFE BEGINS

A number of factors drove Time, Inc., to produce *Life*. Competition for the same markets from radio and motion pictures had become intense: within Time, Inc., itself, the radio program *The March of Time* had become enormously popular since it began in 1931, and became even more so when it went to newsreel in 1935. The availability of machines to mass reproduce photographic imagery was being eagerly taken up with great success in Germany, France, and England, as were the outstanding German photographers and editors who were escaping the country in numbers by the mid-1930s. The documentary thirst, best known in retrospect through the efforts of Roy Stryker and his team at the Farm Security Administration (FSA), was evident throughout American society at the time.[9] There were also the intensely public battles between business and government, unions and bosses, the divisions between right and left occurring throughout the country from shop floors to literary societies. More broadly, the impact of the Depression and Roosevelt's New Deal created conditions that, by 1935, left Time, Inc., committed to growth. Having just the magazines *Time* and *Fortune* in its stable, the company felt it was not exploiting the energy of this period.

Luce's 1936 prospectus for *Life* was—as one would expect, given the circumstances—much broader than his earlier proposals for *Time* and *Fortune*. It dramatically shifted the weight of Time, Inc.'s, energy from the elite toward the popular. Indeed, the first name for the magazine was "Dime." Luce's words gloss the second preferred title: "Show-Book."

> To see life; to see the world; to eyewitness great events; to watch the faces of the poor and the gestures of the proud; to see strange things—machines, armies, multi-

tudes, shadows in the jungle and on the moon; to see man's work—his paintings, towers, and discoveries; to see things thousands of miles away, things hidden behind walls and within rooms, things dangerous to come to; the women that men love and many children; to see and to take pleasure in seeing; to see and be amazed; to see and be instructed.[10]

The essentially photographic nature of this invitation "to see" is immediately striking. The cinematic is also, evidently, incipient in the movement—pans, zooms, close-ups, and cutaways—of its phrasing. The form of consensus building is laid bare; its shuttling becomes clear.

Luce set out to excite interest in what it would be like "to see life" through the pages of *Life*. What would the reader/viewer come to know through such acts of seeing? First, "the world," understood in the next phrase as a fictive presence at events apparently shaping contemporary history (soon, with the increasing presence of camera and journalist recorders, such events would come to be staged as if they were indeed making history). This is immediately followed by a not-so-veiled class contrast. The "faces of the poor" directly evokes the vacant stare of the powerless, the play of glances so structural to FSA photographs, the convention that they amplified by embedding it in the close-up. In contrast, the "gestures of the powerful" conjures historical actors, people conscious that their recorded presence makes history, that their appearance will be minutely studied. Evoked also is a play within the phrase: the power of the rulers, the rich, and the famous is such that even their gestures (the signals of their power), however artificial they might seem, have impact.

And between the two phrases scurries the entire political terrain of democracy led by elites, albeit evacuated of class reference. The "powerful" and the "poor" have been, and always will be, with us. Inequality is eternal and natural, yet part of the power of the rulers is their being tied to this relationship and their capacity to graciously "elevate" the poor by a gesture. The democracy of the list is not the equality of those listed, but the fact that some ("the poor") were listed at all. Both rich and poor are objects of the camera's gaze (the gaze of totality, record, "humanity," "the machine"), but, whereas the powerful are free to take the photograph of the poor as evidence of a situation to be watched, perhaps alleviated, the poor can only submit themselves to being objects of its gaze, if they do not want to retreat into invisibility altogether. This analysis permits us to see who the reader/viewer of *Life* is imagined to be. The poor and the powerful, if they could afford the magazine or deign to look at it, but mostly the intended reader is the millions in between.

What would the everyday life of those living according to *Life* be like? "Machines" is the first item on Luce's list of "strange things," and "the women that men love and many children" is the last. Between these items lies the space traversed by modernity itself since the early nineteenth century. The new machinery finally arrives at the family; having reorganized work, business, and consumption, it is not the foundation of ordinary lives, the valued small things, or the tender mercies of most relationships. The infinite variety of human experience can be contained by these constraints. But it is a constant battle. Luce's language in this prospectus is shaped by modernity in further ways: its *list* form scarcely holds the tremendous differences of type and genus named within it—the "shadows in the jungle and on the moon" can be linked most obviously by the artifice of photography itself. Things "dangerous to come to" (so they can be approached through a blurred picturing of them) need the evocation of women-men-love-children to counteract their otherness. Eventually, however, nothing will be unpicturable.

The clearest indicator of the text's modernity is its framing at the beginning and end by phrases that start "to see. . . ." "To see life" becomes instantly "to see the world," a totality invoked as the overall reference. And, the text ends with three references to visualization that are far from arbitrary: they are essentially modern in their stress on the visual and in the way power is distributed within modes of seeing. This goes quite beyond the emphasis on the reader sitting and looking, which is the obvious target of a picture magazine. "To see and take pleasure in seeing" means discovering, enjoying, exerting, creating, and becoming the photographer. "To see and be amazed" and "to see and be instructed" evoke the nineteenth-century "Nature Teaches" and "God's Hand in Nature," both visible means of organizing the world.

The viewer here is passive, receptive, moved, instructed, and accepting. The magazine itself *is* the spectacle, not a collection of occasion spectacles, such as a gathering of "multitudes" or "armies," but life's constantly replenished sights, an unending variety of images of human experience, often surprising ("unseen") but always essentially similar. The pleasure held out by Luce is that of submission to the spectacle and the fragmentary narratives. At the core of all the excitement, openness, and liberating promise of *Life* lies ideological closure; by being made the primary object of their own fascinated gaze, "the people" are constructed as still signs in a spectacle apparently beyond management and beyond fundamental change because life is always changing, willy-nilly, anyway. At every moment, the imagery of democracy is evoked and betrayed—a rhetoric of freedom disguises a hierarchical "empire of signs."[11]

REHEARSAL

How was Luce's vision realized by the team he had assembled? His first organizational move paralleled modernization efforts made at *Time*. He planned to select outstanding photographs from the stocks of the photo agencies and then shape them mainly around the twin structure of the "Big Newspicture Story of the Week" and a "Big Special Feature."[12] Pirating photographs proved impossible, so he assembled Alfred Eisenstaedt (from Berlin), Margaret Bourke-White (from *Fortune*), Tom McAvoy (from *Time*), Carl Mydans (from the FSA), as well as freelancers such as Robert Capa (based in France). He aimed to capture the markets of mass-

circulation illustrated magazines such as the *Saturday Evening Post,* hoping to steal their advertisers by investing everything in the attractiveness of the "photostory." The goal was nothing less than to position *Life* magazine as the primary vehicle through which Americans would, literally (in the literal sense of taking up something to read), get "to see life."

Everyone involved attested to the unplanned, seat-of-the-pants adventure that it must have been.[13] We can clearly see this when we look at one of the three dummies, such as that of September 24, 1936, two months before the actual first issue. Interestingly, it was given the in-house name "Rehearsal," a pointer to its theatricality and the quality of staging that pervaded it.[14] The idea of the public as a theater in which individuals and institutions try out modes of publicness and enact possible public identities could have been intuited here.

Compare "Rehearsal" to *Life*'s first issue, published November 23, 1936. In one sense, we are comparing something imaginary with something real—but the first was confected, the second constructed. The dummies were circulated to consultants, other media producers, and, above all, potential advertisers. Just how important advertisers were to the magazine is attested by Luce's address to the American Association of Advertising Agencies in 1937. These are the terms in which he asked them to commit their clients' money: "I stand before you as before a court. Your court is also the Appropriations Committee of the American Press: you are the Commissars, you exist as the alternative to the People's Commissariat of Public Enlightenment. Here today I make application . . . that you shall appropriate over the next ten critical years no less than $100 million for the publication of a magazine called *Life*."[15] The ideological program of the publication could scarcely be more explicitly put. But the passage from intention to execution proved, at the outset, unexpectedly rough. The "Rehearsal" dummy attracted a storm of criticism, forcing changes, and obliging Luce to write letters of apology.[16]

"To see life, to see the world . . ." is embodied in the dummy, the most obvious feature being its appearance. Layout was not complete and many more advertisements were to be placed, but the design principle was clear. Information was to be conveyed above all through single images or sequences of them. Writing was reduced to captions or blocks. Impact, argument, and effect—all these are to work visually much more than verbally. The idea of a picture magazine was here taken to a literal extreme.

The opening sections of "Rehearsal" emphasize access to newsreel-type occasions (fulfilling the desire "to eyewitness great events"). A sequence on the U.S. Open golf championship showed highlights of the event with snapshots taken by retired "champ of champs," Robert Tyre Jones II. The world's "great events" of the previous week were assembled under the heading "Bulletin Board" and laid out in a paste-up-style format. The reader sees, as promised, "the faces of the poor and the gestures of the proud." The local is mixed with the international in relatively random fashion. The evident fascination is with American leaders and regions and, internationally, signs of what will become a fixation on the doings of the European, especially British, aristocracy. Edward III and "his American friend Mrs. Ernest Simpson" call on "Turkey's Dictator Kamal Ataturk." "Boy King Peter II" spends a happy summer as a Boy Scout in Yugoslavia. Pope Pius XI is captioned as "ill, old, and frightened by Spanish massacres of churchmen" and pictured blessing refugees at the Castel Gandolfo, where he "thunders feebly against Communism."

This mix of the local and the international did not survive into the first issue of *Life*. Instead, it was redistributed into "*Life* on the American Newsfront," "The Camera Overseas," with a focus on "The English," "Private Lives," a prying society page, and, especially, a profile of Franklin D. Roosevelt. The president was shown in grand but accessible social style via a double-page spread in the manner of a family photo album headed, in fact, "The President's Album." What was at stake in this treatment of the president and these distinctions between the local and the international?

In 1936 the political sphere in the United States was in a state of open contestation. Roosevelt was up for his second term. *Time* and *Fortune* had been largely critical of the president's more socialistic leanings and remained so throughout the period. "The President's Album" included two images of Roosevelt, one showing him at rifle practice in 1917 and the other holding an uncooperative granddaughter. Other images related to his much touted "Roosevelt Boom" on the New York Stock Exchange and to maneuvering among the rich and powerful regarding ambassadorships, as well as political and church visits relating to the war in Spain. There are many power plays dramatized in this apparently innocuous format. The suspicion of Roosevelt simmers in the structure, but overtly *Life* is presenting him as it continued to do during its first years, not only as central to American political life but also as a world leader. These two facts are intimately connected and occur again and again in all departments of the magazine. *Life*'s main project, as I see it, was not simply to exemplify the universal humanism of Luce's credo, but to present his particular vision of American industrial modernity as the best actually existing manifestation of these values. Luce was not, of course, alone in holding these beliefs. They drove his entire class. *Life*'s project, then, might be restated as follows: to define the typical American life by celebrating the strengths of dynamic but ultimately fusible internal, local, and regional differences in contrast to the fascinating but potentially dangerous oddity of external and international differences.

Luce was alert to this contrast—"to see things thousands of miles away, things hidden behind walls and within rooms, things dangerous to come to." On the most obvious level, there is the evident but profound frisson of seeing, for the first time, a picture of the Pope, Churchill, Mussolini, the king of Spain, or a Romanov princess. The strangeness of exotic difference is most marked in "Rehearsal" by the page titled "Seen in

Catalonia," which had a photo of open coffins propped up outside an ancient church with skeletons visible. This could easily be labeled an atrocity by the retreating communist forces, as it is revealed—and the reader/viewer slowly realizes—that these are the remains of Catholic nuns.

Just as powerful in "Rehearsal" is the photo-essay "Hitler Speaks." Almost entirely captionless, it shows a rally at Nuremberg, including Albert Speer's light show and images that could have been stills from Leni Riefenstahl's *Triumph of the Will*. The accompanying text connotes a people in subjection and thrall. Similarly, paintings of Stalin are assembled under the header, "The Communist Dictator as Communists Must See Him." In contrast, a war story from China shows Chiang Kai-shek's people emerging as marginally more heroic than the Japanese invaders. Luce's foreign-policy orientations are evident here, and they remained in the first issues of *Life*, despite changes toward a less confrontational mode. The shocking Catalonia image was replaced by a "Camera Overseas" feature on a city liberated by the fascist forces. The "Hitler Speaks" spread was not used until the third issue (December 7, 1936). And the war story was replaced by a softer one on a Chinese school in San Francisco.

The "Private Lives" pages generated a minor storm of protest from reviewers. A film still showing the new wife of a leading German industrialist in an earlier incarnation as a nude nymph in a forest scene in a minor movie was considered a dreadful lapse of taste.[17] It was withdrawn, and the page was much toned down for the first issue.

LIFE ON THE AMERICAN SCENE

How did *Life* depict the American scene? The imaging of FDR is the least subtle indicator in this context.[18] The lead story of "Rehearsal" was a classic FSA-style study titled "Cotton Pickin'." Shot by Alfred Eisenstaedt, who never worked for the FSA, it concentrated on a single family of Southern sharecroppers, Lonnie

and Mamie Fair of Greenville, Mississippi. The article was similar to James Agee and Walker Evans's classic book *Let Us Now Praise Famous Men* (1941), which itself began as a *Fortune* magazine story (although it was never published by the magazine). Both included a spread that showed the contrast between the Fair family in front of their shack in work clothes and then in their Sunday Best. The narrative positions the family, and others like them, as destined for historical displacement by the arrival of mechanization. "And now come. . . . The Rust Brothers," a header shouted on the following double-page spread, "and their Mechanical Picker." The caption under a photo of Lonnie Fair asked, "If it does mah wo'k, whose wo'k I gwine do?"

The connections between these various photographic and writing projects, and the active exchanges between governmental and news media image making and distributing, are highly suggestive here. On the level of the practitioners, there are profound continuities, despite the radically differing ideological and political objectives of those for whom they are working. There are many stories about the plays between the major individuals. Instances of utter ethical clarity would have been rare.[19]

Sometimes the material itself threw up the contradictions of the moment in an explosive way. This seems to have happened when Margaret Bourke-White presented *Life* editors with a photo-story on the building of a dam in Montana. As they wrote in the introduction to the magazine's first issue, "What the Editors expected—for use in some later issue—were construction pictures as only Bourke-White can take them. What the Editors got was a human document of American frontier life which, to them at least, was a revelation."[20] Bourke-White's feature wiped out the "Cotton Pickin'" story from the "Rehearsal" dummy as the piece about transition from the old to the new. It also brings us to the cusp of two visual regimes of mass-production modernity, to a moment when one subverts the other. The front cover image of "Rehearsal" remained a blank, whereas the front cover of

10,000 MONTANA RELIEF WORKERS MAKE WHOOPEE ON SATURDAY NIGHT

THE frontier has returned to the cow country. But not with cows. In the shanty towns which have grown up around the great U. S. work-relief project at Fort Peck, Montana, there are neither long-horns nor lariats. But there is about everything else the West once knew with the exception of the two-gun shootings; the bad men of the shanty towns are the modern gangster type of gun-waver. The saloons are as wide open as the old Bull's Head at Abilene. The drinks are as raw as they ever were at Uncle Ben Dowell's. If the hombres aren't as tough as Billy the Kid they are tough enough—particularly on pay day. Even the dancing has the old Cheyenne flavor. These taxi-dancers with the chuffed and dusty shoes lope around with their fares in something half way between the old barroom stomp and the lackadaisical stroll of the college boys at Roseland. They will lope all night for a nickel a number. Pay is on the rebate system. The fare buys his lady a five cent beer for a dime. She drinks the beer and the management refunds the nickel. If she can hold sixty beers she makes three dollars—and frequently she does.

Nov. 23rd   9

Right: Figure 1.1. "10,000 Montana Relief Workers Make Whoopee on Saturday Night," *Life,* November 23, 1936. (Courtesy Margaret Bourke-White/TimePix) *Opposite:* Figure 1.2. "Montana Saturday Night: Finis," *Life,* November 23, 1936. (Courtesy Margaret Bourke-White/TimePix)

the first issue of *Life* was a full-page, closely cropped view of part of the Fort Peck Dam, dramatically angled so the massive concrete structure moved like gliding juggernauts, yet seemingly stilled and permanent like ancient temples (see Figure I.1). Toward the bottom, two tiny workmen appear only to register awesome scale. Bourke-White used the devices of modernist photography: composition by repetition and regular variation, broad differences marked by highly con-trasting planes, and lesser differences by a surface modulated by light shadowing. The photo evoked one of the main themes of industrial modernity: the implied independent "life" of the machine dominating over man. Here are the monuments of the modern age, architectural machines so resolutely sure in their declaration of their own eternity, power, and beauty. It is a replay of Charles Sheeler's aestheticizing of the Ford Motor Company's River Rouge plant in 1927.[21]

The late 1920s high modernism of *Life*'s first cover was subverted by Bourke-White's photo-essay on the towns around this Montana construction site. The Fort Peck Dam, the largest earth-filled dam in the world at the time, was a paradigmatic New Deal enterprise. Costing $110 million, it promoted commerce on the Missouri River and provided relief work for 10,000 unemployed. The whole scheme, including dams in the Columbia Basin in Washington State, was supervised by the army. New capital, the latest industrial technology, large-scale social planning, and the people at work: the venture had all the elements of corporate-state modernity.

This points to the New Deal and its relationship with the new corporations and the new welfare state. Both business and government had, to a significant extent, reformed important parts of themselves, and it was these elements that were seeking an historic alliance. While they had to battle, usually by displacement, with conservatives in both business and govern-

ment (and sometimes with each other), their alliance would gradually carry the day. But not in 1936, a year of continuing recovery for the large corporations and continuing misery for the unemployed, especially outside of the North and East Coast. These realities required a complex representation, one that, in artistic terms, brought modernism face-to-face with realism. Again and again, artists were putting modernism to the task of making the real more real, more striking, and more vivid. They did so in order to make their subjects more appealing to those with the power to change the realities, coolly pleading with them to bring the dispossessed into modernity's emergent progress.

Bourke-White's photo-essay on the town of New Deal, Montana, gets as close to its subjects as did Dorothea Lange the migrant workers of California and Russell Lee the sharecroppers of Woodbury County, Iowa. She submitted to *Life* the kind of work she knew was being done for the FSA but had only just begun to be published. Yet, in its stress on the desperate anar-

MONTANA SATURDAY NIGHTS: FINIS

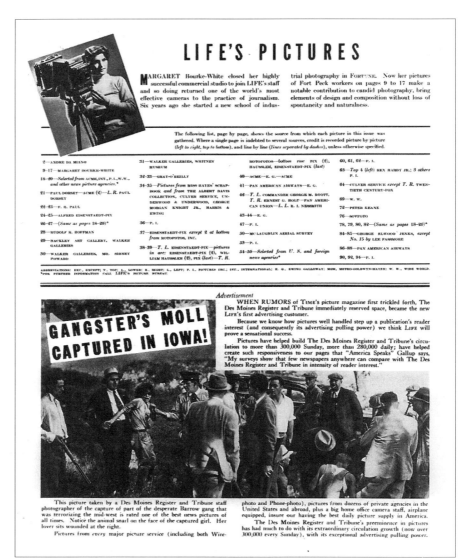

Figure 1.3. "*Life*'s Pictures" and "Gangster's Moll Captured in Iowa!" *Life*, November 23, 1936.

chy of the way of life in these towns, the story itself differs from the FSA picturing of poverty as plight and the celebration of the small town as the desired American heartland. Of the sixteen images in Bourke-White's story, half dramatize the bars and brothels of the shanty towns built in defiance of the army's efforts to regulate the official workers' camps. Only one photograph showed men at work on a tunnel. Ridiculing the economic value of the project, the text embroiders a "Franklin Roosevelt has a Wild West" metaphor. Captions such as "Life in Montana's No. 2 relief project is one long jamboree slightly jogged by pay day," question whether anyone is actually working. The story ends with "Montana Saturday Night," a stunning double-page spread of a crowded bar cut diagonally across the pages, halting at the face of a young girl, glazed eyes staring out, still amidst all this animated noise (Figures 1.1 and 1.2). Below this is a Lange-style, "Migrant Mother" shot of the exhausted mother with her two children clinging to her bruised hands. The social-sexual otherness of this proletarian underclass appears in the flashbulb's glare in all its shocking, sad, strangeness, framed by the driving force of the engineering super project.

PHOTO-REALISM AND THE POSTMODERN

An awareness of the agency of photography itself permeates "Rehearsal" and the early issues of *Life,* as it so evidently did Luce's prospectus. In "Rehearsal" there is a page of images entitled "Released for Publication," which features publicity shots with comments designed to teach the reader not to be fooled by such evident self-interest. Needless to say, no such skepticism was shown toward *Life* staffers, except near the back of the first and subsequent issues there was a feature titled "*Life*'s Pictures," in which there is a listing of photo credits, including a glamour shot of Bourke-White (Figure 1.3). More potentially disruptive is an advertisement on the same page in which the *Des Moines Register and Tribune* clamorously celebrates its skills in photojournalism, in which, indeed, it was nationally renowned as second to none. (A fact demonstrated in January 1937, when its owners and publishers, John and Gardner Cowles, began publishing their own picture magazine, *Look.*) Under the screaming headline "Gangster's Moll Captured in Iowa!" a panorama of figures wrestling against a car is captioned: "Notice the gaze of the captured girl. Her lover sits wounded at right." But this girl, Bonnie Barrow, was not struggling to escape. She is objecting to being photographed.

Color photography appeared in the section devoted to art in *Life*'s first issue, a portfolio of regionalist artist John Steuart Curry's paintings of life in Kansas. The magazine's writers trumpeted, "On looking at what happened to this issue the Editors are particularly pleased that Art is represented not by some artfully promoted Frenchman but by an American." Yet "Rehearsal" featured a long and languid look at the still lifes and nudes of Paul Outerbridge, an American master of understated experimentation with both the techniques and the popular connotations of color photography. One can imagine the mail had this portfolio been published. Like replacing the Fort Peck Dam photo-essay, Curry appears here not simply as a regionalist, but as a creator of images of rural order darkened by natural forces and the strangeness of local custom.

Color photography also enlivened many of the advertisements seen in *Life*'s first issue; it slowly spread into the editorial pages. There are few variations between advertisements in "Rehearsal" as opposed to the first issues. Several of the ads are hymns to the power of photography: Agfa (makers of Plenachrome Film and photographic equipment), Zeiss Ikon (makers of Contax cameras), and E. Leitz, Inc. (makers of Leica cameras). Most advertisements exemplified the ensemble or aggregate aesthetic, like Maxwell House evoking an English gentleman wanting an equivalent to tea and Lucky Strike depicting, in a naturalistic mode, a modern young woman. Many ads were for cars, with Chrysler Corporation taking one stylistic step ahead of Ford. Ford's advertisement isolates an image of the car from the text, which states: "New and modern in appearance, the Ford V-8 for 1937 is powered by a modern V-type 8 cylinder engine." Chrysler, by contrast, adds to their image of the car by sequencing of pictures of it in use, all presented on the inside front cover as a news story: "First pictures and details of the NEW PLYMOUTH." Most of the other ads in this issue are organized around consumption and obsolescence, although few (and fewer as it goes on) are as explicit as Zenith Radio's "The 'Old' is Out; the 'New' is Here!" Finally, the first issue contained an example of an advertisement for advertising: Young and Rubicam's famous "Impact" image—of the moment when a huge fist strikes a man's jaw.

Some features traveled from "Rehearsal" to the early issues of *Life* without change: "Overweather," a study of the remarkable fact that planes flying above clouds gave passengers a more comfortable journey; "Black Widow," a sequence of close-ups of the poisonous spider; and "Greatest Living Actress," a multipage color feature on the life of stage and screen actress Helen

One of the three paintings for Life's gift announcement folder.

LIFE is a Christmas gift that opens new doors. It is a gift of paper and ink—and of airplanes, armies, men, women, surprise, laughter. It is a gift that has never been given before, that is new in its very essence, a gift that opens wider the door of understanding—to reveal the times we live in and record what life today looks like.

Gift subscriptions may still be entered at the Charter rate of $3.50 a year by using the order blank tucked into this issue.

Figure 1.4. *Life* advertisement, *Life*, December 27, 1936.

Hayes. The lives and loves of Hollywood stars were presented in exactly the same manner as stories on the doings of the British royal family. This continued for so long that these two worlds became scarcely distinguishable from one another.

TRANSPARENCY OCCLUDED

By the third issue *Life*'s editors were gloating. "We guessed 250,000, you bought 400,000, newsdealers are asking for 200,000 more." *Life* was a success story,

one that set the terms of its own achievement and continued to do so in the following decades.

Did *Life* resolve its contradictions—the mid-1930s crisis in the U.S. public sphere and those of its own desires to seek a calm, prosperous American way of living in modernity within a larger, relatively hostile world? It recorded and celebrated corporate capitalism within the details of everyday life. It certainly brought together, weekly, the fertile fictions of a nationalist industry, a benevolent government, and an essentially democratic people devoted to the values of community, family life,

Figure 1.5. *Life*
advertisement, *Life*,
December 28, 1936.

and personal independence. They assembled it as snap-shots in a large (but not larger than life) photo album (Figures 1.4 and 1.5). *Life* was a public archive of Americana as it was lived. The encyclopedic thrust of the social reform photographer was there, but like the FSA program, it was tied to a view of the United States that was both general and particular. Photographer Carl Mydans recalled, "We had an insatiable desire to search out every facet of American life, photograph it and hold it up proudly, like a mirror, to a pleased and astonished readership. In a sense our product was inbred: America

had an impact on us and each week we made an impact on America." Luce put the same idea as a morality: "While journalism accepts the abnormal, the hopeful fact is that the photograph can make normal, decent, useful, and pleasant behavior far more interesting than word journalism usually does."[22]

This is an appeal for a world that will resolve the contradictions of capitalist economies and democratic sociality, end the wars between beliefs, and mollify the extremes of violence. This world, Luce believed, could be brought into being by the American middle classes led by the American elites. What a great message to those who were the intended buyers of the magazine and purchasers of its advertised products![23]

Yet, how comfortable this story can become, how quickly! We cannot take these *Life*-makers wholly at their word, however much we might wish to do so. In their desires and ours there is—perhaps only as an historical residue of their achievement—a sharing, or, at least, a coincidence of concerns. Deep down we know that, under capitalism, the Dream can only come to the many at the expense of some. So, we need to ask some hard questions, and to ask them at every stage in the life of *Life*.

On the level of the magazine's visual, graphic, and textual style, we might ask the following: does *Life* become *transparent* in relation to the everyday life of its time? Were there moments when the ideologies that so evidently shape media all over the world disappeared, if only for a moment? At the deeper level of social truth, we might ask this question: Does *Life* represent the truly democratic mediation between citizens and the state, workers and corporations, people and their society? Is anything less than this at stake in our inquiry?

This is, I believe, what is most at stake in our interest in *Life*. Its seduction lies above all in its promise of a political and psychic consensus, one which would leave us free to live out with each other the pleasures, great and small, of sameness and difference. Nothing less than the Social Contract, mid-twentieth-century American style. *Life* got close to its promise, both in style and content, at certain moments, in particular stories—such as "Franklin Roosevelt's Wild West" in its first issue—and on certain pages, albeit by contrast—such as "Seen in Catalonia" in "Rehearsal." But it remains, in fact, a limited artifact, because its vision of consensus was limited. The fact is that *Life* did *not* show normality as the norm

of human life, nor did it do so transparently. To do so was, indeed, the desire driving all those associated with Time, Inc., but it was not their achievement. How could it be, when "the strange things," those "dangerous to come to," were more fascinating, more *there* in the world, than "man's work" and "the women that men love and many children," indeed, when the former made the latter more precious by existing as a threat to them? Difference *within* the nation in all its complexities and in all its complex relays to difference *without:* the mix at the core of *Life* was so unstable that it had to be sustained with enormous effort.

The early years of *Life* were a battle against the drift of history, against the differentiating of nations and the globalizing of the local. This does not contradict its instant and sustained appeal to millions of readers. Indeed, it grounds that appeal in a more subtle valuing of the inner lives of those very readers. Yet, this pressure must have had hard effects within Time, Inc., leading to untold repressions and breakouts. If so, this leads to more questions. How far was *Life* from its ideal, and how did it convey its anger at the failure of the American people to live up to its Dream? How did it indicate, and disguise, its fears at the vacuity of the Dream? Why does *Life* seem more coherent as a project during the years of World War II than before? Why did it all come apart in the 1960s? Did ideological closure—or, as Roland Barthes described it, the moment when good intentions and bad faith can no longer be distinguished—occur then, as it was, indeed, inherent in the project from its beginnings? These are the kinds of questions that can only be answered as we look across the trajectory of *Life*'s work and compare it to other symbols from the period when *Life* seemed to define American modernity itself.

NOTES

1. This is a basic argument in my book Terry Smith, *Making the Modern: Industry, Art, and Design in America* (Chicago: University of Chicago Press, 1993). It is also explored in detail in James Guimond, *American Photography and the American Dream* (Chapel Hill: University of North Carolina Press, 1991).

2. On *Fortune,* see Smith, *Making the Modern,* chap. 5.

3. Cited in Robert Elson, *Time, Inc.: The Intimate History of a Publishing Enterprise, 1923–1941,* vol. 1 (New York: Athenaeum, 1968), 7–8.

4. Noel Busch, *Britton Hadden* (New York: Farrar, Strauss, 1949), cited in Elson, *Time, Inc.,* 82.

5. Cited in Elson, *Time, Inc.,* 126–27.

6. Ibid., 129–30.

7. Smith, *Making the Modern,* 173–89.

8. Advertisement, *Fortune* (April 1943): 11.

9. William Stott, *Documentary Expression and Thirties America* (New York: Oxford University Press, 1973).

10. Henry R. Luce, "Prospectus for *Dime, Show-Book* (*Life*)," June 8–29, 1936. I take these to be Luce's own words, as it was he who presented the case to the Time, Inc., board. But their style is much closer to that of Dwight McDonald and Louis McNeice, young writers for *Fortune* at the time.

11. For a description of the power of the visual image in Japan, see Roland Barthes, *Empire of Signs* (New York: Hill & Wang, 1983).

12. Elson, *Time, Inc.,* 304.

13. Ibid., 275ff; Margaret Bourke-White, *Portrait of Myself* (London: Collins, 1964), chap. 12.

14. "Rehearsal," a dummy for the week beginning September 24, 1936, is available at the front of *Life,* vol. 1, University Microfilms (Michigan: Ann Arbor).

15. Henry Luce quoted in John Jessup, ed., *The Ideas of Henry Luce* (New York: Athenaeum, 1969), 40. It would have been lost on few in the audience that the People's Commissariat evoked by Luce was not only the organization in Moscow, but alluded to media and information agencies of the Roosevelt administration.

16. Comments by Alan Brinkley, based on his access to the closed archives of Time, Inc., as made at the conference "Looking at *Life:* Re-thinking America's Favorite Magazine, 1936–1972," University of Colorado, Boulder, September 14–17, 1995.

17. Ibid.

18. As a demonstration of the FSA's basic populism and its refusal to act as direct propagandist for politicians, director Roy Stryker once proudly boasted that there was only one image of FDR, "the most newsworthy man of the era," in the FSA archive, culled from a news photoservice. See Roy Stryker and Nancy Wood, *In This Proud Land: America 1935–1944 as Seen by the FSA Photographers* (Boston: New York Graphic Society, 1973), 187–88. A number of such images did, in fact, end up in the FSA files at the Library of Congress.

19. There are many studies of individual photographers and their relationships to their employing agencies, including Frank Hurley, *Portrait of a Decade: Roy Stryker and the Development of Documentary Photography in the Thirties* (Baton Rouge: Lousiana State University Press, 1974); Karin Becker Ohrn, *Dorothea Lange and the Documentary Tradition* (Baton Rouge: Louisiana State University Press, 1980); Peter Daniel et al., *Official Images: New Deal Photography* (Washington, D.C.: Smithsonian Institution Press, 1987); and Maren Stange, *Symbols of Ideal Life: Social Documentary and Photography in America, 1890–1950* (New York: Cambridge University Press, 1989). See also Guimond, *American Photography and the American Dream,* chap. 4, especially pages 142–48, and Smith, *Making the Modern,* chaps. 8 and 9.

20. "Introduction to the First Issue of *Life,*" *Life,* 23 November 1936, 3.

21. See, for example, Theodore E. Stebbins and Norman Keyes Jr., *Charles Sheeler: The Photographs* (Boston: New York Graphic Society, 1988), and Smith, *Making the Modern,* chap. 3. *Life* ran Sheeler's 1927 photographs of the River Rouge plant in its August 8, 1938, issue.

22. Carl Mydans, *More Than Meets the Eye* (New York: Harper and Row, 1959); Elson, *Time, Inc.,* 306.

23. See James L. Baughman, "Who Read *Life*? The Circulation of America's Favorite Magazine" (Chapter 2) in this volume. The middle class was evidently the main purchaser of *Life* by the 1950s, but the nature, scope, beliefs, and behaviors of this class were in dynamic formation during the 1930s and 1940s.

2

JAMES L. BAUGHMAN

WHO READ *LIFE*?

The Circulation of America's Favorite Magazine

For several decades in the mid-twentieth century, *Life*, in its size and aspiration, had no equal. Nor could any other magazine inflict more pain. A young Russell Baker, working for the post office in Baltimore in the late 1940s, dreaded *Life*'s arrival. "The great backbreaker was *Life* magazine," he wrote. "Every Baltimorean with a mailbox seemed to subscribe."[1] "The *Life* magazine that everyone remembers," *Chicago Tribune* columnist Bob Greene observed in 1986, "was part of a different age. It was an age during which the world was delivered to people by mail every week."[2]

With reach came influence, or so many thought. In William Brinkley's satirical roman à clef, *The Fun House*, *Life* is the magazine *Vital*, "one of the most important elements in The American Civilization." *Vital* "is the country's really big magazine. In addition: No magazine has such Power. May we repeat that word? *Power*. Nothing has the impact of an article in *Vital*. An article in *Vital* can change overnight an entire nation's habits. . . . No publication so shapes out of the raw raw clay, the raw unknowing clay, what the people of America buy, eat, drive, wear from their skin out, what movies they see, and—not least important, we fancy—what they think."[3]

While Brinkley labored at parody, more than one powerful contemporary took *Life*'s impact seriously. Early in his administration, John F. Kennedy closely monitored and tried to shape *Life*'s treatment of his presidency. Describing Kennedy's attentions, David Halberstam wrote, in his inimitable syntax, "*Life*'s power in Washington for some twenty-five years had been awesome, a dominant national vehicle."[4] For those in show business, "*Life* was king," a longtime staffer recalled. "Starlets, not yet able to get nationwide attention on television talk shows, would do anything to get on the big cover of *Life*, and photographers in Hollywood would have had to be saints to forgo their opportunities, and some weren't. Studios would delay release of their films if *Life* would promise them a spread; Broadway music producers assembled their casts in full costume for expensive 'photo call' rehearsals in hopes of coverage."[5]

Life's quick ascent profoundly affected its founder, Henry R. Luce. Heretofore content to edit and create magazines, Luce, soon after *Life*'s debut, started to regard himself as an opinion maker. He began involving himself (and his magazines) in national politics and foreign affairs. "Harry's third baby, *Life*, was too much for him, the demon in the litter," Wilfrid Sheed wrote. "Up to then he had been a normal-sized editor; but with those thousands of trucks rolling every week just for him, he became the Big Fellow, virtually a principality."[6]

To Luce, *Life* had a special—and essential—role to play in modern America, preserving national unity. "Partly because we are a vast continental nation," he explained in 1961, "it has been the magazine, far more than the newspaper, which has held the country together in nationwide community." For more than a century, the United States "has been the country where the magazine has flourished and achieved a significance far beyond any other country."[7]

In 1948 the magazine enjoyed three times the circulation of Luce's flagship publication, *Time*.[8] "Having *Life*," one Time, Inc., executive said soon after the magazine's start, "isn't like having a baby. It's like having quintuplets."[9] *Life*, Luce remarked in 1937, "is what the public wants more than it has wanted any product of ink and paper."[10] If every *Life* household bought one

bottle of shampoo, Time, Inc., publicists claimed in 1952, the total sales would have the exceeded the whole industry's for the previous year.[11] *Life* had what advertising agencies termed the highest "pass-along factor" of any mass-circulation magazine; that is, a single issue of *Life* was more likely to be "passed along" and read by more individuals than any other periodical. One survey in the late 1930s indicated that fourteen people read each issue; another, in July 1938, boasted a pass-along factor of 17.3.[12] Early in 1972 less than a year before the magazine's death as a weekly, *Life*'s pass-along rate was estimated to be 4.63 persons per copy, giving the weekly a total audience of 25 million.[13]

Life's readership expanded even more in terms of its "cumulative audience," or the total number looking at the magazine in a given period. In 1950 an Alfred Politz market research study, commissioned by Time, Inc., estimated that over thirteen weeks about half of all Americans, ten years and older, had seen one or more copies of *Life*. Four years later, Politz upped the cumulative audience to just over 60 percent. Furthermore, Politz contended that *Life*, over a four-week period and counting the pass-along factor, had a larger audience than five popular television shows.[14]

My own memory of the "pass-along" factor is clear. As small boys in northern Ohio in the late 1950s, my brother and I every other Saturday rode our bikes to Wear's Barber Shop. And there, while waiting to have our hair cut, we could read copies of *Life* while listening to the barbers damn the Indians' trade of Rocky Colavito. A younger, female colleague of mine has a similar recollection; at an Indiana beauty parlor on Friday afternoons in the late 1960s, she sat and leafed through *Life* while her mother had her hair elevated.

Nevertheless, we should distinguish the casual from the regular reader. "The waiting room reader" by definition consumed *Life* less closely than the year-in, year-out subscriber and newsstand patron. Someone leafing through *Life* at a dentist's office or beauty parlor might only scan the magazine. Understandably, then, many advertisers regarded the "pass-along factor" as a grossly inflated measurement. Some agency buyers, *Forbes* reported in 1953, "feel that *Life*'s surprising accumulation of audience represents fewer readers than thumbers, i.e., barber shop customers."[15] Notwithstanding Russell Baker's assurances, not all Baltimoreans subscribed to *Life.*

Any discussion of *Life* magazine—and its supposed effects on public opinion—must begin with certain demographic realities. The first is that magazines were the least popular of the mass media. The total audience for periodicals—even when factoring in the pass-along rate—was smaller than that for any other mass medium, that is, for radio, film, newspapers, and, eventually, television.

Periodical readers were fragmented as well. Although specialization characterizes contemporary magazines, many publishers have long played to subgroups of audiences. Readers today tend to be divided by interests or hobbies; two generations ago, class and educational levels split circulations. Less-educated, poorer Americans preferred specialized magazines like *True Romance* and *True Story,* while their better-educated, wealthier neighbors took general-interest periodicals like *Life* and *Time.* In a 1946 review of research on magazine readership, Paul F. Lazarsfeld and Patricia Salter divided the periodical audience into two groups. The modal readers for *Life* and the *Saturday Evening Post* were thirty to thirty-four years of age, from the professional and skilled labor classes, married and college-educated. The modal readers of romance and detective periodicals were fifteen to twenty-four years old, held unskilled or slightly skilled jobs, were single, and had seven to eleven years of public school education. The audiences truly were separate, Lazarsfeld and Salter found. Just under three-fourths of all *True Confessions*'s readers in 1944 reported *never* reading a general-interest magazine, while a mere 2 percent of those categorized as professionals admitted to examining a detective periodical.[16]

Other class distinctions existed as well. Generally speaking, a majority of those in the bottom income categories did not read periodicals.[17] Simply put, they lacked the discretionary income and the free time of the middle and upper classes. "Magazine penetration," a professor of advertising observed in a 1961 textbook, "is heaviest among the higher income levels."[18]

This was not true for newspapers. Virtually everyone read daily papers. Surveys beginning in 1918 repeatedly showed far more Americans reading newspapers than magazines. "Newspaper reading," one team of historians observed recently, "has cut across class lines, occupations, educational levels, and gender."[19] As Jimmy Breslin noted in his biography of Damon Runyon, the immensely popular Hearst columnist, "Runyon came out of a time when the day's news arrived by ink."[20] As many newspapers cease publication and the survivors surrender their audience to television, we risk losing sight of their importance two generations ago. Bob Greene may remember a world delivered once a week by mail. However, Americans, survey after survey in the 1940s and 1950s indicated, were far more likely to read newspapers. A 1947 *Fortune* magazine feature on how residents in Paducah, Kentucky, kept themselves informed, indicated that 97 percent of all households took the town's afternoon daily. Daily sales amounted to 11,000 compared to *Life*'s weekly circulation of 1,486.[21] Seventeen percent of all Wichita, Kansas, families read *Life* in 1951, compared to 88 percent who read the *Wichita Eagle.*[22]

Radio's reach dwarfed even newspapers. In a mid-1940s survey of 2,571 adults, Lazarsfeld and Harry Field found that 87 percent had a radio, and 84 percent usually read a daily newspaper, compared to just over half, 53 percent, who reported regularly looking at a magazine.[23] In a later study of opinion formation in Decatur, Illinois, Lazarsfeld and Elihu Katz developed a hierarchy of influence in marketing. Personal contacts ranked first, followed by advertising on the radio, then, in newspapers, and finally, magazines.[24]

Life's coverage of World War II appears to have won a special place in the hearts of Americans. Throughout the history of journalism, wars have proven great circulation builders. World War II was no exception. *Life*'s circulation rose from 2.86 million in 1940 to 5.45 million eight years later.[25] "Though we did not plan *Life* as a war magazine," Luce recalled, "that's the way it turned out to be."[26] "World War II," John Corry wrote, "was *made* for *Life*."[27] Again, however, the Lazarsfeld and Field poll discounted *Life*'s primacy. When they asked their respondents which mass medium "did the best job of serving the public during the war," 67 percent chose radio, 17 percent newspapers, and 3 percent magazines.[28]

Other surveys give us a picture of *Life*'s audience. Some studies were commissioned by *Life* and its rivals, others by advertisers anxious to determine the market for different publications.[29] The *Life* readership that emerged was anything but representative of the national population. It was middle class, often very comfortably so, and much less likely to live on a farm or in a small town. Despite the inflated claims of in-house publicists, only one out of every four Americans regularly read Luce's most popular magazine.

Just over two years after the magazine's first issue, *Life*'s own "Continuing Study of Magazine Audiences" estimated that the periodical enjoyed the largest penetration in "the top income class," or "A Group." These were "executives, well-to-do merchants, professional men, prosperous farmers, etc."; most owned cars and their own homes. In fact, of the four general-interest periodicals studied, *Life* had the largest following in the "A Group," comfortably ahead (37.0 to 25.2 percent) of the total circulation leader, the *Saturday Evening Post*. *Life* also led in the "B Group," junior executives, small business people, and professionals, higher salaried white-collar workers, and a few skilled workers. "This group has all necessities of life, but few luxuries," the study explained. Going down the income category ladder, *Life*'s penetration declined: from 37.0 percent in the "A Group" to 14.0 percent in the "D Group," described as "the great mass of working people—manual laborers, farmers, temporarily unemployed. Few own homes." Among the "E Group," *Life*'s readership dropped to 4.9 percent.[30]

This class distortion continued even as *Life*'s circulation exploded during and after World War II. A 1954–55 examination of magazine reading in nonfarm households, conducted by the Daniel Starch group, conveyed the middle-class bias to *Life*'s readership. Among those earning less than $2,999 a year, 9.6 percent reported reading *Life;* the total sample number in those income groups is 17.5 percent. The ratio of *Life* readers rose with each income category, then began falling. *Life*'s main competitor, *Look,* actually had more readers, according to the Starch estimates, among the lower income groups. Comparing median incomes similarly showed *Life* to be above the sample median ($5,425 vs. $4,125).[31]

Life's coverage in the seven Starch survey income categories can be compared to those for *Look* and two different periodicals, the *New Yorker,* with a self-consciously upper-class appeal,[32] and *Parade,* a Sunday newspaper supplement. As expected, *Parade* had the most representative demographics—and was the least attractive to advertisers of pricey items.

Any assessment of *Life*'s audiences after 1950 should take into account the possible effects of television. Although it is tempting to assume that television's arrival adversely affected periodical readership, the immediate, short-term effects should not be overstated. TV-set ownership did not initially hurt most mass-circulation magazines. Although those in homes with televisions spent less time reading periodicals, they did not stop taking them.[33] One of *Life*'s older rivals, *Collier's,* ceased publication in 1957, yet between 1946 and 1954 the total circulation of "the Big Four" mass magazines, which included *Collier's, Life, Look,* and the *Saturday Evening Post,* had risen 33 percent.[34] The percentage of Americans buying magazines actually peaked in 1960, when just under 90 percent of all homes had televisions.[35] Moreover, Starch's own survey suggested that *Life* readers were more likely to own televisions than nonreaders. Of Starch's sample households, 80.2 percent of *Life* "homes" had TVs compared to 65.1 percent of the entire sample. Compared to *Life* homes, readers of periodicals with different demographics, *Parade* and the *New Yorker*, were actually less likely to own TVs, 73.0 and 73.4 percent respectively.[36]

Later in the 1950s, Alfred Politz Research, Inc., on behalf of *Life*'s main rival *Look*, attempted to break down the audiences for nine magazines. *Look*'s publishers undoubtedly preferred a different outcome. The Politz group projected the wholesomely condensed *Reader's Digest* to have the largest audience, 27.5 percent of all Americans twenty years old and over. *Life* finished second with 24.8 percent and *Look* third with 20.8 percent. But, as before, grouping readers by educational level proved more telling. Among those who had attended college, 38.2 percent read *Life* compared to 15.4 percent of those with a grade school education and 26.0 percent of those with a high school education.[37] None of these figures approaches the percentages of the Politz sample base.

Although the Politz group did not categorize the sample by income, some survey questions, notably ones on automobile ownership, convey *Life*'s class bias. Of those households owning a car, 33.9 percent had purchased a new vehicle in the previous two years read *Life*. Of the entire sample, 15.2 percent had bought a new car in 1957 or 1958. Of households with two or more cars, 30.5 percent read *Life;* yet only 11.6 percent of all sample households owned two or more automobiles.[38]

A 1967 W. R. Simmons study of Sunday newspaper and magazine readership in greater Chicago tends to confirm the Politz and Starch data.[39] Just over a quarter of the 4,880 adults surveyed reported reading *Life*. Dividing the sample into five income categories, the Simmons staff found *Life* to be much more popular among the top two income categories (48.2 for those earning $25,000 or more, 40.2 percent for those earning between $15,000 and $24,999) than the bottom two (11.9 percent for those earning under $5,000, 23.3 percent for those earning between $5,000 and $7,999). Of the ten periodicals listed, *Look* enjoyed the highest overall penetration in Chicagoland—28.1 percent—but again, when compared to *Life*, had "worse" demo-graphics. *Look* narrowly trailed *Life* in the top two income levels, while commanding far better numbers among the lower two income levels (23.8 percent for those earning under $5,000 and 22.8 percent for those earning between $5,000 and $7,999). College graduates were more likely to read *Life* (48.3 percent) than *Look* (39.2 percent).[40]

Another Starch study, conducted at about the same time, showed *Life* to be the magazine of the great middle. *Life*'s penetration slowly climbed up the eight income categories for all household members, from 4.6 percent in the first or lowest to 24.9 percent in the sixth income grouping; it then began to decline. By comparison, at least 10 percent of readers in the first six income categories reported reading *Parade* or *Family Weekly*. Once again, the median income for *Life* is above the sample median. And the upper-half median income for *Life* households is $14,187 compared to the total sample upper median income of $10,203.[41]

Possibly too much can be made of such data. *Life*'s reliance on visual imagery undoubtedly gave it greater influence than its audience size alone indicated. A single photograph in *Life* may have, in some instances, moved many more Americans than a stream of dreary, formula-driven newspaper stories and the fatuous generalities—often nothing more than background noise—of radio commentators.[42]

Then, too, audience size does not equal influence. *Who* read *Life* may have mattered much more than *how many*. In their Decatur study, Katz and Lazarsfeld noted that "opinion leaders," those likely to influence friends and neighbors in their communities, read far more magazines.[43] An earlier analysis by Lazarsfeld and others, of voter attitudes in an Ohio county during the 1940 presidential campaign, presented a similar conclusion. Although the percentage of voters surveyed who read magazine articles about the election was small—15 to 25 percent—they tended to be more influential in their community.[44]

That said, *Life* was not an important factor even among the opinion leaders Lazarsfeld and his colleagues interviewed. Faithful subscribers to magazines like *Life* and *Time* routinely read one or more daily newspapers.[45] This multiplicity of sources may explain why respondents in the Ohio study failed to single out *Life* as a source in their decision making.[46] Moreover, Lazarsfeld's colleague, Robert K. Merton, in his study of opinion formation in a New Jersey community in the 1940s, found that opinion leaders, or "cosmopolitan influentials," read *Time; Life* satisfied the less influential, more parochial citizenry.[47]

How could *Life*, with a far larger circulation and much greater and skilled use of photography, lag behind its older sibling *Time* in impact? Part of the problem had to do with definition, both for *Life* and its readers. While attending to news, *Life* never tried to be *Time*. *Life* was much more fun. Both sober-minded parents and their carefree children could equally enjoy the magazine. As a result, though most readers liked *Life*, they did not necessarily take it seriously, or as seriously, as the self-consciously somber news media. Reviewing his 1940 findings, Lazarsfeld speculated that the general-interest periodical "is ordinarily considered as an entertainment publication." Americans did not seek political guidance from magazines like *Life;* they sought to be amused.[48]

Life's influence and place in American culture may be best understood by recognizing the magazine's similarity to a daily newspaper. Not the dour *New York Times* of the 1940s and 1950s but the more typical, lively, and generously illustrated omnibus of comics, gossip, and crime reporting. These dailies offered something for everyone. The formula had been established by Joseph Pulitzer's *New York World* in the 1880s. The *World* presented the affairs of "professional beauty" Lily Langtry traveling across the United States and the story of shipwrecked British sailors eating the cabin boy. And masses of New Yorkers—though not always the influential ones—responded by reading this new type of metropolitan daily.[49]

Luce and the editors of *Life* similarly endeavored to make their magazine entertaining. They followed the metropolitan newspaper model. This included, whenever possible, the mildly salacious. One of the earliest examples of the magazine's raciness came in February 1937, when *Life* carried a photo-essay, "How to Undress for Your Husband."[50] "How To Undress" did not appear in *Life* by chance. In his diaries, John Shaw Billings, *Life*'s first editor, frequently recorded his intentions to enliven the magazine. "I am determined to get charm, sex, and glamor into this issue," he wrote in October 1937. "Hence, a racy spread on zippers."[51] "We need some sex," he remarked a year and a half later. "In the excitement over the approaching war, I must not forget other stuff to give the magazine balance and variety."[52] Luce himself shared such attitudes. *Life*, he told Billings in early 1939, "needs more charming pictures, more boy-and-girl [material], more fun."[53] In that spirit, the magazine in the 1940s four times ran the famous black negligee shot of Rita Hayworth kneeling on a bed.[54] "*Life*'s editors thought it was the best girl picture ever taken," an anniversary issue noted.[55] Although no sports enthusiast—Luce once started leaving a baseball game during the seventh inning stretch, thinking the game had ended—he complained in 1949 that *Life* was neglecting sports.[56]

To varying degrees, the Billings-Luce formula persisted to the end.[57] Longtime editor Edward K. Thompson made breaking news stories the magazine's first priority. But Thompson, longtime *Life* correspondent Loudon Wainwright acknowledged, "encouraged the ardent pursuit of much of the more trivial (and very popular content of *Life*)—the pretty-girl stories, stories about fads and fashions, stories about parlor games and pet elephants." Wainwright himself admitted, "In *Life*'s glossy pages, trivial and vulgar fragments about starlets and hairstyles nestled among splendid color portfolios about the glories of antiquity, titillating items about the weird habits of quirky socialites followed high-minded entreaties for American greatness, powerfully moving black-and-white picture essays illuminating the joys of childhood abutted shocking photographs of starvation victims and of people leaping to their deaths from burning buildings."[58] The October 16, 1964, issue, for example, carried a long feature on Toulouse-Lautrec and nearly as many pages on women's underwear.[59]

Life's opportunistic editorial mix did not go unnoticed. For more than three years after Life's founding, the New Yorker mused, editors had tried to figure out how to run a picture of a naked woman. Life's February 12, 1940, issue ran a feature on a Yale art class with a nude model. "For some reason," read the cutline, "the models at the Yale Art School surpass those elsewhere in figure and face." The New Yorker observed, "This had Yale, it had Art, it had Class, it had America; it had everything, including no clothes on. It was Life's dream come true."[60] In 1947 writer Lloyd Morris praised the periodical's news and cultural values, yet complained that "Life ran two gargantuan portions of 'cheesecake,' and sedulously exploited the 'hyper-mammiferous come-on' of Hollywood starlets and Hollywood models."[61]

Such a mixture raises an obvious question. In the process of making Life more appealing, did Luce and his editors marginalize the magazine? Life's robust circulation and high pass-along rate had been secured at a price. A jumbling of content continually risked confusing readers as to what mattered. An editorial or story promoting higher defense spending was followed by a two-page feature on nylon stockings.[62] Dwight Macdonald, one of Luce's most astute contemporary critics, regarded his editorial variety show as the magazine's greatest fault. "The crowd-catching, circulation-building formulae [of Luce]," Macdonald wrote, "make truth almost impossible."[63]

Pulitzer's World again serves as a useful analogy. Pulitzer had thought that the World's huge circulation made him influential. He assumed that the same readers, poring over accounts of a thirty-eight-year-old woman who discovered she was a man, took in his editorials on the rights of workers and the need for pure milk.[64] In fact, individual readers derived individual satisfactions from a newspaper. Readers, newspaper editors were beginning to learn in the 1930s and 1940s, consumed different portions of the paper and frequently avoided the editorial page.[65] Assertions regarding Life's influence, then, must be qualified by the probability that many readers mimicked Pulitzer's audience two generations earlier.

Some Life readers, to be sure, studied the magazine's long essays, yet many glanced only at the pictures. Consider the February 17, 1941, Life, which published Luce's famous essay "The American Century." Although the United States remained ten months away from direct participation in World War II, war news dominated the issue. The lead story concerned the visit of a Luce favorite, 1940 Republican presidential candidate Wendell Willkie, to Great Britain. Editors allotted two pages to a story on the photo identification badges all defense-plant employees must wear.[66] Nevertheless, there was plenty of copy to amuse the casual or younger reader. A "Hollywood starlet" adorned the cover.[67] Four University of Maryland female undergraduates demonstrated the "Do's and Don'ts of Campus Etiquette." These included "Don't play footsie in the library. Do your date-making outside. What of the student who actually goes to the library to study? Spike heels are out of place on campus. Don't smoke if your escort doesn't. Don't ignore a blind date even if he doesn't look like Clark Gable."[68] Near the end came "Life Goes to a Hollywood Party," a photo-essay on a costume ball in the movie colony. True to the Luce-Billings formula, the essay recorded the gauzy apparel of actresses Virginia Field and Beryl Wallace. Special attention went to another starlet, Juanita Stark, with pictures of her putting on a bare-midriff outfit, later being surrounded by male admirers, and then preparing for bed at 4:30 A.M.[69]

That Life ran such items must be kept in mind. How many readers actually read Luce's plea for American globalism, as opposed to the story of Juanita Stark? Many attracted to the publication, certainly many of the "thumbers" that Forbes later described, absorbed parts of the periodical, not the whole.

Moreover, *Life* remained a magazine, not a radio network or daily newspaper. Its core readership of subscribers and regular newsstand purchasers was overwhelmingly middle class.[70] If *Life* had an influence, it was most routinely exercised over middle-class Americans, most of whom shared Henry Luce's fundamental assumptions about God and the Republican Party. Even Luce once remarked, "Our journalism is concerned mainly with the middle and upper-middle classes."[71]

It remains tempting for some scholars to ignore the class bias to *Life*'s following. Personal histories can be a contributing factor. American scholars born in the 1940s and 1950s often come from the very middle-class households that had read *Life*. And there is the ever-present lamppost fallacy. In conducting research, leafing through bound volumes of *Life* is far simpler than examining a newspaper on microfilm.[72] Radio and television from the period are all but impossible, by comparison, to access.[73]

Convenience alone does not explain *Life*'s appeal to scholars. It *was* a great magazine. If frequently editorially exasperating, freighted with Lucean certainly, *Life* was visually wondrous—and playful.[74] All in all, it is much more delightful to study than competing news media. In a way, the Lucean formula continues to work its magic, only on a new generation of academicians.

That said, scholars should not echo contemporary journalists and popular historians and overstate the publication's power. *Life* undoubtedly shaped the political and cultural values of many Americans. But they were a minority. *Life* was not to be found in most homes and apartments. And many nonsubscribers occasionally sampling the magazine merely looked at the pictures, while having their hair cut or curled.

NOTES

The author wishes to thank David Abrahamson, William Burl Blankenburg, Brian Deith, Erika Doss, Andrew Feldman, Louis Liebovich, Michele M. Michuda, Philip Ranlet, and Sally Stein for their help in the preparation of this chapter.

1. Russell Baker, *The Good Times* (New York: Penguin, 1989), 39.

2. Bob Greene, "One of Life's Lessons in That Things Change," *Chicago Tribune,* 12 November 1986, 2:1.

3. William Brinkley, *The Fun House* (New York: Random House, 1961), 3.

4. David Halberstam, *The Powers That Be* (New York: Knopf, 1979), 361.

5. Thomas Griffith, *How True: A Skeptic's Guide to Believing the News* (Boston: Little, Brown, 1974), 141. See also, memo, W. Rich to F. Norris, 5 July 1940?, Daniel Longwell Papers, box 29, Columbia University.

6. Sheed was commenting on an observation by long-time Time-Lifer Charles Murphy. Wilfrid Sheed, *Clare Boothe Luce* (New York: E. P. Dutton, 1982), 79.

7. Luce address, 10 September 1961, copy in C. D. Jackson Papers, box 58, Eisenhower Library. *Life* staffers to the end continued to speak of the magazine as "national cement." See Chris Welles, "Lessons from *Life*," *World*, 13 February 1973, 22.

8. The January–June 1948 average circulation of *Life* was 5.45 million compared to *Time*'s 1.67 million. *Life* advertisement, *Los Angeles Times*, 19 October 1948, 3:14. See also, "Time, Inc.: In 25 Years, a Publishing Empire," *Business Week*, 6 March 1948, 92.

9. Robert T. Elson, *Time, Inc.: The Intimate History of a Publishing Enterprise,* vol. 1. (New York: Atheneum, 1968–73), 297.

10. Luce address to the American Association of Advertising Agencies, 30 April 1937, reprinted in *The Ideas of Henry Luce,* ed. John K. Jessup (New York: Atheneum, 1969), 40.

11. "Life with *Time*," *Forbes,* 15 August 1953, 15.

12. Elson, *Time, Inc.*,1:342–43. In contrast, the *New Yorker* in early 1937 claimed a pass-along factor of six "enlightened people" per issue. See *Advertising and Selling*, 22 April 1937, 7.

13. A. J. van Zuilen, *The Life Cycle of Magazines: A Historical Study of the Decline and Fall of the General Interest Mass Audience Magazine in the United States during the Period 1946–1972* (Uithoorn, Holland: Graduate Press, 1977), 255.

14. The first study was based on 6,000 interviews conducted between June and November 1949. See *The J. Walter Thompson Newsletter* 5 (31 July 1950): 2, Thompson Collection, Hartmann Center, Duke University; Alfred Politz Research, Inc., *A Study of Four Media: Their Accumulative and Repeat Audiences* (New York; [1953]), 12–15, 116–19. On the "pass-along factor," see Leo Bogart, *Strategy in Advertising* (New York: Harcourt, Brace & World, 1967), 261–62. The

Politz list of TV shows did not include the five most popular, which included "I Love Lucy." All five programs, however, had been in the Nielsen top ten the previous two seasons. See Tim Brooks and Earle Marsh, *The Complete Directory to Prime Time Network TV Shows, 1946–Present* (New York: Ballantine, 1979), 802.

15. "Life with *Time*," 15. See also Robert Vincent Zacher, *Advertising Techniques and Management* (Homewood, Ill.: Richard D. Irwin, 1961), 264; Jackson Edwards, "One Every Minute," *Scribners* 103 (May 1938), 103.

16. Paul F. Lazarsfeld and Patricia Salter, "Magazine Research: Problems and Techniques," *Magazine World* 2 (March 1946):17–18. An excellent historical study that recognized the separateness of magazine audiences is Maureen Honey, *Creating Rosie the Riveter: Class, Gender, and Propaganda during World War II* (Amherst: University of Massachusetts Press, 1984), 7–8, 13–15, 139–40, and chap. 4.

17. Compare tables, breaking down magazine reading by income and profession, in Lawrence C. Stedman, Katherine Tinsley, and Carl F. Kaestle, "Literacy as Consumer Activity," in *Literacy in the United States: Readers and Reading since 1880,* ed. Karl F. Kaestle and others (New Haven, Conn.: Yale University Press, 1991), 172, and Douglas Waples, *The People and Print: Social Aspects of Reading in the Depression* (Chicago: University of Chicago Press, 1938), 148, 150–52.

18. Walter A. Gaw, *Advertising: Methods and Media* (San Francisco: Wadsworth, 1961), 281. See also Henry Foster Adams, *Advertising and Its Mental Laws* (New York: Macmillan, 1920), 43.

19. Helen Damon-Moore and Carl F. Kaestle, "Surveying American Readers," in *Literacy in the United States: Readers and Reading since 1880,* ed. Karl F. Kaestle and others (New Haven: Yale University Press, 1991), 188. In a 1918–19 survey, 46.5 percent reported reading magazines compared to 95.7 percent newspapers. A 1950 study of urban residents narrowed the gap—91.2 to 65.7 percent—considerably. See Stedman, Tinsley, and Kaestle, "Literacy as Consumer Activity," 169, 172.

20. Jimmy Breslin, *Damon Runyon* (New York: Dell, 1991), 20.

21. "One-Newspaper Town," *Fortune,* August 1947, 103, 106.

22. Data are for families within Wichita's corporate limits. Ad for *Parade, Advertising Agency,* May 1951, 122.

23. Harry Field and Paul F. Lazarsfeld, *The People Look at Radio* (Chapel Hill: University of North Carolina Press, 1946), 99.

24. Elihu Katz and Paul F. Lazarsfeld, *Personal Influence: The Part Played by People in the Flow of Mass Communications* (Glencoe, Ill.: Free Press, 1955), 177–78, 180.

25. Figures are January–June averages. Ad for *Life, Los Angeles Times,* 19 October 1948, 3:14. See also Robert E. Herzstein, *Henry R. Luce* (New York: Macmillan, 1994), 396–97, 419.

26. Quoted in Magnus Linklater, "Death of *Life*," *London Sunday Times Magazine,* 11 February 1973, 41.

27. John Corry, "TV: PBS Recaptures the *Life* Magazine Era," *New York Times,* 10 April 1985, 3:21.

28. Four percent listed moving pictures. Field and Lazarsfeld, *The People Look at Radio,* 99.

29. For a review of commercial periodical audience studies in the 1950s, see J. Wesley Rosberg, "A Complete Guide to Readership Reports," *Industrial Marketing,* January 1958, 53–62. See also, Martin Mayer, *Madison Avenue, U.S.A.* (New York: Harper, Pocket Books, 1958), 185–93, 259–64.

30. Otha Cleo Spencer, "Twenty Years of *Life:* A Study of Time, Inc.'s, Picture Magazine and Its Contributions to Photojournalism," Ph.D. diss., University of Missouri, 1958, 282, 289. See also, advertisement, *Life,* 29 January 1940, 74–75; James L. Baughman, *Henry R. Luce and the Rise of the American News Media* (Boston: Twayne, 1987), 94–95.

31. Daniel Starch and staff, *Fiftieth Consumer Magazine Report* (Mamaroneck, N.Y.: November, 1955). Versus *Look, Life* sales representatives in the late 1950s played up the magazine's superior demographics. Curtis Prendergast, *The World of Time, Inc.: The Intimate History of a Changing Enterprise, 1960–1980* (New York: Atheneum, 1986), 44.

32. The *New Yorker's* numbers explain why between 1957 and 1964 the magazine sold more ad pages than any other periodical in the country. Editor William Shawn regularly refused the advertising of goods and services he deemed too cheap or distasteful. Louis Menard, "A Friend Writes," *New Republic,* 26 February 1990, 31.

33. See, e.g., Batten, Barton, Durstine, & Osborn, *What's Happening to Leisure Time in Television Homes* [1951], a November 1950 survey of about 3,000 urban families. In homes without televisions, 69 percent reported reading magazines compared to 60 percent of those with TVs. See also van Zuilen, *The Life Cycle of Magazines,* 156.

34. Leo Bogart, "Magazines since the Rise of Television," *Journalism Quarterly* 33 (April 1956): 156. See also Gaw, *Advertising,* 272–73; Lyndon O. Brown, Richard S. Lessler, and William M. Weilbacher, *Advertising Media: Creative Planning in Media Selection* (New York: Ronald Press, 1957), 44–46; Hollis Alpert, "What Killed Collier's?" *Saturday Review,* 11 May 1957, 9–11, 42–44; "Magazine Paradox—Are They Thriving or Dying?" *Business Week,* 19 January 1957, 88–90, 97; [Harvey Zorbaugh and C. Wright Mills], "A Report on the Impact of Television in a Major Metropolitan Area," [*Puck, the Comic Weekly,* 1952]: 7, 9, 11, 17.

35. In May 1959, 86 percent of all households had one or more TV. See U.S. Department of Commerce, *Statistical Abstract of the United States 1960* (Washington, D.C.: U.S. Government Printing Office, 1960), 520; Stedman, Tinsley, and Kaestle, "Literacy as Consumer Activity," 163.

36. Starch, *Fiftieth Consumer Magazine Report,* 48. See also Bogart, "Magazines since the Rise of Television," 154.

37. Perhaps because of *Life's* comparatively cosmopolitan tone, few farmers took the magazine. Just 8.5 percent of farmers and farm laborers, the Politz survey estimated, read *Life* compared to 22.9 percent *Look* and 11.0 percent the *Post.* Alfred Politz Research, Inc., *The Audiences of Nine Magazines, 1958* ([New York]: Cowles Magazines, Inc., 1958).

The other magazines listed in the survey were *Time, Better Homes & Gardens, Good Housekeeping, Ladies' Home Journal, McCall's,* and *Saturday Evening Post.*

38. Ibid., 53–54. *Life* led *Look* in the car-owning categories, though not the *Digest.*

39. Cook, DuPage, Kane, Lake, McHenry, and Will Counties in Illinois, and Lake and Porter Counties in Indiana.

40. W. R. Simmons and Associates, *Chicago Imprint* (Chicago: Advertising Departments of the *Chicago Tribune* and *Chicago's American,* 1967). The other eight periodicals on the survey were *Better Homes & Gardens, Good Housekeeping, Ladies' Home Journal, McCall's, Reader's Digest, Saturday Evening Post, TV Guide,* and *Time.*

41. Daniel Starch and staff, *Consumer Magazine Report* (Mamaroneck, N.Y.: 1968), 53. The Starch staff conducted the interviews between July 1966 and January 1967. Such figures did not displease advertisers. As Roland Marchand has noted, the advertising community had defined the "mass" audience narrowly. To Madison Avenue, the "mass" only encompassed those citizens with significant amounts of disposable income; that is, the middle and upper-middle classes. See Marchand, *Advertising the American Dream: Making Way for Modernity, 1920–1940* (Berkeley: University of California Press, 1985), 63–66, and Mayer, *Madison Avenue, U.S.A.,* 175.

    If *Life* met the mass persuaders' terms, why did the magazine not survive? The answers are many but related mainly to *Life's* ruinous circulation wars in the 1960s with *Look* and the *Saturday Evening Post.* Advertisers regarded with increasing misgivings circulation gains based almost entirely on heavily discounted subscriptions. Readers paying next to nothing for a periodical, advertisers concluded, were much less likely to read the publication (and the ads) compared to ones for which they had paid a higher rate. See van Zuilen, *The Life Cycle of Magazines,* passim; Thomas C. Leonard, *News for All: America's Coming of Age with the Press* (New York: Oxford University Press, 1995), 169–72; Prendergast, *The World of Time, Inc.,* chaps. 3 and 17; Welles, "Lessons from *Life,*" 20–23; Chris Welles, "Can Mass Magazines Survive?" *Columbia Journalism Review* 10 (July/August 1971): 7–14; "Can Mass Magazines Recover?" *Business Week,* 17 March 1962, 72, 74; David Abrahamson, *Magazine-Made America: The Cultural Transformation of the Postwar Periodical* (Cresskill, N.J.: Hampton Press, 1995), 24 and passim; memo, C. D. Jackson to Luce, 21 October 1961, Jackson Papers, box 77, Eisenhower Library.

42. See., for example, Oscar Patterson III, "An Analysis of Television Coverage of the Vietnam War," *Journal of Broadcasting* 28 (Fall 1984): 397–404. For a careful and persuasive argument for the primacy of photographs in shaping public and congressional sentiments, see David J. Garrow, *Protest at Selma: Martin Luther King, Jr., and the Voting Rights Act of 1965* (New Haven: Yale University Press, 1978), chap. 5.

43. Katz and Lazarsfeld, *Personal Influence,* 310–11.

44. Paul F. Lazarsfeld, Bernard Berelson, and Hazel Gaudet, *The People's Choice: How the Voter Makes Up His Mind in a Presidential Campaign* (New York: Duell, Sloan and Pearce, 1944), 134. See also Paul Lazarsfeld and Patricia Salter, "Magazine Research: Problems and Techniques," *Magazine World,* 15 June 1946, 16–17.

45. Paul F. Lazarsfeld, "The Daily Newspaper and Its Competitors," American Academy of Political and Social Science, *Annals* 219 (January 1942), 36–37.

46. Lazarsfeld et al., *People's Choice,* 135–36.

47. Robert K. Merton, "Patterns of Influence: A Study of Interpersonal Influence and of Communications Behavior in a Local Community," in *Communications Research, 1948–1949,* ed. Paul F. Lazarsfeld and Frank N. Stanton (New York: Harper & Bros., 1949), 203–5. See also Ralph B. Levering, *American Opinion and the Russian Alliance, 1939–1945* (Chapel Hill: University of North Carolina Press, 1976), 13.

48. Lazarsfeld et al., *People's Choice,* 136.

49. George Juergens, *Joseph Pulitzer and the World* (Princeton: Princeton University Press, 1966), 49, 55, 71–72, and passim; Michael Schudson, *Discovering the News: A Social History of American Newspapers* (New York: Basic Books, 1978), chap. 3. See also Gunther Barth, *City People: The Rise of Modern City Culture in Nineteenth-Century America* (New York: Oxford University Press, 1980), chap. 3.

50. *Life,* 15 February 1937, 42–43.

51. Diary entry, 25 October 1937, John Shaw Billings Papers, South Caroliniana Library, University of South Carolina. Billings came to Time, Inc., after working for the *Brooklyn Eagle.* On his muted Peeping Tomism, and *Life's,* see Loudon Wainwright, *The Great American Magazine: An Inside History of* Life (New York: Knopf, 1986), 104–5.

52. Billings diary entry, 25 August 1939, ibid. *Life* subsequently ran a two-page photo-essay on the WPA's efforts to establish standard dress sizes. The magazine ran several pictures of young women, in bras and panties, being measured. See *Life,* 15 January 1940, 24–25.

53. Billings diary entry, 29 March 1939, ibid. See also memorandum, Luce to Billings et al., 15 July 1941, copy in Time-Life-Fortune Collection, Billings Papers.

54. Spencer, "Twenty Years of *Life,*" 350.

55. Quoted in Wainwright, *The Great American Magazine,* 167.

56. *Life* had, in fact, reduced the number of pages devoted to sports, a comparison of issues between October–December 1938 and October–December 1948 indicated. See memorandum, Daniel Longwell to Luce, 2 August 1949, Longwell Papers, box 29, Columbia University. On Luce's ignorance of sports, see Gerald Holland, "Lunches with Luce," *Atlantic,* May 1971, 63.

57. This frequently involved the cover of the magazine. In his unpublished study, O. C. Spencer determined that 393 out of the first 1,039 *Life* covers "had sex appeal." Another 258 concerned the entertainment industry, 139 fashion, and 56 sports. See Spencer, "Twenty Years of *Life,*" 402–3.

    In early 1951 editor Edward K. Thompson denied that *Life* had a "female formula" for covers. "A cover must be just one of two things—attractive, or startling. To millions a pretty girl is both." See

Tex McCrary and Jinx Falkenburg, "New York Close-Up," *New York Herald Tribune,* 22 January 1951, 19, copy in Billings Scrapbooks, box 53, Billings Papers.

58. Wainwright, *The Great American Magazine,* xv, 177.

59. *Life,* 16 October 1964, 82–88, 147–48.

60. "The Talk of the Town," *New Yorker,* 2 March 1940, 9. The picture did not cross one line—the model is not facing the camera but seen from behind. "Tradition and Technique Are Watchwords at Yale's School of the Fine Arts," *Life,* 12 February 1940, 44. Nevertheless, dealers in pornography protested that the magazine was getting away with murder. John R. Whiting and George R. Clark, "The Picture Magazines," *Harper's,* July 1943, 164.

61. Lloyd Morris, *Postscript to Yesterday; America: The Last Fifty Years* (New York: Random House, 1947), 316.

62. See *Life,* 10 June 1940; Billings diary, 30 July 1940, Billings Papers.

63. Dwight Macdonald review of W. A. Swanberg, *Luce and His Empire,* reprinted in Dwight MacDonald, ed., *Discriminations: Essays and Afterthoughts, 1938–1974* (New York: Grossman, 1974), 271–72.

64. Juergens, *Joseph Pulitzer and the World,* 15–17, 32, 49, 50, 54, 92, 278.

65. One of the earliest surveys, of readers in forty-two communities, estimated that between 19 and 33 percent of readers read newspapers' lead editorial. See the Advertising Research Foundation, *The Continuing Study of Newspaper Reading: Summary of Studies 1 to 42 Inclusive,* 16, 68–69. See also Waples, *The People and Print,* 149.

66. *Life,* 17 February 1941, 19–23, 26–27, 61–65.

67. Cobina Wright, the editors explained, "is a young New Yorker of excellent family but limited means who is now making good in Hollywood." Ibid., 17.

68. "Maryland Coeds Demonstrate Do's and Don'ts of Campus Etiquette," ibid., 38, 40.

69. "*Life* Goes to a Hollywood Party," ibid., 84–87, 89.

70. The most stimulating recent study of *Life* acknowledges that readers "were typically white, middle class, and active consumers." Wendy Kozol, Life's *America: Family and Nation in Postwar Photojournalism* (Philadelphia: Temple University Press, 1994), 5, 38, and 91.

71. Luce speech, 27 May 1939, p. 12, copy in Billings Papers, Time-Life-Fortune Collection. *Life's* demise may be partly attributable to its failure to hold its "base" of middle-class readers in its last years, when renewal rates plummeted. See Linklater, "Death of *Life,*" 45.

72. This may prove less true as more libraries, for reasons of space and the magazine's frequent mutilation, house only microfilm editions of *Life.*

73. Radio in many ways has become the forgotten medium. Polls in the 1930s and 1940s repeatedly showed vast majorities regarding radio as the most popular—and the most trustworthy mass medium—especially among working-class Americans. Field and Lazarsfeld, *The People Look at Radio,* 78; Lazarsfeld et al., *People's Choice,* 129–33 and passim; Gerhard Jakob Horten, "Radio Goes to War: The Cultural Politics of Propaganda during World War II," Ph.D. diss., University of California at Berkeley, 1994; William Stott, *Documentary Expression and Thirties America* (New York: Oxford University Press, 1973), 78–84.

74. On *Life's* playfulness, especially in its early years, see James K. Glassman, "One Life to Live," *New Republic,* 9 February 1987, 39–40.

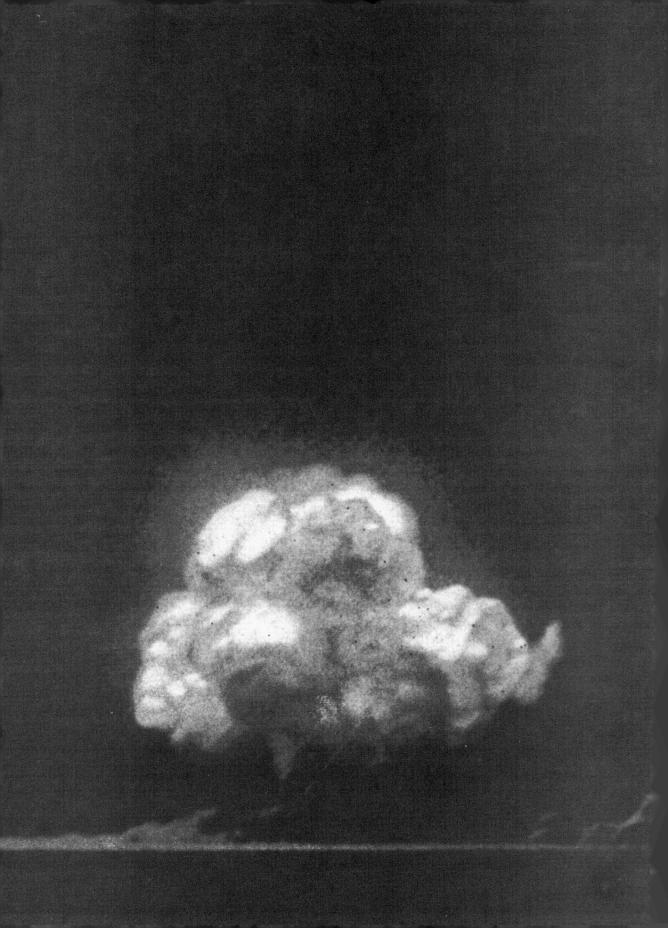

PART TWO   TO SEE THE WORLD . . . TO SEE
STRANGE THINGS—MACHINES,
ARMIES, MULTITUDES, SHADOWS
IN THE JUNGLE AND ON THE MOON

3

KELLY ANN LONG

FRIEND OR FOE

Life's *Wartime Images of the Chinese*

From its first issue in November 1936, *Life* aimed to serve as an eyewitness to world events. It entered the American dialogue about the role the nation ought to play in the international arena at a particular moment when external events called for a well-informed view of East Asia. In informing the public about the Sino-Japanese War of 1937–1945, *Life* editors sought to influence American debates concerning isolationism and interventionism. Through its reporting, *Life* established within the American public a widely shared set of images of the Chinese as the "other."[1] The images and impressions the public held of the Chinese influenced not only the way they acted toward them, but also contributed to the ways in which people defined themselves and the American nation.

Ethnographer James Clifford contends that observers create the other when they impose subjective and cultural views to assess the cultures being observed. Subjecting groups to the scrutinizing gaze, observers objectify and dehumanize individuals within the culture—creating them as the other. Using standards they assume to be universally accepted, observers make invalid comparisons, using norms and values of their own culture as they attempt to interpret the subject group. Asserting the authority to define the other, they stereotype, inappropriately categorize, and tend to "dichotomize the human condition into we-they contrasts and to essentialize the resultant 'other.'"[2]

If we accept this explanation of the creation of other, then *Life* did engage in the creation of the Chinese as the other. Henry Luce, publisher of *Life*, was born in China to missionary parents. Although Luce had a strong affinity for China, he believed in the cultural and moral superiority of the Western world. Luce believed his personal values to be universally acceptable. Reflecting their publisher's outlook, *Life* editors asserted an authority to define and describe, to speak for and about the Chinese.[3] It is worth considering, however, that *Life* could not avoid approaching the Chinese as the other as it sought to make them understandable to its audience. The magazine attempted to form a basis of comparisons through which its readers could become more familiar with the unfamiliar. Although at times these efforts created or perpetuated stereotypes of the Chinese, *Life*'s images of the Chinese did evolve. Constantly attuned to the nuances of complicated foreign policies, *Life* matched its images of the Chinese to emerging policies and to its own hopes for future friendship between these nations. Rather than reinforce a dichotomy, *Life* sought to build a bridge of unity between the United States and China. Only by creating such a bridge could *Life* advocate certain positions and elicit American support for the Chinese.

To build American willingness to support China prior to and after World War II, *Life* tried to depict commonalities between the Chinese and Americans. In so doing, *Life* presented increasingly more favorable, although not necessarily more accurate, views of the Chinese. By establishing a basis of comparisons that had meaning within an American context, *Life* provided for its readership a sense of knowledge about and connection with the Chinese. *Life*'s depiction of the Chinese as the other played a role in its advocacy on behalf of China and possibly in America's increasingly sympathetic regard for China. Only by placing the Chinese under scrutiny of the camera's lens and the editor's pen, thus objectifying the Chinese, could *Life* bring the

Chinese within the American view and make them understood. Only when American's empathized with the suffering of others could the country contemplate making sacrifices on their behalf.

When considering the articles, photo-essays, and photographs for this essay, it is tempting to conclude that *Life*'s efforts were too tentative and too often undermined by editorial inconsistencies. It is easy to discern incongruities, to see missed opportunities, and to be disappointed when *Life* at times failed to recognize contradictions in its interpretations. It should be remembered, however, that *Life*'s representations of the Chinese and the Sino-Japanese War developed in a specific historical context that shaped both its efforts and its reader's reception of images. As Wendy Kozol pointed out in *Life's America: Family and Nation in Postwar America,* "Viewers . . . are historical subjects who read within the contexts of the social spaces they occupy, and therefore we need to examine the historical context within which readers would have seen this picture."[4] Three historical factors significantly shaped the context in which *Life* offered its images of the Chinese.

First, the publication targeted an American audience with a long-standing tradition of regarding the Chinese as inferior beings. In the popular press, Chinese were depicted in stereotypically racist caricatures in political cartoons as early as the mid-1800s.[5] Popular images tended to depict Chinese dress, language, religion, customs, and eating habits as inherently inferior to those of Americans.[6] For years, distorted images of the Chinese had filled the American public imagination. As John Dower noted in *War without Mercy,* words and phrases such as "depraved," "vicious," "pagan savages," and "heathens" were used in Western accounts, which reinforced negative images of the Chinese as a "nameless," "insidious," and "dangerous yellow horde."[7]

Fear of the Chinese also permeated official U.S. policy. With regard to Chinese immigrants, a lingering antipathy existed in some communities that had ousted Chinese during the mining and railway strikes of the late 1800s. The Chinese also had the distinction of being the only group excluded on racial grounds in U.S. immigration acts after 1882.[8] Not until 1942 did Britain and the United States abrogate the treaty provisions that allowed British and American nationals to escape trial in Chinese courts for crimes committed in China. The United States did not repeal the Chinese Exclusion Act and make revisions of immigration policies until the end of 1943. This historical bias against the Chinese, as indicated by governmental policy and within the popular culture, influenced and was reflected by *Life* in its representations of the Chinese.

A second historical factor influencing *Life*'s depictions of the Chinese was the widespread disillusionment and antipathy toward American involvement in war after World War I. Debates pertaining to isolationism and internationalism engaged the most fundamental questions about the nature of the United States and its role in the world. Internationalists argued that it was America's prerogative to intervene against any nation that undermined the principles of democracy. Conversely, isolationists insisted that America's business was America, not the conflicts between foreign nations. The issue of neutrality and a series of neutrality laws established between 1935 and 1937 became central in the debate. Among other provisions, these acts restricted American economic aid to foreign nations at war. The first Neutrality Act, passed on August 31, 1935, forbade American loans to belligerents, banned American travel in war zones, and established an impartial embargo on arms to all belligerents. This act denied the president the authority to distinguish between aggressor and victim, and thus to embargo weapons only to the aggressor nation. However, the president could refuse to invoke the neutrality legislation if he did not find that a state of war existed.[9]

A third factor shaping *Life*'s representations was the economic depression. Debates about U.S. export of munitions to Japan split the public. Some feared that policies prohibiting export to Japan might threaten U.S. economic interests.[10] On the other side, advocates of isolationism contended that American banking and manufacturing interests had led the nation into World War I. They demanded that the United States halt all financial dealings with embattled nations.[11] *Life*'s interpretations of this debate were predicated on an historical basis of friendship with China and an interest in China as a future market or source of raw materials for the United States. Yet when presenting events of the Sino-Japanese War to a divided public, the editors at *Life* faced a difficult task, especially when they presented readers with knowledge that American manufacturers helped to supply materiel used in the Japanese war effort against China. Although Henry Luce was strongly sympathetic to the Chinese, his fledgling publication could not afford to alienate its readers—American manufacturing or business interests, governmental leaders, or the public as a whole.[12]

Given this set of historical factors, the steps *Life* took in its coverage of the Sino-Japanese War were rather bold. The publication devoted pages to the war in China long in advance of direct U.S. military involvement in Asia. In so doing, the magazine asked Americans to concern themselves with a world beyond the West. Although *Life* did not immediately support groups that called for a boycott on Japanese goods, in mentioning the boycotts as early as 1937, the magazine did bring the issue to the attention of its readers. By 1938, however, *Life* supported the boycott on Japanese goods.[13] In 1939 Gallup polls reported that most respondents favored cutting munition supplies to Japan, and *Life* advocated a trade embargo against Japan that year. Also in that year, *Life* predicted that American government intervention in the war was inevitable.[14] Prior to the passing of the Lend-Lease Act in March 1941, *Life* editorialized in favor of loans and military aid to China. As A. T. Steele suggested in *The American People and China*, "In the late 1930s the American people came to a crossroads in their thinking about China. Until then American attitudes toward China, though sympathetic, had been consistently, even persistently, isolationist."[15] *Life* both chronicled and helped the movement of Americans to this juncture.

Figure 3.1. Execution of a Chinese communist, from "The Cruel Chinese," *Life*, December 28, 1936. (Courtesy European)

Yet, in its earliest depictions, *Life* focused on the "otherness" of the Chinese and did not seek to nullify popular representations that construed the Chinese as unapproachably foreign. Some early images contributed to the collective impression of the Chinese as strange, amusing, childlike, and in need of American guidance. In the first issue of the magazine, *Life* devoted two pages to pictures of American-born Chinese girls in San Francisco. Showing girls attired in Chinese dress, an accompanying paragraph explained that these children attend Catholic school where the nuns try to assimilate the "slant-eyed and shy" Chinese youngsters by teaching them to say "very," not "velly."[16]

In December 1936, however, *Life* perpetuated more ill-favored views of the Chinese in a photo spread titled "The Cruel Chinese." The article followed the events of the Sian Incident of December 12, in which Nationalist leader Chiang Kai-shek was kidnapped by Chang Hsueh-liang.[17] *Life* clearly sided with the Nationalists, labeling Chiang the hero and Chang Hsueh-liang the villain. Discussing the Chinese, the editors stated that the "Strangest paradox in Chinese character is the mixture of tenderness and cruelty." The photos suggested a tacit commentary about the nature of life and humanity in China, a commentary that denigrates and sets the Chinese apart from Americans.

The article opens to a photo covering more than half the page of a just-executed Chinese communist prisoner, still seated but beginning to slump forward, head pulled upward from behind by his queue, just moments after the executioner had fired a pistol at point-blank range into the back of his skull (Figure 3.1). The caption said, "Half the town swarmed out to watch his death with customary Chinese stoicism." Not only does *Life* claim to depict life in China, it also claims the authority to interpret and discuss the emotional nature of the Chinese. On the page opposite, under a photo showing a head lying in the street in front of another just-executed man (Figure 3.2), the caption said, "Any tourist in China can buy it (the photo) for five cents. It represents a scene so common that Chinese have grown indifferent to it." Although the crowd in the background of the photograph stands at such a distance that their faces are entirely out of focus and indistinct, the caption describes them as looking on with apathy. The article explained, "Perpetual strife among warlords had made life cheap in a country overcrowded with 450,000,000."[18]

Such characterizations of the Chinese as insensitive to human life and lacking the ability to value human existence as Americans did fit with preexisting popular images of the Chinese as the other. This photo spread reveals both the power of the photograph to turn human subjects into objects and a lack of introspection on the part of *Life* editors who did not seem to consider that showing such scenes to its readers might require of them a stoicism and indifference equal to that of the war-weary Chinese.[19] *Life* editors did not consider at what point the American public might grow indifferent to looking at this and other pictures of slaughtered Chinese purchased at the cost of ten cents an issue.

Figure 3.2. A swordsman slices off head of Chinese communist in front of pedestrians, from "The Cruel Chinese," *Life*, December 28, 1936. (Courtesy European)

Figure 3.3. "Chinese Children Study the ABC of Communism," *Life*, January 25, 1937. (Courtesy Edgar Snow)

CHINESE CHILDREN STUDY THE ABC OF COMMUNISM

The article noted that since 1927 public executions had been confined mostly to communists. Betraying their own indifference to the loss of communist life and implying that communist lives were indeed cheap, *Life* editors obliquely condemned communist factions within the United States as well. Conversely, *Life* de-scribed the KMT, Chinese Nationalists (Kuomintang), as people quite like Americans. Thus, from its earliest issues, the editors supported U.S. recognition of that government and paved the path for public support of a U.S. alliance with the KMT following World War II. Commenting upon the battles between the Chinese

Communist Party (CCP) and the KMT, *Life* editors attempted to accurately depict the strife within the Chinese nation. Yet, such distinctions might have been dismissed by an audience already historically inclined to regard all Asians as alike—and unlikable.

Life was not the sole media organ shaping images of the Chinese in the mid-1930s. Feature films began to depict the Chinese in increasingly sympathetic ways.[20] In January 1937 *Life* turned its camera to the film *The Good Earth,* based on Pearl Buck's novel.[21] Although the story is fictional and Anglos in Oriental make-up portray the lead Chinese roles, the film depicts common Chinese people with names, life stories, and a range of human emotions. The review in *Life* did not help to bridge the gap between fiction and the realities of life for the war-torn in China. For instance, the reviewer said that Luise Rainer, who portrays O-lan, had little opportunity to show emotion because of "the habitual expression of complete submissiveness bred into generations of Chinese peasant women," rather than questioning whether there might be situations in which real peasant women might express outrage or other emotions. In spite of such shortcomings, *Life*'s coverage of the film did help to shape more positive, though not necessarily more authentic, images of the Chinese thereafter. *Life*'s reinforcement of more affirmative images heralded a change in its own depiction of the Chinese.

In its next issue, *Life* turned to real-life events and took a bold step in endorsing the newly established United Front between the KMT and the CCP. Formed in the aftermath of the Sian Incident, the United Front was a short-lived agreement between these Chinese political factions to join together in ousting the Japanese foreign aggressors. By indicating approval of this Chinese effort at cooperation, *Life* may also have implied a tacit acceptance of the Popular Front in America, which sought to form a coalition between socialists, liberals, progressives, and communists in the antifascist struggle.[22]

In an article in January 1937, *Life* for the first time showed faces of Chinese communists as other than victims.[23] Photographs taken by Edgar Snow accompany the article by Agnes Smedley (Figure 3.3). Although the photos are labeled as revealing the new Communist Party, Snow actually took them prior to the formation of the United Front, during his journey in the Yenan area in the fall of 1936.[24] Such mislabeling is only one indication of a conscious effort by *Life* editors to reshape the communists and to represent them in favorable light because they had joined hands with the Nationalists. In an effort to humanize the leaders of the "new" Communist Party, *Life* provided American readers with some of the first glimpses of CCP leaders, including Chou En-lai and Mao Tse-tung. Aligning the communists with American values toward children and education, the article included photographs of children being reared in a remote communist camp. Explaining a photograph of five children seated around a table, Smedley claimed to know that the "deadliest enemy of the Communists" is the Chinese "alphabet" and "traditional culture which keeps knowledge and authority in the hands of the few."[25] Expressing a cautious approval for some communist strategies, *Life* represented these people as actively engaged in giving their children the means to achieve a brighter—less Chinese—future. Suggesting that the CCP intended to modernize along Western lines, *Life* endorsed a negative critique of the traditional, non-Western culture of China, and suggested an unspoken assumption that in seeking to make the Chinese modern, the communists were also making them more like Americans.

Although the editors continued to support the alliance between the KMT and the CCP, ambivalence was also apparent. Captions beneath a photo spread of scenes in Yenan in the February 1, 1937, issue raise as many questions as they answer about the magazine's position on communism, using expressions such as "spinster," "advance agents," and "overworked" to describe communist women. Ironically, the same caption that labels two women as spinsters ends by calling them "girls." Ambiguous statements such as "Unlike Chiang's

New Life Movement, Communists encourage freedom between the sexes" seem geared to arouse questions about the communist's morality and suggest a level of uncertainty in *Life*'s advocacy of the communists.[26]

By July 1937 *Life* began to caution against communism, both at home and abroad. The claim that "Headlines Proclaim the Rise of Fascism and Communism in America" suggests a connection between communism and the rising villain, fascism. For uncertain reasons, this article even lists the address of communist headquarters in New York City. *Life* warned its readers that although eighteen years of "proselytizing" raised only 45,000 members, communism won 5,000 converts in the last year. The editors caution readers about the "zeal, dogmatism, and authoritarianism" with which American communists "worship the gospel of Karl Marx." Once again, this article reflects an editorial ambivalence: after noting the thirty-six arrests of "Mother Bloom: U.S. Communist Heroine," *Life* praised her for representing the best in communism, the "unswerving determination to make life happier for the world's unfortunates."[27]

Others besides fascists and American communists came under *Life*'s scrutinizing gaze. Those in the public who opposed the magazine's editorial positions also became targets. With regard to events in the Sino-Japanese War, *Life*'s examination included groups and individuals who charged that U.S. manufacturers sold materiel to Japan that it in turn used to wage war against the Chinese. These groups called for a boycott of Japanese goods, demanded that embargoes be imposed and the Neutrality Act invoked, and called for an immediate halt on the sale of all war materiel to Japan. In its initial reporting about this debate within American culture, *Life* sided with manufacturing interests and, in so doing, labeled those who opposed them as un-American—as others.

In an April 1937 issue, *Life* flatly rejected the claim that the sale of scrap metal to Japan constituted supplying war materiel to an aggressor. While not denying that much of the U.S. scrap metal sold abroad goes to Japan, the caption to a photograph of a junkyard skirts the issue and focuses upon the positive aspects for America, pointing out that "The scrap-iron boom is sweeping such eyesores as this from the U.S. landscape."[28] *Life* may have only been reinforcing an already established tendency within the public to avoid looking at American culpability. The magazine seems to acknowledge that the United States is the largest source of scrap used to make armaments, but forcefully denies that the Japanese use this scrap metal in their instruments of war. "By no means does most of Japan's scrap go into war machines. But this bogey now excites U.S. Congressmen."[29] Creating a negative image of those who would not look away and insisting that Americans confront this knowledge, *Life* was implying that some people were working outside of the American norm to undermine American interests. Dismissing these individuals as a group of fear-filled pacifist politicians, *Life* also dismissed the validity of their claims.

Perhaps only coincidentally, this issue of the magazine also demonstrates a step backward in *Life*'s efforts to positively represent the Chinese. Although the Chinese government had formerly protested the use of "coolie" to describe Chinese laborers, *Life* continued to label the common Chinese as "peasants" or "coolies." In an article pertaining to the construction of airports, a caption beneath a photograph of Chinese laborers reported, "The maggot-like shadows are a multitude of Chinese coolies" toiling to build an airport.[30] The use of "multitude" evokes images of the Chinese as a horde and so undermines efforts to depict the Chinese as people deserving support. Using "shadows" to describe the people in the photograph, *Life* suggests that the Chinese are ghostlike, unreal, and insubstantial. But most strikingly, and most degrading, the caption dehumanizes the laboring Chinese man or woman by reducing them to insect larvae.

Less than half a year later, however, *Life* reversed its position on the sale of munitions to Japan. Whereas in the spring of 1937 *Life* had denied American participation in Japan's war efforts, by September it divulged without doubt that American manufacturers sold not only scrap metal, but also actual war goods to Japan. Among pictures "pirated" out of China by photographer Walter Bosshard is a seemingly insignificant one of a propeller from a wrecked Japanese plane. One of six photos on the page, its caption noted, "The propeller of the plane, lying by itself, is a Hamilton, made in the U.S."[31] No editorial comment is made, but the editors have clearly acknowledged a U.S. connection to Japan's war machine. Thereafter, *Life* articles consistently depicted the Chinese in positive ways, reflecting a recognition that the magazine could not portray the Chinese in typically racist patterns and at the same time advocate support for them.

One means employed by *Life* to show a more positive view of the Chinese was to emphasize similarities between Americans and the Chinese. In so doing, *Life* sought to cross the boundaries that distinguished "them" from "us" by shaping its images of the Chinese to fit the particular American cultural norms that it chose to value. Not the common citizens of China, but prominent Nationalists formed the basis for these comparisons. It is telling that in a story that hails Madame Chiang Kai-shek as ". . . probably the most powerful woman in the world," *Life* restates the stereotype of other Chinese women as subservient and docile. Only the rare Chinese woman who can be understood in an American idiom can escape such stereotyping; indeed, *Life* claims that the United States educated Madame Chiang for her career as a wife and shows her in domestic scenes with her husband. The article described her as a Bible-reading believer of a Christian God, and the photographs in which American classmates surround her from her college days emphasize her "Americaness." Similarly, Soong Ch'ing Ling and her husband, Sun Yat-sen, father of Chinese nationalism, are associated with things American in an article describing them as "China's George and Martha Washington." Interestingly, when the article said that Soong Ch'ing Ling "sulks" in captivity in Shanghai because she openly opposes the policies of Chiang Kai-shek, it once

again reveals the ambiguous nature of *Life*'s treatment of the Chinese communists and its preference for the Nationalists.[32]

Although *Life*'s partiality toward the Nationalists remained clear, the editors continued to encourage support for the United Front. In an article from October 1937, *Life* praised the efforts of communist troops for striving toward American standards. *Life* captioned a photograph of Chinese youths pouring over books and newspapers "Communists who can read and do."[33] Captions beneath photos describe Yenan as a hygienic area in which soldiers wash hands, use toothbrushes, and play games. One caption stated that the Yenan pictures were purposely staged to convey messages about the healthy conditions in the camp. Nonetheless, the editors published three full pages of photographs that reinforced favorable views of the CCP, as if to wash away former images associated with executions of communists. The article creates the impression of Yenan as a Boy Scout camp rather than a communist army base.

Yet images depicting the plight of the Chinese did not stir the American public as much as reports of a direct attack on American people or property. In December 1937 the Japanese bombed the U.S. gunboat *Panay* and sank three Standard Oil vessels. Headlined "A Terrible Blunder Puts Japan's Ambassador on the Anxious Seat," *Life*'s coverage of the *Panay* incident opened to a full-page photograph that conveyed a self-consciousness on the part of the publication about its position as reporter and shaper of news. The Japanese ambassador, Saito, was sitting on a hard sofa outside Secretary of State Cordell Hull's office (Figure 3.4). A photographer seated to his left turns his camera on the ambassador, who presses against the end of the sofa, apparently in as much discomfort with the presence of the cameras as with the cause for his appointment. Another photographer slides almost under the seat, a leg protruding toward the ambassador. The aggressiveness of the photographers and the obvious discomfort of the ambassador conveyed the message that the spotlight was now on the Japanese.

Right: Figure 3.4. "A Terrible Blunder Puts Japan's Ambassador on the Anxious Seat," *Life,* December 27, 1937. (Courtesy Associated Press) *Opposite:* Figure 3.5. A grief-stricken civilian of Nanking carrying his dying son, wounded by a Japanese bomb splinter, from "The Camera Overseas: The Japanese Conqueror Brings a 'Week of Hell' to China's National Capital of Nanking," *Life,* January 10, 1938. (Courtesy Associated Press)

LIFE

Vol. 3, No. 26

DECEMBER 27, 1937

A TERRIBLE BLUNDER PUTS JAPAN'S AMBASSADOR ON THE ANXIOUS SEAT

Early Sunday afternoon, Dec. 12, on the Yangtze River 27 miles above Nanking, Japanese Navy warplanes swooped down and bombed the U. S. Navy gunboat *Panay* as she was carrying American Embassy officials and other refugees away from the Chinese capital. The ship was abandoned at 2:05 p.m. An hour and three-quarters later she sank, and over her hulk the muddy waters of China's greatest river again rushed on undisturbed to the Yellow Sea. But the concussion of that bombing boomed around the world, sent Japanese and American officials flying for many a day to come.

Ten thousand miles away in Washington it sent Hirosi Saito, Japan's Ambassador to the U. S., scurrying to a hard horsehair sofa outside Secretary of State Hull's office (*above*). The Japanese are a proud and dignified people, and a Japanese Ambassador is the personal representative of a ruler whom 69,000,000 people regard as divine. But as he perched on the anxious seat, submitting to the American ordeal by candid camera, tough little Ambassador Saito looked neither dignified nor divine. Though protesting that the bombing was "completely accidental," he called it a "terrible blunder" as he waited to offer his country's humblest apologies to Secretary Hull and to receive the sternest reception that a foreign diplomat has had from a Secretary of State since 1917.

At the same time the *Panay* was sunk, three Standard Oil vessels were also destroyed by Japanese bombs, and several British gunboats were attacked. In the course of China's invasion, repeated forays by the Japanese military against American and British life and property have brought repeated apologies from the Japanese Government—and nothing more. This time, grave and grim in the face of more such apologies, the U. S. Government was apparently set for a showdown.

Life's treatment of the incident also foreshadowed what became an apparent slant in its coverage of the war thereafter—a direct connection between American commercial interests and the battles taking place in Asia. While linking Japan to the idea of a threat to America, *Life* also made it clear that this threat was economic. Rejecting the arguments of isolationists who insisted that American vessels should have been removed from China long in advance of the incident, *Life* defended the right of the United States to have such representation in China. The editors argued that the *Panay* was in Chinese territory to uphold the Open Door policy, which is "America's historic policy toward its rivals for rich, weak China's trade and resources. It is based on the principle that no single nation shall be allowed to gobble up the whole Chinese feast." The wealth of China's natural resources is juxtaposed against its apparent helplessness as a nation. America, through historic precedent, has a right, and the editors later suggest, a duty, to save China from exploitation by others.

Japan, clearly, is the foremost opponent. Once regarded as just another nation dividing up China's ample pie, Japan posed a greater threat to American economic interests as it increased aggressions in China. In reaction to this incident, *Life* editors finally endorsed a boycott of the sale of goods to Japan, but also sought to reassure Americans who feared the loss of trade. China, the editors suggested, may prove to be not only a resource for raw materials, but also a suitable replacement market for Japan. Applauding the U.S. government for maintaining an isolationist stance and for demanding an apology with remuneration for damages, the article closed by mentioning that a direct assault on American vessels provided just cause for the United States to enter the war.[34]

Although the *Panay* bombing occurred nearly a month earlier, *Life*'s January 10, 1938, issue had photographs from film taken by Universal photographer Norman Alley. The sequence opened with an American flag draped over a coffin being hoisted from a ship's hull.[35] *Life*'s editors pointed out the power of the media to construct interpretations of news events, noting that film footage of "Universal's 'Panay Incident'" already played to applauding audiences in theaters across the United States. *Life* was emphasizing the fact that the film had been edited and manipulated by the studio. The editors did not, however, discuss the fact that they also carefully selected, edited, and arranged a series of photographs to convey a particular message about the chronology of events in order to point a condemning finger and to build upon a growing antipathy toward Japan.

Compounding the charges against Japan, this issue of *Life* also carried the story of the refugee flight from the pillaged city of Nanking. A short article titled "China's Refugee Millions Stampede Up the Yangtze" described the Nanking survivors as "numberless droves of half-starving men and a few surviving women." Using "droves" and "millions," *Life* may be suggesting that the sheer number of victims presents a problem too large to try to solve. *Life* also makes a perplexing claim in stating "What is happening in China makes trivial in numbers if not in emotion the migrations of European refugees in the World War."[36] *Life* editors may be openly challenging racist sentiments by suggesting that Chinese deaths are less worthy of sympathy than those of Europeans. Or, by employing the tentative "if," the editors may have been encouraging the audience to empathize with the Chinese.

It is worth noting that in this same issue of *Life*, "Rape of Nanking" included some of the most graphically horrific war images of one of the greatest atroci-

THE CAMERA OVERSEAS: THE CHINESE CONSIGN TO HIS ANCESTORS ONE SMALL CITIZEN

Wartime burial of a Chinese child whose parents were prosperous enough to buy him shoes. Other dead (notice foot in left foreground) lie under woven-straw matting. Coffins are piled in rear. Nobody dawdles at this work. China's Generalissimo Chiang Kai-shek and 400,000 soldiers are trying to hold off some 140,000 Japanese striking from north and south to unite their armies, drive Chiang inland or destroy his whole force. Standout career open to the homeless young Chinese now is guerrilla warfare against the Japanese.

Figure 3.6. "The Camera Overseas: The Chinese Consign to His Ancestors One Small Citizen," *Life*, February 21, 1938. (Courtesy Pictures Inc./ TimePix)

ties in twentieth-century history. Turning to the article, the reader's eye is drawn by the most dominant photograph, on the first of two pages, the head of a Chinese man, severed from the body and set on a tangled barbed-wire barricade outside the city of Nanking. The victim's mouth is stuffed open with what appears to be his own tongue. At the top of the left-hand page, another photograph leaves no uncertainty that the Japanese ruthlessly destroy what Americans value—home and family. A nameless civilian Chinese, an old man,

cradles a child as he tries to step his way through the wreckage of the city torn asunder (Figure 3.5).[37] Driving home the point that the Chinese—helpless, defenseless victims—desperately need salvation from abroad, *Life* created some of its most damning images of the Japanese without focusing the camera on the Japanese. Instead, it focused upon the consequence of Japanese aggression to make it clear that such people were destroyers of American values.

Life focused again in February 1938 upon the civil-

Page 9

Vol. 4, No. 25

LIFE

JUNE 20, 1938

A CHINESE MOTHER WEEPS AS DEATH FALLS FROM THE SKY UPON CANTON

The most terrifying news since the World War is presented in the pictures on the following pages. They show what airplanes can do to a city of a million, what they did to South China's Canton, what they will doubtless do in the next European War to Paris, Berlin or London.

On May 28 the Japanese Navy's air fleet went seriously about the job of utterly destroying Canton so far as air bombing could. They had sporadically bombed Canton before, but Canton had come to be the great transshipping point for munitions that had entered China through British-owned Hong Kong and were bound for the armies to the north. During the morning and afternoon of May 28 Japanese planes circled mercilessly over Canton, methodically dropping their 500-lb. bombs. They hit their "military objective" four times, the Wongsha station of the north railroad, but they incidentally killed 700 Cantonese, wounded 1,000. Cantonese charged that they also swooped down to machine-gun Red Cross workers (see the next page) who had run out to rescue the wounded. For the impotent civilians there was nothing to do but squat and cry, like the poor coolie mother who in the picture above grieves for her dead daughter. The next day and the next and the next the Japanese planes returned to drop their loads, though on the fourth day some Chinese planes returned from the north and

fought them off. At this the Japanese took a two-day recess until the Chinese planes had gone back to the front. Then they began another series, this one lasting, up to June 10, for eight consecutive days. They came over in squadrons of half-a-dozen, 50 at a time, sometimes in three shifts, morning, afternoon and by moonlight.

They first made shambles of the railway stations to Hankow and Hong Kong, then went for government buildings, schools, factories, tenement districts, the Sun Yat-sen Memorial Hall, power plants and even the U. S.-owned Lingnan University. The total dead on June 10 was 3,000; the wounded 5,000. Half of Canton's 1,000,000 had scuttled out of the city, but the people had frozen into a kind of stolid rage, without panic. One boy was seen giving a glass of water to his mother, who lay pinned under a huge stone.

On June 3 the U. S. State Department voiced general disapproval of the "ruthless bombings of unfortified localities." On June 8 it specifically protested the Japanese bombing of Lingnan University. Great Britain and France also protested this outrageous device of modern warfare. Japan replied that the air raids on Canton were a success and therefore would be continued, that Canton was fortified and that most of the victims were killed by "careless anti-aircraft fire."

Figure 3.7. "A Chinese Mother Weeps as Death Falls from the Sky upon Canton," *Life,* **June 20, 1938.**

ian Chinese to bring home the message that not only military personnel were being killed. A full-page photograph headlined "The Camera Overseas: The Chinese Consign to His Ancestors One Small Citizen" was employed as an editorial. It was a picture of the limp body of a dead child suspended by a worker whose fist clutches the child's shirt and pants at belly level (Figure 3.6). The child's drooping arms extend backward toward the earth into which the body will be placed. A stack of adult-sized coffins awaits to the left

in the background, and two women, faces out of focus, work to prepare another. Facing toward the camera, two laborers stand above a tiny coffin open at their feet. The tender age of the victim reinforces a message about the indiscriminate hand of war. The caption simply stated "Wartime burial of a Chinese child whose parents were prosperous enough to buy him shoes."[38] The caption's pointing out of the economic status of the parents, and the goods purchased as a result of that status, suggest that *Life* also wanted its readers to consider the loss of potential customers in deaths like this child's.

In a similar way, an article from June 1938 titled "A Chinese Mother Weeps as Death Falls from the Sky upon Canton" connected middle-class American mothers with Chinese mothers. The woman kneels in the foreground in front of a child whose body is half hidden behind her, dead face turned toward the camera (Figure 3.7). The caption, which reinforces the helplessness of the Chinese, stated "For the impotent civilians there was nothing to do but squat and cry like the poor coolie mother who in the picture above grieves for her dead daughter." It is sadly ironic that *Life* diminished its message with "coolie," as if it were too much trouble to inquire about the woman's actual occupation and station in life. In this article on the bombing of Canton, *Life* used a caption it first introduced under a picture of dead soldiers from the Spanish civil war, "dead men have died in vain if live men refuse to look at them," to justify its graphic depiction of death. Perhaps the editors hoped to stir readers' memories to create a connection between the deaths of Chinese and those of white-skinned Europeans.[39]

Carrying its coverage of the Sino-Japanese War into the 1940s, *Life* occasionally focused upon nonwar images of the Chinese then circulating in the American popular culture. An article in February 1940 explained a new American craze: "Confucius Say: America Go Crazy over Chinese Philosopher." *Life* furthered readers' acquaintance with inane expressions, crude parodies of Confucian axioms, such as "Girl with future should beware of man with past." The fad included singer Guy Lombardo's hit, "Confucius Say"; women's Confucius Say dresses; a best-selling book of two hundred "witty daring" Confucius remarks; and Confucius parodies in Walter Winchell's column and comedians Jack Benny's and Fred Allen's radio programs.[40] This commodification of things supposedly Chinese indicated a proprietary attitude toward China, and *Life*'s participation in marketing these images helped reinforce a sense of connection between America and China.

Life's presentation of this association between the American consumer and China was an intentional and, perhaps, essential step in its efforts to garner support for China. Indeed, one of Henry Luce's most powerful essays arguing for interventionism, "The American Century," focused on American commercial interests and the potential of markets in China. Published in *Life* on February 17, 1941, the article said, "We are *not* in a war to defend American territory. We are in a war to defend and even to promote, encourage and incite so-called democratic principles throughout the world." Conspicuous among these principles was capitalistic interest in other nations. When Luce maintained that America had already exported its ideology and culture to willing, recipient nations, the commercial and the cultural were inextricably mixed: "Once we cease to distract ourselves with lifeless arguments about isolationism, we shall be amazed to discover that there is already an immense American internationalism. American jazz, Hollywood movies, American slang, American machines and patented products, are in fact the only thing that every community in the world, from Zanzibar to Hamburg, recognizes in common. Blindly, unintentionally, accidentally and really in spite of ourselves, we are already a world power in all the trivial ways—in very human ways."[41]

Luce described China as offering economic prosperity to America. Calling forth an old dream of the China market, Luce wrote, "Our thinking of world trade today is on ridiculously small terms. For example, we think of Asia as being worth only a few hundred millions a year to us. Actually, in the decades to come Asia will be worth to us exactly zero—or else it will be worth to us four, five, ten billions of dollars a year."[42] As potential consumers of American goods, the Chinese, Luce argued, had become others worthy of support.

In articles that followed, *Life* urged an alliance with the Chinese on the ground that they would be allies when, not if, America entered the war. The idea that America stood to profit economically lay beneath these messages. In articles discussing voluntary humanitarian networks in China, Americans were depicted as champions of democracy who would guide a struggling democracy such as China. In June 1941 *Life* focused on U.S. relief efforts, especially United China Relief and China fund-raising groups in which Henry Luce personally made large investments. Americans working on behalf of China included school children raising funds; the wealthy, such as John D. Rockefeller III, who participated in ritzy relief benefits; Hollywood celebrities appealing for aid on radio programs; and a variety of local business leaders initiating campaigns. To Americans who had remained aloof for five years while the Chinese suffered, *Life* stated, "The job of saving the children and the people of China rests heavily now in the hands of Americans."[43] This image of Americans as saviors of the struggling Chinese became a theme in *Life*'s reporting throughout the 1940s.

Prior to the December 7 Japanese attack on Pearl Harbor, *Life* played a part in moving the American public toward a state of war readiness. It is nearly impossible now to distinguish the actual impact of *Life*'s editorials and imaging of the Chinese from other influences, including other media and the war in Europe. It might be claimed that *Life*, however brief, succeeded in positively reshaping the images Americans held of the Chinese. Conversely, it could be argued that *Life* simply helped Americans transfer longstanding antipathy against Asians from the Chinese to the Japanese, bringing racist targeting more into conformity with the emerging national economic and strategic interests. *Life* seems to have succeeded most fully in employing the rhetoric of consumerism in its efforts to persuade it readers. Hope that China would be a future market for the United States underscored many of *Life*'s articles prior to and after U.S. entry into the war.

Following U.S. entry into the war in 1941, Luce, a steadfast supporter of Nationalist leader Chiang Kai-shek, turned the publication policy for *Life* back to support for the Nationalists and renunciation of the communists. Theodore "Teddy" White, who had formerly written press releases for the KMT, was employed to write for *Time* and *Life* in 1939 and became a well-noted China correspondent. Although they would later break over publication policy and censorship issues after Whitaker Chambers took over as foreign editor for *Time*, in the beginning, White and Luce shared the belief that Chiang Kai-shek was the "best leader China could provide." Although White often offered frank criticism of the Chiang regime, he also wrote articles that supported Luce's preference for the Nationalists. Such is the case in a March 1942 article in *Life* in which White provided a laudatory biographical account of Chiang Kai-shek.[44]

Over time, however, White and other correspondents became increasingly disillusioned with the corruption they witnessed in the Chiang regime. Yet reports critical of the Nationalists rarely got through the press censorship in the wartime capital of Chungking, and the stories that did get out were cut, polished, and sometimes radically altered back in New York at Time, Inc.'s, editorial offices. In his recent work, *China Hands*, Peter Rand noted, ". . . Luce's achievement was the use to which he put facts in his publications so that they represented what he wanted them to." Nevertheless, when White returned briefly to the United States in 1944, he was surprised that Luce let him publish an article critical of China in *Life*. In "*Life* Looks at China," published in May 1944, White tried to correct myths and misconceptions about China, suggesting that American images of China were inaccurate: popular images of China as the treaty-port nation were outdated; images attached to Madame Chiang Kai-shek were unreliable; and the image of the Nationalists as fascists was also incorrect. Although he agreed that a corrupt political clique dominated the KMT, he did not include Chiang in that assessment. White explained that a KMT blockade of the communist areas prohibited securing accurate information to make a fair assessment of the Communist Party. The CCP's appeal to peasants and the working class put it in conflict with the KMT, which attracted China's middle class. Given these class tensions, White predicted that civil war was inevitable.

In criticizing the U.S. government for only partially keeping promises made to China, White helped to establish what would become a theme in *Life* at the end of the war. He urged Americans to reassess and reaffirm support for China, specifically the Nationalists, stating "The Chinese people are possessed of an affection for America which is one of our greatest assets in foreign affairs. To keep the permanent friendship of this great nation, almost any price is small." The appeal of a China aligned with American values and aspirations marks his closing statement. If the United States does not deny its obligation to help China, he asserted, "we shall find on reaching China vital forces eager to join us in pursuing the ends we consider the true ideals of America."[45]

Having gained access to the communist territories later in 1944, White wrote "Inside Red China." The article suggested that a political truce between the KMT and the CCP might be in the making. White reported that the CCP wanted the United States to recognize that it has power against the Japanese, that its army and government function as a democracy, and that it will go to great lengths to be friends with the United States. Although White undermined these claims by stating that the CCP only supports democracy because it pays, he added, "In proclaiming their friendship with the U.S. the Communists at present are sincere and if their friendship is reciprocated it can become a lasting thing." In prophetic closing words, White said, "Presently it wants American friendship more than any other single conditioning force for the future of China. . . . In victory they will remember who were friends and who stood coldly aloof."[46] Despite this prescient warning, White did not explicitly urge American alliance with or help for the CCP. Moreover, subsequent editorials indicated that these appeals for friendship with the CCP did not move *Life*'s editors or readers.

Following the end of the war in August 1945, concern about whether China would be embroiled in civil war and whether it would become communist or democratic became a major concern of *Life*'s editors. In No-

vember 1945, in "China Reborn," Charles Murphy expressed hope that differences between the KMT and the CCP will be resolved.[47] Murphy did not disparage communism entirely, but he said that internationalism was its greatest difficulty. In a pattern of the time, he downplayed the communist threat in China, suggesting that those labeled communists were not all true adherents. Reflecting a growing apprehension about a military coalition between the CCP and Moscow, Murphy said there was certainly already a political alliance. This suspicion about an affiliation between the Chinese communists and the Soviet Union recurred in *Life* thereafter.

Growing fear that a communist China might foreclose American possibilities in China pivoted *Life* into a fervent anticommunist campaign. Mere months after the war, *Life* editors began to distinguish in more forceful terms the differences between the Chinese it deemed like, and those it deemed unlike, Americans. This turn is evident in mid-November 1945, in "China: What Price Peace?" the editors call for U.S. internationalists to stand behind their former promises to support wartime friends in China, warning that China will face civil war if America does not make good on assurances made to the KMT. Then, conjuring forth the magazine's earliest images of the communists as cruel and inhuman, the editors cautioned readers about what it presumes to know as the true nature of the CCP: "But the Chinese Communists differ from other countries' Communists in an important respect: instead of just preaching and politicking, they shoot and they control."[48]

In December 1945, while striving to allay fear of a communist victory in China, Charles Murphy heightened the anxiety over a potential alliance between China and the Soviet Union in "Crisis in China." Murphy assured readers that the communist position is hopeless without direct help from Russia. He does concede that, "At their best the Communists introduced a genuine democracy into the bottom of Chinese life—the bottom where the hundreds of millions are."[49]

Nonetheless, debunking claims of American apologists who depicted the communists as agrarian democrats, Murphy reported about destruction of property, the killing of village elders, ruthless imprisonment, and the silent, scared people in communist regions. In conjuring forth an image of Chinese multitudes, Murphy fed a dread of millions unified under a political system antagonistic to the ideals of America.

By 1946 the Chinese communists had once again become the other—unfamiliar and unlike Americans—in the pages of *Life*. Fear of pervasive communist threat emerged in articles such as Henry P. Van Dusen's, which claimed that the Chinese communists were showing themselves to be truly like the Russians. Van Dusen confirmed reports out of North China, based on hearsay, of communist brutality, terrorism, and tyranny. Creating an image of a monolithic enemy, he stated, ". . . the Chinese Communists are committed to a single ultimate aim—domination of all China." Such sweeping statements about the CCP would provide fertile ground for later claims that communists wanted to conquer and dominate the world. Van Dusen evoked a fear that America might become embroiled in war again. He warned, "China in Communist hands would be the most probable, one may almost say certain, prelude to World War III."[50]

By the late 1940s *Life* articles were helping set the stage for the charges of "un-Americanism" that would be launched against the "Old China Hands" during the red scare that would later consume the nation's energies. Pointing to a failure in American foreign policy toward China in the days following the communist victory in Mainland China in October 1949, these articles helped arouse a widely asked question—Who lost China? Reporting in increasingly anticommunist tones years before that event, *Life* asserted that the Chinese communists were becoming aggressively anti-American. In March 1947, under the bold headline "Struggle for the World," *Life* predicted that communism doomed Western civilization. James Burnham opened the article, "The Third World War began in April 1944"

and proclaimed that an international, monolithic communism based in the Soviet Union aimed to create a communist world empire. With regard to China, blame was assigned to American advisers who urged Chiang to take communists into his government. Burnham said, "The objective of the Communists is not to make China a unified democratic nation but to turn it into a Communist totalitarian province."[51] In language reminiscent of Luce's "The American Century," Burnham argued for an American empire to counter a communist world empire.

In January 1949 *Life* editors seemed to acknowledge that the communists would win mainland China. In cautioning readers that a communist victory in China was a victory for the Soviet Union and a disaster for the United States, they strengthened the image of a monolithic foe, the other diametrically opposed to Americans values.[52] By May 1949 *Life* once again showed pictures of Chinese kneeling before the executioner's gun, photos strangely reminiscent of its earliest coverage of the Chinese in 1936. The photographs show Nationalists shooting fifth columnists, and the article explains that Shanghai citizens wished for a quick communist takeover in the hope of averting a terror campaign.[53] These images of the Chinese as executors and executed once again placed the Chinese people, Nationalists and communists alike, outside of the American norm, hearkening back to former notions of the Chinese as others who did not value human life.

Despite occasional articles that questioned the character of even the Nationalist Chinese, *Life*'s strongest antipathy was reserved for the communists. *Life*'s reporting supported a policy of containment and furthered a fear that eventually paved the way for American entry into war in Vietnam. This fear that communist China would eventually mean a communist Asia was clearly expressed by Gen. Claire Chennault in July 1949, when he warned that a CCP takeover in China would mean the spread of communism throughout Asia. In predicting that the raw materials of Asia would be denied to the United States and that its markets would be closed,

Chennault clearly established the nature of this threat—a loss to America's commercial interests.[54] When in fact Mao Tse-tung announced the People's Republic of China in October 1949, *Life* clearly drew the line between the Chinese who were friends and the Chinese who were other—the enemy. In no uncertain terms, *Life* sounded the battle cry, "The Communist regime now completing its conquest of the Chinese mainland is an enemy of the U.S. and of all that the U.S. stands for in Asia and elsewhere."[55]

In the early 1950s this vitriolic antipathy toward the communists pervaded *Life*'s reporting. As America entered the Korean conflict, tensions increased and depictions of demonic Chinese communists grew. Reports of brainwashing, the murder of clergy, and imprisonment of Americans filled the magazine's pages. In January 1950 "The Conqueror from the Caves" provided a portrait of Mao and predicted that the communist revolution would follow three stages: nod head, or official politeness; shake head, or official toughening; and chop head, a period of confident communist rule.[56] Photographs of communist executions of landlords in "speak bitterness" sessions filled pages in January 1953.[57] While *Life* articles vilified the communists, little attention was paid to the violence associated with Chiang Kai-shek's takeover of Taiwan. One article focused on a prison camp run by the Nationalists on Green Island, where those labeled as communists were interred.[58] The article was laudatory and uncritical of the Nationalists. With regard to the mainland, however, by 1954 *Life* editors attributed to Red China a plan to "subvert and control the whole world" and proclaimed that "China is an enemy of civilization."[59]

Life's earnest efforts to build a bridge of friendship between the United States and China in the 1930s and early 1940s gave way to a vituperative denunciation of mainland China in the early 1950s. The bridge of friendship was made impassable by governmental policies on both sides, supported by the popular media in both nations. The nature of reporting in *Life* and other journals in the 1950s effectively blocked the formation of a public opinion that could support or sustain a dialogue with the communists. In place of language evoking the historical friendship between nations, a stalemate between bitter enemies set the tone for reporting. Ironically, the Japanese, who once had been depicted as others more villainous than even the Chinese communists, emerged as American friends and were lauded in the press.

From its earliest issues, *Life*'s editors claimed that their photographs could almost take a reader to the scene. By the 1950s, however, communist China was not a place readers wanted to be taken too, even if the Chinese government had allowed it. Yet, even as short-lived American interest in China receded, *Life* continued to exert an influence on popular images of the Chinese. These images neither shaped nor completely reflected U.S. foreign policy, but they may have sanctioned or helped to set in motion a set of attitudes and actions toward mainland China during the Cold War.

The media's ability to create images of others is not a thing of the past. The influence and implications of image shaping is worth contemplating even today. In Beijing in the mid-1990s, a television documentary on Beijing TV-1 depicted events in the Sino-Japanese War. Among hundreds of images that flashed across the screen as a narrator described the "Rape of Nanking," were many that had originally appeared in *Life* magazine. These included the severed head lodged in the barbed-wire barricade, the old man cradling his child, and the limp body of the child carried to his coffin. We can only speculate about how those images used within American culture more than fifty years ago were received in China in the 1990s. Their use evokes a perplexing set of questions concerning how pictures once employed within one culture to represent and shape images of others are later used by those very people in that different culture and historical context. Perhaps it confirms the inherent power of the photographic image to transcend time and place. Or, it may prove the power of words and historical context to shape or reshape the meanings of an image.

At different times and from different needs, a nation's peoples conceptualize other cultures and other people as like or unlike themselves. Images and impressions we hold of others influence not only the way we act toward those others, but also contribute to or even make possible self-definition, whether as nations, ethnic groups, or individuals. James Clifford said that scrutinizing a culture's perceptions of others evokes ". . . a substantial and disquieting set of questions about the ways in which distinct groups of humanity (however defined) imagine, describe, and comprehend each other."[60] Perhaps more disquieting are questions about how perceptions of others influence action, or inaction, toward those others.

Scenes of death and destruction in China filled pages of *Life* magazine for years. Pictures flashed before the eyes of common people in the United States, touching sentiments, but failing for many years to provoke action. Such images led, perhaps, to a numbing of sensitivity, to a sense of distance from the scenes depicted. *Life*'s images of the Chinese could horrify, sicken, and impress, but they were, after all, just pictures of others.

NOTES

1. For demographic information on *Life*'s readership, see James L. Baughman, *Henry R. Luce and the Rise of the American News Media* (Boston: Twayne Publishers, 1987), 92–95. Baughman stated that "No magazine in American history had passed the half-million mark so soon after its initial release. . . . *Life* had a circulation of seven hundred sixty thousand." Over 15 percent of the American adult population read *Life*. That readership was predominantly middle class.

   Chinese names are rendered in the transliteration system employed by *Life* throughout the period on which this study focuses rather than in the pinyin standard now acceptable in international journalism.

2. James Clifford, *The Predicament of Culture: Twentieth-Century Ethnography, Literature, and Art* (Cambridge: Harvard University Press, 1988), 258.

3. For a discussion of the authority implied in ethnographic studies, see ibid., 8.

4. Wendy Kozol, *Life's America: Family and Nation in Postwar America* (Philadelphia: Temple University Press, 1994), 172. In Kenneth Shewmaker, *Americans and Chinese Communists: A Persuading Encounter* (Ithaca: Cornell University Press, 1971), 5–6, it is suggested that in critiquing American journalists and observers who encountered the Chinese communists in the 1930s and 1940s, it is easy "to look backward and condemn . . . (but) one of the historian's tasks is to understand events in their proper context."

5. American popular perceptions of the Chinese is a topic addressed in several significant texts. See, for example, A. T. Steele, *The American People and China* (New York: McGraw-Hill, 1966); Eugene Wong, *On Visual Media Racism* (New York: Arno Press, 1978); John W. Dower, *War without Mercy: Race and Power in the Pacific War* (New York: Pantheon Books, 1986); Gina Marchetti, *Romance and the "Yellow Peril"* (Berkeley: University of California Press, 1993); and Philip P. Choy, Lorraine Dong, and Marlon K. Hom, eds., *Coming Man: 19th-Century American Perceptions of the Chinese* (Seattle: University of Washington Press, 1995).

6. Alexander Sexton, *The Indispensable Enemy: Labor and the Anti-Chinese Movement in California* (Berkeley: University of California Press, 1971), 19, cited in Wong, *On Visual Media Racism*, vi.

7. Dower, *War without Mercy*, 155.

8. Ibid., 164–65. Dower pointed out that "the Chinese had been singled out by name as undesirable immigrants in no less than fifteen federal laws, or parts of laws, passed between 1882 and 1913—a dishonor done to no other nationality."

9. For a more developed discussion of the Neutrality Acts, see Robert H. Ferrell, *American Diplomacy: The Twentieth Century* (New York: W. W. Norton, 1988); Michael Schaller, *The United States and China in the Twentieth Century* (New York: Oxford University Press, 1979); and Robert D. Schulzinger, *American Diplomacy in the Twentieth Century* (New York: Oxford University Press, 1990).

10. For further discussion of U.S. relations with China during this period and American attitudes toward the Sino-Japanese War, consult Warren I. Cohen, *America's Response to China: An Interpretive History of Sino-American Relations* (New York: John Wiley, 1971); K. Holly Maze Carter, *The Asian Dilemma in U.S. Foreign Policy: National Interests versus Strategic Planning* (New York: M. E. Sharpe, 1989); Robert A. Hart, *The Eccentric Tradition: American Diplomacy in the Far East* (New York: Scribners, 1976); Harold Isaacs, *Scratches on Our Minds: American Views of China and India* (Armonk, N.Y.: M. E. Sharpe, 1980); Anthony Kubek, *The Red China Papers* (New Rochelle, N.Y.: Ar-

lington House Publishers, 1975); Michael Schaller, *The United States and China in the Twentieth Century* (New York: Oxford University Press, 1979); and Waldo Heinrichs, "The Middle Years, 1900–1945, and the Question of a Large U.S. Policy for East Asia," in *New Frontiers in American-East Asian Relations* (New York: Columbia University Press, 1983).

11. Schulzinger, *American Diplomacy in the Twentieth Century,* 159.

12. For a discussion of Luce's attempts to influence policy makers about the Sino-Japanese War, see Patricia Neils, *China Images in the Life and Times of Henry Luce* (Savage, Md.: Rowman and Littlefield Publishers, 1990). For a discussion of the influence of advertisers and business interests upon *Life,* see Robert E. Herzstein, *Henry R. Luce: A Political Portrait of the Man Who Created the American Century* (New York: Scribners, 1994) and James L. Baughman, *Henry R. Luce and the Rise of the American News Media* (Boston: Twayne Publishers, 1987).

13. There was an American Committee for Non-Participation in Japanese Aggression, a citizens group headed by Henry Stimson, that informed publishers of Japanese activities in China and urged the public to support boycotts, embargoes, and alliance with China.

14. "Twenty-Two Years after, America Ponders Its World War Lesson," *Life,* 17 April 1939, 13–15.

15. A. T. Steele, *The American People and China* (New York: McGraw-Hill, 1966), 20.

16. "Chinese School," *Life,* 23 November 1936, 24–25.

17. The Sian (Xi' an) Incident took its name from the city nearby the hot springs where Chang Hsueh-liang kidnapped Chiang Kai-shek. Michael Schaller noted that "On December 13, 1936, news reached the outside world that the KMT dissidents at Sian had seized Chiang in order to compel him to form a new United Front" (*The United States and China in the Twentieth Century,* 45).

18. "The Cruel Chinese," *Life,* 28 December 1936, 50–56.

19. Wendy Kozol stated that "Photography has the ability to establish a terrain of the Other by turning the subject into an object captured by the film and put on display as a spectacle." Kozol, *Life's America,* 24.

20. Eugene Wong stated that the Hollywood film industry of the 1920s created images of the "hostile, threatening, and savage Asiatic based largely upon the Chinese." The industry began to depict more favorable yet no less stereotypical images of the Chinese in the 1930s. Wong, *On Visual Media Racism,* 70.

21. "Movie of the Week: The Good Earth," *Life,* 18 January 1937, 50–56.

22. Richard M. Fried, *Nightmare in Red: The McCarthy Era in Perspective* (Oxford: Oxford University Press, 1990), 12–13.

23. Agnes Smedley, "The Chinese Communists," *Life,* 25 January 1937, 9–15.

24. Snow traveled in the communist areas of the Northwest from June 1936 to October 1936. Edgar Snow, *Red Star over China* (New York: Grove Press, 1938), 13.

25. Smedley, "The Chinese Communists," 12.

26. "An Army of Fighters Chinese Communists Takes Possession of China's Northwest," *Life,* 1 February 1937, 42–45.

27. "Headlines Proclaim the Rise of Fascism and Communism in America," *Life,* 26 July 1937, 19–27. See also Chapter 4 in this book, "The Pitiless Spotlight of Publicity: *Life* and the World War II–Era Exposure of American Extremists," by Brett Gary.

28. "The Junkman's Pile Moves toward the Munitions Factory," *Life,* 19 April 1937, 64–68.

29. "Japan Wolfs U.S. Scrap," ibid., 62–68.

30. "Chinese Coolies Level off an Airport . . . ," *Life,* 19 April 1937, 62.

31. "The Chinese Outfight the Japanese as Shanghai Blazes," *Life,* 13 September 1937, 23–27.

32. "Mei Ling ('Beautiful Mood') Helps Her Husband Rule China," *Life,* 16 August 1937, 17–21.

33. "The Camera Overseas: Chinese Communists to the Rescue," *Life,* 11 October 1937, 100–3.

34. "A Terrible Blunder Puts Japan's Ambassador on the Anxious Seat," *Life,* 27 December 1937, 9–13.

35. "A Universal Cameraman Documents American History: 'The Panay Incident,'" *Life,* 10 January 1938, 11–17.

36. "China's Refugee Millions Stampede Up the Yangtze: Nanking Citizens Board Steamer," *Life,* 10 January 1938, 32–33.

37. "The Japanese Conqueror Brings a 'Week of Hell' to China's National Capital of Nanking," *Life,* 10 January 1938, 50–51.

38. "The Camera Overseas: The Chinese Consign to His Ancestors One Small Citizen," *Life,* 21 February 1938, 54.

39. "Death from the Air: The Bombing of Canton," *Life,* 20 June 1938, 9–13. Vicki Goldberg argued that "*Life*'s orotund sermon on the power of photographs was a partisan plea for the chance to print dramatic pictures and pull more subscribers." Vicki Goldberg, *The Power of Photography* (New York: Aberville Press, 1991), 198. *Life* editors argued differently, claiming that they wanted readers to face the brutality of war and more importantly, the importance of the antifascist fight. Nonetheless, they acknowledged that pictures could not awaken in a viewer the same fear or terror that actual events conjured forth in real participants.

40. "Confucius Say: America Go Crazy over Chinese Philosopher," *Life,* 19 February 1940, 30.

41. Henry Luce, "The American Century," *Life,* 17 February 1941, 62, 65.

42. Ibid., 65.

43. "China Relief: U.S. Opens Purse," *Life,* 23 June 1941, 59–67.

44. Peter Rand, *China Hands: The Adventures and Ordeals of the American Jounalists Who Joined Forces with the Great Chinese Revolution* (New York: Simon and Schuster, 1995), 193. Working with Hollington Tong for the Chinese Ministry of Information (MOI), "Teddy" White fed stories to the foreign press that writers for the MOI developed. Theodore H. White, "Chiang Kai-shek," *Life,* 2 March 1942, 70–80.

45. T. H. White, "*Life* Looks at China: Through the Blockade One of Its Correspondents Brings This Firsthand Report," *Life,* 1 May 1944, 98–110.

46. T. H. White, "Inside Red China," *Life*, 18 December 1944, 39–46.

47. Charles J. V. Murphy, "China Reborn," *Life*, 12 November 1945, 112–24.

48. "China: What Price Peace?" *Life*, 19 November 1945, 36–37.

49. "Crisis in China," *Life*, 17 December 1945, 106–18.

50. Henry P. Van Dusen, "China's Crisis," *Life*, 2 September 1946, 36–37.

51. James Burnham, "Struggle for the World," *Life*, 31 March 1947, 59–80.

52. "Challenge in Asia," *Life*, 3 January 1949, 24.

53. "The Shanghai Gesture, 1949," *Life*, 23 May 1949, 48–49.

54. Claire L. Chennault, "Last Call for China," *Life*, 11 July 1949 , 36.

55. "And Now Formosa," *Life*, 19 December 1949, 24.

56. Robert Doyle, "The Conqueror from the Caves," *Life*, 23 January 1950, 80–90.

57. "Red China Reforms a $2/_3$-Acre Landlord," *Life*, 19 January 1953, 14–17.

58. John Osborne, "Free China's Forbidden Green Island," *Life*, 26 April 1954, 83–92.

59. "Behind the Face of China," *Life*, 14 June 1954, 24–25.

60. Clifford, *The Predicament of Culture*, 26.

4

BRETT GARY

THE PITILESS SPOTLIGHT OF PUBLICITY

Life *and the World War II–Era Exposure of American Extremists*

The phrase "pitiless spotlight of publicity" and its variations first appeared in the 1930s and 1940s in response to the threat of foreign-inspired subversion in the United States. The phrase conveyed the hope that exposing and publicizing extremist groups—especially fascists and communists—would be a salutary, democratic response to such threats, since it was believed most Americans would reject radical ideas if adequately informed about the actual foreign influences behind them. One of the most respected antifascist investigators in the "Brown Scare" era, Reverend L. M. Birkhead, founder of Friends of Democracy, Inc., and publisher of the journal *Propaganda Battlefront*, used the phrase "publicity spotlight" to explain his purposes in exposing the propaganda strategies, financial links, political connections, and ideological profiles of domestic right-wing groups and individuals.[1]

Congressman John McCormack used the same language to describe the goals of the 1938 Foreign Agents Registration Act, which called for the "pitiless spotlight of publicity" directed against groups disseminating "vicious propaganda of foreign origin." The McCormack-Dickstein Committee found significant Nazi and communist activity in the United States in the mid-1930s and argued that exposure and registration of these groups would generate "an aroused and intelligent public opinion," which the committee's report described as the "surest safeguard for those fundamental principles of American liberty." Without public exposure, the committee warned, "such activity will increase in scope and . . . will inevitably constitute a definite menace."[2]

Henry Luce's *Life* magazine also found a threat to American society—especially to domestic unity and U.S. foreign-policy interests—in fascist and communist activity at home and abroad. From 1937 to 1947 *Life* consistently took the position that aiming a visual or editorial spotlight on un-American groups and ideas was more democratic, more respectful of the Bill of Rights, and less subject to abuse than were laws that censored or made such groups illegal. Like the American policy makers it reported on, and the millions of readers it reached on a weekly basis, *Life*'s cautiously tolerant position about freedom of speech and association shifted rightward as the war-era crises deepened and as the temporary wartime rapprochement with the USSR turned to global competition against it at war's end, reflecting (and perhaps shaping) mainstream opinion. While *Life* consistently claimed that the intense beam of journalistic and congressional exposure was the surest safeguard for American democracy, its editorial commitment to tolerance and freedom of press and association diminished as the war approached—because of its anxieties about the native fascists' capacity to disunify Americans, its disgust with the Nazi-Soviet pact and the American communists' subsequent shifts in policy and rhetoric, and its growing suspicions of invidious Soviet influence over American liberals, especially as World War II ended.

By the early Cold War *Life* enthusiastically vilified left liberals and openly supported what it described as the need for "responsible" Red hunting. Its main question was whether the House Un-American Activities Committee (HUAC) or fellow-traveling liberals were more damaging to American democracy. Never quite settling on an answer, it averred that at least HUAC had capacity to shine a searching spotlight on those who hid their real loyalties and intentions from the Ameri-

can public. I suggest, then, that while the metaphor of the "pitiless spotlight" remained a consistent one for *Life* as an expression of the need to expose supposedly antidemocratic and subversive forces in the American body politic, the tone and urgency surrounding its invocation changed from essentially a Popular Front rejection of restrictive legislation and "nervous liberalism" (to use New Deal liberal and poet Archibald MacLeish's apt phrase) in the 1930s, to a postwar vindication of anticommunist fervor. *Life*'s shift is a telling chronicle of the ideologically restrictive national security logic that overtook American political culture from 1937 to 1947, where the mainstream commitment to civil liberties existed in a tense and often unbalanced relationship with the perceived imperatives of rooting out domestic subversion.

During the Popular Front period, from 1935 to 1939, few within the larger community of liberal government officials, writers, churchmen, and scholars believed that American-based Nazi activities could be ignored. Congressional and Justice Department investigations, reports by private organizations such as Friends of Democracy, the American Council Against Nazi Propaganda, and the B'Nai Brith Anti-Defamation League, and a plethora of left-liberal journal and book-length reports all indicated that there was a large and well-financed Nazi movement flourishing in the United States.[3] The movement's activities included disseminating propaganda through numerous German-American organizations, sympathetic German-American newspapers, shortwave radio broadcasts beamed from Germany, and through official German channels. By the late 1930s and early 1940s, many interpreted the Nazi infiltration of the United States through a prism that compared it to the fate of Austria, Poland, Belgium, Norway, France, and other European nations that had been undermined by fifth columnists who had prepared the way for Nazi military conquest. For those concerned with ubiquitous profascist materials in the United States, subjugated Europe provided compelling evidence of the power of the Nazi strategy for conquest through rumor, propaganda, and campaigns of disunity.[4]

The question of what to do about Nazi activities in the United States was problematic, however. The tension between security-oriented liberals (who proposed speech and association-restrictive measures) and free-speech liberals (who opposed such measures) is reflected in *Life*'s effort to work out a consistent position toward the far right. *Life* frequently took a stance similar to that expressed by Archibald MacLeish (a Luce friend and employee who broke with Luce over the Spanish civil war): MacLeish regularly took to task those so frightened by fascism and communism that they were willing to restrict fundamental freedoms by making party affiliation and extreme political speech illegal. To MacLeish, this was the paradox of strangling democracy in order to save it, and he warned that the greater danger to American democracy came not from conservatives or even reactionaries, but from the "nervous liberals" who would "preserve the gentle heifer of liberalism from the fascists [by shooting] her through the head."[5] Prior to the Nazi-Soviet pact in August 1939, *Life* echoed this speech-protective position, counseling tolerance to government and citizens' groups alike, contending that it and other responsible parties shine the pitiless spotlight on extremist groups and that the United States should avoid any measures that restricted fundamental liberties for its citizens and denizens.

In the fraught and fractious political landscape of the Popular Front era, *Life*'s position was progressive, promoted by the interwar generation's most dedicated civil libertarians. Likewise, *Life* made vital distinctions between the far right and left and generally avoided linking Nazism and communists as essentially the same "totalitarian" menace, unlike some American foreign affairs journalists who frequently used the phrases "Red Fascism" and "Brown Bolshevism" to encapsulate these ideologically opposed movements.[6] For much of the press the similarities between Nazism and communism were more important than the differences, and totalitarianism was widely used in the mid-1930s

to describe modern dictatorships in general. But for *Life*, which always had an eye on foreign-policy matters, the animus between Hitler and Stalin, and the significant differences in their ideologies and systems seemed more important than whatever common features they might have had—until the Nazi-Soviet pact when *Life* began to consistently invoke the "red fascism/brown bolshevism" trope to suggest that the two systems were equally treacherous.

Prior to the Nazi-Soviet pact, however, *Life* was far less critical of American communists and tended to depict Popular Front iconography rather uncritically. Meanwhile, it visually and rhetorically vilified the American far right, confidently and unapologetically connecting it to the Nazi menace abroad. From its inception in 1936, *Life* provided visually compelling coverage of the Third Reich, race-hate doctrines, Nuremberg spectacles, foreign-policy machinations, and fifth-column campaigns. Therefore, when it exposed the anti-Semitic hate sheets and Bundist military parades in the United States it had already created an elaborate visual context to explain to its readers where the American fascists fit into a worldwide Nazi and fascist movement. American Nazis flying the swastika and goose-stepping on Long Island or New Jersey parade grounds were damned by the visual context of Leni Riefenstahl's elaborately choreographed rallies and Nazi artifacts, such as swastikas, brown-shirted troops, saluting youths, Hilterian mustaches, and anti-Semitic propaganda.[7]

Most important, *Life* created the context for understanding the fascist movement in the United States by spotlighting Nazi propaganda organizations and fifth column–like subversion throughout the world. Pictorials from 1937 to 1940 regularly showed the Nazis indoctrinating youth and sowing seeds of destruction. With a full-page photo of the commanding presence of Nazi politician Hermann Göring "thundering into the microphone," *Life* explained that "Germany Speaks to the World" and that Göring and his minions had not just "brought the German people under strict control"

Germany speaks to the world

Thundering into the microphone is Hermann Göring, star performer of German Nazism. His voice and those of his colleagues and minions have for the past five years given daily moral and intellectual drills by radio to 67,000,000 Germans. Having brought the German people under strict control, these imperious voices are now broadcasting to the world at large in a mighty effort to sow the seeds of fascism in foreign lands.

Right: Figure 4.1. "Germany Speaks to the World," *Life*, February 14, 1938. *Opposite:* Figure 4.2. Members of the German-American League, from "At Camp Siegfried, on Long Island. . . ," *Life*, March 29, 1937. (Courtesy European)

but had also turned to "broadcasting to the world at large in a mighty effort to sow the seeds of fascism in foreign lands" (Figure 4.1).[8]

The article said "Europe is Now Waging A War of Propaganda by Short-Wave Radio" and was illustrated with arrow-strewn maps of the Nazi capacity to beam its shortwave propaganda all over the globe. *Life* warned, "Today the radio, through the development of short-wave transmission, has become an insidious device with which the great powers of Europe are fighting one another for the mental and spiritual mastery of many hundred million people."[9] By June 1940—as

France fell to the Nazis—*Life* presented photographic evidence that there were "Signs of Nazi Fifth Columns Everywhere," in Canada, Paraguay, Brazil, Mexico, and the Americas, as well as in China, Italy, Austria, Hungary, Rumania, Czechoslovakia, Poland, Bulgaria, Greece, Netherlands, Denmark, France, England, and Belgium.[10] For *Life*, this Nazi fifth-column movement justified a growing intolerance of fascist activity in the United States.

As Germany became more aggressive abroad, as anti-Semitism grew more violent, and as American Nazis themselves became more violent, *Life*'s rancor grew and so did its insistence that responsible parties—like the Dies Committee—expose the American Nazi movement as a dangerous source of hatred, violence, and potential American disunity. Yet, at the same time, it generally counseled tolerance and nonviolence.

In its first photo-essay on the American Nazi move-ment in 1937, "The 'American Nazis' Claim 200,000 Members," *Life* used six photographs and only one-half column of text.[11] Visually, it highlighted a snarling, saluting Bundsführer Fritz Kuhn, whom *Life* dubbed the "No. 1 American Nazi," and exposed more generally the culture of militarism American fascists displayed. The photo-essay featured a German-American League rally at Camp Siegfried in New Jersey, implicitly asking whether it was possible to wear Nazi-styled uniforms, use Nazi rituals and poses, and still be American (Figure 4.2). The written text suggests that being American meant eschewing military paraphernalia and "long, windy speeches," and certainly not polluting emblems of Americana by placing foreign flags and symbols in either equal or superior positions to the American flag. The Bundists' iconographic un-Americanness was reinforced by the text's explanation that besides their declared objectives of "fighting Commu-

nism, Jews and the American Jewish boycott of German goods," they "Presumably [were] also in favor of an American Fascist dictatorship." A second page of photographs visually elaborated the German-American Bundists' aggressive failure to assimilate into American democratic culture.

As Figure 4.2 shows, older German-American women, middle-aged men, younger men, and even small boys gave the Nazi salute, suggesting the possibility that generations of American-born children might be inured to democratic principles if the Nazis had their way. Lest readers worry too much, *Life* tried to quell a potential public reaction by reporting that most German-Americans were loyal Americans and that the Bundists had "no more bitter enemies in the U.S. than the non-Nazi Germans."[12]

Months later, *Life* reinforced the essentially foreign nature of fascist culture when it published an extensive photo-essay on American fascists and communists. Putatively comparative and equally critical, a theme emerged in this pictorial treatment that defined *Life*'s Popular Front–period coverage of the two movements: the American fascists were shown as being unequivocally more menacing and un-American than the communists. With the title "Headlines Proclaim the Rise of Fascism and Communism in America," *Life* reported on the twin threats by exploring the problems of labor violence in Michigan and Pennsylvania that had accompanied the wave of sit-down strikes in 1937.[13] Explaining that the nation's newspapers had "shrilled and boomed with alarms of the growth and imminent armed clash of fascist and communist forces in the U.S.," *Life* assured its readers—the "non-alarmist, democracy-loving citizens" who have "scratched their heads" over this violence—that after sending its reporters and artist Thomas Hart Benton to the Detroit area for the Fourth of July weekend, it could report that the headlines were hysterical in their excess. First of all, the ideologies of these competing creeds made them unacceptable to all but fringe Americans; "real Communism is an arduous doctrine and discipline which

has only 45,000 adherents in the U.S." Second, the "prerequisites of real Fascism are usually a genuine proletarian menace, a middle class driven to despair by disorder and want, and a leader. None of these has yet appeared convincingly in the U.S."[14]

The text suggested that good political leadership, as demonstrated by the governors of Pennsylvania and Michigan, would handle the problem. Benton's sketches completely deflated both movements, creating undifferentiated members engaged in entirely mundane activities like playing and listening to music, drinking beer, going to the zoo, engaging in conversation, and waiting peacefully in lines for ball games. The sardonic captions accompanying the sketches diminished any sense of danger posed by these groups, deflating any seriousness of purpose they might have had. As Erika Doss observed, "The visual truth inherent . . . in Benton's on-the-spot sketches would show *Life*'s view of the situation, namely, that neither organized labor, even with its red infiltrators, nor vigilante alarmists, were a serious threat in America."[15]

The overall tone of the pictorial does not show equal disdain for the far right and far left. Photographs in the beginning pages show Klansmen, marching Nazis, and White Russian fascists as elements of the antilabor, vigilante far right, composing a rather nasty collective portrait of a violent and intolerant movement. By contrast, only the final two pages of the pictorial focus on the American Communist Party, and the comparison is instructive. While the text dismisses the Communist Party as making more noise and drawing more attention than it deserved, the visuals show a completely different face of radicalism: indeed, *Life* ends the photo-essay with an affectionate close-up of Mother Ella Bloor (Figure 4.3), whom it calls "the grand old woman" of the U.S. Communist Party who "represents the best in Communism—its unswerving determination to make *Life* happier for the world's unfortunates."[16] Quite simply, *Life* never gave this kind of gentle stroke of visual and textual affection to an American Nazi, nor did it ever suggest that there was

MOTHER BLOOR: U.S. COMMUNIST HEROINE Ella Reeve ("Mother") Bloor is the grand old woman of the U. S. Communist Party. She represents the best in Communism—its unswerving determination to make life happier for the world's unfortunates. Having served her cause for 45 years and been arrested for it 36 times, Mother Bloor at 75 is a lively, indefatigable propagandist and member of the Party's ruling Central Committee.

Figure 4.3. "Mother Bloor: U.S. Communist Heroine," *Life,* July 26, 1937. (Courtesy Alfred Eisenstaedt/TimePix)

a positive impulse behind fascist ideology as there was to communism.

In fact, this dissimilar visual treatment of the American right and left remained consistent in the Popular Front period. Although the textual treatment did occasionally use the "red fascism, brown bolshevism" trope, the communists consistently received more sympathetic visual treatment. Other examples of the pre–Nazi-Soviet pact comparisons are instructive, because they reveal *Life*'s disgust at the violence, anti-

Semitism, and thuggish attitude of the American Nazis, and its belief that the communists, while potentially revolutionary, did not spout hatred, violence, and disunity, and were not, therefore, as threatening to the body politic.

Overall, *Life*'s visual emphasis resulted in different treatments of the far right and the left. The German-American Bundists and native fascists (different groups with similar outlooks) were more vilified because they were visually more connected to and appeared too

NAZIS HAIL GEORGE WASHINGTON AS FIRST FASCIST

Protesting allegiance to the U. S. flag is a leitmotiv of all Nazi assemblies in this country. On Feb. 22 the German-American Bund of New Jersey undertook to manifest its patriotism by holding meetings in honor of Washington's Birthday. In Hackensack its members hired a hall, procured a picture of Washington, hung it beside the swastika. Highlight of the evening was a speech by the Rev. John C. Fitting, Bund official, hailing Washington as "the first Fascist" and as a "realist" who knew democracy could not work. Bundsman Fitting praised Washington's courage, related by way of illustration that at 15 young George "rode a horse to death because the horse would not give in."

Figure 4.4. "Nazis Hail George Washington as First Fascist," *Life,* **March 7, 1938.**

much like their fascist counterparts abroad. The American fascists could not extract themselves from the web of visual and ideological associations connecting them to Nazi fifth columns worldwide: their uniforms, insignia, parades, hate-filled publications, and violent oratories made them seem a part of the Nazi juggernaut not to be dismissed as just crackpot, fringe Americans. While *Life* insisted that the real Nazi problem was in Berlin, its "pitiless spotlight" made it clear that the American far right was dangerous and un-American.

Unlike the communists, there were no points at which American fascists were accorded sympathetic, or even neutral, treatment. The only question was whether, and how, they should be tolerated by policy makers and Americans.

Life captured American fascists in action at four main sites: at Camp Siegfried, Yaphank, Long Island; at rallies and meetings at Madison Square Garden; in the Yorkville district of Manhattan; and in the Detroit area.[17] It consistently exposed the fascists' false Americanism and tendency to intermingle symbols of Americana—especially the flag and photos of George Washington—with Nazi insignia. A stunning half-page photo from March 1938 with the headline "Nazis Hail George Washington as First Fascist" (Figure 4.4) shows how the Bundists tried to pitch themselves as America-loving patriots while engaging in Nazi rituals. The photo was accompanied with minimal commentary, presumably because the patent offensiveness of a framed reprint of a Gilbert Stuart painting of George Washington sandwiched between an American flag and a swastika flag, foregrounded by a saluting Bundist, spoke for itself. The text explained how the Bundists wanted to claim an indigenous American lineage, against complaints that they were a foreign-based organization. The article was not sympathetic: "Protesting allegiance to the U.S. flag is a leitmotiv of all Nazi assemblies in this country," Life reported, but such allegiance was belied by the speech "hailing Washington as . . . a 'realist' who knew democracy could not work."[18]

Life also focused on the domestic fascists' brute tactics. Violence frequently broke out at Nazi meetings and rallies, partly because antifascists were at those rallies to protest, but mostly, according to Life, because the Nazis used incendiary speech, brooked no opposition, and ordered their young storm troopers to beat up unfortunate interlopers. A May 1938 photo-essay on Nazi violence against Jewish-American veterans of World War I showed sharp contrasts: bloodied, middle-age World War I veterans juxtaposed to bottle-wielding, smiling, saluting, swastika-bedecked young fascists. As Life noted "there could be no question of where popular sympathy lay. For blatant bad taste, noisomely offensive to the great mass of Americans, it would be hard to beat the swastika-waving and propagandizing of the 'American Nazis.'" Despite that offensiveness, and instead of demanding retaliation, legal or otherwise, Life counseled restraint and tolerance. Suggesting that the real threat to American democracy resulted from legislative efforts

to restrict such groups or from equally thuggish retaliation against unwanted speech, Life said that "any suppression of unpopular minorities is the denial of democracy, the entering wedge of tyranny. Americans who detest Adolf Hitler's methods will not wish to pay him the compliment of imitation."[19]

This was the line maintained by the editors for a time. In its major prewar exposé of the fascist front in the United States, including the Nazis, the native anti-Semites, and hard-core isolationists, Life reiterated its faith in the power of negative publicity instead of restrictive legislation. The title of a seven-page March 1939 photo-essay, "Fascism in America: Like Communism It Masquerades as Americanism," suggested that readers would get a comparative treatment. The article focused, however, on the extreme right's anti-Semitic propaganda sheets and on its leading "voices of hate." Throughout, Life maintained that exposure was a sufficient, and democratic, antidote to the hateful ideas and spokespersons it illuminated. Contending that "public exposure is the best treatment for such festering sores in the body politic," the article averred that most Americans were driven to revulsion and anger against the images before them. Life asked its readers to "keep cool" and also called for the Dies Committee to do its job, as the congressmen had "virtually ignored" the "leading spokesmen of Fascist sentiments in America."[20]

The photo-essay began with a blatant juxtaposition: a full-length photo covering the left two-thirds of the page was of a forty-foot-tall mural of George Washington dwarfing five brown shirts standing in the foreground holding Nazi and American flags (Figure 4.5); in the page's lower-right corner a photo one-sixth the size of the fascist one of Abraham Lincoln was part of the "Communism Is 20th Century Americanism" mural at the national party headquarters. Here readers learned that at the Nazi's Madison Square Garden "Pro-American Rally" in celebration of Washington's birthday, "speakers for three hours derided American democracy, praised Nazi Germany and its ideals,

Figure 4.5. A 40-foot picture of George Washington serves as the backdrop at a Bund rally, from "Fascism in America," *Life*, March 6, 1939.

preached hatred and expulsion of the Jews and 'Jewish Communism' from America" and "greeted mention of the names Hitler and Mussolini" with "loud cheers" while "loud laughter greeted a speaker's sneering reference to 'Franklin D. Rosenfeld.'"[21]

In the text, American communists were not depicted as being especially trustworthy. Linking the two movements with the red-fascism/brown-bolshevism trope, *Life* warned that both were dangerous because of their foreign connections and, referring to their respective murals, their duplicitous methods of hiding behind false patriotism: "at bottom they are no more unlike than the red and black on a roulette board.... Each derives its inspiration and guidance, if not its pay, from a foreign government which presents the model of a superstate run by supermen. Each calls its doctrine Americanism and skulks behind the symbols and heroes of America while working to destroy the American democracy which it despises." *Life* also explained what made the Nazis far worse. Especially damning was the Nazi use of fear. Because, *Life* said, Americans had historically been susceptible to fear-mongering, and were vulnerable again because of economic dislocation, the Nazi strategy of using fear as a weapon was "one profound difference which makes Fascism a far graver menace to Americans than Communism." A huge difference was that the communist's "alien ideal" of wealth redistribution had already alienated most Americans: "[T]he Communist Party in America has in 20 years acquired 100,000 active members and some 129,900,000 enemies," making the communists unattractive, even silly, to most; by comparison, fascist appeals to fears and hate-filled doctrines made them a serious, if underestimated, threat.[22] Beyond these brief written comparisons, the bulk of the essay was comprised of photographs of the fascist menace.

Two full pages assaulted the reader with the distorted, hate-filled propaganda espoused by the fascists, and two more offered the grim visages of the leading "voices of hate." Explaining that the movement consisted of "over 800 organizations devoted to spreading anti-Semitic, anti-democratic, pro-Fascist doctrines through the land," *Life* offered "Some Samples of Anti-American Propaganda" by reproducing the mastheads of newspapers, pamphlets, insignia, poster-art, and other vehicles of fascist ideology in the United States. Highlighted newspapers included *Liberation,* the organ of William Dudley Pelley's Silver Shirts; the *National American Bulletin* (replete with swastika in its masthead) published by the American National Socialist Party; Father Coughlin's weekly, *Social Justice;* Gerald B. Winrod's *The Revealer;* and the *National American,* official organ of the American National Socialist Party. These pamphlets and handbills captured the crude visual and rhetorical style of the anti-Semitic attacks aimed at the Federal Reserve, Hollywood, and the Roosevelt administration.[23] Following the hate sheets, *Life* offered its readers a two-page gallery of the leading hate-mongers, including Silver Shirt leader William Dudley Pelley, George Christians, Gerald E. Winrod, and James True—many of whom *Life* profiled again in an April 1942 photo-essay called "Voices of Defeat," and most of whom were subsequently indicted (but unsuccessfully prosecuted) by the Justice Department for seditious conspiracy.[24]

In the remaining pages of the exposé *Life* went inside a fascist "cell" in Chehalis, Washington, to provide some explanation for the attraction 1930s small-town Americans held for fascism. It found "no guttural-voiced 'hyphenated Americans' [meaning German-Americans] but simple folk of the kind to be found in any American small town." Fearful for their jobs and small businesses and "groping for something to fight back at in a bewildering, swift-changing world," the cell members "were easy meat," *Life* said. "Losing their faith in democracy," they had accepted the Nazi line that democracy had failed and all politics were reduced to a global struggle between communism and fascism. *Life* reminded its readers that they, however, should not lose faith in democracy and its protections and processes, nor should they lose faith in their own good judgment, the moderating effects of popular opinion, and the democratic tradition of tolerance. Most of all, they should resist "the temptation to smash the Fascists . . . by the brute methods of suppression of free speech, free press, free homes and free assembly." Confidently, *Life* noted, "Public opinion, the weapon of democracy, has vanquished all such mass hysterias in America's past, and will again."[25]

Life was not so reassured, however, by Congressman Martin Dies's apparent inability or unwillingness to do his job of prosecuting communists as head of the Dies Committee. Consistently frustrated by Dies's excessive attention to the political left, his headline-grabbing (and ultimately foolhardy) accusations, his unreliable witnesses, and the damage his work did to the goal of effectively exposing dangerous forces in America, *Life* repeatedly demanded that Dies shift his focus and improve his techniques.[26] Bemoaning Dies's methods, it visually ridiculed the "big, bluff Congressman Dies" for looking a lot like a drooling hayseed in a full-page photo (Figure 4.6), and for bringing disrepute to the weapon of exposure by indiscriminately accusing liberals and radicals alike of being communists. Even after enactment of the Nazi-Soviet pact in August 1939, when Dies's charges seemed more credible to *Life,* his tactics still offended *Life*'s sense of propriety and its concern for democratic procedures.[27] Indeed, Dies's wrecking-ball methods were especially bothersome because of the damage he had done to the cause of "responsible" Red hunting; as *Life* began to call for the exposure of American communists, Dies's legacy rankled *Life* because he had elicited such scorn for the whole cause.[28]

Overall, *Life*'s Popular Front–era treatment of the American far left was surprisingly benign. Though frequently faulting the communists as un-American, the visual spotlight drawn on the communists was generally (although not entirely) soft and even humorous. The communists' ideas were more compassionate than the Nazis; they were not racist, anti-Semitic, or physically and rhetorically violent like the native fascists. Nor were they photogenic in the same way: they did not wear uniforms like Nazis and fas-cists and thus were not "caught in the act" of being iconographically un-American. Additionally, anti-democratic methods of Red-baiting in the United States—A. Mitchell Palmer's post–World War I Red scare and the buffoonish Martin Dies and HUAC's irresponsible methods and accusations—made *Life* think twice about what they endorsed.

In a November 1937 piece on a Madison Square Garden celebration of the Soviet Union's twentieth anniversary, where 20,000 communists and sympathizers "swarmed," sang, hissed Hitler, cheered Stalin, and watched the play *One Sixth of the Earth, Life* noted that the participants were like fascists in that they too adopted the use of "spotlights, spectacles, and style" in their gatherings.[29] Despite these similarities, the accompanying photographs included party chairman Earl Browder and his wife standing with clenched fists, three thousand new party members who pledged their "complete devotion to the Leninist struggle for socialism, for a Soviet America," fifty members of the Abraham Lincoln Brigade, and sympathetic close-ups of a tired, handsome young black couple resting on one another. By comparison to the Nazi rallies, the visual scene was neither silly nor outlandish, and there were no outbreaks of thuggish violence to show or report.

Life also presented accounts of communist leisure activities that were downright bucolic. Photographs from a Bronx County birthday party for Mother Ella Bloor, "matron saint of American Communists, symbol of the militant working-class woman," showed Mother Bloor "glistened with sweat as she spent 8 hours greeting 10,000 friends." There was a beauty contest to honor Mother Bloor. The different beauties wore sashes with slogans that read LONG LIVE THE PEOPLE'S FRONT, STOP JAPANESE AGGRESSION, and AGAINST UNEMPLOYMENT, and the winner was festooned with a banner inscribed FOLLOWING THE EXAMPLE OF MOTHER BLOOR.[30] Elsewhere *Life* showed a Madison Square Garden rally in May 1939, where 20,000 members of the Young Communist League looked a lot like any other dancing collegians "getting

BIG, BLUFF CHAIRMAN DIES, ANTI-C.I.O. AND ANTI-COMMUNIST, LISTENS TO A WITNESS

A witness points to anti-Nazi, anti-church Red propaganda in U.S. The poster is titled: "The Attack on U.S.S.R."

CONGRESSMAN DIES ON RED TRAIL;

NEW DEALERS, MOVIE STARS ACCUSED

Since Aug. 12 the Special House Committee Investigating Un-American Activities in the United States, with Martin Dies of Texas as chairman, has been making daily, front-page headlines. On its first day of hearings in Washington, the Committee, which is delegated to investigate all evidences of Communist, Fascist and Nazi activity in America, heard testimony about the "American Nazis" (LIFE, March 29, 1937, Sept. 13, March 7). Next day it switched to Communism and stayed there.

Opening its doors to anybody who cared to come in and call anybody else a Red, the Dies Committee heard that hundreds of C.I.O. officials are Communists or their sympathizers. It heard that the C.I.O.'s Pacific Coast leader, Harry Bridges, belongs to the Communist Party under the name of "Harry Dorgan" and that a "high official" of the Labor Department is protecting him from deportation. It heard that the American League for Peace and Democracy, and most other anti-fascist, anti-war, pro-Labor and pro-civil liberties organizations of grownups and college students are dominated by Communists. It heard that Communists, putting on a false face of democracy and gloving their guiding hands, have duped such citizens as Vassar President Henry Noble MacCracken and Emporia Editor William Allen White into serving as sponsors for their organizations. It heard that eight middleweight New Deal officials belong to the Peace and Democracy League. Also drawn more or less innocently into Communist service, it heard, have been such Hollywood stars as Robert Taylor and Shirley Temple.

To see some of the Committee charges and charges, turn the page.

Figure 4.6. "Congressman Dies on Red Trail; New Dealers, Movie Stars Accused," *Life*, September 5, 1938. (Courtesy Underwood and Underwood)

in the groove" by doing the "sociological swing." Describing photos of young "communist cats" jitterbugging away, *Life* noted (quite favorably), "For several years Communists have soft-pedaled revolution, waved the American flag, ballyhooed American institutions and fads." Given this, *Life* reminded its readers that these class conscious dancers should not be confused "with sobersided Nazis."[31]

Reporting on young communists dancing, however, was the last time *Life* made light of communism in the United States before World War II. News of the Nazi-Soviet pact in August 1939, quickly followed by the Nazi invasion of Poland, the outbreak of war in Europe, and the Soviet invasion of Finland, made *Life* reexamine its previous soft pedaling of the communists and shift focus to communist deception.

From the Popular Front era through the end of World War II, *Life*'s position toward the American

Figure 4.7. "Stalin's No. 1 U.S. Stooge Finds Out That U.S. Laws Have Teeth," *Life*, November 6, 1939. (Courtesy Hart Preston/TimePix)

communists reflected the state of U.S.-Soviet relations. Its ferocity depended on whether or not American communists were espousing American foreign-policy interests or hewing to the Soviet line. When American communists showed too much fealty to Soviet leaders and their foreign-policy explanations, they were portrayed as antidemocratic stooges who undermined American interests. They too deserved a harsh spotlight.

Life used a November 1939 piece about Earl Browder's arrest for a series of passport violations (acquiring two under false names and then twice denying he had ever had a passport) to highlight the similarities between American communists and Nazis. A photo of a glaring Browder topped the page (Figure 4.7), and underneath in bold letters he was identified as "Stalin's No. 1 U.S. Stooge." The text that followed contemptuously analyzed the place of the Communist Party in

America, claiming that party members had "damned themselves as no Red-baiter could have" when they responded to Browder's arrest by accusing the Justice Department of "Gestapo" tactics, but especially by changing positions on the nature of the Nazi menace by echoing Soviet pronouncements that the recently begun European war was an "imperialists" war. On the next page, under a headline reading "American Communists and Nazis Both Hide Foreign Allegiance behind False Front of Patriotism," *Life* used a series of photographs and captions to assert that both groups were foreign-controlled and essentially the same. One image showed the mustachioed Browder sitting under a photo of Stalin; juxtaposed with a photo of Fritz Kuhn meeting with Hitler, *Life* completed the "red fascism/brown bolshevism" argument by directing readers' attention to "Browder's startling resemblance to Hitler in this picture." On the final page of the three-page spread, there was a picture of Browder in jail, a photo from a vagrancy arrest in Indiana in 1936. The text explained *Life*'s changed tone: "The crude and blatant American Nazis of the German-American Bund never fooled anybody by using George Washington as a backdrop for their swastika-flaunting and heil-Hitlering. But the American Communists have, until lately, been slicker and more plausible." Until the Nazi-Soviet pact and the Nazi invasion of Poland, when "Overnight obedient U.S. Communists . . . became as hot to keep America out of war with Germany as they had previously been to get her in. . . . Thus they have made it nose-plain that their first loyalty is not to America but to Russia, they are just as truly Stalin's stooges as the Bundsmen are Hitler's."[32]

In a rather opportunistic about-face, *Life* then acknowledged the good work the Dies Committee had been doing in "piling up plenty of substantiating facts & figures" about these false patriots who had thoroughly discredited themselves. Reporting that the "air is cleared" and "nobody needs to be afraid of the Communists any longer," *Life* noted with relief that between party disintegration, the attorney general's new focus

on communists, and outraged public opinion, the American people would not be misled any longer. Then, in a line that ironically foreshadowed its post–World War II logic, *Life* said the real problem with this communist deception about its loyalty to Moscow was that it "tainted all liberal and labor movements with suspicion of their own deceit and disloyalty, so the real danger now is that the reaction against Communists will be used—just as Hitler and Mussolini used it—to discredit all liberals and unionists."[33]

Finally, in a November 1939 report on the beating of several communists at the hands of a Detroit mob, *Life* all but joined in the cheering. With two photos showing "Reds" being kicked, stomped, and "yelling for mercy," the text explained that a mob of 1,500 had "stood ready and truculent" to meet communists who gathered to celebrate the USSR's twenty-second anniversary. When the party loyalists emerged from their meeting, the crowd closed in on them, "Fists and clubs were swinging. Red heads bled. An A. F. of L unionist cheered through a megaphone: 'Boys, you're doing a very good job. This is one of the most patriotic scenes I've ever witnessed. Next time they try to hold a meeting we'll hang them to lamp poles.'"[34] This time *Life* made no comment about resisting the incitement to vigilante violence, and it made no argument that Americans avoid reverting to mob action.

As the nation moved toward war, *Life*'s tolerance of the far right and far left diminished precipitously, especially as the domestic fascist and communist propaganda and policy positions echoed the official Nazi and Soviet lines. When the United States went to war in December 1941, *Life* rejected its own soft but consistent prewar commitment to a civil libertarian interpretation of First Amendment protections. *Life*'s anxieties about internal security and national unity made it adopt a more speech-restrictive policy toward the far right, and it increasingly demanded (and applauded) legal action against those who it saw as being divisive purveyors of seditious hate propaganda. It rejected the interwar liberal interpretation about the World War I–era civil liberties abuses. "That the Wilson government misused its war powers and was much to blame for suppressing free speech" was misguided, *Life* argued. The article quoted approvingly Attorney General Biddle's suggestion that perhaps sedition laws should once again have to include not just acts, but speech as well. As *Life* explained, "the written word in this war is more dangerous than in World War I and . . . in consequence, a seditious utterance may have to be considered the equivalent of a seditious act." It applauded the impression that Biddle was "stiffening his attitude."[35]

Overall, however, *Life* disapproved of Biddle's comparatively mild policy. A fourteen-page April 1942 exposé on the domestic fascists was aimed at toughening that policy by mobilizing public opinion against them. Arguing that Nazi-inspired defeatists were destroying American unity, *Life* intensified the spotlight it had aimed at these same fascists in its March 1939 "Voices of Hate" photo-essay. The April 1942 report, "Voices of Defeat," looked at them again and leveled the additional wartime charge of sedition against them, demanding federal action. It should be recalled that in the March 1939 piece, *Life* said that public opinion was enough to curtail fascist influence. By April 1942 it still wanted to rely on public opinion, but an angry public opinion, and it demanded quick federal action so that wartime statutes against seditious speech could be used to prosecute the unrepentant isolationists and hate-mongers it profiled here, which included Mrs. Elizabeth Dilling, Col. Robert R. McCormick, Father Charles Coughlin, Gerald L. K. Smith, the Reverend Gerald Winrod, William Dudley Pelley, Lawrence Dennis, and Joe McWilliams. *Life* hoped to anger the American people about the disunifying hate groups active during wartime and to provoke them to demand that the attorney general act to silence the defeatists. According to *Life*'s own follow-up account, it succeeded in this provocation.

"Voices of Defeat" exclaimed in bold letters, "While our country fights for its life, some Americans sow lies and hate inside our lines. They abuse free speech and spread Hitler's propaganda" and were seditious in intent: "The fact is that subversive doctrines are widespread in the United States today. . . . They want the same thing that all our enemies want—to knock America out the war or end our fight against world aggression." Having grown impatient with First Amendment protections for such speech, *Life* claimed it had First Amendment rights too, which included the right to "name names and describe some of the activities that are going on behind our lines."[36]

Organized according to region, the article surveyed the nationwide movement, its key spokesmen, groups, propaganda organs, and its Nazi-inspired rhetoric. It reminded its readers that they may just be "crackpots," but they were dangerous nonetheless: "in time of war, especially an all-out war for national existence, crackpots who spread enemy propaganda are a dangerous luxury."[37] *Life*'s investigators went to Los Angeles, Wichita and Topeka, Kansas, Chicago, Muncie and Noblesville, Indiana, Detroit, New York City, and Boston. At each stop they found leaders, followers, and newspapers whose propaganda themes echoed and intended to aid the Nazi war cause.

Life concluded this unusually extensive print-based exposé by drawing a line between security and liberty, arguing that the emergency did not permit as much liberty in wartime as in peace. The nation's interests were better promoted by the punishment of arguably seditious speech than by the preservation of First Amendment protections for decidedly defeatist speech: "The defeatists and disunionists will try to take refuge behind the privileges of free speech. But let it be remembered that the laws of free speech contain no provision which permits a little group of spiteful men to indulge in unbridled abuse and falsehood in an attempt to thwart this nation from winning a victory over its enemies."[38] In subsequent weeks, *Life* was proud to announce that the "Voices of Defeat" article had had a dramatic impact in mobilizing public opinion. One week after it published "Voices of Defeat," the magazine received 382 letters of approval and 57 of condemnation.[39] More important, the article had provoked the American people "to bestir themselves against their own fifth column." According to *Life,* the article generated 43,000 letters to the Justice Department urging action against Coughlin's *Social Justice* and the far right hate sheets. After receiving this flood of letters, *Life* said, "the Department of Justice roused itself at last from a brown study of the war and advised the Post Office to bar *Social Justice* from the mails. The American people are not in a mood for trifling and the pressure on Government authorities for strong action against moral traitors is rising every day."[40]

At least *Life* was not in a trifling mood. When wartime riots broke out in Detroit in the summer of 1943, it argued that Nazi-inspired hate speech, coupled with Detroit's migration history, made Detroit less a melting pot than a boiling pot, one brought to a boil by rumor and propaganda, the two major tools of the Nazi's divide-and-conquer strategy. The axis strategy of "exploiting existing lines of discontent," especially along race lines, had "led to a sort of psychological suicide" in Detroit.[41]

When *Life* investigated labor violence and vigilantism in Detroit in 1937, it noted the existence of Klansmen, White Russian fascists, Bundists, and other hate groups, but downplayed their threat. When it returned to Detroit in August 1942, it found that "demagogues of every persuasion" had planted seeds of violence.[42] And, in July 1943 *Life* reported that those seeds had borne rotten fruit, claiming that "Americans maul and murder each other as Hitler wins a battle in the nation's most explosive city." In a stunning seven-page pictorial on the Detroit race riot of June 1943, entitled "Race War in Detroit," *Life* said that the bloody riots were a consequence of Nazi propaganda and a Nazi victory (Figure 4.8). Reprinting the work of Detroit *Times* photographers who captured ground-level action in riots that killed 31, injured 600, and saw 1,800 arrested, *Life* reported, "Americans everywhere can see what happens when race prejudice, rumor-mongering and hate propaganda do their worst in a great American city." Even though

the basic cause "was an old, ugly fact in U.S. life: prejudice and misunderstanding between the white and black races" and the riots were not planned by "foreign agents [or] local Fascists," they were "definitely a victory for Adolf Hitler and other enemies of the U.S."[43]

The photos are dramatic in their action, primarily showing black men being chased, surrounded, pummeled, tripped, clubbed, pulled off buses, slapped, beaten into submission by white mobs, and threatened by white police. Black men are clearly the victims of the wild violence, and the white mobs who bullied and beat their victims were repeatedly described as carrying out Hitler's work on American soil. In one dramatic photograph of a policeman falling backward into the arms of another policeman after being hit by a bottle thrown from the crowd, the caption read: "By a weird trick of mob psychology, the white rioters raised the cry of 'Hitlerism!' when the police tried to stop their abuse of Negroes. They yelled, 'Just like Germany,' when the police turned tear gas on them. One white youth snarled 'Yah, you damn Gestapo' at the policemen who seized him for beating a Negro." *Life*'s final comment was that apparently the white mobs "did not realize they were the ones who looked and acted like Nazis."[44]

Violence, like in Detroit, and the continued presence of fascist voices in the nation at war made *Life* intolerant of forces of disunity. It continued its criticism of the Justice Department's "comparatively mild" policies toward the far right. When the Justice Department eventually handed down its second seditious conspiracy indictment in the *U.S. v. McWilliams* case (most of the defendants had been depicted in either the "Voices of Hate" or "Voices of Defeat" pieces), *Life* was pleased, but still a bit perturbed at how long it had taken Attorney General Biddle to act. In the name of an aroused American public, *Life* proclaimed it had "always been hard to understand why some Americans were being sent overseas to face death from fascist bullets and bayonets, while others spread lies and propaganda behind the lines at home." This had happened, *Life* explained, because Biddle had been too solicitous of constitu-

THIS NEGRO (CENTER) HAS JUST BEEN SLUGGED BY YOUNG WHITE HOODLUMS IN DETROIT'S RACE RIOT AND IS FRANTICALLY TRYING TO ESCAPE BEFORE THEY HIT HIM AGAIN

RACE WAR IN DETROIT

Americans maul and murder each other as Hitler wins a battle in the nation's most explosive city

Last summer LIFE reported that Detroit was seething with factional bitterness and warned: "Detroit is Dynamite. . . . Detroit can either blow up Hitler or it can blow up the U. S." (LIFE, Aug. 17). Last week some of Detroit's dynamite exploded in the bloodiest race riots the country has had since 1919. White and black Detroiters slugged, clubbed, gouged, stoned, kicked, stabbed and shot each other until 31 were dead, more than 600 injured and 1,800 arrested. Detroit's news photographers (one of whom is shown in the picture above being threatened by Negrobeating hoodlums) did an outstanding job of recording the truth about the riots. On these nine pages LIFE presents some of their best pictures so that Americans everywhere can see what happens when race prejudice, rumor-mongering and hate propaganda do their worst in a great American city.

After several thousand soldiers in full battle dress put down the riot, a fact-finding committee appointed by Governor Kelly of Michigan went to work to determine its causes. But most Detroiters already knew the causes. Said the Detroit *Free Press:* "Detroit has been building steadily for three years toward a race riot." Named by the *Free Press* and other observers as contributing largely to last week's riot were: 1) Detroit's abominable housing situation, which condemns thousands of white and Negro war workers to living in slums, tents and trailers. 2) the tremendous migration of white and Negro war workers from the South since 1940; 3) "race" strikes and friction in war plants (a month ago 20,000 Packard workers walked out because three Negro workers were up-graded to the assembly line); and 4) juvenile rowdyism, which has increased during the war (last month 100 white and Negro youths fought a pitched battle in a Detroit playground). C. I. O. leaders blamed the Ku-Klux Klan for the riot, and Negro spokesmen charged that Detroit police and the "pussy-footing" attitude of Mayor Edward J. Jeffries were responsible for much of the violence. Although the riot was definitely a victory for Adolf Hitler and other enemies of the U. S., there was no evidence that it had been planned by foreign agents, local Fascists or anyone else. It broke out suddenly on a hot Sunday night, and its basic cause was an old, ugly fact in U. S. life: prejudice and misunderstanding between the white and black races.

The "incident" which started the riot was a fist fight between a Negro and a white man on a crowded bridge leading from the Belle Isle public amusement park to the city proper. A rumor quickly spread among other Negroes on the island that whites had killed a Negro mother and her baby and thrown them in the water. (This was completely false.) The rumor reached Hastings Street in "Paradise Valley," the old Negro slum section where Champion Joe Louis once lived. Bands of Negro hoodlums broke into pawnshops, stole some guns, looted white-run stores and stoned automobiles driven by whites. A doctor answering a late call was beaten to death. Police who rushed to the area were fired on and they fired back. Of the 31 known dead in the riot, 15 were Negroes shot by city police. White gangs, barred from the Negro area by police guns and tear gas, took over Woodward Avenue, Detroit's main thoroughfare, where they hauled isolated Negroes from autos and streetcars, beat them up and set fire to their cars. In most cases the police were either too outnumbered or too indifferent to stop these white attacks. The action photographs on these pages show the white mobs who raged unchecked through the heart of Detroit until the troops arrived on Monday night.

CONTINUED ON NEXT PAGE 93

Figure 4.8. "Race War in Detroit," *Life,* **July 5, 1943. (Courtesy Corbis)**

tional niceties and had "leaned over backward to preserve the right of free speech in wartime." Now that it had the seditious conspiracy indictment, the Justice Department could finally prosecute the native fascists, which *Life* supported without reservation.[45]

Through the end of World War II and into the Cold War, *Life* remained ambivalent about ensuring First Amendment protections for those perceived as anti-democracy in purpose and deed. It remained steadfast in its conviction, however, that the pitiless spotlight of exposure was a democracy-serving tool, one that enlightened and protected Americans as it shifted its glare to left-wing activities and influence.

Life's treatment of the threat of communism in the United States and Soviet machinations abroad was dominated by one overarching precept, one that became a central tenet in the conservative attack on liberalism: American policies were deeply flawed because communists had too much influence within liberal policy-making circles.[46] By war's end *Life* began to Red-bait American liberals by defining the problem of communism in the United States and abroad as a problem of liberal susceptibility and weakness. Shouldering the responsibility for left-wing influences in America became liberalism's burden. Not only did liberals have to accept their responsibility for communist influence, they also had to accept the onus of making sure that the inevitable and necessary Red hunts did not abuse civil liberties. To make these arguments, *Life* relied less on visual evidence about communist influence and more on arguments about language and its importance in the struggle for domestic and global security. In so doing, *Life* articulated a line of argument that echoed throughout postwar journals, from the left-leaning, anti-Stalinist *Partisan Review* to the then centrist *Commentary*. In short, that line was that the struggle against communism was just as grave as the struggle against fascism; that anyone who aided the Soviet cause needed exposure as a dupe or traitor; that propaganda was a key battleground in the struggle for global loyalties; and that fellow-traveling liberals had left the United States severely weakened.[47]

At the end of the war *Life* began developing a semantics-based critique of liberalism when it compared America's uncertain postwar aims and inadequate propaganda campaigns to the Soviet's overt expansionist ambitions and their equally clear propaganda stratagems.[48] In a July 1945 essay titled "America and Russia: To Equal the Communist Talent for Persuasion We Must Develop Persuasiveness of Our Own," *Life* said that American interests had to be better defined and more clearly trumpeted in a worldwide propaganda competition, a competition that hinged on who best seized the rhetoric of democracy, social justice, and progress: "Russia is the No. 1 problem for America because it is the only country in the world with the dynamic power to challenge our own conceptions of

truth, justice and the good life." Although most Americans at war's end did not want to go to war with the Soviets, most also "don't like to see Russian institutions, Russian standards of 'democracy' and 'freedom of the press' spreading into the power vacuums of Eastern Europe." Therefore, American propaganda needed to subvert Soviet efforts to lay claim to those powerful symbols and words. Liberal susceptibility to communist influence had created a dire problem. The Soviets were not just territorial expansionists, but lexical ones as well: when Americans "try to base their case on an appeal to the superiority of democratic principles, they discover that the Russians have stolen their language." Who was to blame for this lexical theft? Fellow-traveling liberals were blamed for, wittingly or not, ceding the language of democracy to the Soviets.[49]

Life argued that from the Popular Front era through the end of the war, fellow-traveling liberals had permitted the Soviets to get away with claiming that it too stood for democratic ideals. Reclaiming the language of democracy and attaching it to American institutions and policy initiatives was one of the great postwar challenges, *Life* predicted, because "[i]n this battle of definitions, this war of semantics, the Russians have practically everything rigged in their favor." Indeed, the United States had become disadvantaged because fellow travelers, some of whom were still in positions of influence, had permitted this to happen, both by allowing Soviet infiltration of all kinds of institutions and because they themselves had debased the language of politics by agreeing to and employing Soviet-propagated uses of that language. Thus, the language of politics had become undependable because words had no clear meanings. If the Soviets could claim to be democrats, *Life* asked, what did the word mean?[50] And, if Marxists could claim to be liberals, then what did that label refer to?

These implied questions became central to *Life*'s unyielding assault on any liberals who did not immediately take a staunch anti-Soviet position and who did not endorse domestic purges. (Henry Wallace and his followers were the most high-profile exemplars of liberal internationalists who rejected Cold War thinking at home and abroad, and *Life* insistently pilloried Wallace and company as embodiments of that strain of American liberalism that had been the entering wedge for communist influence.) Developing the argument that fellow-traveling liberals had allowed communists to destroy the language of democracy by rendering it unintelligible, *Life* explained in a September 1945 editorial titled "Some Big Words," "that the political vocabulary of bourgeois America is sadly confused. American Marxists, by appropriating to themselves words like 'liberal,' have certainly contributed to the confusion." Making the problem worse, these Marxists, hiding under the protective label liberal, were everywhere: "in Hollywood, on college faculties, in government bureaus, in publishing companies, in radio offices, even on the editorial staffs of eminently capitalist journals." If liberals did not "face up to this task" of retarding this communist influence at home, the piece warned, "they will soon find that they have no ground for defending those individual liberties whose sacredness they have always taken for granted."[51] *Life* upped the rhetorical ante by making the threat of postwar communism equal in danger to the threat of prewar and wartime fascism and by accusing those who recoiled from the necessity of a domestic purge as being the moral, and actual, equivalents of those who had appeased Nazi Germany.

In this end-of-the-war vitriol, *Life* said that two camps were emerging in America: those who demanded a fight with the Soviets and the "masochists," who, not wanting to offend the Soviets, had adopted an "attitude that sounds curiously like the one the appeasers had toward" Nazi Germany. While backing off from this accusation by asserting that neither position was entirely satisfactory, *Life*'s emotionally laden analogy indicated how hard its ideological line had become by war's end. In fact, in the same editorial, *Life* suggested that American democracy ran the risk of making itself defenseless against its enemies; ironically, it

continued, the very fellow travelers who had surrendered the language of democracy were themselves protected by the democratic privileges they had made vulnerable—as long as those rights and liberties remained in place.[52]

If fellow travelers and American communists were the equivalents of Nazi appeasers and seditionists, then they would have to be dealt with in similar ways. So, therefore, the same speech and association-protective First Amendment positions that had made the United States vulnerable to the far right's divide-and-conquer strategies during the war now made it vulnerable to communist subversion in the postwar world. Arguing that communism "must . . . be fought at all times and in all places" in a 1947 editorial titled "Struggle for the World," *Life* set the stage for demanding what it called "responsible" Red hunting.[53] By "responsible" it meant that a purge of leftists was necessary, but it must take place with global propaganda values in mind. In other words, the purge needed to be accomplished without undermining claims about the United States as the protector of democratic values and practices. While throwing accusatory language at the communists and fellow travelers, it demanded that "responsible" liberals clean their house of these "appeasers" because they were more attentive to democratic procedures. *Life* was not so entirely keen on a postwar witch-hunt, however, that it felt it should be undertaken at any cost. In fact, it wanted one engineered by liberals themselves because it feared what would happen if reactionary forces in the United States were responsible for the purge. Turning the job over to conservatives, perhaps even to "antidemocratic hands . . . would indeed be a tragedy for America."[54]

Life's position at the war's end demanded that liberals protect the civil libertarian tradition from reactionary forces, but they should not make the country too vulnerable by being overly solicitous of that tradition. If they failed, *Life* warned, reactionaries like Martin Dies, John Rankin, and J. Parnell Thomas were ready to seize the moment. Heading into the postwar world, *Life* saw American democracy challenged by an ill-defined foreign policy, inadequate propaganda, a susceptible and weak-willed liberalism, and an intolerant and reactionary conservatism waiting to take over the responsibility for the domestic and global struggles against Soviet communism, which made *Life* nervous.

As U.S.-Soviet suspicions grew, the "pitiless spotlight" aimed at American communists became more intense. Because of Smith Act prosecutions, HUAC hearings, the Truman administration's federal loyalty oaths, and other efforts to purge America of left-wing activities, American communists sought cover. Therefore, the damnable images *Life* could have used against them were virtually nonexistent, especially compared to the domestic fascists. While the communist act of self-preservation denied *Life* of visual evidence, the process of going underground became evidence of the left's duplicity. That American communists acted in secret and operated through front organizations only reinforced suspicions that they were un-American, controlled by foreign interests, and served foreign interests. Between 1945 and 1947 *Life* asked two different sets of questions about domestic communists: who were they and what did they represent? And, they also wanted to know what kinds of tactics could be used against them to diminish their threat without traducing agreed-upon commitments to civil liberties.

A March 1945 editorial titled "'Un-American Activities': What Are They? The Successor to the Dies Committee Is Trying to Find Out" asked about acceptable tactics for the coming struggle against domestic communism. *Life* knew that Martin Dies's "prejudiced and primitive methods" could not be endured in the postwar period, especially since the concept of democracy was a crucial battleground of the ideological and lexical wars between the United States and its enemies. Because efforts to identify communism in America were part of a worldwide struggle, the record of ineffectiveness established by Dies's House Un-American Activities Committee was as unacceptable as were its unscrupulous, undemocratic

techniques. The new members of HUAC were wisely asking advice from friends and foes of the original committee, including the editors of *Life,* who offered a critical summary of Dies's legacy as their advice: "avoid Martin Dies's obvious bias and errors. Toward the end he ran a one-man show, issuing 'committee reports' which the other members had not even read. He attached as much importance to gossip and opinion as to evidence and fact. The 'facts' he got were often wrong and seldom corrected." As a result, the committee's reputation and effectiveness were laughable. Therefore, the new HUAC had to "play fair" and should "focus on *activity,* not thoughts." Most important, it should wield the main weapon it had at its disposal, the spotlight of publicity: ". . . we bear in mind that the main function of this congressional investigating committee is not to convict, not to indict, not necessarily even to propose legislation, but to *study* and *expose.*" *Life*'s final bit of advice to HUAC was straightforward—target those whose "political activity . . . pretends to be what it is not."[55]

This problem of uncovering hidden activities, especially activities that served the interests of foreign powers, led *Life* once more to the "red fascism/brown bolshevism" construction. In the war's aftermath, it was unequivocally clear to *Life* that communism and fascism were moral and tactical equivalents: "Both of the world's great revolutionary organizations—the Communist Party and the Nazi Party—are adept at the masquerade. They employ sympathizers to perform innocently or at least legally what they can not effectively do themselves." American communists were, therefore, both un-American and dangerous. Exposing communist-front activities, instead of writing legislation aimed specifically at them, kept HUAC on the side of the Bill of Rights and damaged those groups and individuals exposed by the committee. This enhanced, not weakened, democratic practices: "And if the labels are correctly affixed, our Bill of Rights will survive its foes and our political fortunes may be safely left to the good sense of the American people."[56] If HUAC could do this, it would mirror what *Life* claimed it was doing in the arena of journalism.

Life's most significant effort at exposing and labeling communist activity was the July 1946 publication of a twelve-page article by the young Harvard historian and Americans for Democratic Action (ADA) liberal Arthur Schlesinger Jr. titled "The U.S. Communist Party."[57] In general, the Schlesinger piece is a fascinating effort to explain the appeal of Communist Party affiliation along psychological lines (only those with weak personalities are attracted), to explore its leaders (who are Moscow's dupes), to understand its shifting policy positions (evidence of Moscow's influence), and to determine what kind of threat American communists pose (their clandestine activity is their chief threat). The question of communist secrecy emerged as the central problem in Schlesinger's analysis, and the liberals' potential liability for communist damage emerged as the central warning.

Like *Life*, Schlesinger argued that repressive legislation was dangerous because it drove the party further underground and made it near impossible to assess communism's real presence in America. This, he argued, had been the result of reckless witch-hunts by Dies, Rankin, and others in the past. What the American public needed, he suggested, was a sober analysis of the extent and nature of communist influence, a problem difficult to assess because of covertness and considerable party membership turnover. Beyond estimates of membership (roughly 65,000 card-carrying members in 1946), what he could offer was speculation into the psychology of members and evidence as to how the party functioned. Members, he said, operated with a kind of religious devotion to the idea that the party "alone knows the path to salvation." The members' discipline and devotion, he added, "can only be duplicated in a religious order or in a police state."[58]

Ideologically, party members had two main goals—to support and advance the cause of the USSR and to promote the establishment of socialism in the United States. Therefore, American interests were always subordinate to Soviet interests. This "subservience to Soviet foreign policy" had been its most consistent feature and was evidence of just how much power the Soviet Comintern representatives had in the U.S. party. As a result of foreign influence, the party developed "a corruption, both of the mind and of the heart, which is alike contemptuous of reason and careless of truth." Because of persecution, the party had been forced to operate clandestinely through underground cells—in Washington, D.C., where "well-known Communist sympathizers are on the staffs of some senators and congressional committees"—and, especially, through trade unions. The most important thing to know, Schlesinger wrote, was that "[t]he Communists spread their infection of intrigue and deceit wherever they go."[59]

Finally, Schlesinger turned to the problem of the relationship between liberals and communists. He suggested that liberals were susceptible to communist influence because of their "innocence, laziness and stupidity." Thus, hundreds of fronts, youth organizations, foreign-language groups, newspapers, and other seemingly benevolent liberal organizations were used by Moscow to "disseminate bits and pieces of the communist line." In Los Angeles, for instance, where a "frenzied 'popular front' atmosphere" existed, "Communism flourishes along with the other weird cults," particularly in Hollywood where intellectuals were doing Soviet bidding through film. From Schlesinger's point of view, communists had had their most disastrous effect on liberalism by dividing and neutralizing the left, thereby aiding conservative and reactionary interests in the United States and potentially making the liberal left irrelevant in American political life, because they had been the dupes to whom the "Communists [had] succeeded in hiding their true face."[60]

Schlesinger's call for liberals to purge their ranks of communists echoed *Life*'s argument that communism had really become a problem for liberals and of liberalism. As Schlesinger explained, "In its larger aspects the Communists are engaged in a massive attack on the moral fabric of the American left. . . . It is imperative for the American liberals, if they wish to avoid total bankruptcy, to get back to a sense of moral seriousness and of absolute devotion to the facts." They could do so by exposing the communists and fellow travelers in their midst and by taking responsibility for the damage they had done by serving Moscow's interests. This would make it possible for noncommunist and anticommunist liberals—like Schlesinger's ADA—to get back to the job of defining and defending American interests.[61] Schlesinger offered, and *Life* endorsed, the ADA justification for liberal anticommunism: to restore liberal credibility in order to ensure that conservative and reactionary voices were not dominating postwar American politics. Neither *Life* nor Schlesinger had any compunction about the need for a purge.

Life wondered, however, whether "responsible Red-hunting" was possible. It was certainly desirable. In a 1947 article titled "Red-Hunting," subtitled "Here Are Rules for Three Legitimate Kinds by Which the Pitfalls Can Be Avoided," *Life* suggested that it was necessary and possible to find a balance between the liberals' foolish strategy of not paying adequate attention to domestic communists and the excesses of the World War I–era Palmer Raids and Martin Dies's star-chamber

proceedings. Acknowledging that previous "Red-hunt" episodes had been an embarrassment to American democracy, *Life* asked the central question confronting those who were concerned about matters of security and liberty: "Is our country in more danger from the Communists or from the pitfalls of the chase?" By drawing on the familiar "red fascism/brown bolshevism" trope and the appeasement analogy, *Life* implicitly answered its question: "To argue that Communism is not so bad as Nazism, for example, as some 'liberals' still like to do, is a complete waste of time." Tried and true democratic methods could be employed to expose the communists, techniques that both recognized Bill of Rights protection and informed the court of public opinion about their dangerous presence. Thus, to J. Parnell Thomas, HUAC's new chair, *Life* said, "the committee's chief weapon should be neither handcuffs nor shotgun; it should be a searchlight."[62] *Life,* like Schlesinger, demanded that liberals hold and shine the light. Failure to do so would make noncommunist liberals fatally responsible for either unleashing reactionary forces or for abetting Soviet subversion. Neither possibility was acceptable. Liberalism's—and democracy's—best bet remained, *Life* suggested, the "pitiless spotlight of publicity."

NOTES

1. For a biographical sketch of Reverend L. M. Birkhead, see E. J. Kahn Jr., "Democracy's Friend," parts 1–3, *New Yorker,* 23 (26 July 1947): 28–36, (2 August 1947): 28–39, (9 August 1947): 28–38.

2. See U.S. House, *Investigation of Nazi and Other Propaganda,* February 15, 1935, 74th Cong., 1st sess., H. Doc. 153.

3. Among the many articles in mainstream journals, see, for instance: Johan J. Smertenko, "Hitlerism Comes to America," *Harper's Magazine,* November 1933, 660–70; Ludwig Lore, "Nazi Politics in America," *Nation,* 29 November 1933, 615–17; Raymond Gram Swing, "Patriotism Dons the Black Shirt," *Nation,* 10 April 1935, 409–11; Charles Angoff, "Nazi Jew-Baiting in America," parts 1–2, *Nation,* 1 May 1935, 501–3, 8 May 1935, 531–35; Harry F. Ward, "The Devel-

opment of Fascism in the United States," *Annals* 180 (July 1935): 55–61; Robert Lewis Taylor, "The Kampf of Joe McWilliams, *New Yorker,* 24 August 1940, 32–39; Dale Kramer, "The American Fascists," *Harper's Magazine,* September 1940, 380–93; Albert Grzenski, with Charles Hewitt Jr., "Hitler's Branch Offices, U.S.A.," *Current History and Forum,* 26 November 1940, 11–13.

4. For further discussion of this argument, see Brett Gary, *The Nervous Liberals: Scholars, Lawyers, and the War on Propaganda, 1919–1947* (New York: Columbia University Press, 1999), chaps. 2 and 6.

5. "Freedom to End Freedom," reprinted in Archibald MacLeish, *A Time to Speak: The Selected Prose of Archibald MacLeish* (Boston: Houghton Mifflin, 1940), 131–37.

6. See Les K. Adler and Thomas G. Paterson, "Red Fascism: The Merger of Nazi Germany and Soviet Russia in the American Image of Totalitarianism, 1930s–1950s," *American Historical Review* 4 (April 1970): 1046–64; and Thomas R. Maddux, "Red Fascism, Brown Bolshevism: The American Image of Totalitarianism in the 1930s," *Historian* 40, no. 1 (November 1977): 85–103.

7. See, "The Camera Overseas: Nazi Germany Puts on Its Greatest Show Every Year at Nurnburg," *Life,* 27 September 1937, 98–99; "The Camera Overseas: Fascist Mussolini Visits Nazi Hitler and Two Dictators Look Silly Together," *Life,* 18 October 1937, 96–97. See also "Christmas in Nazi-Land," *Life,* 27 December 1937, 60; "Germany Speaks to the World," *Life,* 14 February 1938, 32–34; "Inside Nazi Germany—1938," *Life,* 31 January 1938, 25–28.

8. "Germany Speaks to the World," 32–34.

9. Ibid., 33.

10. "These Are Signs of Nazi Fifth Columns Everywhere," *Life,* 17 June 1940, 11. See also, "Spanish Propaganda Pictures Appeal to World to Take Sides in Civil War," *Life,* 25 October 1937, 51–54; "The Camera Overseas: Fascists March through London's Worst Riot in 11 Years," *Life,* 25 October 1937, 100; "A Brick Fells Britain's Fascist Leader," *Life,* 1 November 1937, 74; "How 40,000,000 Italians Are Made to Think Alike," *Life,* 15 November 1937, 106–7; "How to Start a Fascist Movement: A Specimen from Belgium," *Life,* 14 March 1938, 36–38; "Canadian Fascists Give Dominion a Headache and Opponents the Bum's Rush," *Life,* 18 July 1938, 9–11; "Close-Up: Herr Doktor Goebbels," *Life,* 20 March 1939, 60–68; "U.S. Readers Can Now Examine Adolph Hitler's Creed in Full," *Life,* 20 March 1939, 28–29; "A Nazi Fifth Column and Communist Allies Are Active in Mexico," *Life,* 10 June 1940, 51–52.

11. "The 'American Nazis' Claim 200,000 Members," *Life,* 27 March 1937, 20–21.

12. Ibid., 20.

13. "Headlines Proclaim the Rise of Fascism and Communism in America," *Life,* 27 July 1937, 19–27.

14. Ibid., 19.

15. Erika Doss, *Benton, Pollock, and the Politics of Modernism: From Regionalism to Abstract Expressionism* (Chicago: University of Chicago Press, 1991), 180.

16. "Headlines Proclaim the Rise of Fascism and Communism in America," 27.

17. See, for instance, "German-Americans and Italian-Americans Hold a Fascist Rally at Yaphank," *Life,* 13 September 1937, 31.

18. "Nazis Hail George Washington as First Fascist," *Life,* 17 March 1938, 17.

19. "U.S. Veterans Lose Battle with Germans in Manhattan," *Life,* 2 May 1938, 18–19. For another account of violence and thuggery at a Nazi rally, see "It Can Happen Here," *Life,* 6 March 1939, 22–23.

20. "Fascism in America," *Life,* 6 March 1939, 57–63.

21. Ibid., 57.

22. Ibid.

23. Ibid., 58–59.

24. For discussions of these unsuccessful seditious conspiracy prosecutions in the cases of *U.S. v. Winrod, et al* and *U.S. v. McWilliams, et al,* see Leo Ribuffo, *The Old Christian Right: The Protestant Far Right from the Great Depression to Cold War* (Philadelphia: Temple University Press, 1983), 178–224; Francis Biddle, *In Brief Authority* (Garden City, N.Y.: Doubleday, 1962), 233–51; Gary, *The Nervous Liberals,* chap. 6.

25. "Fascism in America," 62.

26. "Congressman Dies on Red Trail; New Dealers, Movie Stars Accused," *Life,* 5 September 1938, 11.

27. "Disloyal Foreign Agents Deserve No Toleration but Dies Smear Points to Danger of Wide Red-Hunt," *Life,* 6 November, 1939, 23.

28. In another photo, *Life* visually ridiculed Dies's star witness, "Mrs. Elizabeth ('The Red Network') Dilling Warns the Senate against Felix Frankfurter," *Life,* 23 January 1939, 16–17.

29. "New York Communists Dramatize 20 Years of Soviet Rule," *Life,* 29 November, 1937, 59–61.

30. "Mother Bloor Is 76," *Life,* 15 August 1938, 25.

31. "Young Communists 'Get in Groove' at Party Rally," *Life,* 22 May 1939, 24.

32. "Stalin's No. 1 U.S. Stooge Finds Out That U.S. Laws Have Teeth," *Life,* 6 November, 1939, 21–23.

33. Ibid., 23.

34. "Communists Hailing Soviet Anniversary Are Beaten by War Veterans in Detroit" *Life,* 27 November 1939, 34. Several other pieces showed communists being beaten, jeered, and burned in effigy: see "Browder at Yale: No. 1 Communist Cheered and Jeered by Student Mob," *Life,* 11 December 1939, 30; and "Communist Popularity Hits Record Low in New Incidents on West Coast," *Life,* 18 December 1939, 24.

35. "Voices of Defeat," *Life,* 13 April 1942, 86–100.

36. Ibid., 86.

37. Ibid., 88.

38. Ibid., 100.

39. See samples in letters to the editor, *Life,* 4 May 1942, 4–6.

40. "Newsfront," *Life,* 26 April 1942, 26.

41. "Rumor Clinic," *Life,* 12 October 1942, 88–91.

42. "Factions: They Breed Hatred and Strife in Detroit," *Life,* 17 August 1942, 18–19.

43. "Race War in Detroit," *Life,* 5 July 1943, 93–99.

44. Ibid., 97.

45. "U.S. Indicts Its Two Top Fascists," *Life,* 17 January 1944, 15–18. Not wanting to be perceived as having rejected constitutional protections of speech and association, *Life* noted that even the American Civil Liberties Union had announced that it had found no civil liberties violations in the indictment and would not help defend the alleged conspirators.

46. See, for instance, "U.S. Is Losing the War of Words," *Life,* 22 March 1943, 11.

47. For a discussion of *Partisan Review* and *Commentary,* see Richard Pells, *The Liberal Mind in a Conservative Age* (New York: Harper and Row, 1985), 121–27.

48. For its wartime critique of American propaganda efforts compared to the Nazis' campaigns, see "U.S. Is Losing the War of Words," 11.

49. "America and Russia: To Equal the Communist Talent for Persuasion We Must Develop Persuasiveness of Our Own," *Life,* 30 July 1945, 20.

50. Ibid., 20.

51. "Some Big Words," *Life,* 24 September 1945, 32.

52. "America and Russia," 20.

53. "Struggle for the World," *Life,* 21 April 1947, 38.

54. "What Is 'Liberalism'?" *Life,* 7 January 1946, 26. For a discussion of the need for greater American propaganda, see "Money for Truth," *Life,* 14 April 1947, 40.

55. "'Un-American Actvities': What Are They? The Successor to the Dies Committee Is Trying to Find Out," *Life,* 26 March 1945, 30.

56. Ibid., 30.

57. Arthur Schlesinger Jr., "The U.S. Communist Party," *Life,* 29 July 1946, 84–96.

58. Ibid., 85–87.

59. Ibid., 87, and quoting Harold Laski, 88 and 90.

60. Ibid., 93–96.

61. Ibid., 96.

62. "Red Hunting," *Life,* 3 March 1947, 32.

5

PETER BACON HALES

IMAGINING THE ATOMIC AGE

Life *and the Atom*

Central to the atomic age is the visual: pictures that promise to carry the meaning of this epoch, to represent its complexities with new forms, so that we might understand and embrace it. Declaring a universal event, universal hope, and universal peril, the atomic age has presented itself as a global age, transcending boundaries of language, class, education, and culture, and demanding a new universality of form and rhetoric to match. Yet it is a peculiarly American mythos—promoted and exploited throughout the world, but originating here, where the atomic age began.

To the people of Japan, and to most of the peoples of the world, the dominating image of the atomic age is one of holocaust—horrible pictures of blindness, deafness, pain, disease, loss, and death. But this is not what Americans saw when they opened their magazines, journals, and newspapers from August 1945 to the comprehensive test-ban treaties of the early 1960s. For them, the dominant image was the atomic cloud, rising mightily from an indeterminate landscape, towering to the sky (Figure 5.1). Though there were important exceptions to this campaign of imagery, the dominant American version of the atomic age was a presentation for a witness, a passive consumer located at some distance, protected and privi-

TOWERING ABOVE THE NEW MEXICO DESERT THE COLUMN OF HOT GASES CREATED BY FIRST ATOMIC EXPLOSION LIGHTS THE GROUND AND THE CLOUDS OVERHEAD

FIRST ATOMIC BOMB

Epoch's opening is shown in color

The first atomic explosion, which has been called the beginning of the second epoch in history, is the only authentic epoch-making event to be recorded in full color. In the picture above, color film has preserved an infinitesimal fraction of the explosion's appalling light. It shows the great luminous cloud which zoomed into the stratosphere after the first brilliant flash. Inside the cloud were battered atoms of the air surrounding the explosion and of the vaporized steel tower which had held the bomb. Nine miles away, smeared with sunburn lotion to protect them from long-range ultraviolet burns, were the scientists who developed the bomb. As they watched the light of the explosion the earth trembled and they danced for joy.

Figure 5.1. "First Atomic Bomb," *Life,* **November 19, 1945.**

leged. And the dominant theater of presentation was America's premiere picture magazine, *Life.*

Through *Life* the atomic age truly found its form, as symbol and myth—that is, as a visual icon and as a narrative, whether condensed into a photo-essay or stretched across a decade of sustained presentation and modulation. Inserted into *Life's* universal visual democracy, into its combination of folksy intimacy and overbearing authority, into its breathy pseudodocumentary seaminess and its cult of visual pleasure, the atomic bomb and its terror found a form of cultural legitimacy. If we wish to study the atomic age, we must start with the pages of *Life.*

The iconography of that atomic era is interesting. From the earliest representations of the atomic explosion to the last, we can observe subtle variations on a single, compelling, ever-repeated image: the mushroom cloud, rising above enemy lands, paradise islands, or wasteland deserts. One theme of *Life*'s presentation of the atomic age was the reassuring pleasure of that sight. But to study this magazine and its complex dance with the forces of atomic destruction and promise is to find something far more interesting than a string of illustrations; it is to discover a narrative, sometimes forceful and sometimes hesitant, but rarely direct, that proposed the path from a terrifying dark present to a shining future. To look at *Life* in this regard is to discover a complex set of stages in America's accommodation to the atomic bomb, beginning with incomprehension and ending with something beyond dispassion, something closer to acceptance. More than a simple response to the realities of atomic warfare and the exigencies of time, this myth of the atomic age was also a process of cultural adaptation in which the dominant cultural institutions of the time directed the flow of images and meanings.

Using the mass-market picture magazine *Life* to propose this narrative of accommodation affords us more than the benefit of condensation. *Life* was the preeminent popular outlet of the immediate postwar years. From its first issue in the fall of 1936 *Life* was a sellout; by 1937 it was selling a million copies every issue; in 1956 circulation peaked at 5.8 million paid subscribers, with a pass-through readership estimated at 75 million or more.[1]

To reach this level of success, *Life* mastered a form of mass-culture production that spoke to and spoke for middle-class Americans. *Life* reflected its audience's beliefs and predilections, and re-presented those beliefs in a language of comfortable and comprehensible symbols. But *Life* also directed and modified the beliefs of its audience: it was a teacher of values, shaping American attitudes by careful choices in what made up the weekly "news" and how it went into American homes, doctors' offices, dentists' waiting rooms, and all the other places where a copy might be found.

Writing in 1948, *Life*'s publisher, Henry Luce, pro-posed for his magazine something close to a mission: "Life as it is lived in America today is a strange and wonderful tension between the particular problems of little people (all of us and our families) and the surge of great 'historic forces.' . . . If we can bring together in one magazine a feeling for all the little 'human' problems and all the little episodes of human life together with an awareness and intelligent disclosure of the 'great historic' forces—that surely will be a great achievement."[2]

The politics of the atomic age formed one of the central strains in *Life*'s combination of reportage and propaganda. Week after week through nearly two decades between the end of World War II and the development of a comprehensive test-ban treaty, *Life* found something of interest in the atomic age and its products for "the little people" and something for the "surge of great historic forces." For *Life*'s editorial staff and its readers, the atomic age was one of the central issues facing postwar America; looking at the atomic culture, *Life* found the basic lessons facing American democracy in a time of peril and promise.

The role of interpreter and spokesperson conformed to the larger vision *Life* had of itself. From its first issues, *Life* was a magazine devoted to the modern consolidation of technology, power, capital, and government, and it consistently advocated programs and projects that reflected this centralization. Beginning with the cover story of the first issue on the Fort Peck dam project, *Life* had used its trademark blend of photographs, visual layout, captions, and human-interest stories to create a broad if unspoken narrative celebrating the taming of nature in service to human progress.

To intervene in this moment of doubt and confusion, to still fears (or direct them), and to awaken and direct middle-class America's image of itself and its country was a natural extension of the larger mission *Life* had carved for itself. And yet the magazine was but one part of a larger chain of cultural and political institutions not only reassuring, but also exploiting the fears and doubts of a nation in the uneasy transition between two eras.

Figure 5.2. "A Jap Burns" and advertisement for Campbell's soup, *Life*, August 13, 1945. (Courtesy Campbell Soup Company)

Life's coverage of the atomic age began on August 20, 1945, two weeks after the bombing of Hiroshima. Printing lag time had made it impossible for the magazine to rush a pictorial account into print, and editors chose to use the time to devise a complex and comprehensive coverage of the atomic bomb and its implications. This delay was significant, for it reminds us of the particular role *Life* proposed for itself—not as a journal of news competing with radio and daily newspapers, nor even as a "news weekly" that organized and edited the week's events (that was the role of *Life*'s sister-publication, *Time*), but rather as an interpreter and director of interpretations, a shaper of attitudes. *Life*'s editors saw the events of early August as so momentous that to present them in disjointed form, to present them without appropriately spectacular visual materials, would be to abrogate their position in American mass culture.

It is worth noting what *did* show up in the magazine during that week of the bombings of Hiroshima and Nagasaki and the Japanese surrender (August 13, 1945), because it provides important clues to the context within which *Life*'s editors and writers presented the circumstances of atomic warfare. The cover story represented one theme: a celebration of the new Air Force jets, presenting technology as the key to a new, victorious democratic alliance. But this was actually the third of three articles that anticipated the final days of the war against the Japanese. First was a double-page spread called "The Jap Homeland: Allies Give It a Terrific Beating," which included nine photographs depicting the aerial and sea attacks on the islands of Honshu. "Besides the . . . lands . . . over which U.S. ground troops may soon have to fight," the article said, "these pictures showed what an unmerciful beating the Jap has been taking." The final paragraph accompanying this spread contained the only direct report of the atomic bombing, a brief statement inserted at the one point in the issue where its absence would have compromised *Life*'s reputation for newsworthiness. "And something far more terrible was yet to come," read this insert. "On August 5 an American plane dropped the first atomic bomb on the Jap base at Hiroshima. Said President Truman, 'If [the Japanese] do not now accept our terms they may expect a rain of ruin from the air, the like of which has never been seen on this earth.'"[3]

Life's photo-essay packaged the atomic bombing of Hiroshima as a continuation of conventional warfare, intensified by divine right. Truman's warning of "a rain of ruin from the air" echoed warnings from the Old Testament and the Book of Revelation and proposed that the atomic bombing was a divine act rather than one of human retribution.

This sense of retribution depended on that most essential of wartime propaganda strategies, the dehumanization and demonization of the enemy. The air force pictures of August 13 showed no people—only ships, buildings, and landscapes battered by Allied attack. But turn the page, and you would have seen in gruesome sequence, from flamethrower attack to final grisly death, the immolation of a Japanese soldier in Borneo (Figure 5.2). This essay presented the Japanese in their most demonic guise, as "the enemy," implacable, fanatical, "the Japs" who "fought from caves, from pillboxes, from every available hiding place." "Easily the most cruel, the most terrifying weapon ever developed . . . but so long as the Jap refuses to come out of his holes and keeps killing, this is the only way." This concluding paragraph, originally meant to describe the flamethrower, had by August 13, 1945, come to suggest instead the new and more powerful superweapon, even more cruel, yet by implication equally necessary to punish the inhuman enemy.[4]

These early pieces had three of the essential elements that dominated the postwar presentation of atomic warfare: packaging the bomb as a continuation of other, accepted forms of conventional aerial warfare; presenting its use as a necessary shocking strike to halt an irrationally suicidal enemy; and marking its difference as an indicator of Biblical retribution, the product of God wielded by the righteous against the unrighteous.

Between the immolated soldier and the striking flight views of America's first jet airplane were pages of very different pictures and text. Opposite "A Jap Burns" was a color advertisement for Campbell Soup Company's cream of mushroom soup titled "Mushrooms: Fresh from the Hothouse." On the next page was a pair of spreads full of happy Caucasian babies—one a color ad for soaps, the other a black-and-white piece on the orphaned children of German ss soldiers. These images provided the context within which atomic warfare was couched—a context of normalcy, of safety and pleasure, of innocence and continuity. This duality— of violence and disruption set against the reassuring safety of the everyday—recurred repeatedly as *Life* developed its stance on the atomic age.

On August 20, 1945, *Life* published its full treatment of the atomic bombings of Hiroshima and Nagasaki, the end of the war, and the opening of the atomic age. In so doing, the magazine's editors asserted their postwar role as interpreters of a disturbing new era in human history. The boldly graphic spread on the destruction of Hiroshima and Nagasaki, with its telegraphic headlines and air force aerial views, formed the opening salvo in that first presentation. It proposed the bombings as the end of things; "B-29s Almost Finished Job," the headline said, between views of the atomic cloud and aerial photographs of the destroyed cities. "Strategic bombing . . . had already ripped the guts out of Japan's great cities," the article said, and the pictures of Tokyo and Kobe were virtually indistinguishable from those of Hiroshima. And the text ended with a quote from an air force general: "Wouldn't it be an odd thing if these were the only two atomic bombs ever dropped?"[5]

The second spread, symmetrically located toward the end of the issue, proposed a great beginning, "a new era," in which American "scientists have harnessed nature's basic force," "the end of one world and the start of a new one." In an uncharacteristically wordy history of the Manhattan Project, *Life* proposed that the atomic bomb was the result of high intellectual and moral courage, sacrifice, and utopian planning.[6]

Surprisingly, within this reassuring package of words, images dominated. They dominated as pictures, and as word-pictures. The unifying element of the Manhattan Project history was the story of the Alamogordo test explosion some months before, "that stormy morning on that outlandish terrain," the event "no one really could describe . . . a phenomenon unique in human experience" and an event shot through with visual spectacle, pleasurable and terrifying—the atomic sublime.[7] Into this tale of endings and beginnings, these first visuals of the atomic age overlaid a different duality—of panorama and of microcosm. Aerial views of cities destroyed offered a distanced, omniscient rationality within which Hiroshima before and Hiroshima after looked not significantly different: cleaned, perhaps even sanitized, of the traces of an unpleasant and now impotent enemy. What was missing were pictures of the destruction from below, from the human standpoint rather than the gods'. Such pictures remained censored and suppressed for years, leaving the field to these dispassionate representations of rationalized destruction.

In the panoramas of the second essay, however, a more complex discourse appeared—a discourse of spectatordom and spectacle. *Life*'s staff artists presented paintings of men at work in a dramatic desert landscape dominated by a looming tower, turning, overwhelmed, from the blast of this new creation and, as tiny silhouettes, staring in awe at the rising "pillar" that, the caption tells us, "blossoms" before them. "Here was . . . the prize at the end of a death race between nations," "a light of unearthly brilliance . . . awesome . . . so spectacular that observers were too stunned to pay much attention to the air blast and the sound . . . a huge fiery cloud of many colors, . . ." a sight so intense that "an observer who had the temerity to face the explosion suffered temporary blindness and permanent damage to his vision. . . ."[8]

This last word-picture is important: it presents a symbolic first casualty of the atomic age—"an observer," not a victim but one whose folly was lack of self-restraint and whose punishment was loss of sight. The image is drawn obliquely from the ancient Greek stories of Prometheus, who stole fire from the gods and was punished for eternity, and of the inventor-scientist Daedalus, whose overambitious child flew too close to the sun and fell into the sea after his father's invention failed.

This opening on the atomic age thus served to locate the new in ancient Western myths and contexts. But more prominent, and more significant, was the imbedding of this new age within the European Romantic traditions of visual pleasure, spectatordom, emotion, and nature known as the sublime.[9] *Life*'s presentation of the atomic test at Alamogordo proposed atomic holocaust as a natural phenomenon, in which Promethean science awakened natural forces, and these forces released visual spectacles that overwhelmed the witness with visuality rather than death or injury. In this opening document of the atomic age, humans did not die; no one suffered radiation injury or burns, no one was underneath the explosion or within it. Instead, they, and we, were above it, or far away, in some zone of spectatordom. I say "we" because it is important, I think, to propose two interrelated sets of spectators: the observers who we see in the pictures and *Life*'s middle-class readers then (and ourselves, now). Opening the pages of *Life,* readers became witnesses, and that witnessing was visual first and most of all an essential part of the atomic sublime.[10]

Life's viewers accepted a passive relationship with the overwhelming destruction they witnessed; they were neither threatened by, nor responsible for, this phenomenon of nature. They found themselves in league with Truman, echoed by *Life,* who said that the destruction of Hiroshima and Nagasaki were forms of Biblical vengeance upon an aggressor for which Americans need not feel guilt.

Such a picture, literal and figurative, proposed an

impossible equation, or at least, an equation contradicted by other elements of the emerging mythology of the atomic age. Humans had created this new nature; they must then somehow be implicated in its effects. But this was where a different iteration of the atomic sublime applied: an awesome nature located not in the vast powers of the mushroom cloud but in the submicroscopic order and beauty of the atom. This was a theme proposed in August 20, 1945, in the photo-essay "The Atomic Bomb," *Life*'s attempt to educate its readers about the physics of the atomic age. In images that alternated representations of minuscule particles with accounts of near-infinite releases of energy, "millions of electron volts," "enormous atomic explosion[s]," and the creation of a new element, plutonium, the article offered magical entry into the subatomic universe. Viewers turned the page to see dramatic pictures of mysterious "atom-smashing machines" and dark-suited, serious scientists ministering to the machines or grouped in the foreground discussing their experiments.[11]

To look at *Life*'s articles, picture-essays, and news reports on the atomic age over the next decade is to be struck by how fully that August 20, 1945, issue encompassed the developing mythology of the atomic age. To trace this path in issue after issue is to see not so much transformation or development, but an unfolding of the implications contained in that first issue. As the pictures of Hiroshima and Nagasaki appeared in the magazine, for example, they served not as shocking counters to this aestheticized view, but as variations on the romantic sublime, as meditations on ruins rather than condemnations of the makers of ruins. Both types presented the deflection of horror into the distance, in photographs of destruction that presented the wrecked city without inhabitants, a ruin brought on by natural cataclysm, earthquake, perhaps. Or, like the paintings of the German romantic Caspar David Friedrich, they offered moral lessons—as was the case, for example, in a photograph in the October 15, 1945, issue titled "Statue of Christ Lies Intact in Bombed Nagasaki."[12]

Against this dispassionate, distanced view came the recurrent and increasingly spectacular images of atomic explosions. In November 1945 the Manhattan Engineer District released the first color photographs of the New Mexico test. "First Atomic Bomb: Epoch's Opening Is Shown in Color," blared the *Life* headline (see Figure 5.1). The full-page picture showed a brilliant eruption set against a dawn sky, a spectacle of nature set in a mass-culture icon of nature worship: the desert at sunrise.

The text was in its own way even more radical, for it endowed this beauty with the power of absolution. Here is the accompanying paragraph:

> The first atomic explosion, which has been called the beginning of the second epoch in history, is the only authentic epoch-making event to be recorded in full color. In the picture above, color film has preserved an infinitesimal fraction of the explosion's appalling light. It shows the great luminous cloud which zoomed into the stratosphere after the first brilliant flash. Inside the cloud were battered atoms of the air surrounding the explosion and of the vaporized steel tower which had held the bomb. Nine miles away, smeared with sunburn lotion to protect them from long-range ultraviolet burns, were the scientists who developed the bomb. As they watched the light of the explosion the earth trembled and they danced for joy.[13]

Here was the bright sublime, "appalling," yet "brilliant," "luminous," "great," and "authentic."

This joyous, celebratory, and redemptive dance with divinity did not encompass the mythology of the atomic age as *Life* presented it. Instead, it served as one pole of a radical bifurcation, between spectacle and victim, between the omnipotent eye watching over all and the helpless subject, small, terrified, powerless. This was the theme presented in the photo-essay immediately preceding "First Atomic Bomb." Titled "Imaginary 36-Hour War," the discussion of an early report on the possibilities of atomic warfare proposed a dark sublime of terror and impotence, laced with adjectives of gothic disintegration: the "ghastliest," most "terrible," "devastating" catastrophe.[14] This proposal, of the reader as victim, and the human brotherhood a brotherhood of pain and death, drew, if only obliquely, on references in a pair of earlier reports on the destruction at Hiroshima and Nagasaki. The Hiroshima account, titled "What Ended the War," contained most of the benevolent tendencies we have traced: presenting the ruins of Hiroshima as vestiges of a natural catastrophe, mediating the images of destruction with its remarkable view of the mushroom cloud over Nagasaki, and even reasserting the image of the bombing as a return of the "terrible swift sword" of divine vengeance. But it also reported the lingering torture of radiation injury.[15]

Look at an October 1945 photo-essay titled "Tokyo Express Arrives in Bomb-Scarred Hiroshima." Here again, the pictures and captions in a nine-page spread sought to normalize the bomb. Beginning with a picture of the train arriving at Hiroshima station, the article said the "bomb blast blew away sheds but did not destroy track bed" and "Tokyo's stationmaster, who sold Photographer Eyerman a second-class ticket to Hiroshima for 165 yen ($11) and thought Americans should not pay." Featuring pictures of soldiers jamming a coach, the scenery, including mountains, a "rural shrine, a quaint structure," and "schoolchildren, carrying their books and parasols," the photo-essay finally ended with pictures of the victims. Yet even these showed children of Hiroshima in "colorful, full-length knickers" and parasols, marred only by their "nose and mouth masks of gauze." And the morbid connotations of those masks, *Life*'s caption editors reassured readers, was that this was simply a common Japanese custom, originally adopted by "the Japs in the '20s as a safeguard against influenza," which suggests a correspondence between the plague of Hiroshima and the flu, both in intensity and in natural origin.[16]

The last double-page photo spread showed "atomic bomb victims . . . suffering from burns and fractures." But even these two views were defused by their caption. The first criticized the medical conditions of the hos-

pitals, an indictment, it seems, of Japanese response rather than Allied generosity. The second caption was more striking—"Photographer Eyerman reported their injuries looked like those he had seen when he photographed men burned at Pearl Harbor . . ."—a double reference to the continuousness of atomic and conventional warfare and the atrocity of Pearl Harbor.[17] The final picture, a full-page image, showed a family praying at a Buddhist temple in Hiroshima.

This early presentation of human injury hinted at the November warning on the consequences of atomic warfare. The double image—the dark sublime of the victim and the bright sublime of the witness—did not include the Japanese casualties of Hiroshima and Nagasaki. They were, as article after article recapitulated, the legitimate casualties of war, provoked by Japanese imperialism and contained only with this overwhelming retributive weapon.

This, then, was the way *Life* introduced the atomic age. On one side, the bombings at Hiroshima and Nagasaki were the powerful ends of an older era, in which a wise and divinely sanctioned Allied leadership conquered tyranny and imperialism. On the other side was the beginning of a new age—the atomic age. Here the atomic bomb was subsumed under a larger rubric: atomic energy, a force of divine origins, a force of nature, benignant and awesome when folded within the larger rationality of science and the benevolent meritocracy of the American scientific establishment.

Over the next decade, this double narrative of endings and beginnings reappeared in more and more sophisticated form. It was perhaps most effective in the story of "Peace City," published in September 1947. There, *Life* reported, "a startled world read that Hiroshima, proclaiming itself the new world mecca for peace, had held a carnival. . . . Hiroshima seemed to have risen from the dead." From this day forward, *Life* said, Japan had relocated itself from the narrative of endings to the narrative of beginnings. To emphasize this proposal, *Life* ended its narrative with the story of Kiyosji Kikawa, "a survivor [who] hopes his wounds will serve peace." Here for the first time, *Life* called a Japanese casualty of the atomic bombings a "victim," a telling shift from its previous terms—"casualty" and "survivor," morally neutral terms for military losses. Yet it was this victim's wish "to be sent to the U.S. so doctors can experiment with my body. It does not matter if I die as long as I can be of some use to a world at peace." Named a "victim," Kiyosji Kikawa ended up a self-proclaimed martyr, sacrificing himself to absolve his fellow Japanese for their wartime aggression, absolving the Americans for the horror of their retribution.[18]

If "Peace City" declared the absolution of the Allies, it also accompanied anxiety in America. Articles on the radiation injuries of the Japanese surfaced periodically; their goal was to remind American readers not of what had happened to the Japanese, but of what might happen to Americans. As Russian advances in atomic and nuclear technology brought the possibility of massive atomic warfare home to middle-class households, however, the visual imagery of *Life*'s photo-essays rose eloquently to respond with the beauty and managed theatrics of the atomic sublime. Picture spreads on the scientific miracles of atomic energy ranged from the homely (as in "25 Million-Volt Cancer Treatment" of 1949) to the spectacular. Scientists posed heroically, deep in thought or tending their technological tools, reinforcing the call for "the little people" (to remember publisher Luce's words for his readers) to place their faith in a centralized scientific, governmental, and military elite, and embrace the receding mirage of world-government and global weapons control. These themes represented the mediating forces over atomic terror. At the other extreme was an evermore sophisticated, and seductive, aesthetic of atomic pleasure and witness. Between 1948 and 1952 we can see such a mythology evolve, as the images of spectatordom recurred, bringing the celebrity and the everyman soldier before the altar of atomic grandeur, and as the images appeared in more and more compelling and seductive guise.

This mythology did not develop spontaneously. Between 1945 and May 1952 the images *Life* published came not from their photographers but from the army's Manhattan Engineer District (the M.E.D. was the formal military entity known colloquially as the Manhattan Project) and its quasicivilian successor, the Atomic Energy Commission (AEC). At M.E.D. headquarters, military leaders, like Gen. Leslie R. Groves, and public-relations specialists, like George Robinson, worked with civilian press representatives to orchestrate and regulate the mythology of the atomic age.[19]

Life, then, served as one within a chain of institutions shaping the postwar narrative of the atomic age. To see the AEC releases and to trace the carefully managed events where the press first watched an atomic test from News Nob in Nevada is to witness an orchestrated propaganda campaign designed to create obedience to the centralized powers of the state. In this early, tightly controlled stage of atomic imagery, the most-repeated narratives told of benevolent militarists and benevolent scientists seeking permanent global peace through the development of preventive atomic weaponry. And *Life* obediently presented this narrative in stories about the first atomic tests at Bikini, in special reports from the various atomic weapons labs, and in full-page or even double-page spreads of spectacular color photography of atomic clouds. That is one aspect of the atomic culture: a campaign by centralized forces to neutralize or direct fear. But it is not the only theme nor, I suspect, the dominant one. Too many disruptions and counter events unsettled this crusade, and each disruption tore at this program of directed propaganda.

To a large extent, this undermining force resulted from the failure of the government and military authorities to fully regulate press coverage. As long as the M.E.D. and the AEC maintained strict controls over the content and form of reportage and imagery, the result was a coherent and persuasive knitting of ideology and mythos. Before 1952 these agencies controlled who entered the test sites, where they stood, what they saw, and when they left. At such events, "staged" took on an increasingly literal flavor, and the resulting texts

WHEREVER YOU LOOK THERE'S DANGER IN LAS VEGAS

Little Las Vegas, Nev. is a wide-open town that is quite accustomed to spinning as dizzily as a roulette wheel. But even for Las Vegas last week was a full week. The first shock came Tuesday night when the town's 13 bookies met and decided to quit business rather than pay a 10% federal tax. Only a few hours later, at 3 a.m. on Wednesday, Marion Davies flew into town with an old friend, "Uncle Horace" Brown, and married him (*p. 41*). Dozens of citizens, and some newsmen too, forgot all about the bomb tests at nearby Frenchman Flat and swarmed to the ceremony instead. After the surrenders by the bookies and Miss Davies, residents of Las Vegas were hardly surprised on Thursday morning when a fleecy white atomic cloud drifted in toward the city, producing a picture (*above*) that illustrates two of the riskier aspects of life in the 20th Century. The cloud's performance, however, was not just for Las Vegas—it announced that U.S. GIs had been given an awesome preview of the war of the future (*next page*).

Figure 5.3. "Wherever You Look There's Danger in Las Vegas," *Life,* **November 12, 1951. (Courtesy Corbis)**

came to resemble official scripts and the pictures either came directly from the press kit or were made under close watch by public affairs officers and security police. The results sounded and looked like stage dramas, even down to the lighting and the proscenium-style angle of view.

In 1952, after seven years, the AEC loosened its hold. Reporters and photographers were given freer access to the sites, especially the newer ones in the deserts of Nevada. Tests in the South Pacific had meant press representatives stayed on naval vessels or they landed on small cordoned beachheads at neighboring atolls, locations scouted and designed by military representatives.

Everything changed in Nevada. While the sites themselves remained off-limits and AEC or army vehicles shuttled press representatives to and from designated locales, the visual boundaries of those sites were porous. In part this was the result of a change in the venue for atomic testing and the establishment of testing seasons in the deserts of Nevada. Enterprising photographers began to stake out the test sites, producing memorable pictures. One of the most celebrated was *Life*'s "Wherever You Look There's Danger in Las Vegas," a "Picture of the Week" published in November 1951 (Figure 5.3).[20]

At first, this new freedom did not bring a corresponding counterimagery. As the army began bringing soldiers into the atomic testing arena, it sought to reassure Americans that the dangers were minimal. One method was to invite newsmen to the spectacle zone; the result was better than the AEC had imagined. Not simply recapitulating the older controlled views from the South Pacific sites, these new pictures dramatically increased the theatrical effects and inserted them within familiar American landscapes and stories: the Great American Desert and the movie western, most of all. There were now images of awestruck observers and spectacular pictures by *Life*'s star photographers using state-of-the-art lighting techniques and trademark photographic tricks and novelties (shots into concave and convex mirrors, mushroom clouds reflected in military sunglasses or goggles, and the like). These brought an upsurge in the aesthetics of the sublime, with soldiers and newsmen vying to look more awestruck about the visual pyrotechnics and more blasé about the dangers.[21]

This was, however, only half of the strategy. At Eniwetok atoll and Bikini, where the first hydrogen-bomb tests were being concurrently held, strict secrecy took precedence. Such a bifurcation was essential from a security standpoint; the desire of American political and military figures to keep the H-bomb far from Russian eyes was powerful, and the experiments themselves were highly speculative. Whereas the events at News Nob in Nevada were predictable, controlled, and photogenic, the events at Eniwetok atoll were not.

Two trends quickly surfaced to undercut the monopoly on the atomic mythos. The disconcerting flow of events formed the first: from accidents at Eniwetok to the Russian development of the H-bomb came a situation no military censor could control, nor patriotic editorial board ignore or suppress. But these events could be interpreted within the pages of the magazine; and here, in the decisions of editors and writers, lay a second phenomenon—a decisive trend toward a certain darker and more alarming vision on the part of *Life*.

The period from mid-1949 to spring 1954 did not lack disturbing events to feed this trend. In September 1949 President Truman announced that the Russians had exploded their first atomic weapon. Three years later, American scientists blasted their first hydrogen thermonuclear device, and within a year the Russians had followed suit. Just months into 1954, a hydrogen-bomb test at Eniwetok atoll went out of control, shooting fallout far into the atmosphere and claiming the atomic age's first innocent victims—Japanese fishermen on a trawler named the *Fukuryu Maru*.

None of these events could be ignored, but there were ways of interpreting and presenting them that might ameliorate their terror and downplay their implications. In this regard, *Life*'s editors seem to have chosen a double path. On the one hand, the magazine presented its readers with spectacular images that might rouse any adult to panic and any child to nightmares. Such was the case, for example, with its presentation in September 1952 of the earliest images of the human effects of atomic war—the Japanese photographs of the hours and days after the bombing of Hiroshima and Nagasaki (Figures 5.4 and 5.5). These images, crumbling and damaged, showed people—no longer "Japs," no longer "the enemy," but simply people—hurt and helpless, terrified, wandering in shock,

"burned children," half-destroyed hospitals, and desperate families caring for their doomed offspring.[22]

The editor's opening text, with its melodramatic declarations and compelling language, amplified the powerful new imagery. Here for the first time, Americans saw pictures of the radiation-sick "walking dead." They read captions like HURT AND HOMELESS, DOOMED CHILD, STRIPPED HOSPITAL, LAST DRINK, and longer descriptions drenched with emotional and symbolic power.

Such a potent combination was also applied to *Life*'s April 1954 special photo-essays on the implications of the H-bomb for domestic terror. "5-4-3-2-1 and the Hydrogen Age Is Upon Us," in the April 12 issue, included images of worried American scientists and military men and views of American cities overdrawn with graphic circles of destruction and underscored by phrases like "scientists were astonished" and "a stunned nation." *Life*'s writer used the code word of the sublime—"awesome"—early in this issue-spanning series, but countered with words like "menace" and "horror" toward the end.[23]

Both the magazine and the larger culture the era produced undercut the effect of this darker, more terrible face on the symbolism of the atomic age. The immense popularity of the atomic sublime had, by 1954, made spectacular images of atomic tests a virtual staple of the magazine, and after each terrifying disruption came the recurrent images of awe and beauty, reinserting atomic holocaust in the context of spectacular nature, succoring fears and neutralizing terror. Thus, the week after "5-4-3-2-1 and the Hydrogen Age Is Upon Us," *Life*'s editors chose to run the first cover image of the atomic sublime, "The Awesome Fireball," on April 19, 1954 (Figure 5.6). One week later, the "Speaking of Pictures" section of the magazine featured an interior decorator who liked to collage images and had used an early color picture of the atomic cloud in his work. The next week, "Fire and Ice" devoted two double-page spreads to the beauty of atomic destruction.[24]

This process had a double effect. On one hand, the

newly emboldened writers and editors may have been supporting (inadvertently or purposefully) the national agenda by awakening fear and then leaving political figures to direct it toward patriotism and subservience to the state. We must not forget, after all, that this was not only the period of atomic escalation but also the era of the Korean War, when American men were drafted, fought, and died in Asian lands to counter an intangible communist threat. To demonize communism as a global menace rather than a local Korean dispute, to set the hardships of conventional war against the greater horrors of atomic war, was to press American democracy further toward a warlike culture of sacrifice and obedience.

The recurrent imagery of atomic sublimity served in some senses both to render acceptable the concept of atomic war and to neutralize it. This tendency—to numb emotion through repetition—was one side. The other was the more diffuse and uncontrolled process of normalization and domestication that occurred as pictures of atomic explosions and even of atomic-war ca-

sualties appeared inserted in the complex texts of the magazine itself. For readers did not just read one article or look at one picture-essay. They paged through the magazine, and what appeared before and after the atomic imagery served to recontextualize it—a process graphically brought home to us now when we come upon spreads of atomic images set next to an ad asking if readers had "trouble sleeping," or thin columns of pictures of mushroom clouds set beside parallel columns of ads for headache medicine and shoe polish, or a promise of an auto-adjusting television inset with images promising domestic salvation, opposite a multipicture spread titled "A-Bomb vs. House" (Figure 5.7).[25]

Some of the double-page spreads seem on the face of it almost impossibly fortuitous: to sell insurance with one spread, to propose the anxieties of the atomic age as the rationale for insomnia with another. But the circumstance that brought these conjunctions ranged from pure chance to a highly complex and orchestrated program of sequencing watched over by the editors and approved by advertisers.

Right: Figure 5.6. "Color Photographs Add Vivid Reality to Nation's Concept of H-Bomb," *Life,* April 19, 1954. *Opposite:* Figure 5.7. Advertisement for Westinghouse televisions and "A-Bomb vs. House," *Life,* March 30, 1953. (Courtesy Westinghouse and J.R. Eyerman/TimePix)

In this regard, exigencies of printing technology shaped the narratives within each issue, but so did the decisions of advertisers. The process of setting up the "book" on each issue illustrates this complex interconnection. In the office of the managing editor, each week the walls became vertical mock-up boards for the final version, and as the week went on, the editorial and advertising sales staffs arranged and rearranged the sequence, the size of ads and articles, the scale of indi-

vidual pictures, and all the other elements that made up the finished product. Because color was slower to produce and more expensive, the location and nature of the color essays and ads were determined relatively early and remained stable.[26] The pictures of the atomic sublime, then, were fixed set-points in the issue's sequencing, and the rhetoric of the entire issue revolved around them to a marked degree.

To see the effects of this, look at the full-page spreads

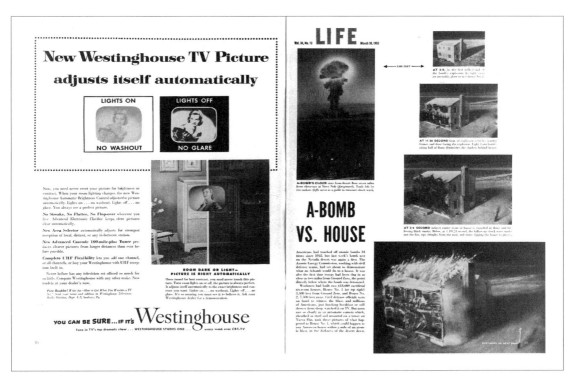

from the August 13, 1945, issue (Figure 5.2) and the September 29, 1952, issue in which "Uncensored" appeared (Figure 5.5). In the 1945 issue, the Campbell soup ad was the prime determinant of the spread and its location, for the Campbell Soup Company had a contract for a preordained location within the magazine and a set color format. Thus, *Life*'s editors included the image of the flamethrower death, knowing what it would run against. In the 1952 issue, editors made a deliberate choice to use "Uncensored" as their lead editorial essay, literally putting the imprimatur of *Life* on the upper-right corner of the image of huddled victims at Nagasaki. This bold editorial decision, with its significant shift in stance and its spectacularly horrifying visual imagery, required that the editors conclude (quite possibly in consultation with the advertisers) that the combination would be neither offensive nor ineffective.

It is striking to look at this particular double-page spread not simply for its juxtaposition of a domestic interior with the flattened terrain of atomized Nagasaki, but for its counterpoising of two forms of domestic anx-

iety, in both of which families are threatened and sundered by environmental poisons, one of a supremely terrifying sort, the other of a mundane and everyday variety. To look at these two is to see the ways in which the editorial page must have served to awaken anxieties about family disintegration by an outside threat—a phenomenon similar to the ways neighborhoods experience a sudden rise in the purchase of fire extinguishers after a local house has burned. To say that this response trivialized the atomic holocaust would, however, be to misunderstand the ways *Life* penetrated into the intimate spheres of domestic life and the ways its horrifying imagery awoke a nationwide huddling fear.[27]

In the end, *Life*'s weekly interpenetration of images and themes served to insert the atomic age into the narrative of everyday life. Holocaust pictures might increase the sales of insurance, but ads for tourist havens and bad-breath cures served to neutralize that atomic anxiety as well, by presenting it as only one among many bodily, family, domestic, national, and global concerns. Just how effective was this neutralizing may have been hinted at in a series of articles and editorials that appeared in *Life* and elsewhere in the late 1950s and early 1960s. There, politicians and editors wondered just why it was that Americans were so much less willing to respond to warnings about atomic warfare. On July 20, 1959, *Life*'s editors went so far as to decry "public apathy" toward fallout-shelter programs. And both politicians and editors looked with alarm at the appearance of a large, articulate nuclear-protest movement in the United States and abroad.

The editors of *Life* never appear to have noticed the possibility of a connection between their magazine's marketing the imagery of the atomic age and a developing immunity to political and cultural exploitation of atomic fear. When *Life* presented its viewers with the last glorious, even-mannered representations of the atomic sublime in 1962, it marked the end of an era and signaled the immersion of atomic imagery into the sea of symbols that made up postwar American,

and global, culture. Today, a new generation of Americans has reached adulthood, a generation for whom the mushroom cloud is a historical curiosity and not a symbol laden with import and charged with emotion. For these global citizens, the combination of human terror, scientific utopianism, and aesthetic pleasure that marked the atomic sublime has shifted from the center of modern culture to its edges, and now, perhaps, approaches a cultural oblivion. As the last survivors and victims of Hiroshima and Nagasaki die of old age and as the children of Cold War terror approach old age and death, new symbols and images replace those once so central to an era. And perhaps it is because of this diminishment in cultural relevance that we can begin, as historians, to analyze and understand the ways in which the highly charged visual imagery of atomic holocaust came to play a central role in Cold War American culture.

NOTES

I first wrote of this subject in 1989; a revised early draft appeared as Peter Hales, "The Atomic Sublime," *American Studies* (Spring 1991). Some segments of this essay also appeared, in similar form, in Peter Bacon Hales, "The Mass Aesthetic of Holocaust: American Media Construct the Atomic Bomb," in *Yearbook of the Japanese Association for American Studies* (Toyko: JASA, 1996), 110–30, in 1996. None of the research for this work would have been possible without the assistance of the Rare Books and Manuscripts Collection at Northwestern University and its curator, Russell Malone. I am also grateful to the National Endowment for the Humanities, which, some years ago, funded the early stages of my research in the subject, and to the Institute for the Humanities of the University of Illinois, Chicago, under whose auspices I was able to write early drafts for the larger study of which this is a part.

1. I am extrapolating here from James L. Baughman's report that the pass through—"the highest pass-along factor of *any* periodical"—reached as high as 17.3 per copy in 1938. Market research reported that, by the mid-1950s, more than 60 percent of all Americans over ten years of age had seen at least one issue. Baughmann's analysis is quoted from his presentation at the symposium, "Looking at *Life:* Rethinking America's Favorite Magazine," University of Colorado, Boulder, September 14–17, 1995. See also Chapter 2 in this book by Baughman.

2. Loudon Wainwright, *The Great American Magazine: An Inside History of* Life (New York: Knopf, 1986), 173, and in Wendy Kozol, Life's *America: Family and Nation in Postwar Photojournalism* (Philadelphia: Temple University Press, 1993), 39.

3. "The Jap Homeland: Allies Give It a Terrific Beating," *Life*, 13 August 1945, 32–33.

4. "A Jap Burns," *Life*, 13 August 1945, 34.

5. "The War Ends," *Life*, 20 August 1945, 25–31.

6. "Manhattan Project: Scientists Have Harnessed Nature's Basic Force," ibid., 91–111.

7. Ibid., 91.

8. Ibid.

9. The history of the sublime begins with Edmund Burke's *Philosophical Enquiry into the Origins of Our Notions of the Sublime and the Beautiful,* published in 1757; but Burke was in fact reclaiming a concept that reached back to the first century philosopher Longinus, in his work *On the Sublime* (New York: E. Mellen Press, 1985); Burke's position concerning the necessary presence of an edifying terror was countered by Kant's more sensational determination of the state—see the *Critique of Judgment* (Oxford: Clarenton Press, 1964), 99–100. An important general reference on the term and its meaning is Thomas Weiskel, *The Romantic Sublime* (Baltimore: Johns Hopkins University Press, 1976). On the American sublime, see Mary

Arensberg, ed., *The American Sublime* (Albany: State University of New York Press, 1986); Elizabeth R. McKinsey, *Niagara Falls: Icon of the American Sublime* (New York: Cambridge University Press, 1985); and Earl A. Powell, "Luminism and the American Sublime," in John Wilmerding, ed., *American Light: The Luminist Movement, 1850–1875* (Washington, D.C.: National Gallery of Art, 1989).

10. Readers will note that I am proposing the concept of the sublime not simply as a convenient trope for the experience of passive awe at the sight of infinite force; I am proposing that the pictures and written imagery that shaped and gave order to this "new thing" (to use the words of William L. Laurence, describing the Alamogordo test explosion) came from an explicit visual and cultural tradition. I have not argued this case in the text, but I will suggest the shape of such an argument. American conceptions of nature-as-spectacle follow a direct tradition. Writers and critics of landscape in particular referred often to the romantic concepts of the sublime and the beautiful as articulated by Burke and Kant, and the concept of the picturesque as it emerged as a mediating term in British landscape design and theory in the late eighteen and nineteen centuries.

The most influential theorists of American aesthetics, in particular the philosopher-politician Thomas Jefferson and the painter-philosopher Thomas Cole, formed one connection that imported this form of nature-aesthetics from Europe. Scientists, and especially those scientists whose writings on American nature and the American landscape were most popular and widely read (and I am thinking here of the government scientist-explorers Clarence King and Ferdinand Vandeveer Hayden) also promoted the notion of spectatordom and intuitive learning from nature. Finally, a huge segment of American art, from elite painters like Cole and Albert Bierstadt to the popular photographers, like Eadweard Muybridge, Carleton E. Watkins, and William Henry Jackson, carried this conception into the twentieth century and into popular and mass-culture imagery. By mid-century these proposals for a democratic audience gaining wisdom from an intuitive apprehension of nature had become the staple of mass-culture imagery, including such diverse outlets as Kodak film advertisements and tourist brochures. When *Life* presented the atomic sublime to its viewers, it did so in this broad context: on many of the pages before or after the photographs and illustrations of atomic clouds, readers might find equally spectacular images of natural landscape, whether in highly popular series like those *Life* subsumed under the rubric of "The World around Us" or in the ads for Arizona vacations, railroad excursions, Pontiacs and Plymouths, or Kodak films and cameras.

11. "The War Ends," 25–31.

12. "What Ended the War," *Life,* 17 September 1945, 37–39; "Bombed Nagasaki," *Life,* 15 October 1945, 37. This is the text accompanying this "Picture of the Week": "A Stone head of Christ, dislodged by the atomic bomb blast at Nagasaki, lies before the ruins of a Roman Catholic cathedral . . . like a stony symbol of the moral problem facing a people who profess to follow His teachings: whether even the urgencies of war

should permit such violation of individual life as the atomic bomb had committed. Last week President Truman reminded Congress, 'Civilization demands that we shall reach at the earliest possible date a satisfactory arrangement for the control of this discovery.'"

13. "First Atomic Bomb: Epoch's Opening Is Shown in Color," *Life,* 19 November 1945, 107.

14. "Imaginary 36-Hour War: How Next War Might Be Fought," *Life,* 19 November 1945, 27.

15. "What Ended the War," 37–39.

16. "Toyko Express Arrives in Bomb-Scarred Hiroshima," *Life,* 8 October 1945, 27–30.

17. Ibid.

18. "Peace City," *Life,* 1 September 1947, 39–42.

19. It was Gen. Leslie R. Groves, for example, whose alarm at the reports of radiation injury at Hiroshima and Nagasaki resulted in a special press excursion to the Alamogordo test range to view the landscape of atomic destruction, and the release of that first color image of the Alamogordo test. And it was Groves and his adjutants who had recruited one-time *New York Times* reporter William Laurence to serve as chief press representative on the Manhattan Project. I have discussed this at length in my cultural history of the Manhattan Project; see Peter Hales, *Atomic Spaces: Living on the Manhattan Project* (Urbana: University of Illinois Press, 1997).

20. "Wherever You Look There's Danger in Las Vegas," *Life,* 12 November 1951, 37.

21. "AEC Plays Host to Camera, Newsmen, and TV at Blast on Yucca Flat, Nevada," *Life,* 5 May 1952, 36.

22. "When Atom Bomb Struck—Uncensored," *Life,* 29 September 1952, 19–25.

23. "5-4-3-2-1 and the Hydrogen Age Is Upon Us," *Life,* 12 April 1954, 23–33.

24. "The Awesome Fireball," *Life,* 19 April 1954, cover and 21–25; "Speaking of Pictures" *Life,* 26 April 1954, 14–15; "New Ivy Pictures Show Fire and Ice," *Life,* 3 May 1954, 52–55.

25. The range of combinations ran from the simply inappropriate (hope chests, last-minute Christmas gifts, "fast help for headache" set around a column on the Atomic Bomb Casualty Commission, *Life,* 12 December 1959) to the garishly tasteless (color images of Libby's "Leaner Meats" across from the decimated mannequins in "Victims of Yucca Flat," *Life,* 16 May 1955). The very nature of scanning the pages of *Life*—how long one might spend on a given pair of pages, whether one found surcease in the ads—begs further discussion.

26. This reconstruction is based upon a discussion with Richard Stolley, who was *Life*'s managing editor later and a bureau chief during the atomic years.

27. In this regard, I am drawing not only from my own personal experience of the atomic age during my American childhood, but also from interviews I have conducted for an upcoming study of the Cold War American cultural landscape.

PART THREE   TO SEE MAN'S WORK . . .

TO SEE AND BE INSTRUCTED

6

ROLAND MARCHAND

LIFE COMES TO
CORPORATE HEADQUARTERS

During the first year of its meteoric success, *Life* magazine invited its readers to participate vicariously in an array of parties and celebrations. In its regular "*Life* Goes to a Party" feature, *Life* seemed to go everywhere—from a Polish wedding in Cicero, Illinois, to a public dance hall in New York City to a picnic for Iowa Emigrants in Los Angeles. It even took its readers to a "camping" party of sit-down strikers in a Woolworth's store in Detroit.[1] Not once, however, did *Life* go to a corporation's headquarters. Nor did anyone find this surprising. After all, it was the role of *Fortune,* Henry Luce's favorite among his array of publications, to carry out that task. And *Fortune* did so—two or three times every month.

Even though *Life* did not actually go to corporate headquarters, it had profound effects in many corporate boardrooms nonetheless. One of these impacts was direct and immediate. Launched with what awestruck observers characterized as "a Himalaya" on the landscape of promotional campaigns, *Life* sold an unprecedented 1,500 pages of advertising before its first issue appeared. Critics in the advertising trade press marveled at the "witchery" of Luce's prospectus for *Life,* circulated everywhere in the business world. "[A]fter reading it," according to *Advertising and Selling*'s "Promotion Parade" column, "spellbound repre-

Figure 6.1. Advertisement for Dodge, *Literary Digest*, June 10, 1933. (Courtesy DaimlerChrysler)

sentatives of other publications began to spout paragraphs of it in their sleep."[2]

Dummies of the forthcoming picture magazine also circulated everywhere. As he had with the prospectus, Luce invited comments and criticisms of these mock-ups, a tactic that gave numerous business and media figures a sense of participation in the new phenomenon. Never in the nation's history, *Advertising and Selling* proclaimed, had it seen "ad buyers go in the Bag" for a new venture as they had for *Life*. That journal's sketch of Henry Luce in mid-November observed that "the eyes of our little advertising world are on the present new baby—*Life*."[3]

For several months *Life* sold out quickly on the newsstands and could not manage to publish enough copies to meet the demands of an "astronomical market."[4] This conspicuous and instantaneous success, amplified by its own breathless self-promotion, insured its

continued scrutiny by business eyes. Within two months, the trade press noted that *Life* had "bred a host of imitators." Ads for *Life* dramatized its mounting circulation figures in week-by-week tabulations and claimed for it the earthquakelike status of a "*natural phenomenon.*" These ads for *Life* impressed on business leaders the breadth of the new magazine's audience and its equal appeal to both men and women ("Life Delivers Whole Family Readership as No Other Medium Can").[5] Henry Luce, himself, avowed to those assembled at the annual convention of the American Association of Advertising Agencies that *Life* ". . . evidently is what the public wants more than it has ever wanted any product of ink and paper."[6]

Life's advertisements asserted that "its *pictorial journalism* satisfied a peculiarly *modern* hunger. . . ."[7] Its overwhelming popularity invited observers, then and afterward, to think of *Life* as the culmination, if not the full embodiment, of the graphic revolution of the interwar years. More precise interpreters of *Life*'s place in the explosion of visual imagery in the 1920s and 1930s have noted how extensively *Life* drew upon the graphics ferment of the previous decade. Wider attention to *Life*'s impact reveals that it represented not so much a culmination of a graphics revolution but that it spurred forward the new visuality to broader triumphs in ways that went well beyond the mimicry it inspired in a plethora of other picture magazines.

The power of *Life* to influence the graphics revolution lay not only in its apotheosis of the photograph as a story-telling medium, but particularly in its evident success in finding a way to reach a broad segment of the public through a language that audiences enjoyed and understood. Even a relatively complex story, *Life*'s photo-essays seemed to confirm, could be made simple by telling it through pictures. Moreover, *Life* demonstrated this aptitude for reaching the general public at a particularly timely moment—in the immediate wake of the election of 1936. This conjunction proved crucial to a second significant impact of *Life* magazine on the nation's corporate headquarters, one ultimately of larger significance than simply a new advertising medium.

The second way in which *Life* came to corporate headquarters was soon dramatically evident. In the two years immediately following the appearance of *Life*, communications that emanated from corporate offices, including the dreary corporate annual report, blossomed with unprecedented visual embellishment. A few corporations such as Swift & Company and B. F. Goodrich had incorporated photographs and drawings into their annual reports prior to the mid-1930s, but within eighteen months of the appearance of *Life*, scores of corporations had brought a dramatic new visuality to these stodgy balance sheets. Hundreds of companies had initiated or overhauled their in-house magazines and newsletters to carry their corporate messages to employees through photographs and pictographs. Corporations had taken a new step toward using visual splendor and the truthful and forceful reporting of company news through the photographic image.

This sudden corporate conversion to a new visuality and to a quest for an everyday vernacular can certainly not be attributed entirely to the influence of *Life*. The pictographs of *Fortune* also made an evident impact. *Life*, as students of its origins have observed, had itself emerged as the product of a mass of influences—cultural, journalistic, and technological—that had been promoting a new amplitude of pictorial consciousness. Not the least of these influences had been a rising awareness of photography's power to communicate and of the manipulability of the pictorial image through such high-art innovations as the photomontage. Even beyond Time, Inc.'s, own *The March of Time* newsreels and its visually stunning *Fortune*, with its embryonic photo-essays and its stable of future *Life* photographers, advertising itself had demonstrated the effectiveness of new visual techniques.[8] Many of the visual formulas employed in *Life*—the bleed photos, the story-telling sequences of movie stills, and the melding of photos and captions—had been foreshadowed by striking magazine advertisements between 1931 and 1936 (Figure 6.1).[9]

Still, the most powerful currents of influence ran in the other direction—*from* the successful new magazine *to* corporate headquarters. *Life* came to big business as a revelation, albeit as one among several similar revelations. A public that had just proved its economic illiteracy, by voting overwhelmingly for Franklin D. Roosevelt and the New Deal in 1936, might yet understand corporations and the free-enterprise system. *Life* seemed to have demonstrated a capacity to capture the emotions of a mass audience (what Wendy Kozol has called "the immediacy of its emotional address").[10] By inviting Americans to gaze at ostensible images of themselves—in the form of weekly picture albums of an encompassing variety of people engaged in both familiar and fascinating activities—*Life* caught the attention of business leaders desperate to discover the language and imagery through which to restore the public's faith in the free-enterprise system. Many public relations managers and CEOs thought that they recognized something in the style of *Life* that they might use in their efforts to reach and influence these Americans.

What was it that prompted this reaction? By 1936 corporate leaders almost unanimously saw themselves as having been cast in the role of national villains and the entire business system as suffering from "vicious public attacks." Even the mildest assessments of the situation concluded that "the government was giving business a black eye with the public."[11] By 1937 one advertising agency president was reminding fellow business leaders that there was "not a town or city of any consequence" in the nation in which industry had not been forced to shelter itself against a "constant black rain of vilification and abuse."[12] From 1935 onward, at every convention of business leaders, influential voices had called out fervently for their fellow businessmen to get out their ideological message. Even as the corporations had continued during the Depression to apply all their ingenuities to selling their products, critics in the advertising press reiterated, American business had failed to sell *itself* and the free-enterprise system to the public. "[I]ndustry . . . has not told its story," was their constant refrain. Businessmen had "lost the confidence of the public more completely than at any previous time in the memory of living men."[13]

While some corporations, along with such organizations as the National Association of Manufacturers (NAM), had tried to do this before and during the presidential election of 1936, their efforts had been dismissed by other business leaders as maladroit and ineffectual. With a rising shrillness, corporate spokesmen excoriated their fellow executives for failing to phrase industry's message in a mainstream vernacular. "This is a personal world," observed ad executive Arthur Kudner in reflecting on how big businesses had "grown corpulent in speech." Kudner enjoined corporate leaders to "let both your words and your acts be simple" and to "let your personality be more in the guise of Clark Gable than Scrooge."[14] By 1935 NAM, itself, was calling for education of "an inflammatory type" in "economic facts" that would reach "for the heart and emotions of the people rather than their brains." Paul Garrett, head of public relations for General Motors, complained that business executives were "notoriously aloof from the play of human emotions, of the public we want to influence." A contributor to *Advertising and Selling* confronted business leaders with perhaps the most exasperating challenge to learn to speak in the public vernacular: "If Mr. Roosevelt learned to talk their language, starting as *he* did, you and I can, too."[15]

Business and advertising periodicals took up the cry for corporations to speak the people's language. Business should cast off its "dignity complex"; it should "take its hair down," stop using "big words or abstract concepts," and make itself understood "by every waitress, truck driver, and voter in the land."[16] Dismayed by their sudden loss in popularity and harangued constantly by advertising men about their negligence and incompetence in explaining their companies and the free-enterprise system to the public, corporate spokesmen grasped eagerly at a variety of tactics for getting reacquainted with average citizens and learning their vernacular. Explaining an economic system and a corporation's entire operations in a noncorporate language seemed a much more formidable task than simply advertising products. At least, the trade press made it seem so. No matter how plain and folksy the company tried to make its communications, new voices always emerged to berate business for its stuffy approach and call for a new tactic or idiom that would be even more simple and more dramatic. *Printers' Ink* praised Sears, Roebuck and Company for "good will" advertising, which was "unusually human, of the fireside variety." Business leaders should recognize how good public relations could be cultivated, *Printers' Ink* implied, when a "giant business institution figuratively pulls up a chair and has a chat with its friends. . . ."[17]

Along with such intimacy went simplicity. "For the

mass mind," urged an article in *Advertising and Selling,* "put your copy in low gear." The success of Walt Disney's *Snow White and the Seven Dwarfs* carried a message for big business, *Advertising Age* concluded: "They like it simple."[18] Bruce Barton, the most effective of all the insider critics of corporate publicity, urged businessmen in 1936 to wake up to a certain "quality of mind" pervasive among the new, politically potent public that was failing to heed the messages of big business. "They would rather not put forth the effort to read," Barton observed just months before the launching of *Life,* "but they will look at pictures."[19]

Company executives also worried desperately about reaching labor unions. As labor unions increasingly flexed their muscle, corporate leaders sought to regain what they imagined nostalgically as close and trusted communications with their own working force. They implored each other to "Sell . . . the Labor Relations Program," to the workers, or coaxed them more simply, "Let's Tell the Employees." Paul Garrett of General Motors, head of the largest of all corporate public relations departments, admonished his fellow executives in 1936 that "Every day more than 28,000 'General Motors people' are casting a vote for or against us in a sort of informal nation wide poll with their friends."[20] Both for the sake of its own labor relations and as a tactic in developing a base among its employees for reaching a wider audience with a corporate image campaign, Garrett insisted, public relations had to begin at home. Bruce Barton, broadcasting the same message to all of big business, urged corporate executives to recognize that their employees alone, in many large companies, comprised a constituency larger than that of many U.S. senators. Major corporations should look inward in their efforts to "heighten and intensify their good will." In their competition with Franklin Roosevelt for public favor, they should recognize the "employee of almost any large corporation" as the true "forgotten man" of the age.[21]

Even when they recognized the logic of this strategy, however, corporate leaders remained confused and frustrated in their efforts to discover the proper vernacular. Initially, they perceived themselves as addressing *two* crucial, yet distinct, audiences—the voting middle class and their own working force. Awkwardly, they sermonized in high moral generalities to the public while they tried to use a proletarian lingo for conversations with their employees. In seeking to reach across what they still perceived as a vast social and cultural gulf between themselves and their ethnically distinct working force, they fell into a confusion and incoherence they had rarely confronted as advertisers of products. In consumer advertising they had facilely associated the public as consumers with middle-class status; but the threat posed by their own employees now persuaded some of them to shudder at their inability to speak to these workers.[22] Certainly many of the efforts of individual corporations to communicate in a worker's dialect resulted in phony phrasing and unconvincing portraits. As William Bird observed, corporate leaders were casting about desperately in the mid-1930s, particularly in the wake of the 1936 election, for some "new vocabulary" in which to reach their crucial constituencies.[23]

In their attention to the new phenomenon of the picture magazine, there soon appeared several explicit imitations of *Life* in company literature, the fusing of what they had perceived as two, separate audiences. The dramatic simplicity of the news or feature story told in pictures seemed to span the social classes—it spoke to those of limited literacy but did not seem to talk down to those of higher intelligence or status. Such a blurring of class lines appealed strongly to corporate leaders. A picture magazine—a genre that Henry Luce himself had envisioned as simple and dumbed-down—might offer a formula for effective conversations with workers who were also voters and aspirants to middle-class status. Perhaps company publications should image their audience in the *Life* fashion as a broad and ostensibly classless amalgam, reachable through stories told with pictures.[24]

The discovery of the "picturability of the commonplace," which editor Wilson Hicks ascribed to *Life* pho-

Figure 6.2. Court House Square, from "Muncie, Ind. Is the Great U.S. 'Middletown,'" *Life*, May 10, 1937. (Courtesy Margaret Bourke-White/TimePix)

tographers and editors, suggested another lesson that the picture magazine might teach employers.[25] Constantly warned that the public viewed industry as "cold and heartless," corporate executives had pondered various methods to "humanize" the corporation and thus remove some of the "curse of bigness." The picture story suggested itself as one way through which the corporation might place itself in the context of everyday, common experiences without surrendering its dignity. Through photographs, with their connotations of realism and sincerity, a company might both romanticize its structures and personalize the human relations within its corporate family. And, by telling its story in *Life*-style, through close-ups of an average family or employee, it might both enhance its humanized image and contribute to the economic literacy of its employees and stockholders. The founding of *Life* coincided almost exactly with the rising impulse to discover America's essence in "the average"—a phenomenon that Warren I. Susman so deftly traced in its multifaceted

expression from the mid-1930s onward. These trends and notions induced corporate spokespeople to train their sights on such imaginary figures as the "average reader" of so popular a weekly as *Life* magazine.[26]

Life, even within its first year, began to display some of this fascination with the average and with imaging what Wendy Kozol has called "*Life*'s imaginary collective."[27] In June 1937 a photo-essay on college life emphasized the notion of a typical campus and a typical student. Already *Life* had seized upon the phrase "from Maine to California" as its shorthand for the concept of the average or typical in American behavior, styles, and institutions.[28] Early in May, moreover, *Life* had made a point of "visiting" Muncie, Indiana—the locus of Robert and Helen Lynd's sociological studies of "Middletown"—in order to make available to its readers "an important American document" (Figure 6.2). Overlooking all the reasons that the Lynds had given for choosing a decisively nontypical American city for their studies (Muncie was exceptional in the small size of its immigrant and African American populations), *Life* proclaimed that Margaret Bourke-White's photographs of Muncie had "set down for all time . . . the average 1937 American as he really is." In visiting Middletown, *Life* had essentially visited "every small U.S. city from Maine to California." Already, *Life* was employing a single "exemplary site" to shape its stories as inquiries into the life and attitudes of the typical American through an "ordinary" individual, family, or community.[29]

In what form did the graphics revolution embedded in *Life* and the new magazine's mirroring of America come to corporate headquarters? Coincidentally, with the appearance of *Life,* a massive resurgence erupted in the publication of house organs by business corporations. Almost simultaneously, an outburst of graphic display transformed that most stately, esoteric, and unadorned of all corporate documents—the annual financial report. The first nine months of 1937 witnessed the launching or revival of more than four hundred company magazines, an increase of 45 percent over the previous year.[30] Many adopted a modern semblance in shameless imitations of *Life* and *Look.* The new vogue in annual reports emerged with such visual impact in 1938 that the entire trade press bore astonished and enchanted witness to such signs of a new and intelligent political awareness on the part of corporate America. Now certain companies, as *Business Week* put it, were finally getting "in step with new mass trends."[31]

Corporate house organs were hardly new in the mid-1930s; they had enjoyed great popularity among business executives during the post–World War I era. The Depression, however, had taken a heavy toll on all such "unnecessary" company expenditures.[32] Their massive resurgence in 1937 testified not so much to improved corporate finances as to the urgency felt by corporate leaders to communicate with their own workers and to attempt to restore public confidence by cultivating loyalty within the corporation. As the house organs proliferated and modernized, the influence of the picture magazines became evident. *Caterpillar Magazine* was "almost entirely photographic," observed *Printers' Ink Monthly* in September 1938, its text "consisting wholly of captions." *Kroger Magazine* incorporated sequences of photographs, and International Harvester's house organ included photographic double-page spreads. General Electric's *New Graphic* adhered strictly to *Life*'s tenets. It made "lavish and intelligent use of pictures" and "never uses text when a picture will describe what is intended to be described." A single issue, *Printer's Ink Monthly* reported, contained 167 illustrations, most of which were "photographs of all types."[33] In 1938 *Printers' Ink Monthly,* itself, adopted a *Life*-style cover with a single bleed photograph.[34]

The corporate annual report was not a new phenomenon in the late 1930s. These financial statements to stockholders, scorned even by some publicly held companies until they were required by the New York Stock Exchange and, eventually, by 1934, by the Securities Exchange Commission, had been long regarded as among the most boring and abstruse of all documents.[35] Even critics of the ineffectiveness of the corporate annual report in the early 1930s accepted its tediousness and opaqueness, calling only for reforms that would prevent it from deceiving stockholders.[36] A few companies utilized this communication to stockholders as a medium for public relations in the 1920s and early 1930s. Such companies as Swift and Company, Goodyear Tire Company, and General Foods rarely neglected at least to picture their various brands of products, sometimes in color. But the majority of corporations, with austere dignity, embellished the pages of incomprehensibly labeled figures with nothing more visually alluring than the company logo.

In more than a score of corporations, annual reports for the 1937 year witnessed an astonishing metamorphosis. Bethlehem Steel directed its report to employees as well as stockholders, as did the Jewel Tea Company, Kimberly-Clark, Caterpillar Tractor Company, and General Mills. The Johns-Manville Corporation, Monsanto Chemical, Eastman Kodak, and Du Pont issued special employee editions of the annual report or published excerpts from it in their employee magazines. By the beginning of 1939, according to *Nation's Business*, some forty-two corporations had adopted this practice and more were "joining the procession."[37] The Monsanto's "Employees Edition" of its annual report, according to *Printers' Ink Monthly*, was now "executed in a distinctly informal and conversational style." President Edgar Queeny led off with the invitation, "Let us sit down together and talk for a little while about our business."[38]

In dozens of other remodeled annual reports, corporations inserted photographs, charts, and pictographs.[39] United Air Lines, which had included nary an illustration in its eight-page report for the year 1935, suddenly doubled the number of pages for the following year, adding three graphs, four photos, and a full-page map. By the end of 1938 their annual report was boasting a photo on the cover and five pages of pictographs. One of several internal photos had a bar graph superimposed on it for dramatic effect. At Caterpillar Tractor Company, an even more striking metamorphosis occurred. From an austere, pictureless twelve-page booklet in small format at the end of its 1936 year, Caterpillar's annual report burst forth at the end of 1937 with five graphs, nine drawings, and thirty-one photographs with captions. It was now addressed to employees as well as stockholders and boasted both a larger format and greater length. A year later it was further "simplified" and incorporated full-page bleed photographs and pictographic graphs and charts to "make it even more understandable."[40]

Meanwhile, General Foods announced that ". . . instead of issuing the conventional, sedate periodic corporation report," it would report to employees four times a year on both its finances and its current activities. The new publication would take the form of an "eight-page tabloid newspaper."[41] International Harvester addressed its report to both stockholders and employees, embellishing it with full-page photographs. The Jewel Tea Company prepared its annual report for the 1936 fiscal year in the form of a special booklet entitled "A Report to the Jewel Family." Enlivened with "a

great many pictures and charts," the booklet explained the company's finances on a "dollars per employee basis," thus bringing it "into the range of average experience." Nearly every account of a company's conversion to a "report to employees" mentioned that the traditional annual report had been "re-written in simple language" or phrased "in words which employees can understand." Illustrations and tabular spreads had "humanized" the reports for both stockholders and employees.[42] Annual reports by the end of 1937 had taken on so decidedly a public relations and employee relations dimension that the business press broke into cheers for such business "progressivism."[43]

One of the most striking corporate conversions to the *Life*-like style occurred at the Johns-Manville Corporation. In October 1937, speaking at the convention of the Association of National Advertisers, company president Lewis H. Brown said, "for well over a year" public relations had been "the No. 1 job on my list." Warning his fellow executives that "every company which fails to do its part in this job of making friends for industry is, in fact, contributing to the possible destruction of not only its own business but of our whole system of private enterprise and representative government under the Constitution," he suggested that they follow his model of setting aside 10 percent of the corporation's sales and advertising budget for public relations.[44]

Making friends, Brown insisted, required that corporations "reverse all our previous methods." "We must start at the bottom," he said, "and we must learn to speak a language that will reach everyone." In selling goods, company salespeople and advertisers had never really sought to reach the nonconsumers—the "great percentage of the public at the base of the pyramid." But now industry, in competition with "matinee idol" politicians, needed desperately to reach the entire voting public. If advertisers had long realized that they had to translate products "into one syllable words" before the public could understand and accept them, now even more did they need to "sweat . . . blood" to discover the simple words and ideas "the masses will understand." In the process, they needed to "personalize and humanize business." "[L]et's keep it as simple as an old shoe," Brown exhorted the leaders of big business, "and as small-town as a Cape Cod or Iowa village."[45]

In company publications, Brown's humanizing initiative took the form of "folksy talk" and *Life*-style photographic spreads. In newspaper advertisements in Johns-Manville plant communities, photographs of the company's factories came to life through speech balloons and replied to questions from "Mr. Average Citizen." In "an informal, breezy manner," the factories explained their contributions to community welfare. Johns-Manville began to fire off "policy bulletins" to the homes of company employees that explained "in non-technical language the company's official stand on topics of vital interest to workers."[46] In March 1938 Johns-Manville Corporation issued yet another traditional annual report in which its balance sheet ("undoubtedly to the great perplexity of its 7,138 stockholders" *Time* magazine observed) was still phrased in a "bewildering fashion."[47]

Almost simultaneously, the company "startlingly reversed . . . [its] field" by issuing a profusely illustrated, eighteen-page "report to jobholders." This document provided employees with "substantially the same information as is given to stockholders" but in what Brown described as "A B C language" and *Time* called "a notable simplification of a balance sheet."[48] According to *Forbes* magazine, over two hundred corporate executives wrote to Johns-Manville requesting information on devising such a report.[49]

In its company magazine, and even in its annual report to stockholders, Johns-Manville Corporation mobilized the new graphics for the shaping of its corporate persona. Not a single photograph, chart, or graph had appeared in the company's annual reports before

1937. Its report to stockholders for 1938, however, achieved a comparative visual splendor; it contained a pictorial supplement replete with photographs (at least forty), many pictographs, and a photomontage cover.[50] Meanwhile, the company had also developed a monthly entitled *News Pictorial.* "Radically different from the conventional 'house organ,'" according to *Advertising Age,* its pictures were "packed with warm human interest." This photo-intensive "pictorial news sheet for employees [*sic*]," the company declared, had been "frankly adapted from *Life.*"[51]

Johns-Manville's advertising agency and public relations advisor, the J. Walter Thompson Company, proved no less brazen in appropriating *Life*'s graphic style for itself. Proclaiming that the assignment to interpret business and its policies to an uncomprehending public was "falling right in the lap of advertising men," the agency stressed its experience in "*explaining* something . . . so forcefully, so imaginatively, so simply that the mass mind can grasp it." In 1937 J. Walter Thompson published a booklet entitled "A Primer of Capitalism, Illustrated," which emphasized, through

Figure 6.3. *People: Monthly Bulletin of the J. Walter Thompson Company,* July 1937. (Courtesy J. Walter Thompson Company)

"plain words" and simple "school primer" drawings, the agency's capacity to reduce sophisticated economic concepts to "plain words, simple drawings, and a human viewpoint." "This is a Cow," its text commenced.[52] On pages dominated by cartoon illustrations, the agency explained, "The Cow is the mother of capitalism. . . . Under private capitalism, the Consumer, the Citizen, is boss. . . . In state capitalism, the politician is boss. . . . He tells consumers what they can buy. . . ." Other advertising agencies did not take the concept of the primer so literally, but still composed their own versions of common-man's copy. The N. W. Ayer agency talked unassumingly about "Joe and the Corporate Surplus," while Batten, Barton, Durstine, and Osborne, Inc., bragged that its own cartoon figures had given a Ripley's Believe-It-or-Not crowd-pleasing quality to the institutional messages of one public-utility company.[53]

To publicize its insights into modern modes of corporate public relations, J. Walter Thompson converted its monthly news bulletin in early 1937 into a *Life*-style format complete with large-bleed photographs on the cover. Its title, *People,* was superimposed over the cover photograph in the form of a *Life*-style slug (Figure 6.3). Although *People* carried more extensive articles than *Life,* with more extended texts, it self-consciously highlighted dramatic photographs. Some of its photos of people, in direct imitation of some of the early *Life* issues, were cast in "cut-out" or silhouetted form.[54] In phrasing redolent of its readership evoked in *Life*'s prospectus, J. Walter Thompson's *People* spoke of the need for the corporations to reach "people from all classes and descriptions; people to be influenced, persuaded, and informed. People who are eager to know the 'inside' on almost everything."[55]

Even within the most staid and aloof of the nation's corporations, such as the United States Steel Company, the graphics revolution found expression. The industrial giant adopted a heavily pictorial style in the dramatic photographs of some of its advertisements and in its new company magazine in 1936.[56] In that respect, under the goading of advertising man Bruce Barton and writer and consultant Samuel Crowther (who urged the company to reach out through the new company magazine to "get . . . sound economics" over to both its brightest workers and to those "in the lower ranges of intelligence"), this giant corporation had already fallen into step with the thrust toward dramatic visuality. Then, in late 1937 and early 1938, provoked by the recent burgeoning of illustrated annual reports, U.S. Steel began, in the words of *Advertising Age,* to "humanize itself" by explaining to its employees "Why We Have Stockholders" and "How We Earned Our Living." Its accounts, U.S. Steel explained, were no more complicated than those of a family household, just as

Figure 6.4. *GM Folks,* October 1938. (Courtesy General Motors)

the corporation, itself, ". . . in spite of its size," was "just a corner store for steel, iron, and other products."[57]

Pleased with the results and "impressed by the fact that only a small portion of the public will bother to read and analyze technical accounting reports," the corporation moved at the end of 1939 to phrase its annual report (to both stockholders and employees) in the kind of "clear and simple" wording that would make U.S. Steel better understood by everyone. Still, Thomas Lamont, partner in J. P. Morgan and Company and member of the U.S. Steel board of directors, continued to goad the corporation's public relations staff to make the report ever clearer to the "lay reader." In an apparent play on words once used to characterize children's books or playthings, Lamont defined the proper level of explanation as "little words for little fingers."[58] By 1940 the annual report of the behemoth of American corporations, which had contained as late as 1938 no embellishment whatsoever beyond the corporate logo, featured a multitude of photos and graphic displays. A night photo of its South Works in Chicago, with its blaze of operations reflected in water, would aptly have graced a cover of *Life*.[59] In many respects, the photographic imagery of *Life* and of the humanized corporation were now indistinguishable.

Of all the major corporations, none paid *Life* magazine the flattery of imitation so fulsomely as did General Motors. While General Motors' public relations activities had expanded rapidly from 1932 to 1937, it had postponed a long-contemplated corporate house organ in favor of a wide range of other projects.[60] But, in 1938 General Motors concluded that the time had come to invest heavily in a magazine for all its employees. Debuting in May 1938, *GM Folks* unabashedly mimicked *Life* magazine (Figure 6.4). Full-page cover photos against a red border and title slug that echoed the now-famous *Life* cover aimed to present the General Motors worker the same kind of "mirror" of himself that *Life* had sought to provide middle-class Americans through its "search for beauty in the commonplace."[61]

GM Folks served multiple purposes for the corporation. Through special inserts, replete with pictographs, it conveyed to employees a simplified account of the company's finances and its benefit plans for workers. It also, through extensive pictures and close-ups of "individual members of the family," acquainted employees with the entire organization, helping them to better "know each other." Above all, according to General Motors' chief of public relations, the pictures in *GM Folks*, "though chosen for their news appeal, say in effect that we are wholesome, normal people all working together to our mutual benefit."[62] Not only was the magazine "styled on the order of *Life*," it also cultivated a *Life*-like picture album of an all-American culture shared by all General Motors employees. "We go to the movies, listen to concerns, stage our own shows," avowed one institutional ad featured on the back cover of the September 1939 issue of *GM Folks*. "We take our vacations, engage in sports, follow our hobbies, do our share of traveling. All told, we're pretty typical American folks."[63]

Although *GM Folks*, with its emphasis on the company's rank and file, deliberately spurned *Life*'s predilection to humanize big corporations by depicting them as extensions of the personalities of their chief executives ("General Motors Is Chiefly Alfred P. Sloan, Jr., Chrysler Corp. Is Chiefly Walter P. Chrysler"[64]), it humanized General Motors in a manner more consonant with the corporate desire to identify itself with its own workers and the hero of the age, the common man. *GM Folks* fully embodied what Terry Smith has defined as "*Life*-style modernity"—the broad picturing of everyday life, with its finely calibrated admixture of the typical and specific.[65]

Did *Life* magazine, then, provide the answer to that panicky quest of corporate America to discover what William Bird has called a "new vocabulary" for conversing with the broad public and with its own employees? Certainly it did not provide the entire answer, or even exercise a predominate influence. The rising cadre of public relations experts were zealously scrutinizing every form of popular culture for cues to an effective lexicon of the American vernacular. And, as

Bird suggests, they discovered it as much in the newer media of film and radio as they did in even the most successful of popular print media.[66]

Still, some of *Life*'s impact was strikingly evident and unhesitatingly acknowledged. This was apparent in the format, style, and even content of a number of company magazines and was acknowledged by proponents of the new visuality in corporate annual reports. In almost every venue, the corporate visual style and the visual style of *Life* seemed indistinguishable. The trade press treated the words *simple* and *graphic* as synonyms and spoke of pictographs as the counterpart to the photograph in simplifying corporate messages through "illustrated statistics."[67] What is less certain, but intriguing to ponder, is the possibility of a much vaguer kind of influence—that of the contribution of *Life* to the appreciable, if wavering, advances of corporate leaders as they struggled to define the audience for their urgent public relations messages. In the mid-1930s business had remained confused about the nature of its audience. Was it talking to an uncomprehending proletariat, to emotional masses, envisioned as vast crowds in the streets and capsulized in the phrase "the mass mind," or to something so abstract as the "public at large"? Many of the corporate communications of the emerging public relations crusade of the mid-1930s had been crudely argumentative, laughably inept in their effort to acquire a proletarian voice, or equally ludicrous in their inability to cast off a residual pompousness. Few factory workers were likely to be enraptured by the stilted attempts to explain economic principles through the feigned voice of "Joe the worker." Richard Tedlow has observed that advertisements directed to workers often seemed to represent "mere examples of management talking to itself."[68] Many individual corporations, in their initial efforts to speak in the language and imagery of the common man, drew unconvincing portraits and spoke in transparently phony voices.

The voice of the photograph—and visual imagery in general—evaded such obvious pretense. To the extent that *Life* encouraged corporate leaders to concentrate more on visual style in their communications to employees and the public, it certainly contributed to a modulation of their inclination toward preaching and didacticism. And in *Life*'s broad, encompassing reach—not only to a middle class but to all who might wish to envision themselves as middle class—it may well have assisted corporate America in overcoming a fractured vision of its audience as divided between a misled, middle-class public and an alien throng of crude, plebeian workers. *Life* provided a helpful image of a non–class-segregated, non–class-conscious public in which industrial workers, at least in their lives outside of labor-union participation, constituted an integral part of the nation. As General Motors characterized all of its employees in a 1939 advertisement, "we're [all] pretty typical American folks."[69] This corporate conception of workers less as stereotyped proletarians and more as common men who preferred a more middle-class image of themselves continued to advance until it dominated the thinking of corporate leaders in the postwar era. By then, the image of workers fully enjoying middle-class lives had become a pervasive part of the theme relentlessly promoted by American business—the notion of a classless America.

By the end of World War II, some corporate annual reports, in the words of a staid accountant, were illustrated so profusely as to fall into the category of "pictorial display of the Mother Goose type." A large proportion boasted covers in dramatic color. Among those that found "a happy medium between ballyhoo and self-repression," the majority carried cover illustrations. Sixty percent used color and a larger percentage carried photographs.[70] For several years, *Financial World* had even sponsored awards for the most spectacular annual reports.[71] During the war, such companies as Kraft & Company had brought out new company magazines in *Life* look-alike style, and nearly every major corporation, and virtually every subdivision thereof, had begun to record its contributions to the war effort in photo-filled, *Life*-style books and pamphlets.[72] By 1947 the Du Pont employee magazine, in conventional *Life* style, was visiting some of the company's employees at a "Splash Party." The "just folks" image of the corporation, united from top to bottom by visible commonalities, seemed imperceptibly to have drawn upon models established by *Life*'s humanizing of figures, great and small, through candid photos and attention to their leisure pursuits. When *Life* came to corporate headquarters in the late 1930s, in the view of some of the critics of previous corporate public relations, business executives came to their senses and began more comfortably to address both their workers and the public as a unified audience of "just folks" in the *Life* image of ordinary people.

NOTES

1. "*Life* Goes to a Party," *Life,* 22 March 1937, 72–73; "*Life* Goes to a Party," *Life,* 29 March 1937, 72–73; "*Life* Goes to a Party," *Life,* 12 April 1937, 82–85; "*Life* Goes to a Party," *Life,* 21 June 1937, 88–92.

2. *Advertising and Selling,* 19 November 1936, 26, 36, 77.

3. Ibid., 26, 77; "Henry Luce," *Advertising and Selling,* 1 January 1937, 50.

4. *Advertising and Selling,* 20 May 1937, 29; Robert T. Elson, *Time, Inc.: The Intimate History of a Publishing Enterprise, 1923–1941* (New York: Atheneum, 1968), 297–98.

5. "Life Delivers Whole Family Readership as No Other Medium Can," *Advertising and Selling,* 25 February 1937, 41; *Sales Management,* 1 November 1937, 27–29; *Life,* 25 January 1937, 8; *Advertising and Selling,* 28 January 1937, 11.

6. Elson, *Time, Inc.,* 308.

7. *Life,* 3 October 1938, 68.

8. Wilson Hicks, *Words and Pictures* (New York: Harper and Row, 1952; reprint, Arno Press, 1973), xiv, 21, 29–31, 38–40; Neil Harris, "Graphic Art for the Public Welfare," 95, and Ellen Lupton and J. Abbott Miller, "A Time Line of American Graphic Design, 1829–1989" in *Graphic Design in America: A Visual Language History,* ed. Mildred S. Friedman and others (Minnesota: Walker Art Center, 1989), 45; Sally A. Stein, "The Composite Photographic Image and the Composition of Consumer Ideology," *Art Journal,* 39 (Spring 1981): 41–43; Terry Smith, *Making the Modern: Industry, Art, and Design in America* (Chicago: University of Chicago Press, 1993), 340–41.

9. John Tebbel and Mary Ellen Zuckerman, *The Magazine in America* (New York: Oxford University Press, 1991), 167, 169, 228; James L. Baughman, *Henry R. Luce and the Rise of the American News Media* (Boston: Twayne Publishers, 1987), 43, 83–84; Jackson Lears, *Fables of Abundance: A Cultural History of Advertising in America* (New York: Basic Books, 1994), 324–29; John Kobler, *Luce: His Time, Life, and Fortune*, (Garden City, N.Y.: Doubleday, 1968), 87, 100; Elson, *Time, Inc.,* 135–36, 189, 205, 270–72; Roland Marchand, *Advertising the American Dream: Making Way for Modernity, 1920–1940,* (Berkeley: University of California Press, 1985), 149, 302–3, 307–9; advertisement, *Saturday Evening Post,* 15 July 1933, 41; advertisement, *Saturday Evening Post,* 13 January 1934, 48–49; advertisement, *Saturday Evening Post,* 17 February 1934, 80–81; advertisement, *Saturday Evening Post,* 1 February 1936, 46; advertisement, *Literary Digest,* 17 June 1933, 17.

10. Wendy Kozol, *Life's America: Family and Nation in Postwar Photojournalism* (Philadelphia: Temple University Press, 1994), 23.

11. Donald B. Davis, "Public Must Be Given Facts about Big Business," *Printers' Ink,* 31 October 1935, 32; *Tide,* 10 (January 1936): 16–17, 22; Bruce Barton, "The Public," 4 December 1935, Barton Speeches File, Batten, Barton, Durstine, and Osborne, Inc., (hereafter BBDO) Archives, New York City; H. A. Batten, "Public Relations," 28 April 1937, 38, box 34–31, N. W. Ayer & Son Archives, New York City.

12. Batten, "Public Relations," 3.

13. *Advertising and Selling,* 5 December 1936, 34; *Advertising and Selling,* 15 July 1937, 22; *Advertising Age,* 12 October 1936, 20; *Advertising Age,* 19 October 1936, 12; "What Right to Profits?" *Printers' Ink,* 22 November 1934, 7, 10; Davis, "Public Must Be Given Facts about Big Business," 32; *Tide* 10 (July 1936): 36; *New York Times,* 4 December 1936, 47; *Factory Management and Maintenance,* 94 (March 1936): 96–97; S. H. Walker and Paul Sklar, "Business Finds Its Voice," *Harpers Magazine,* January 1938, 112, and March 1938, 428; Colby Chester, "Business Team Play," enclosure to Verne Burnett to Edward R. Stettinius Jr., January 22, 1936, box 565, Edward R. Stettinius Jr. Papers, Alderman Library, University of Virginia (hereafter, Stittinius Papers); Edwin S. Friendly to Lammot Du Pont, 14 November 1936, acc. 1662, box 33, E. I. Du Pont de Nemours and Company Papers, Hagley Library (hereafter, Du Pont Papers); Colby Chester, "Industry's Basis of Cooperation," in J. George Frederick, *For Top-Executives Only: A Symposium* (New York: The Business Bourse, 1936), 378.

14. Arthur Kudner, "The Job Ahead," *Atlantic Monthly,* March 1937, 339, 342–43.

15. National Association of Manufacturers, "Proposed Education Program for Next 12 Months," 20 March 1935, acc. 1662, box 51, Du Pont Papers; Paul Garrett, "The Importance of the Public," typescript for speech, 20 October 1934, 8–9, pamphlet file, General Motors Library, Detroit (herafter, GM Library); *Advertising Age,* 31 January 1938, 33; *Advertising and Selling,* 9 September 1937, 36.

16. *Advertising Age,* 31 January 1938, 33.

17. "Seeks Farmer Good-Will" *Printers' Ink,* 14 November 1935, 67–68.

18. *Advertising and Selling,* 18 November 1937, 38; *Advertising Age,* 28 February 1938, 12.

19. Bruce Barton, "Winning Public Approval," speech manuscript, 12 May 1936, 6, BBDO Archives.

20. *Factory Management and Maintenance,* June 1936, 206–7; *Advertising and Selling,* August 1938, 34; *Advertising Age,* 21 February 1938, 1–3; General Motors Corporation, *Annual Report for Year Ended December 31, 1935* (New York: General Motors Corporation, 1936), 5.

21. Don Hogate to Paul W. Garrett, 16 March 1938, GM Library; Barton, "Winning Public Approval," 14; *Printers' Ink Monthly,* January 1938, 14–15; *Advertising Age,* 18 May 1936, 44; *Advertising Age,* 22 November 1937, 6; William D. Kennedy, "Workers Are People," *People,* July l937, 5, 27, J. Walter Thompson Company Archives, John W. Hartman Center for Sales, Advertising and Marketing History, Duke University (hereafter, JWT Archives).

22. *Advertising Age,* 3 January 1938, 22; Burton Bigelow, "Should Business Decentralize Its Counter-Propaganda?" *Public Opinion Quarterly* 2 (April 1938), 322–23; Richard Tedlow, *Keeping the Corporate Image: Public Relations and Business, 1900–1950* (Greenwich, Conn.: JAI Press, 1979), 66.

23. William L. Bird Jr., "The Drama of Enterprise: DuPont's *Cavalcade of America* and the 'New Vocabulary' of Business Leadership, 1935–1940," paper presented at Society for Cinema Studies, May 1990; William L. Bird Jr., "Enterprise and Meaning: Sponsored Film, 1939–1941," *History Today* 39 (1 December 1989), 24–30; William L. Bird, Jr., *"Better Living" : Advertising, Media, and the New Vocabulary of Business Leadership, 1935–1955* (Evanston, Ill.: Northwestern University Press, 1999).

24. Loudon Wainwright observed that Henry Luce, during the experimental stage in the development of *Life,* "apparently thought of the picture magazine as something of a simpleminded alternative to *Time.*" Loudon Wainwright, *The Great American Magazine: An Inside History of* Life (New York: Knopf, 1986), 12.

25. Hicks, *Words and Pictures,* 35.

26. Warren I. Susman, "The People's Fair: Cultural Contradictions of a Consumer Society," in Warren I. Susman, *Culture as History: The Transformation of American Society in the Twentieth Century* (New York: Pantheon Books, 1984), 212–13, 219–20, 227. On *Life's* emphasis on typicality, see its own ad in *Life,* 10 January 1938, second cover; on the close-up as adapted by the corporation, see *GM Folks* 1 (May 1938), second cover, 2.

27. Kozol, *Life's America,* 18. *Life,* 10 January 1938, second cover. According to *Life's* official historian, Robert Elson, the *New Yorker* neatly summarized these claims to capture the nation's essence when it complained about *Life's* "trick of taking a couple of snapshots of somebody somewhere and announcing that 'This is America.'" Robert R. Elson, *The World of Time, Inc.: The Intimate History of a Publish-*

ing Enterprise, Volume Two: 1941–1960 (New York: Atheneum, 1973), 24.

28. *Life,* 7 June 1937, 29, 39–40.

29. *Life,* 10 May 1937, 16. On this point, see particularly Kozol, *Life's America,* 9, 13, 22.

30. *Advertising Age,* 11 October 1937, 28.

31. *Business Week,* 16 July 1938, 30.

32. Industrial Relations Section, Princeton University, *Employee Magazines in the Depression,* pamphlet, 1933, Baker Library, Harvard School of Business Management, 1, 7–8, 11.

33. *Printers' Ink Monthly,* September 1938, 19–20, 59, 61.

34. *Printers' Ink Monthly,* January 1938, cover; *Printers' Ink Monthly,* March 1938, cover.

35. N. Loyall McLaren, *Annual Reports to Stockholders: Their Preparation and Interpretation* (New York: Ronald Press, 1947), 6–7, 32; Richard A. Lewis, *Annual Reports: Conception and Design of Annual Reports* (Zurich: Graphics, 1971), 8; Jasper Grinling, *The Annual Report* (Aldershot, GB: Gower Publishing Company, 1986), 7–8.

36. Anderson F. Farr, "The Annual Corporate Report," *Harper's Magazine,* March 1934, 421–32; Anderson F. Farr, "Give the Stockholder the Truth," *Scribner's Magazine* 93 (April 1933), 228–34.

37. *Nation's Business,* April 1939, 38; *Advertising Age,* 25 April 1938, 17.

38. *Printers' Ink Monthly,* July 1938, 54.

39. Neil Harris places the outburst of graphic display in corporate annual reports in the context of the emergence of a similar visual consciousness among museums, libraries, and other cultural institutions. See Harris, "Graphic Art for the Public Welfare," 95.

40. *Advertising Age,* 7 February 1938, 20; Caterpillar Tractor Company, *Annual Report to the Stockholders of Caterpillar Tractor Company for the Year Ended December 31, 1936* (Chicago: Caterpillar Tractor Company, 1937), passim; Caterpillar Tractor Company, *Annual Report to Stockholders and Employees for the Year Ending December 31, 1937* (Chicago: Caterpillar Tractor Company, 1938), passim; Caterpillar Tractor Company, *Annual Report to Stockholders and Employees for the Year Ending December 31, 1938* (Chicago: Caterpillar Tractor Company, 1939), passim, box 26, folders 81–82, F. Hal Higgins Collection, University of California, Davis (hereafter, Higgins Collection); *Printers' Ink Monthly,* July 1938, 55.

41. *Advertising Age,* 22 November 1937, 4.

42. "Employee Reports Bring Results," *Forbes,* 1 April 1938, 22; *Printers' Ink Monthly,* July 1938, 17, 55; International Harvester Company, *Industrial Power Facts,* booklet, December 1937, passim, box 91, folder 64, Higgins Collection.

43. "Will Washington Now Alter Its Course?" *Forbes,* 15 March 1938, 23; "Employee Reports Bring Results," 22; *Printers' Ink Monthly,* July 1938, 16–17, 54–55. On Swift, see Swift and Company, *Year Book, 1936* (Chicago: Swift and Company, 1937), passim, Swift and Company Archives, Chicago, and "Profits for All," *Printers' Ink,* 7 January 1937, 21, 24.

44. *Sales Management,* 15 November 1937, 19, 86.

45. Ibid., 18–20, 86; *Advertising and Selling,* 2 December 1937, 48.

46. *Advertising Age,* 31 January 1928, 20; *Business Week,* 16 July 1938, 31.

47. "Simplicity for Employees," *Time,* 21 March 1938, 68, 70.

48. *Printers' Ink Monthly,* July 1938, 55; *Business Week,* 12 March 1938, 15; *Business Week,* 16 July 1938, 30; "Simplicity for Employees," 68, 70.

49. "Employee Reports Bring Results," 22.

50. Johns-Manville Corporation, *Annual Report to the Stockholders of Johns-Manville Corporation, Year Ended December 31, 1938* (New York: Johns-Manville Corporation, 1939), passim, Historical Corporate Reports Collection, Baker Library, Harvard Business School (hereafter, HCR Collection). For comparison, see the Johns-Manville annual reports for 1936 and 1937.

51. *Business Week,* 16 July 1938, 31; *Advertising Age,* 31 January 1938, 20.

52. *People* 1 (August 1937), 20–21, 23, JWT Archives; *Advertising Age,* 16 August 1937, 30; Stanley Resor to Lenox R. Lohr, 21 July 1937; J. Walter Thompson Company, "A Primer of Capitalism, Illustrated," booklet, 1937, box 57, folder 28, National Broadcast Company Papers, State Historical Society of Wisconsin.

53. *People* 1 (August, 1937): 20, JWT Archives; *Advertising and Selling,* 18 November 1937, 38, 48; *Advertising Age,* 28 February 1938, 12; advertisement, *Printers' Ink,* 20 May 1937, 11; Resor to Lohr, July 21, 1937; "Joe and the Corporate Surplus," box 34–3l, N. W. Ayer Archives Center, National Museum of American History, Smithsonian Institution, Washington, D.C.; BBDO, *Newsletter,* 24 October 1936, n.p.; BBDO, *Newsletter,* 29 October 1937, 4, BBDO Archives.

54. Wilson Hicks referred to these early experiments in *Life* as instances of "physically abused photographs." Within this category, he included photos that were "cocked at precious angles" or "rounded, ovalized, or scalloped into cooky [sic] shapes, or silhouetted." Editor John Billings called them "cookie cutouts." See Hicks, *Words and Pictures,* 42–43, and Elson, *Time, Inc.,* 304.

55. *People* 1 (April 1937), cover, second cover, 8, 11; *People* 1 (July 1937), 5–6, 27; *People* 1 (August 1937), cover, 23.

56. Advertisement, *Saturday Evening Post,* 16 November 1935, 86–87; advertisement, *Saturday Evening Post,* 8 February 1936, 66–67; *U.S. Steel News* 1 (August 1936), second cover; Edward R. Stettinius Jr., "Memo to Heads of Departments," 3 May 1937, box 47, and Samuel Crowther to Myron Taylor, 4 January 1936, box 64, Stettinius Papers.

57. *Advertising Age,* 25 April 1938, 12; *U.S. Steel News,* 2 (December 1937), 20; *U.S. Steel News,* 3 (January 1938), 18–19.

58. Thomas Lamont, comments written in pen in E. M. Voorhees to Lamont, 21 February 1940, box 227, Thomas Lamont Papers, Baker Library, Harvard School of Business Management (hereafter, Lamont Papers). See also, Lamont to Myron Taylor, 24 September 1937, and Lamont, "Memo for Edward R. Stettinius, February 3, 1938," box 227, Lamont Papers.

59. Edward R. Stettinius Jr., "The Mutual Responsibility of Business and the Public," typescript of speech, 11 April 1940, 7–8, box 227, folder 16, Lamont Papers; United States Steel Corporation, *37th Annual Report of the United States Steel Corporation for the Fiscal Year Ended December 31, 1938,* (New York: U.S. Steel Corporation, 1939), passim; United States Steel Corporation, *38th Annual Report of U.S. Steel Corporation for the Fiscal Year Ended December 31, 1939,* (New York: U.S. Steel Corporation, 1940), passim; United States Steel Corporation, *39th Annual Report of the U.S. Steel Corporation for the Fiscal Year Ended December 31, 1940* (New York: U.S. Steel Corporation, 1941), passim, HCR Collection.

60. These other public relations projects ranged from expensive fair exhibits and public relations road shows ("Parade of Progress") to institutional advertising that included even labor union publications. General Motors had considered a corporation magazine in 1931. One "obstacle," in addition to the heavy cost, was "the possibility that the wage earning groups . . . have not the mental calibre to benefit enough from a magazine of this high quality" and thus a fear that such a magazine "would go quite over . . . [the] head of a man on the line in a Chevrolet plant." The example of *Life* was not available to General Motors in 1931. See Paul W. Garrett to Public Relations Committee, 27 November 1931, box 550, Stettinius Papers.

61. Elson, *Time, Inc.,* vol. 1, 352. Carl Mydans, a *Life* photographer, later recalled that the magazine's staff "had an insatiable drive to search out every facet of American life, photograph it and hold it up proudly, like a mirror, to a pleased and astonished readership." Quoted in Elson, *Time, Inc.,* vol. 1, 307.

62. *GM Folks* 1 (May 1938), second cover; Paul Garrett, "Industry's No. 1 Problem Defined," pamphlet, 9 February 1939, 8, pamphlet file, General Motors Library, Detroit (hereafter, GM Library).

63. Paul Garrett, "Large Scale Business and the Public," typescript of speech, 25 March 1939, n.p., GM Library; *GM Folks* 2 (September 1939), fourth cover.

64. "Detroit Faces Its First Great Strike," *Life,* 18 January 1937, 11. On *Life*'s penchant for a "journalism of persons," see Baughman, *Henry R. Luce and the Rise of the American News Media,* 45–46.

65. Smith, *Making the Modern,* 442–43.

66. Bird, "Enterprise and Meaning," 24–27, 30; Bird, "The Drama of Enterprise," n.p.

67. *Advertising Age,* 21 February 1938, 2; *Advertising Age,* 12 September 1938, 2; *Printers' Ink Monthly,* January 1938, 12–13.

68. Tedlow, *Keeping the Corporate Image,* 66. On this point, see also Howell John Harris, *The Right to Manage: Industrial Relations Policies of Big Business in the 1940s* (Madison: University of Wisconsin Press, 1982), 96, and Bird, "Enterprise and Meaning," 24–25.

69. *GM Folks* 2 (September 1939), fourth cover.

70. McLaren, *Annual Reports to Stockholders,* 34, 268–70.

71. Lewis, *Annual Reports,* 15.

72. See *The Kraftsman,* 1 (March–April 1943), cover and passim, Kraft General Foods Archives, Morton Grove, Ill. The hundreds of volumes of photo narratives of corporate war service are so numerous as to preclude citation.

7

DAVID MORGAN

THE IMAGE OF RELIGION IN AMERICAN
LIFE, 1936–1951

The portrayal of religion in *Life* during the early years of the magazine visualized an old narrative with a new twist. Images of religious subjects offered a definition of America that stressed the traditional importance of Protestantism, but also celebrated Roman Catholicism as a moral force in the world. Long the object of Protestant curiosity, Catholic ritual was regarded as both exotic and idolatrous.[1] But in the pages of *Life*, Roman Catholicism enjoyed an affirmation and a sympathy that no mainstream American periodical had ever allowed. This chapter considers the cultural politics of visual representations of religion in *Life*, both Protestant and Catholic Christianity, as well as non-Christian religions.

Religious subjects were especially common in the first fifteen years of *Life*, and certain religions and subjects undeniably prevailed.[2] To understand why, it is important to grasp how the magazine's editors and its founder, Henry Luce, a committed Protestant and son of Presbyterian missionaries, regarded the appeal of the photograph. The documentary photographs in *Life* were intended to capture the spectacle of world events and the behavior of contemporaries, particularly the character of "great men," exposing things as they were, reducing their complexity to the lapidary terms of facts, or what Henry Luce and his editors called "news."

The editors' understanding of image making was that truth was visible and made to be documented with the camera. The "journalistic job" of "articulating a language of pictures," as the editors conceived it, consisted of a search for the direct and seductive power of visual representation.[3] Telling the truth visually and empirically was the mission *Life* promised its readers. The photograph was a reliable measure of reality. Thus, *Life* could advertise itself as a provider of everything one would need to know about the world.[4] An early ad for the magazine stated that *Life* promised "to reveal the times we live in and record what life today looks like."[5] Sign and referent intermingle in the magazine and offer the viewer a revelation of the world. Inscribed as an oracle in the ad was the magazine's editorial animus, composed by Henry Luce as notes for a new picture magazine: "to see life [*Life*], to see the world, to eye-witness great events." The slippage from life to *Life* and back again naturalized the magazine's photographs and its editorial policy such that seeing *Life* was seeing the world. The act of representation became as transparent as looking through a window. To see the photographs in the magazine was to be an eyewitness before the unfolding of world events.

Making the viewer a spectator, poised before the spectacle and drama of life, was the chief strategy of *Life.* Another ad of the same time, this one for *Time,* Henry Luce's earlier success, said that reality was a great drama "so richly complex and so hard to follow without *Time*'s help."[6] The news was "the greatest show of all," a "tremendous, marching pageant," an epic theatrical production that the ad portrayed as both the world and the world as it was represented by journalists. The pictorial news magazine was a service in an age of global complexity, a reliable way of making order out of confusing events that threatened to overwhelm the viewer without the theatrical relation that *Life* and *Time* afforded by offering a choice seat before "the great world drama." However dissimulating human folly may be, *Life* pledged itself to be a clear-eyed representation of the show for its viewers.

The structure of appearances on the global stage took two forms: the soliloquy and the pageant. Accordingly, religion was treated most frequently as the acts and personalities of significant individuals and as the public performance of ceremonies and rituals that were meant, like everything else, to be seen through the organ of mass spectacle—the photograph. To these a third category can be added, the exotic and curious, in which, nevertheless, spectacle remained the paradigm. In all three categories religion dominated as ritualistic pageantry, the priesthood of personalities, and outlandish spectacle or ethnographic peculiarities. *Life* interpreted religion's role in the modern world as inherently conservative: as guardian of democracy, as the locus of traditional authority, as the seat of ethnic identity, and as a pure expression of national heritage. Religion was consistently associated with the old and traditional. Even in the present, religion was properly about the past. Moreover, mainstream Protestantism and official Roman Catholicism were the baseline against which all other forms of Christianity and all world religions were measured.

Life indulged its editorial preference for pageantry and personality with each story about domestic and global Catholicism. In its fifth issue (December 21, 1936) the magazine boasted, for instance, of displaying for the first time the complete array of Catholic cardinals in an article devoted to prospects for Pope Pius XI's successor.[7] Arranging the sixty-six cardinals, or "Princes of the Church," in a gallery of four full pages spread out like baseball cards or Hollywood press photos, the editors estimated the likelihood of each candidate's election. The cardinals were portrayed as religious celebrities.

In 1936 and 1937 the first archbishops of the new sees of Los Angeles and Detroit received coverage as did a Polish wedding, an Italian family at prayer, the Vatican, a Mass, a magnificent estate given to the Jesuit order, nuns dancing, playing tennis, and preparing food, and a debutante at first communion. In every instance photographs documented traditional ceremony

THE AGA KHAN OF THE ISMAILI MOSLEMS MARRIES HIS NIECE AT BOMBAY

For the first time as religious head of his family, the Aga Khan, President of the League of Nations Assembly, lately performed the wedding ceremony for his niece in Bombay.

Above, in palm beach suit, he leans back while the bride squats before him, entirely covered with a blanket of woven flowers. The groom is under the flowers at extreme left.

Flanking the Aga Khan are (*right*) his 26-year-old son, the Aly Khan, already married to an Englishwoman, and (*left*) the groom's father, Sir Abdoola Haroon, a Sind merchant.

Figure 7.1. "The Aga Khan of the Ismaili Moslems Marries His Niece at Bombay," *Life,* January 31, 1938. (Courtesy Associated Press)

and ritual, official portraiture, or the picturesque deviation from tradition, as with the nuns. In 1938 a photographic essay on the celebration of "A Solemn High Mass" in St. Patrick's Cathedral foregrounded the mystery and pageantry of the rite, explaining visually and in text what the Mass meant, even going so far as to define the doctrine of transubstantiation and to differentiate it from the Protestant theology of Holy Communion. Combining portrait shots of Cardinal Hayes with panoramic images of the cathedral's nave and sanctuary and the company of priests and attendants at the altar, the article applied the favorite categories of popular photojournalism—personality and spectacle—to the Catholic Mass.[8]

The treatment of spectacle often shifted when *Life* represented non-Western religions. The role of personality changed such that the heroic individual, the prince of the church, or the aged patriarch was eclipsed by exotic architecture, teeming urban scenes, and barren landscape or crowds of pilgrims and worshipers. If the personality was not eliminated, it might be reconfigured as the type or character such as the Aga Khan, the leader of the Ismaili Muslims in India (Figure 7.1).[9] Islam was characterized as "totalitarian" and as "an impersonal Semitic creed," and was therefore bound to be denied the privileged status of the personality, a feature of Western individualism.[10] This stands in marked contrast to the frequent packaging of American Protes-

THE SPIRIT OF U. S. PROTESTANTISM BREATHES FROM THIS FORMAL PORTRAIT OF THE REV. DR. EDWIN A. BRIGGS AND FAMILY IN THE METHODIST PARSONAGE AT BOONE, IOWA

A Practical Man of God

HERE IS THE LIFE OF A TYPICAL U. S. PARSON

Photographs for LIFE by Alfred Eisenstaedt

In his 37 years, Edwin A. Briggs has accumulated no wealth. He is not well known outside his community. Yet in the railroad town of Boone, Iowa, he holds a unique position. As pastor of the First Methodist Church he is, more than almost any other man, the servant of his people. To his 1,400 parishioners he acts as adviser in daily affairs, officiator at birth, marriage and death, consoler in time of grief, at moments of stress physician to their souls. He must also manage a large institution, pick his way through conflicting opinions, act as model to his neighbors, meet the world with unimpeachable good humor and compassion.

The Rev. Dr. Edwin A. Briggs is one of 40,000 pastors who minister to nearly 8,000,000 U. S. Methodists, our largest Protestant group. How such a man lives is described with wit and charm in Hartzell Spence's best-selling book, *One Foot In Heaven* (Whittlesey House, $2.50). It will be further shown in the movie Warner Bros. is now fashioning from Mr. Spence's tribute to his father, the late Rev. William Spence of Mason City, Iowa. Meanwhile, LIFE presents, as an important U. S. document, this essay on Dr. Briggs and his family. For like William Spence, Edwin Briggs typifies the best in Protestant ministry. Of him, too, it can be said that, "the words of *Onward Christian Soldiers* leap at you when he enters the room."

CONTINUED ON NEXT PAGE   55

Right: Figure 7.2. "A Practical Man of God," *Life,* February 3, 1941. (Courtesy Alfred Eisenstaedt/TimePix)

Opposite: Figure 7.3. *American Gothic,* by Grant Wood, 1930. (Courtesy Art Institute of Chicago)

tantism and Catholicism in *Life.* While there was no shortage of characters to represent in American Christianity—*Life* enjoyed documenting eccentric Protestant preachers from raving Pentecostalists to Father Divine—feature articles were dedicated to the installation of important Protestant clergymen and the promotion of Catholic priests to prestigious church office. One religion feature in 1940 covered the ordination of a Presbyterian minister in Philadelphia. The story was told with photographs of carefully posed elder clergy's laying on of hands, the young preacher's vows, views of his childhood home, his parents, and himself at work in his study.[11] Photographer Alfred Eisenstaedt and the editors used the solemn ritual and the personalized treatment of the event to document the making of a religious personality who was consumed by his vocation and able to present impeccable credentials. A University of Pennsylvania and Princeton Theological Seminary graduate who had toured Europe and the Holy Land, the young clergyman was not in the least eccentric, picturesque, exotic, or bizarre.[12]

Another photographic essay by Eisenstaedt focused on a Methodist clergyman, documenting a week in his personal and professional life in Boone, Iowa. Published in 1941, one month after an article on a patriotic British parson, and subtitled "Here Is the Life of a Typical U.S. Parson," the essay urged a national consciousness of American Christianity in the light of international events and framed its view in the ethos of the individual person.[13] The Reverend Dr. Edwin A. Briggs and his family incarnated for Eisenstaedt and *Life* the "spirit of U.S. Protestantism," as a caption beneath a family portrait stated (Figure 7.2). Borrowing the formal severity of Grant Wood's iconic *American Gothic* (Figure 7.3), Eisenstaedt's photograph of the family heavy handedly accentuated Midwestern pride, self-restraint, filial obedience, and thrift. The nine-page spread praised the austerity of the clergyman's life, his manliness, his selfless commitment to his vocation, the hard work and frugality of his wife, and his children's

orderliness.[14] Readers responded positively to what one called the "flesh-and-blood realism" of Eisenstaedt's photography and to the "much-needed, magnificent revelation of what it means to be an effective, hardworking liberal Protestant minister."[15]

Patriotism and the search for the American character became dominant concerns in *Life*'s treatment of religion during and after World War II. Indeed, the principal occasion for the appearance of images of religious subjects in *Life* from the late 1930s to the early 1950s was opposition to fascism and communism. Henry Luce and the editors of *Life* were convinced that Christians everywhere ought to oppose totalitarianism. A 1943 editorial said, "both in Germany and in the occupied countries, the churches, Catholic and Protestant, stand today as focal points of resistance to the Nazis. Of all the institutions of Europe, they alone have survived unamended and uncompromised."[16] From the late 1930s to the Cold War, *Life*'s editors repeatedly used images of a religious nature to underscore the violence, oppression, and destruction carried out under the auspices of totalitarianism. According to *Life*, Christianity, but also Buddhism, Hinduism, and other religious traditions, fostered a tenacious spiritual resistance to totalitarian regimes and served to broadcast totalitarianism's blatant disregard for the spiritual values held dear by Americans. Luce made no secrets about his support for Britain and France and for the necessary rearmament of the United States.[17] Essayist Walter Lippmann also frequently wrote in favor of rearmament. One such essay of October 28, 1940, which advocated a greatly expanded naval force as the "weapon of freedom," included a full-page photograph of naval cadets in the chapel at Annapolis, staring intently at the altar and, according to the caption, "absorb[ing] the spirit of the navy."[18] In the summer of 1941 a similar photograph of West Point cadets in an Episcopal Church service was said to picture "the spiritual sanctuary of U.S. military might. Here is undoubtedly the outward and visible sign of the soul of the U.S. Army." West Pointers were described as quintessentially Amer-

On his rounds, Parson French of Church of England looks over a new bombing. His chief jobs are to get people evacuated promptly, to find new quarters and to provide small necessities.

Figure 7.4. Parson French of Church of England on his rounds, from "*Life* on the Newsfront of the World," *Life*, January 6, 1941. (Courtesy Black Star)

ican and prepared to return to Europe to repeat their performance in World War I.[19]

Life's portrayal of religious activities outside of the United States from 1937 to 1941 was dominated by pictures of regimes threatening world peace. Thus, the king of Bulgaria, monarch of a precarious Balkan state teetering on the edge of communist annexation, was featured in a 1937 photograph kissing the cross of the Greek Orthodox Church. Another item in the same year proudly proclaimed in its title the editorial view of

Life: "Religion Thrives in Godless Russia." Items in subsequent issues showcased the church in Russia and White Russian Orthodox émigrés outside of the Soviet state. Two articles in 1938 lamented the plight of the Jews in Europe, the second after the Nazi violence of Kristallnacht. In the following year, Lutheran Finn military men were shown taking an oath of loyalty in their church in an organized resistance to the Soviet threat.[20]

The editors at *Life* were careful to work religion into the major pieces. For example, most references to the valiant resistance put up for religious reasons or to the destruction of religious buildings were sandwiched within larger contexts of reporting the news. A story in 1941 focused on a popular entertainer and a parson as two individuals instrumental in maintaining public morale against Hitler's aggression. Photographs showed the parson interacting with children and inspecting bomb damage to a fifteenth-century church (Figure 7.4). A photographic essay from the year before appeared after the Germans had begun their bombardment of Britain and surveyed the medieval city of Churchill, England, replete with a seven-hundred-year-old church. Entitled "What We Fight For," the article was careful to point out that the rose bushes in the church graveyard were planted in 1787, "the year the U.S. Constitution was signed." Local worshipers were shown on their way to and in the church. One sculpture, a caption pointed out, was a memorial to a "Churchill parish man who fought in the Crusades."[21] Religion was a venerable link both to the distant, heroic past and to the historic American struggle for liberty. A brief note from Winston Churchill accompanied the article, commending the pictures to *Life*'s readers. In addition to religious subjects, the essay surveyed the lives of Churchill's inhabitants from its local nobility to a middle-class schoolmaster and an unemployed man named Charlie Turner. At stake for Britain, and for America, *Life* wished to say, was the very heritage of the church and the life of free society, which could not be separated from one another.

Given his frustration with President Franklin D. Roosevelt's persistent and politically motivated public avowal of isolationism and the overwhelming unwillingness of the American people to become involved in what most regarded as the distant problems of Europe, Luce turned to religion to augment national resentment for Hitler and Mussolini and to help bring American democracy into world leadership. Roosevelt, he complained in a 1941 essay, had failed to make American democracy succeed materially. "Our only chance now to make it work is in terms of a vital in-ternational economy and in terms of an international moral order."[22] Luce's strategy was to posit an American spirit or national consciousness manifest in religious belief to which he could appeal over against the ingrained isolationist sensibility of so many Americans. In a major editorial article in which he presented his argument for increased American involvement in the war effort, Luce diagnosed what he considered an American illness: an anxiety due to a lack of resolution, a crisis of identity, which he traced to a hesitation to rise to the occasion of world leadership.[23] America's problem was that it failed to grasp its destiny, to mature in its appointed time, in the "American Century," the title of Luce's essay. He included "churchmen" in the blame for this national failure.

For the same reason that *Life* had denounced arch-isolationist Father Charles Coughlin as an anti-Semitic "voice of hate," the magazine's editors considered it important to portray American religion as mature, manly, decisive, and as the secure bastion of American identity or spirit.[24] Accordingly, consistent with its solemn portrayal of Christianity as a faith fitting for the image of the United States as globally prestigious and as the seal and charter of American exceptionalism, *Life* distanced American Protestantism from the grassroots evangelicalism of the nineteenth century. A caption beneath one of Eisenstaedt's photographs of a Methodist church service in 1941 pointed out that "the day of religious emotionalism in U.S. Protestant churches has for the most part passed away with the old revival meeting, the prayer meeting, and the camp meeting."[25] *Life* depicted revivalist evangelicalism that was still operative in Southern and Pentecostal practices as exceptionally odd, anachronistic, or the consequence of deprivation. The sober and civic-minded Christianity of mainstream Protestantism and Catholicism became a touchstone in the revitalization of national will and the call to global dominance.

Religious sectarianism had always bothered the editors of *Life*. From the beginning, the magazine portrayed rural Southern evangelicalism as culturally back-

Figure 7.5. Two photographs from Erskine Caldwell and Margaret Bourke-White, *You Have Seen Their Faces,* which appeared in *Life,* November 22, 1937. (Courtesy Margaret Bourke-White/TimePix)

ward, a fossil of a former age. Revivalists and evangelists were frequently discussed in terms of having flamboyant lifestyles funded by contributions from devout followers.[26] In November 1937 *Life* ran several images on "sharecropper religion" from a book by staff photographer Margaret Bourke-White and writer Erskine Cald-

well, son of a Georgia Methodist preacher. The book, *You Have Seen Their Faces,* was a condescending lament of Southern poverty, race relations, and religion, all viewed as manifestations of a system of cultural retardation. *Life* reproduced photographs of the ecstatic religion of poor Southern blacks and whites, transmitting intact the book's judgment that Southern religion only provided a mechanism of escape from egregious social conditions into the ritualized "hysterical behavior" of "religious frenzy" (Figure 7.5). Caldwell's text and Bourke-White's photographs indicted the church for substituting an ecstatic primitivism for social action.[27] Yet, whereas Caldwell and Bourke-White promoted social reform in the tradition of the Roosevelt's Farm Security Administration, *Life* was concerned to christen the new stature of American Christianity by distinguishing it from its peculiar abuses.[28]

Even the familiar institution of Sunday school in the pages of *Life* was to be distinguished from former days. In another Eisenstaedt photo-essay, a cover story on religious education in a Pennsylvania Presbyterian congregation, the Protestant Sunday school appeared as a modernized component of church life. The article stressed that the facility, management, pedagogy, and curriculum of the Sunday school had been updated to the standards of progressive education. Moreover, although the Bible remained the "basic guide" in the Sunday school, its interpretation "has been broadened" such that in nearly all classes "democratic principles and a social order based on religious teachings are being stressed."[29]

Life's editors avoided, even marginalized, Protestant sectarianism and understood Protestantism to mean mainstream Protestant denominationalism (i.e., Presbyterianism, Congregationalism, Methodism, and Episcopalianism). While *Life*'s articles took greater care to explain Catholic doctrines, in part, no doubt, because American Protestant readers were ignorant of them, the magazine's interest in the two preeminent forms of American Christianity was not sectarian or doctrinaire. The national purpose that Christianity served in the editorial policy of *Life* was indifferent to the fine points of doctrine. Mainstream American Protestantism and Roman Catholicism constituted a faith ready to testify to the mission that awaited the nation. The political message of Sunday schools that taught democratic principles (rather than, say, narrow-minded theological ones) was not lost on readers, one of whom wrote in response to the article, "I sincerely believe if Europeans had a Sunday School or two like the one at the First Presbyterian Church, Lancaster, Pa., they would not be having wars."[30]

The two forms of Christianity were not identically deployed in *Life*. Somewhat different uses were found for each, although they were directed to the same end of the war effort. Protestantism pertained principally to the domestic scene, while Catholicism sounded an international note. In the pages of *Life*, Roman Catholicism played a preponderant role in global opposition to communism and fascism. Having blamed Roosevelt for thwarting "effective American leadership in international co-operation" before his conversion to internationalism, Luce valorized Catholicism as the spiritual voice of opposition that he found wanting in domestic politics.[31] Catholicism exhibited the structural integrity and singular leadership under Pius XII to challenge totalitarianism in a way that the United States was disinclined to do before the attack on Pearl Harbor. Following the Nazi bombing of Guernica, Spain, an image in *Life* showed Catholic Basques celebrating as if in defiance, French nuns were shown feeding Spanish refugees, and the democratic movement in Czechoslovakia was linked directly to the Greek Catholic Church in articles of 1937 and 1938. Catholics in Mexico were also seen struggling against an antireligious socialist government.[32] Catholic religious leaders were frequently seen voicing opposition to totalitarianism and offering assistance to those brutalized by military aggression. One headline in 1938 announced that U.S. Catholic priests joined Pope Pius XII in opposing totalitarianism's "deification of the State which has brought such trouble to [the Catholic] Church abroad." *Life* saw Pius XII as a special force in world politics, and one article noted especially that his election was opposed by Nazis and fascists.[33]

Once the United States had entered the war, *Life*'s propaganda efforts intensified. A photograph in a story about the Nazi destruction of an Egyptian liner and the imprisonment of those on board highlighted the role of Protestant missionaries and Catholic priests in ministering to their fellow captives. Another photo underscored a Singapore church's contribution to the city's preparations against Japanese invasion. The only words quoted by *Life* from the homily of the new primate of England, Archbishop of Canterbury, on the day of his sumptuous enthronement were predictable: "This is not the moment to speak much of war—but a German victory . . . would mean an end of the Christian movement."[34] And in what would become an established practice of Christmas issues, a suite of Christian art images appeared in the December 22, 1941, issue. The point, however, was not simply an artistic celebration of Christmas iconography. Americans were uneasy about joining forces with communists in China and the USSR. *Life*'s Christmas 1941 issue, therefore, attempted to bridge the cultural and political distance as it had months earlier with Russia by foregrounding the production of ink drawings of the Christmas story by Chinese artists at Catholic University in Beijing. Several of the images reproduced in *Life* were the work of a young Chinese artist who was not Christian, but remained in university, the article said, with the prudent encouragement of the Chinese government. The government's policy of supporting students was proof of a wise ally. "China," the article said, "even in the midst of battle, holds to the spiritual and cultural values which America and China alike are now fighting to preserve."[35]

As the war developed, *Life*'s editors began to emphasize a new theme: the Allies would win only by cultivating a spirituality rooted in Christianity. This theme addressed Luce's belief that confidence, or faith, in America's mission in the world had declined since the First World War. In the wake of Pearl Harbor, the choice was seen as black and white, as Luce put it in an editorial two weeks after the attack: "Every American . . . must find a spiritual rebirth or lose his soul alive." Luce indulged in religious rhetoric in order to mobilize the American public: Hitler was the "anti-Christ," Pearl Harbor was "The Day of Wrath," and Americans were "the principal trustees in this century of human freedom under God."[36] The large number of letters to the editor commending the editorial registered the appeal of Luce's message and rhetoric.[37]

This viewpoint persisted and was clearly articulated in an essay by John Foster Dulles, lawyer, Presbyterian layman, future secretary of state (under Dwight D. Eisenhower), and newly elected chair of the Federal Council of Churches' "Commission to Study the Bases of a Just and Durable Peace." Said to be Henry Luce's favorite *Life* contributor, Dulles wrote an essay for the 1942 Christmas issue entitled "A Righteous Faith," which argued that the twentieth century had brought Western democracies to a stand still and marooned them in a spiritual wasteland. World War I marked the turning point, a moment when Americans "so lost our faith in our own institutions that we felt it necessary to shelter them from contact with the outer world. We sought only to be left alone."[38] Isolationism was the loss of faith in America's global purpose. Dulles merged faith in American commerce and the ideal of liberty with Americans' traditional Christian belief. Indeed, he attributed the victory of World War I and the domination of the world by France, Britain, and the United States, countries whose combined numbers made up less than 10 percent of the world's population, to the "great faiths" of the three nations. Dulles embraced the imperial achievements of Great Britain and the Manifest Destiny of the United States as shining examples of benevolence and the global dissemination of moral influence. Speaking for the Protestant membership of the Federal Council of Churches, Dulles said, "Protestant Churches of America are awake to the spiritual need that faces our nation." The "righteous faith" of the American citizen was faith that "our nation will again become a dynamic moral force in the world," a view that renewed the idea of American exceptionalism evident in Puritanism and later millennial visions of America's formative example to the world.[39]

In fact, only a few issues prior to Dulles's essay, *Life*

ran a long special feature on "The Puritan Spirit," which portrayed the original Puritans as a decisive group led by a firm and confident faith in their divinely elected destiny, a "faith that victory comes from God." Puritan violence against the Indians was depicted as necessary for self-preservation in the face of alien aggression and as akin to divinely sanctioned Jewish militarism in the Old Testament. The Puritans were praised for carving out a home in the "aboriginal wilderness of New England" and laying down their own charters, churches, laws, and schools. *Life* saw them as the origin of the American spirit because they "started doing the things that all Americans have sought to do ever since."[40] *Life*'s readers agreed. One reader surely confirmed the hopes of editors that the message of the need for a return of American confidence had gotten through:

> The Puritan spirit of our forefathers has lived on to make America the greatest democracy in the world.
>
> America, now engaged in the greatest struggle of its history, will win this war of survival with the conviction and spirit that man must stay free.
>
> America will play a major role so that all peoples over the world will enjoy freedom in the post-war world.[41]

As the war progressed, *Life* returned to its discontent with Roosevelt and the American public's uncertainty regarding the role of the United States in international affairs. Fearful of a return to prewar isolationism, *Life*'s staff wrote editorials and commissioned articles from sympathetic writers. A powerful editorial of July 5, 1943, called "The American Purpose," reiterated the view that the turning point for American loss of confidence had followed the First World War. The editorial accused Americans of abandoning their dream and urged them to rededicate themselves to the belief "that in founding the United States of America we were summoning all the people of the earth into the green pastures of liberty."[42] This editorial view was applied to economic and foreign policy problems facing a postwar United States in two essays by *Time* editor John K. Jessup.[43] Jessup called for a

friendlier attitude in the government toward business (a subject of *Life*'s criticism of the prewar Roosevelt) and stipulated several areas of desired reform in order to stimulate corporate development and a foreign policy that highlighted international trade, the formation of a world court, and greater communication between the State Department, Congress, and the people.

While Luce steered increasingly to the right and directed what James Baughman has called a "new partisanship" in his magazines, *Life* differentiated "true American nationalism," with its divinely elected national mission and its commitment to moral law descended from God, from the religious patriotism of Nazi Germany.[44] In fulfilling its special mission to the world—spreading "the sanctity of the individual"—America was "not a thing in itself like other nations, but an instrument in God's hand to advance the cause of freedom."[45] A 1944 Easter editorial cited four articles of the "American faith" identified in a recent book by Ralph Gabriel, *The Course of American Democratic Thought.* Americans, according to Gabriel and many others, had historically believed in individual liberty, human progress, the unique national mission of the United States, and in the existence of moral law. The editorial affirmed each of these and contended that moral law was derived from God. Indeed, belief in the divine origin of moral law was all that kept America from placing the state in charge of life, opening the way to the "national religion of Germany." Luce and his colleagues did not seek to install a cult of civil religion, but committed themselves during the war to a distinctly Christian position. Religion, they insisted—the revealed religion of the Easter resurrection—was of the "first importance" in national life and "the only possible framework for the news." A spate of letters to the editors affirmed the particularly Christian version of American faith advocated at *Life*. "May the Christian flag and Old Glory always stand in the chancels of our churches with perfect compatibility," wrote one reader. Another wrote, "It would be a rich reward if 'The Easter Message' which you have so strongly presented penetrated pulpit and pew into producing a new enduement of the Pentecostal power of the Gospel." And a third letter lauded *Life*'s willingness to discuss in print "the very foundation stone of our American ideology."[46]

When the war came to a close and Americans manifested new divisiveness, which threatened to unravel the national unity achieved during the war, *Life* called for religious unity, but insisted on unity that was conducive to a distinctive community of belief. In an Easter editorial in 1945 the magazine opposed the tension among Protestants and Catholics in the United States and praised religious accord. While the editors applauded John D. Rockefeller Jr.'s recent call for interdemoninational cooperation to foster a "new era of Christian unity," they cautioned that secularism, not sectarianism, was the "real enemy" of religion. Traditional Christianity must not give up its missionary charter lest it lose its message for the world. The search for unity needed to be conditioned by "hard thought and creative theology" in order to overcome the "scandal of divided Christendom."[47] *Life* hailed the gathering of world Protestants in 1946 to form the World Council of Churches as "proof that Protestantism, always weakened by arguments among denominations, was making progress in its long attempt to unify itself spiritually and ecclesiastically."[48] It was Christianity with a missionary (but not Fundamentalist) bite that *Life* wished to identify as characteristically American. Shorn of its backwoods provinciality and sectarian intolerance, American Christianity was now ready to provide the moral imperative for the international role awaiting the nation. This may account for why *Life* did not dismiss the new popular preacher Billy Graham, but recognized him with national coverage in 1949 and 1950 as spokesman for a new and cosmopolitan evangelicalism that distanced itself from the antagonistic Fundamentalism of the 1920s.[49]

As the line was drawn between East and West in the years following the war, *Life* moved toward associating Christianity with democracy. The West was defined by democratic values that were fixed in humanity's spiri-

tual nature. Partisans considered this fully corroborated by the opposition raised by Christian churches against the scourge of Soviet-style communism. In a 1946 Easter editorial, *Life* asked "why men pray" and answered that prayer-in-unison "symbolizes the democratic character of Christian brotherhood."[50] In what became a commonplace notion used to underscore the fundamental difference between East and West, the editorial asserted that it was "no accident that democracy, which can work only when free individuals are morally responsible, has flourished best in Christian lands."

A few months later Dulles wrote a major article on the problems posed by Soviet foreign policy. American response should begin with religious belief, said Dulles, "The most significant demonstration that can be made is at the religious level. The overriding and ever-present reason for giving freedom to the individual is that men are created as the children of God, in His image. The human personality is thus sacred and the state must not trample on it."[51] The rhetoric only became more religiously intense and explicit in a two-part report a year later on the condition of "organized Christianity abroad," assigned by *Life* to Paul Hutchison, managing editor of the leading Protestant magazine, *Christian Century*. Hutchison portrayed the global enmity of communism and Christianity as a struggle for Christian liberty: in Europe the advance of communist interests was being outstripped by Christian socialist and democratic parties; in Asia and the rest of the non-Western world Christianity and other religions were reaffirming the certainty of "unshakable moral standards" or laws that shape human destiny.[52] Everywhere this meant a mounting rejection of totalitarianism. Hutchison characterized the collective position of the Christian socialist parties in Europe as "fundamentally opposed to communism" and as possessing a view of life "which must be preserved at all costs if Western civilization is not to lapse into slavery."[53] In his writing about the Western attacks on Soviet communism, Hutchison said that it was "as much a religion as a system of politics and economics."[54]

Not only was communism a religion, it was the hideous caricature of religion, the diametric opposite, the "supreme enemy" of true Christianity, the anti-Christ. Recalling anti-Catholic propaganda that stretched all the way from the Reformation to modern American evangelical denunciations of the Pope, Hutchison compared Soviet communism to the papacy. Communism had "its heresy trials, its excommunications, its saints, its martyrs, its demonology, its ruling hierarchy, its pope, its consecrated priesthood. . . . Save in the purposes for which they exist, there is little difference between the international of the Kremlin and of the Vatican."[55] As anachronistic as the comparison was, and out of character with *Life*'s celebration of the Catholic church as anticommunist, likening the Kremlin to the Vatican allowed Hutchison to underscore the Orthodox church's domestic struggle against the Soviet government. In any event, it was not a comparison that Pius XII would have made. The comparison reveals that, for Hutchison and many others, American Christianity remained Protestant. Hutchison's larger point was that communism was now (Protestant) Christianity's evil adversary, a dark and rival faith, employing premodern techniques of coercion and indulging in self-glorification and authoritarianism with which there could be no compromise. "How can there be any true accommodation or even a prolonged truce between these two faiths?" he asked. *Life* took this position in the following years when urging political leaders not to compromise with the Soviets.

Coordinated with the attack on the new Soviet enemy, in 1946 articles in *Life* on the nation's former foe, Japan, shifted toward portraying the revival of religion, a Westernization of belief, and an expected upswing in Christianity.[56] One item even reported that some Japanese had been Christian since the sixteenth century and had escaped persecution by concealing crosses inside Buddhist statuary.[57] This latent Christianity helped build a bridge to the former enemy, now a crucial outpost for Western democracy and a highly visible example of capitalism's power to transform a broken state ravaged by totalitarianism into a flourishing capitalist economy and free society.[58]

Editorials in *Life* after the war clearly tried to distinguish between the humanitarian ethic of the "brotherhood of man" and religion as a revealed truth that required the spiritual rebirth of anyone who would affirm it and put its precepts into practice. The magazine explicitly advocated a Protestant interpretation of the incarnation and resurrection of Jesus in editorials published near Easter and Christmas each year in the second half of the 1940s.[59] Although some of the editors may have regretted the new tone and explicit advocacy, it was important to Luce because he believed that individual freedom was divinely ordained.[60] Without a clear sense of Christian faith in divine revelation, Western democracy would forfeit its metaphysical underpinning. This proclaimed a traditional American theme of the importance of belief for the security and prosperity of the republic.[61] One of these editorials sounded a somber Calvinist note by subordinating the "brotherhood of man" to the "fatherhood of God" in order to affirm an enduring foundation for human morality. The editorial expressed suspicion of anything "man-made," for if a code of ethics was "man-made, it can be remade by other men."[62] Another editorial at this time said that rights were part of the "God-given nature of the individual" rather than "social dispensations granted by the state."[63] The threat of secularism, fatalism, relativism, totalitarianism, socialism, and atheism uniformly consisted of denying the divine source of human freedom. In contrast to the patriotic fervor of American Christianity during the war years and shortly thereafter, by 1949 *Life* baldly announced, "Our civilization, for all its churches and all its churchgoers, is predominantly a secular, godless civilization."[64]

This grim assessment was directed against what the editors considered the Harry S. Truman administration's less-than-hard-line attitude toward the USSR. But there were deeper affinities at work. *Life* rejected the humanist view of religion as no more than a good intention in a world that mercilessly devoured any-thing less than a resolute determination backed by force. In this light it is possible to discern a theological disposition in *Life* during the postwar years that un-derscored the human capacity for evil personified in the threat of the Soviet Union. The theological current that *Life* embraced was the "Christian Realism" or so-called "neo-orthodoxy" of the reformed theologian at Union Theological Seminary in New York, Reinhold Niebuhr, who came to repudiate liberal Protestantism as unrealistic and incapable of confronting the reality of human brutality and the necessity of God's un-compromised sovereignty.

A former socialist and pacifist, in the late 1930s and early 1940s Niebuhr became deeply skeptical of Chris-tian socialist sensibilities and the Social Gospel (which *Life* at the same time discerned in many Methodist clergy for their "uncritical softness toward Russia"). In 1941 Niebuhr helped found the Union for Democratic Action with other New York leftist intellectuals who were likewise disillusioned by Stalin and alarmed at the rise of fascism in Europe. *Life* and Luce affirmed Niebuhr's newly negative assessment of liberal Protes-tantism, "whose faith at times seems no more than vague good will."[65] In practical political terms this meant for Niebuhr a hard-line approach to Soviet "truc-ulence" and a rejection of pacifism. In church politics it meant a vigorous move toward global Protestant unity, which *Life* did much to herald. Although Niebuhr publicly expressed distrust of Luce in 1941, recognizing in him a hyperpatriot who did not take human depravity seriously, by the mid-1940s Niebuhr was willing to associate himself (however briefly) with *Life* on the cause of anti-Soviet foreign policy.[66]

The global mission of Protestant unity for *Life* was linked to a reinvigorated Christianity that carried abroad the cultural DNA of American democracy. A Christmas editorial in 1943 praised the ecumenical movement of world Protestantism gathered under the umbrella of the World Council of Churches and "strengthened by certain developments in Protestant

theology," namely the work of Niebuhr, who, along with John Foster Dulles, was active in the movement to-ward international Protestant unity.[67] The editorial identified a "reassertion of Christianity" in the new the-ology, which moved between the "the old Fundamen-talists, on the one hand, and the Modernists on the other." Central to the new development was an em-phasis on the idea of a Christian community as the "nu-cleus, or heart, of the world community, organically re-lated to it, and inspiring in it a higher spiritual realization." The editorial looked for the possibility of a "long-awaited religious revival; a revival born in the hearts of the citizens of our time." Nothing, at least for the editors of *Life,* could have been a better spiritual brief for the United States. The spirit of Puritanism was about to return, and America's time of regression was to be repealed: "The lackadaisical days when it did-n't matter much whether you were a Christian or not, may be numbered."

No term in Niebuhr's gloomy, scolding discourse was freighted with such contempt as the "sentimental-ity" he attributed to the sunny disposition of an irre-sponsible political liberalism and liberal Christianity. The word designated the failure of liberal optimism to take sin, evil, and human depravity seriously, which, ac-cording to Niebuhr, threatened profound danger in the West's dealings with communism.[68] Neoorthodox re-alism and the denunciation of political and religious "sentimentality" were adopted by *Life* to designate the romantic isolationism of an earlier day as well as the deluded hopes of Truman and his secretary of state, Dean Acheson, who maintained that a peaceful coexis-tence could be struck with the Soviets. In an unusually caustic editorial, *Life* said Truman's policy was a "source of weakness" and a "pietistic fraud."[69] Soviet commu-nism was "prodigious evil," and anything short of rigid opposition was "the way to suicide." *Life* agreed with Niebuhr's assessment of the international face-off be-tween East and West; to win the battle against com-munism it was necessary to be willing to go to war.[70]

The neoorthodox idea of a Christian community

appealed to *Life*'s brand of photojournalism, because it leant itself to the photo-essay survey of America. During and after the war readers were treated to such visions of religious community at the heart of American life as Sunday school, the small-town choir, women praying for their soldier sons and husbands, a Northern pastor who transformed a backward Southern community with his ministry, and two adorable Sunday school students.[71] Each of these stories offered a public reflection on what it was to be an American, and to belong to a national community with its religious vocation on the global stage nourished by the local life of average citizens.

To these icons of community and the global influence of American democracy *Life* contrasted the secularist vision of the world as a determinist, materialist nightmare whose single aim was the destruction of democracy and the elimination of personal freedom. A 1947 editorial applauded what the magazine called "a marked trend [among scientists] . . . toward believing that at the heart of reality there is mystery."[72] Science itself was bearing witness to the need for "believing in God," as the editorial's subtitle put it. Response to this and the other explicitly religious editorials was bristling and extensive. *Life* printed several long letters following each editorial. While one clergyman cheered the affirmation of Christ's divinity in a 1947 Easter editorial, other readers condemned the editorial's appeal to mystery and mysticism as "running away from the great challenge of our time."[73] Responding to the science editorial, another reader complained of the "growing tendency in *Life* to propagandize the notions of dogmatic theology and to deplore or to ridicule science." The reader asked for an "explanation of this gradual policy change," decried the heavy-handed editorial approval of religion, and insisted that religious coverage had surpassed its appropriate boundaries: "Have the staffs of *Life* and *Time* been converted? Or have they decided that only a mass dose of oldtime religion will save the republic? Or do they believe a holy war is in prospect and are they choosing sides?"[74] The editors denied that they were

dogmatic or opposed to science. They said their fear was "scientism—the unscientific dogma that science always knows best."

There was an undeniable editorial change at *Life* between 1936 and 1946. From the beginning the magazine had consistently rejected totalitarian forms of government and had seen religion as a crucial force of opposition. Only as a result of the war and its massive destruction and Luce's frustration over Truman's response to Soviet postwar aggression did *Life* espouse the belief that religious faith preceded government as the source of American freedom. In 1947 a Thanksgiving editorial contrasted the Pilgrims' sense of metaphysical certainty regarding their mission in life to the modern existential experience of meaninglessness and despair. Even democracy was no longer fully adequate for human happiness and meaning: "no triumph of democracy will remove all human sadness and doubt. For that the only prescription is the grateful consciousness of individual responsibility not only to ourselves and to our neighbors, but to a living God."[75] Accordingly, *Life* could even speak of democracy as Christianity's tool of assault on communism: In an impoverished and restless world North America has become a major bulwark of the Roman Catholic Church and its best hope in the battle against communism.[76] Courted by presidential candidate John F. Kennedy in 1960, Luce agreed to an evenhanded treatment of the Catholic senator because of his tough stand against communism.[77]

What confronts the late twentieth-century viewer of *Life* during the early decades of the Cold War is a familiar and perennial theme in American history: the longing to reestablish the Christian identity of the nation as its moral backbone and purpose in the world. American Protestants have long used the media. Indeed, one media historian has even argued that evangelicals virtually invented the mass media in America in the early nineteenth century.[78] But Protestants were no longer the only player on the stage of this mass-circulation magazine. Roman Catholics from around the world joined American Protestants to visualize Christianity as a moral force capable of enjoining the communist threat and nourishing democracy while preserving the Protestant character of the nation. The "American Century" was to be Protestant at home and ecumenically Protestant and Catholic abroad.

NOTES

1. See Jenny Franchot, *Roads to Rome: The Antebellum Protestant Encounter with Catholicism* (Berkeley: University of California Press, 1994), and John Davis, "Catholic Envy: The Visual Culture of Protestant Desire," *The Visual Culture of American Religions,* ed. David Morgan and Sally M. Promey (Berkeley: University of California Press, 2001), 105–28.

2. I examined 750 issues of *Life* from the first issue of 1936 to the final weekly issue of 1951, the first fifteen years of publication, identifying 683 instances of the visual depiction of religion. I counted every instance of the occurrence of a religious image, excluding advertisements. Those images that were clearly Christian but not identifiable, were coded "Unidentifiable Christian"; those that depicted Christian art or some aspect of early Christianity during the New Testament period were gathered in a separate category called "Christian art/historical Christianity." Such religious traditions as Universalist/Unitarian (four instances) and Mormon (six instances) were counted with Protestantism due to their historical association with that tradition. The groups break down as follows: Protestant, 219; Roman Catholic, 216; Unidentifiable Christian, 80; Christian art/historical Christianity, 78; Eastern Orthodoxy (including Russian Orthodox Church), 20; Buddhist, 18; Jewish, 13; Hindu, 10; Islam, 8; Shinto, 5; Spiritualism, 4; Oceanic, 2; Vodou, 2; Native American, 2; Sikh, 1; Pagan, 1; Masonry, 1; Baha'i, 1; Chinese, 1; South American (non-Christian), 1 (with a total of 683).

3. Quoted in Robert T. Elson, *Time, Inc.: The Intimate History of a Publishing Enterprise, 1923–1941,* ed. Duncan Norton-Taylor (New York: Atheneum, 1968), 284.

4. An ad in 1937 boasted that the quantity of visual information managed by the magazine was so comprehensive that "some mythical *Life* reader set off on a desert island without newspapers, radio, telephone, or other means of communication, might have got, from *Life* alone, a fair idea of what was going on in the world" (*Life,* 15 March 1937, 5). The editors reprinted the following excerpt from a reader's enthusiastic endorsement of *Life:* "I don't give a darn when Television now arrives, as with a copy of *Life* before you no one needs any further appeal to the eye on current events. And *Life* gives us many scenes that Television won't touch for a long time to come" (*Life,* 14 December 1936, 7).

5. The ad was on the inside back covers of all issues in December 1936.

6. *Life,* 28 December 1936, inside back cover.

7. "Princes of the Church," *Life,* 21 December 1936, 22–25. Another Luce enterprise, *The March of Time,* was touted in *Life* for its unprecedented documentation of the Vatican, an effort "at which all others failed" and an achievement that was "one of the greatest newsreel scoops of all time, a visual document of such value that its place in camera history is assured" (*Life,* 26 February 1940, 26).

8. "A Solemn High Mass Is Celebrated: Catholic Rite at St. Patrick's Told in Pictures," *Life,* 21 March 1938, 32–38.

9. "The Aga Kahn of the Ismaili Moslems Marries His Niece at Bombay," *Life,* 31 January 1938, 53.

10. "Turkey," *Life,* 8 April 1940, 82.

11. Because it is not possible to reproduce a large number of images, I have placed the citation of a large number of images in the endnotes for the convenience of the reader's further interest.

12. "Young Philadelphian Is Ordained a Minister in the Presbyterian Church," *Life,* 6 May 1940, 50–52, 54, 56.

13. "*Life* on the Newsfronts of the World," *Life,* 6 January 1941, 26–27.

14. "A Practical Man of God: Here Is the Life of a Typical U.S. Parson," *Life,* 3 February 1941, 55–63. When, in a light-hearted piece, *Life* portrayed "quiet-hearted denominations" such as "sedate Unitarians and Congregationalists" as cavorting and less than serious, readers lamented the story and corrected the editors (*Life,* 16 September 1940, 88ff; editorials, *Life,* 7 October 1940, 2, 4).

15. Letters to the editor, *Life,* 17 February 1941, 2.

16. Editorial, "Christmas," *Life,* 27 December 1943, 28. German clergy such as Dietrich Bonhoeffer and Martin Niemöller, who resisted their church's accommodation of Nazism, would have told quite a different story.

17. See, for instance, Luce's editorial written after touring Europe, Henry R. Luce, "America and Armageddon," *Life,* 3 June 1940, 40, 100. For discussion of Luce's political views during the period under question here, see James L. Baughman, *Henry R. Luce and the Rise of the American News Media* (Boston: Twayne Publishers, 1987), 129–57; also Robert E. Herzstein, *Henry R. Luce: A Political Portrait of the Man Who Created the American Century* (New York: Scribners, 1994).

18. Walter Lippmann, "Weapon of Freedom," *Life,* 28 October 1940, 44–45, 110.

19. "The Spirit of West Point," *Life,* 7 July 1941, 56–57.

20. "The Assassins of Southeastern Europe Mark Their Victims," *Life,* 29 March 1937, 52; "Religion Thrives in Godless Russia," *Life,* 3 May 1937, 56–58; "Church in Russia and White Russians," *Life,* 15 November 1937, 103; "*Life* on the American Newsfront," *Life,* 6 December 1937, 21; "European Jews," *Life,* 18 April 1938, 46–55; "For a Diplomat's Murder Nazi Germany Takes an Awful Revenge on its Jews," *Life,* 28 November 1938, 17; "Lutheran Finns," *Life,* 30 October 1939, 77.

21. "*Life* on the Newsfront of the World," 26–27; "What We Fight For," *Life,* 18 November 1940, 92–93. *Life*'s portrayal of war needs to be situated within an emerging history of the visual treatment of war in European and American journalism and the history of photography. For a fascinating study of more current news coverage, with a helpful bibliography, see Michael Griffin and Jongso Lee, "Picturing the Gulf War: Constructing an Image of War in *Time, Newsweek*, and *U.S. News & World Report*," *Journalism and Mass Communication Quarterly* 72, no. 4 (Winter 1995): 813–25.

22. Henry R. Luce, "The American Century," *Life,* 17 February 1941, 64.

23. Ibid., 63: "In the field of national policy, the fundamental trouble with America has been, and is, that whereas their nation became in the 20th Century the most powerful and the most vital nation in the world, nevertheless Americans were unable to accommodate themselves spiritually and practically to that fact. Hence they have failed to play their part as a world power—a failure which has had disastrous consequences for themselves and for all mankind."

24. "Fascism in America," *Life,* 6 March 1939, 60.

25. "A Practical Man of God," *Life,* 3 February 1941, 63.

26. See "The Case of the Child Bride," *Life,* 15 February 1937, 15; "*Life* on the American Newsfront," *Life,* 3 May 1937, 25; "Mass-Baptism in LA," *Life,* 14 June 1937, 10–11, 13; "The South of Erskine Caldwell," *Life,* 22 November 1937, 50–51; "Holiness Faith Healers: Virginia Mountaineers Handle Snakes to Prove Their Piety," *Life,* 3 July 1944, 59–60; "Daddy Grace: Grandiloquent Negro Preacher Has a Half-Million Faithful Followers," *Life,* 1 October 1945, 51–56, 58; "New Mrs. Divine: Cult Leader Marries White Woman Who Is Much Younger Than He Is," *Life,* 19 August 1946, 38. Some articles praised the efforts of clergy from the North who moved to poor and rural areas in the South to take up ministries of reform and social improvement. See, for example, "Walkin' Preacher of the Ozarks," *Life,* 25 December 1944, 65–66, 69–70; "Mining-Town Minister: A Young Presbyterian Preacher Applies Practical Christianity to a West Virginia Coal-Mining Town," *Life,* 24 June 1946, 49–51.

27. Erskine Caldwell and Margaret Bourke-White, *You Have Seen Their Faces* (New York: Viking, 1937), especially 144. The book has recently been reissued with an introduction by Alan Trachtenberg (Athens: University of Georgia Press, 1995).

28. For a critique of the book and its images in light of Farm Security Administration (FSA) photography, see James Guimond, *American Photography and the American Dream* (Chapel Hill: University of North Carolina Press, 1991), 117–19. Guimond contended that Caldwell and Bourke-White were much less sympathetic toward their subjects than FSA photographers were to theirs.

29. "Sunday School: With Modern Methods It Works for God & Country," *Life,* 2 June 1941, 72.

30. Letters to the editor, *Life,* 23 June 1941, 6, 8.

31. Luce, "The American Century," 63.

32. "Showing Itself in Spain, Italy Offers to Withdraw," *Life,* 1 November 1937, 66; "An Army Corps of the Spanish Loyalists Skis to Refuge in France," *Life,* 25 April 1938, 27; "Czechoslovakia Is a Republic Surrounded by Dictators," *Life,* 8 November 1937, 100; "Sudeten Germans Hear Their Leader," *Life,* 30 May 1938, 64; "The Camera Overseas," *Life,* 10 January 1938, 48; "Mexico: Can a Socialist at Home Be a Good Neighbor Abroad?" *Life,* 11 April 1938, 55.

33. "100,000 Catholics at U.S. Congress," *Life,* 31 October 1938, 20–21; "Pope Pius XII," *Life,* 13 March 1939, 13–17. A long essay by Frederic Sondern Jr. praised the Pontiff as a great statesman and a leader dedicated to world peace; another article stressed the Pope's favorable treatment of the American military. Frederic Sondern Jr., "The Pope: A Great Man and Great Spokesman Works for the Peace of the World," *Life,* 4 December 1939, 86–95; "Pope Greets Americans in Vatican," *Life,* 26 June 1944, 86A–86D.

Yet Pius XII maintained Vatican neutrality in the war and was sharply criticized after the war for not having done more to resist Nazism in particular, see, for instance, Guenter Lewy, *The Catholic Church and Nazi Germany* (New York: McGraw-Hill, 1964), and Gordon C. Zahn, *German Catholics and Hitler's Wars: A Study in Social Control* (Notre Dame, Ind.: University of Notre Dame Press, 1989), 212–14. This is a subject that remains hotly debated—see David Van Biema, "A Repentance, Sort of," *Time,* 30 March 1998, 60. Among the most cited studies of Pius, the Nazis, and the Holocaust are Saul Friedländer, *Pius XII and the Third Reich: A Documentation,* trans. Charles Fullman (New York: Knopf, 1966), and Carlo Falconi, *The Silence of Pius XII,* trans. Bernard Wall (Boston: Little, Brown, 1965). More recent studies include Robert G. Weisbord and Wallace P. Sillanpoa, *The Chief Rabbi, the Pope, and the Holocaust: An Era in Vatican-Jewish Relations* (New Brunswick: Transaction Publishers, 1992), and, particularly critical of Pius, John Cornwell, *Hitler's Pope: The Secret History of Pius XII* (New York: Viking, 1999) .

Pius's defenders have argued that he did what he could. For a brief, balanced discussion, see Kenneth L. Woodward, *Making Saints* (New York: Touchstone, 1996), 295–300. Whatever Pius XII may have failed to do during the war, *Life*'s greatest use of him occurred immediately before and during the early days of the war, although *Life* never ran anything unfavorable toward Pius. A February 26, 1940, piece on a nineteen-minute film of the Vatican produced by *March of Time* (which *Life* touted as "one of the greatest newsreel scoops of all time") documented the pontiff before an advisory body gesticulating expressively as he discussed "international peace" (26–27). Another article of the same year pictured the Pope in a cruciform manner with the headline: "Peace Pope Beseeches God with Outstretched Hands to End the War" (*Life,* 25 March 1940, 24). After this, however, Pius XII did not appear in the pages of *Life* until June 26, 1944, when a four-page pictorial featured the Pope greeting American soldiers in the Vatican and argued in detail for the special favors the pontiff bestowed on Americans that he had withheld from German and Italian military officials before the Allied occupation of Rome (86A). A fall 1944 article praised the Pope's measures to save Rome from the war's destruction (*Life,* 4 September 1944, 103). In January 1945 a "Papal Christmas" was featured (*Life,* 15 January 1945, 26–28). And in the October 29, 1945, issue Pius XII appears proudly in a papal portrait, his final appearance in *Life* during the war.

34. "Prison Ship," *Life,* 15 December 1941, 116; "Malay Jungle War," *Life,* 12 January 1942, 35; "New Primate of England," *Life,* 1 June 1942, 34–35.

35. "The Story of Christ in Chinese Art," *Life,* 22 December 1941, 40.

36. Henry R. Luce, "The Day of Wrath," ibid., 11.

37. Letters to the editor, *Life,* 12 January 1942, 2, 4.

38. John Foster Dulles, "A Righteous Faith," *Life,* 28 December 1942, 49. For further discussion of Dulles's views, particularly his belief that Christian ethics was to be part of a lasting peace and that Protestantism in the late 1930s was about to undergo a spiritual rebirth that would affect global politics, see John Chamberlain, "John Foster Dulles," *Life,* 21 August 1944, 92. For a helpful overview of Dulles's views on religion and world politics, see Michael A. Guhin, *John Foster Dulles: A Statesman and His Times* (New York: Columbia University Press, 1972), 116–28. On Luce and Dulles, see Townsend Hoopes, *The Devil and John Foster Dulles* (Boston: Little, Brown, 1973), 311. For a collection of Dulles's writings on patriotism, religion, and international affairs, see *The Spiritual Legacy of John Foster Dulles: Selections from His Articles and Addresses,* ed. Henry P. Van Dusen (Philadelphia: Westminster Press, 1960).

39. Dulles, "A Righteous Faith," 50. On exceptionalism, see the historiographical review by Michael Kammen, "The Problem of American Exceptionalism: A Reconsideration," *American Quarterly* 45, no. 1 (March 1993): 1–43; on millennialism, see James F. Maclear, "New England and the Fifth Monarchy: The Quest for the Millennium in Early American Puritanism," *William and Mary Quarterly,* 3d ser., 32 (April 1975): 223–60; and Nathan O. Hatch, "The Origins of Civil Millennialism in America: New England Clergymen, the War with France, and the Revolution," *William and Mary Quarterly,* 3d ser., 31 (July 1974): 407–30.

40. "The Puritan Spirit," *Life,* 23 November 1942, 74–88.

41. Letters to the editor, *Life,* 14 December 1942, 2.

42. "The American Purpose," *Life,* 5 July 1943, 39.

43. John K. Jessup, "America and the Future, I—Our Domestic Economy," *Life,* 13 September 1943, 105–6, 108, 110, 113–14, 116; and John K.

Jessup, "America and the Future, II—Our Foreign Policy," *Life,* 20 November 1943, 105–8, 110, 113–14, 116.

44. Baughman, *Henry R. Luce,* 142–48.

45. "The Easter Message: Faith in America Asks a Greater Faith in God," *Life,* 10 April 1944, 38.

46. Letters to the editors, *Life,* 1 May 1944, 2.

47. "Christianity and Creeds," *Life,* 2 April 1945, 28.

48. "Protestants Plan for Peace," *Life,* 18 March 1946, 31–35.

49. "A New Evangelist Arises," *Life,* 21 November 1949, 97–98, 100; "Billy on Dixie," *Life,* 27 March 1950, 55–56; on Billy Graham and the older style of Fundamentalism, see Robert T. Handy, *A Christian America, Protestant Hopes, and Historical Realities,* 2d rev. edition (New York: Oxford University Press, 1984), 189; and Betty DeBerg, "The Ministry of Christian Art: Evangelicals and the Art of Warner Sallman, 1942–1960," in *Icons of American Protestantism: The Art of Warner Sallman,* ed. David Morgan (New Haven: Yale University Press, 1996), 123–47. Graham no doubt merited the attention in the minds of *Life*'s editors because of the evangelist's ardent anticommunism as well as the patriotic tenor of the ministry that launched him into national exposure, the Chicago-based Youth for Christ, which William Randolph Hearst (as well as *Time* magazine) had made such a point of covering immediately following the second world war—see William Martin, *A Prophet with Honor: The Billy Graham Story* (New York: William Morrow, 1991), 95, 101, 165–67. See also Joel A. Carpenter, *Revive Us Again: The Reawakening of American Fundamentalism* (New York: Oxford University Press, 1997), 161–76, 226–27. Graham also represented a moderate wing among conservative Protestants, separating himself from Fundamentalist zealots and making a formal break in the early 1950s; see George Marsden, *Reforming Fundamentalism: Fuller Seminary and the New Evangelicalism* (Grand Rapids, Mich.: William B. Eerdmans Publishing Company, 1987), 53–71, and Martin, *A Prophet with Honor,* 204–24. My thanks to Jay Green for helpful conversation on this issue.

50. "Why Men Pray," *Life,* 22 April 1946, 36.

51. John Foster Dulles, "Thoughts on Soviet Foreign Policy and What to Do About It, Part II," *Life,* 10 June 1946, 122.

52. Paul Hutchison, "Does Europe Face Holy War?" *Life,* 23 September 1946, 61–62, 64, 66, 68; and Paul Hutchison, "Religion around the World," *Life,* 10 March 1947, 112.

53. Hutchison, "Does Europe Face Holy War?" 64.

54. Hutchison, "Religion around the World," 116. *Life* had already published a full-page image of the enshrined Lenin, "God of Communists," as he was revered by Soviet pilgrims at the sacred site of his tomb, "Lenin: The God of Communists Lies for His First Entombed Portrait," *Life,* 5 February 1940, 68–69.

55. Hutchison, "Religion around the World," 116.

56. "Kyoto's Shrines," *Life,* 17 June 1946, 51–54; Hutchison, "Religion around the World," 115–16.

57. "Hidden Crosses," *Life,* 25 March 1946, 93–94.

58. For an enthusiastic account of Catholicism and Protestantism in China, see Archbishop Paul Yu-Pin, "Christianity in China," *Life,* 13 January 1947, 39–40; and Bishop Ralph A. Ward, "Protestants Are Strong," *Life,* 13 January 1947, 42–44, 46.

59. "Christian Disunity," *Life,* 23 December 1946, 24; "The Road to Religion," *Life,* 7 April 1947, 36; "Creator and Created," *Life,* 22 December 1947, 24; "Tidings of Great Joy," *Life,* 27 December 1948, 20; "God's Underground," *Life,* 18 April 1949, 34.

60. Matthew Fox reported that an editor at *Time* asked Luce's friend, Reinhold Niebuhr, "to intervene with their boss who was getting 'more pious and conservative'" during this period; see Richard Wrightman Fox, *Religion USA: Religion and Culture By Way of* Time *Magazine* (Dubuque, Iowa: Listening Press, 1971), 51.

61. For a discussion of the theme of republicanism in connection with religious visual culture in the nineteenth century, see David Morgan, *Protestants and Pictures: Religion, Visual Culture, and the Age of American Mass Production* (New York: Oxford University Press, 1999).

62. "The Road to Religion," 36.

63. Editorial, "The Mindszenty Case," *Life,* 21 February 1949, 30.

64. "God's Underground," 34.

65. Editorial, "The Methodists," *Life,* 10 November 1947, 38; editorial, "Christian Disunity," *Life,* 23 December 1946, 24. On Niebuhr, see Martin E. Marty, *Modern American Religion,* vol. 2, *The Noise of Conflict, 1919–1941* (Chicago: University of Chicago Press, 1991), 52–53, 321–30. On Niebuhr and Luce's religious thought, see Wrightman Fox, *Religion USA,* 52–63.

66. On Niebuhr's suspicions of Luce and the fundamental ways in which the two differed, see Richard Wrightman Fox, *Reinhold Niebuhr: A Biography* (New York: Pantheon, 1985), 202; on Niebuhr's contribution to *Life* and his quick distancing from what Wrightman Fox calls "*Life*'s unnuanced fist-shaking," see Wrightman Fox, *Religion USA,* 228–29.

67. "Christmas," *Life,* 27 December 1943, 28. Niebuhr was among the delegates of American Protestants who prepared for the first conference of the World Council of Churches (wcc); see "Workers for Church Unity," *Life,* 17 May 1948, 108–10. He spoke at the historic conference of the wcc in Amsterdam; see "Protestants Form a World Council," *Life,* 13 September 1948, 38–40.

68. Reinhold Niebuhr, "The Fight for Germany," *Life,* 21 October 1946, 72: "[I]t has been the unfortunate weakness of both liberalism and liberal Christianity that they have easily degenerated into sentimentality by refusing to contemplate the tragic aspects of human existence honestly." At the first meeting of the World Council of Churches

in 1948 Niebuhr denounced as "insufferable sentimentality" the hope of many Christians that "this conference will speak some simple moral word which will resolve by love the tragic conflict in the world community" ("Protestants Form a World Council," 40).

69. Editorial, "This Way to Suicide," *Life,* 22 January 1951, 36.

70. According to Niebuhr, Franklin D. Roosevelt had "succumbed to sentimentality" when he thought that he could convince the Russians of a mutual trust; see "For Peace, We Must Risk War," *Life,* 20 September 1948, 39.

71. Cover, *Life,* 7 April 1947; "American Sunday. *Life* Documents a Day," *Life,* 8 March 1943, 73–80; "Small Town Choir," *Life,* 11 May 1942, 83–86; "The Women Say Their Wartime Prayers," *Life,* 13 September 1943, 69–71; "Praying Boys: Atlanta Sunday-School Intercedes for Allied Leaders," *Life,* 22 November 1943, 49–50, 52; "Outlaw's Bridge: A small Southern Community Shows How a Church Can Lead the People," *Life,* 20 March 1944, 47–48, 50, 52; "Congregational Convention: Heirs of the Pilgrim Faith Meet to Preach and Practice Democracy," *Life,* 8 July 1946, 41–42, 44; "Life Goes to Sunday School," *Life,* 7 April 1947, 136–38, 141; "Church Builder: A Country Minister Works By Hand to Put Up the Place He Preaches In," *Life,* 22 November 1948, 135–36, 138; "Presbyterian Church," *Life,* 10 January 1949, 75–84; "Great American Churches," *Life,* 1 January 1951, 80–87.

72. "Science: A Mystery Story," *Life,* 23 June 1947, 30.

73. Letters to the editors, *Life,* 28 April 1947, 8.

74. Letters to the editors, *Life,* 14 July 1947, 7, 8.

75. Editorial, "Thanksgiving," *Life,* 24 November 1947, 38.

76. "Catholics Hold Huge Conference in Canada," *Life,* 14 July 1947, 25.

77. Wrightman Fox, *Religion USA,* 23; Baughman, *Henry R. Luce,* 182–83.

78. On evangelical Christianity and the mass media in North America, see David Paul Nord, "The Evangelical Origins of the Mass Media in America, 1815–1835," *Journalism Monographs,* no. 88 (1984), 1–30; Leonard I. Sweet, ed., *Communication and Change in American Religious History,* (Grand Rapids, Mich.: William B. Eerdmans Publishing Company, 1993); R. Laurence Moore, *Selling God: American Religion in the Marketplace of Culture* (New York: Oxford University Press, 1994). On Pat Robertson and televangelism, see Stewart M. Hoover, *Mass Media Religion: The Social Sources of the Electronic Church* (Newbury Park, Calif.: Sage, 1988). On the visual aspects of nineteenth-century evangelical publications, see Morgan, *Protestants and Pictures.*

8

WENDY KOZOL

GAZING AT RACE IN THE PAGES OF *LIFE*

Picturing Segregation through Theory and History

In 1956 *Life* published a five-part series titled "Segregation," which included a two-page genealogical chart of the Reverend and Mrs. William J. Faulkner and their family.[1] In the center of the layout is a color photograph of the couple with pictures of their children and grandchildren below them. Above are smaller black-and-white photographs of their ancestors. Staff writer Robert Wallace explained that what makes this a "typical" Negro family is the "fact that they have an admixture of white stock." He used this "fact" to destabilize the notion of racial purity: "A glance at the faces of the entire group raises this question: Who, or what, is a Negro?" To ask this question in 1956, a highly contested moment in American race relations, locates *Life*'s representation of race in a historically specific, yet politically ambiguous space. What is the magazine saying about race? And why is the family central to the "glance" at racial determination?

With an estimated postwar audience of twenty million, mostly white, middle-class readers, *Life* had great influence in shaping their knowledge about African Americans.[2] Thus, articles and photographs like these were more than reflections, more than just pictures of black experiences in the segregated South. As Wallace's question suggests, an a priori prerogative to define "who or what is a Negro?" and thus to represent race, structures this series' depiction of segregation. The shift from *who* to *what* foregrounds the objectification at the heart of this classification. "Gazing at" in my title calls attention to the centrality of looking at another in the process of defining race. Indeed, photojournalism's presumably neutral and objective gaze at race is anything but raceless. Instead, the presumption of neutrality reinforces the racial divisions in American society that depend on visual codes to define differences.

Since *Life*'s readers during the 1950s were primarily middle-class and white, one could easily argue that this series on segregation reinforced hegemonic white society by defining blacks as the Other. Yet such a generalized claim simplifies the historical complexities of seeing and being seen. We must be careful here not to assume a singular or monolithic gaze. In recent years theorists have argued that since spectators occupy multiple subject positions, looking is framed by and shaped by those social locations.[3] *Life* photographers used a variety of formal visual strategies, such as point of view and composition, to align the viewer's gaze with the camera's and/or the subject's gaze. The photographic subjects also gaze, both within the composition and in interaction with the camera, which further complicates acts of looking. Moreover, the diversified nature of production at the magazine raises questions about the authorship of the gaze.

Typically, *Life* did not give credit to, although at times we can speak of an authorial voice, either a writer or photographer with a byline.[4] This series, for instance, identified Robert Wallace as the writer for four of the five installments, but only the fourth segment assigned a photographic byline to Gordon Parks. In addition, it was the editors, not the photographers, at *Life* who had the power of selection and layout. Finally, photographers rarely participated in writing the text, a crucial part of anchoring meanings to visual images.[5] Therefore, when I discuss "*Life*'s gaze," I refer to the final product that readers saw, since this ultimately was the magazine's statement to its viewers. The concept of multiple gazes, however, enables us to be sensitive to

the diverse perspectives embedded in this product. As Catherine Lutz and Jane Collins explained, multiple gazes are "the source of many of the photograph's contradictions. . . . It is the root of much of the photograph's dynamism as a cultural object and the place where the analyst can perhaps most productively begin to trace its connection to the wider social world of which it is a part."[6]

The racial gazes in this series were not merely oppressive ones that constructed an inferior and exploited other, in part because the magazine was critical of racial violence and generally supportive of African Americans' civil rights. At the same time, in addressing the social and political conditions for African Americans, this series also reproduced normative ideals that in turn reinforced the racial identity of its readers. In other words, whiteness is never absent from this discourse. As Evelyn Brooks Higginbotham has argued, race is "a social construction predicated upon the recognition of difference and signifying the simultaneous distinguishing and positioning of groups vis-à-vis one another. More than this, race is a highly contested representation of relations of power between social categories by which individuals are identified and identify themselves."[7] This chapter takes up the question of multiple gazes and their contradictions to explore how *Life* represented postwar race relations. In other words, when *Life* responded to the Civil Rights movement in the postwar period, why did the camera gaze at black and, as we will see, white families? Moreover, what can we learn from this five-part series on segregation about looking as a historical act?

Film and photography scholars have increasingly examined the power of visual apparatuses to construct ways of seeing that reproduce and/or challenge social relations. Feminist film theorists, for example, often understood the gaze as inherently one of male privilege.[8] These scholars relied on psychoanalytic theories to examine how visual apparatuses appeal to male desires through processes of objectification. Recently, critics have made important arguments for complicating the ways in which we understand acts of looking.[9] They argue that a theory of the gaze that relies only on gender dualism excludes race, sexuality, and other key social relations from analysis. Linda Williams, for example, writes that while "psychoanalytically derived models of vision . . . have enabled the analysis of certain kinds of *power*—the voyeuristic, phallic power attributed to a 'male gaze'—they have sometimes crippled the understanding of diverse visual pleasures. . . ."[10] Looking is not always about controlling; there are times when we look with empathy, shared desires, etc. For instance, did *Life*'s readers perceive the degree of whiteness in the faces of the Faulkner family as reinforcing ideals of racial equality and assimilation so prevalent at the time? Or did it provoke anxieties about sexuality and racial purity? This ambiguity resonates with another ambiguity in the genealogical chart. All of the family members stare out, some smiling, some reserved, some perhaps even skeptical of the camera. What did these various looks say to the viewers? Can we read resistance, or alternatively compliance, in these smiling or unsmiling faces?

A related problem with psychoanalytic models is the tendency toward an ahistorical or universalizing theory.[11] Jane Gaines, for instance, has pointed out that "framing the question of male privilege and viewing pleasure as the 'right to look' may help us to rethink film theory along more materialist lines, considering, for instance, how some groups have historically had the license to 'look' openly while other groups have 'looked' illicitly."[12] In other words, theories of looking need to account for the historical relations of racial privilege and exclusion that permit certain gazes (such as the white male gaze at women of color), while taboos prohibit other gazes. For instance, a reading of the genealogical chart that relies on psychoanalytic theory can explain how visual images activate racist fears and desires. While drawing on earlier ways of seeing (such as nineteenth-century racial theories about physiognomy[13]), *Life*'s argument about racial mixture took place amid the heated politics of the 1950s Civil Rights movement. Notably, the text suppresses any dis-

cussion of interracial sexuality or sexual violence. As we will see, a historical perspective reveals that beyond psychic fears and desires, this suppression promoted racial equality as part of postwar national ideals of progress at the expense of examining sexuality in racial violence.[14]

The crucial point is that visual images do not merely reflect historical conditions but rather mediate those historical forces to shape social understandings of political struggles.[15] In this regard, photographic historians have pushed debates about the gaze from the psychoanalytic to the social. They have explored the power of the camera's surveilling gaze to classify social groups, implicating photography in such processes as class formation and the colonizing power of the nation state.[16] As Lutz and Collins wrote, "the crucial role of photography in the exercise of power lies in its ability to allow for close study of the other and to promote, in Foucault's words 'the normalizing gaze,' a surveillance that makes it possible to qualify, to classify and to punish."[17] When *Life* turned the camera's "normalizing gaze" to classify African Americans, it aligned 1950s assimilationist concepts of race with postwar national ideologies about liberal progress, equality, and domesticity. The series accomplished this effect by focusing on African American families, such as the Faulkners. In a magazine that routinely represented news events through the lens of domesticity, picturing African Americans as members of nuclear families legitimized them. Notably, the genealogical chart is reminiscent of numerous layouts in *Life* that simulated family photo albums.[18] In eliding difference, however, this visual attention to African Americans as family members came at the expense of representations of political activism.

Although *Life*'s editors tended to promote conservative political positions, especially in Cold War politics, the magazine accepted African Americans' demands for legal equality. The five-part series stands out as a privileged statement on race by the editors, apparent in the extended length of the series, its promotion on the covers, and lavish use of expensive color plates. Yet this series offered a complex and often contradictory commentary about Southern race relations in 1956, a crucial moment in the Civil Rights movement when increasingly violent responses to integration by whites challenged major successes like *Brown v. Board of Education* (1954) and the Montgomery bus boycott (1955). While condemning racial violence, the journalistic pressure to be objective (and perhaps also a desire not to alienate Southern readers) resulted in the inclusion of a sympathetic photo-essay about white segregationists. Pictures of white families in this photo-essay complicated the representation of domesticity and race. Even a surveilling or normalizing gaze is not monolithic, since domesticity normalized both African Americans and whites, but with highly different consequences. Varied images of domesticity expose how multiple gazes both reproduced dominant ideals and functioned as a site of contestation over social and political meanings.

This demonstrates the complex role of "looking" in the politics of contemporary social movements. Increasingly since the postwar period, political activism has become dependent on visual media for publicity.[19] How visual representations depict activism, therefore, is crucial to audiences' perceptions about social problems and of the people working to alleviating those problems.

As the essays in this volume demonstrate, *Life* defined the terms of visuality at mid-century. Particularly acute consequences occurred in depictions of postwar race relations, since efforts to represent African Americans within the narrative and visual conventions of the magazine competed with, and at times contradicted, the prevailing social and political agendas.

Civil-rights struggles, including economic boycotts, school and housing integration, and voting-rights efforts, were among the most contentious issues facing postwar Americans. As Michael Omi and Howard Winant have observed, "The postwar period has indeed been a racial crucible. During these decades, new conceptions of racial identity and its meaning, new modes of political organization and confrontation, and

new definitions of the state's role in promoting and achieving 'equality' were explored, debated, and fought out on the battlegrounds of politics."[20] As one of the most prominent sources of visual news, *Life* magazine was instrumental in *showing* white Americans these struggles and defining the terms of debate. The editors explained in the introduction that the 1956 series was produced in response to the national crisis created by the 1954 Supreme Court decision, *Brown v. Board of Education.* From the outset, then, the editors framed their discussion of segregation around the theme of crisis— one that directly linked civil rights to national concerns. *Life* mediated, rather than merely reflected, historical relations by focusing on the socioeconomic problems of African Americans, as opposed to white racism, as the crucial challenge affecting blacks.

The representation of history in this series established at the outset the definition of race as a social problem. The first installment discussed the slave trade, economic and social conditions of slavery, and the political conflicts leading up to the Civil War. The photo-essay began with contemporary photographs of West Africa and captions that claimed that these images showed a social world that had not changed in four hundred years.[21] This idealized image of Africa placed the continent and its peoples outside of historical time. The essay then included paintings (commissioned for this series) of an Ashanti court and a coffle of West Indian slaves. While condemning the brutality and exploitation of slavery, the text also pointed out that whites were not the only ones to use slaves and Africans routinely enslaved each other, thus diminishing Euro-Americans accountability. Significantly, in this historical review there is only one picture of a black leader, Booker T. Washington. The discussion of abolitionism featured William Lloyd Garrison, not the many African Americans who fought for the end of slavery or against lynching. Instead, the series presented blacks only as victims of oppression, as the social problem that the (white) nation must resolve.

The second installment referred to the war briefly

and then turned to the rise of the Ku Klux Klan, lynchings, and Jim Crow laws.[22] One especially disturbing photograph of a lynching from 1919 demonstrates how a sympathetic gaze that condemned racial violence nonetheless also reinforced white paternalism.[23] This image shows an African American burning on a pyre in front of a jeering crowd of men looking into the camera. The composition encourages us to gaze first at the foreground, which establishes an intimacy with the subject of the violence. Hence, the camera's and the viewer's gaze aligns against the white men who unself-consciously stare back. At the visual level, then, the camera's gaze challenges the white lynchers' gaze. The photograph and the accompanying text on lynching, however, remain part of a now-distant past, since there is no discussion of later racial violence or African American struggles for justice. As with the pictures of contemporary Africa, the layout disconnects the viewer's gaze from historical responsibility and, instead, aligns it with a national gaze at a localized problem.

Figure 8.1. A group of eminent black churchmen outside the U.S. Supreme Court, from "Momentous Reversal in the Court," *Life,* September 10, 1956. (Courtesy Edward Clark/TimePix)

In the introduction, the editors announced their intention to publish a separate essay on northern racism, but, to my knowledge, this was never done.[24] Instead, civil rights was portrayed as a regional issue that reinforced a common historical myth of Southern racial exceptionalism.[25] After the lynching photograph, the text reported on the 1954 Supreme Court decision, accompanied by a two-page low-angle shot dramatically depicting the facade of the court building (Figure 8.1).[26] Jumping from 1919 to the present, this symbol of American judicial ideals narratively signifies the nation's progress on race relations. The inscription across the pediment of the building, EQUAL JUSTICE FOR ALL, is clearly readable at the top of the image. On the steps of the building a group of African American clergy kneel in prayer. The caption explains that they are praying "for the speedy integration of public schools." Associating the clergy with national ideals was consistent with the magazine's view of African American struggles as part of a steady American progression toward greater democracy.[27]

This image itself is rife with ambiguity, since the monumental scale of the building dwarfs the figures. The camera's gaze places the viewer in a powerful position, as we look down at these small figures with heads bowed. These figures could be read as nonthreatening (because small), obedient (kneeling with bowed heads), or, by contrast, as part of a greater national ideal of freedom and democracy. In this regard, it is significant that the series discussed race relations and segregation only in terms of the South. For instance, *Life* explained that the legal doctrine of separate but equal "was emphatically the will of the white South, and the other sections of the nation acquiesced. But, in the 1930s the opinion in the north, east and west, a majority of the people, began to change. There-

FACES OF THE CONTEMPORARY AMERICAN NEGRO

The mixture of stocks found in the Faulkner family on the preceding pages is also found in Negro society as a whole. In this cross-section of Chicago professional, business and laboring men, non-Negro characteristics are pronounced—Byron Minor (*top row, left*) and Byron Turnquest (*second row from top, third from left*) have reddish hair. Thomas Pitts (*second row from bottom, extreme left*), one of whose grandparents was an American Indian, appears to be more Indian than Negro. Some, such as David Kilgore (*second row from top, second from left*), have an almost pure Negro ancestry. But others, such as Archibald Le Cesne (*bottom row, second from left*), contain so strong an admixture of white blood that, if they were not proud of their Negro heritage and did not choose to live in Negro society, they would be accepted ♥ "white."

Opposite: Figure 8.2. "Faces of the Contemporary American Negro," *Life,* September 10, 1956. (Courtesy Jerry Cooke/TimePix) *Left:* Figure 8.3. "Mr. and Mrs. Albert Thornton," *Life,* September 24, 1956. (Courtesy Gordon Parks/TimePix)

upon the court too began to change." Framing segregation as a Southern problem protected the nation from the taint of racism even when the editorial tone was supportive of civil rights.

The next essay in the series is concluded with a full-page color photograph of twenty-five African American men (Figure 8.2).[28] Unlike the Faulkner family genealogical chart, here none of the men look at the camera. They all pose in three-quarter profile, and the viewer can now look with impunity since the subjects

do not look back. The caption points out "non-Negro" characteristics, such as a man with reddish hair, another who appears to be "more Indian than Negro," and those with light skin who, "if they were not so proud of their Negro heritage and did not choose to live in Negro society, they would be accepted as white." Although the writer argues against concepts of racial purity, an essentializing quality persists as we are invited to peer at skin color and other physiognomic characteristics.

Figure 8.4. Professor Thornton at a segregated bus station, from "A Professor's Injured Pride," *Life,* **September 24, 1956. (Courtesy Gordon Parks/TimePix)**

The layout relies on physical characteristics to construct a racial gaze that once again suggests that we can *see* race. Indeed, even as the text points out the problems with miscegenation laws that try to determine race through the percentage of blood, this photo-essay reduces race to a biological essence. Here, as elsewhere in the series, *Life*'s gaze at race also addressed whiteness. The captions repeatedly emphasized the closeness or distance of skin color to whiteness. In the discussion of the Faulkners, the text reads, "One branch of the family . . . has such light skin that it is accepted as white. Many U.S. Negro families have such a branch. Since 1900 several hundred thousand Americans having a portion of Negro ancestry may have 'passed' or become 'white.'"[29] The shift from a historical review to this discussion of genealogy and passing appears curious only until we consider these images within the context of *Life*'s liberal humanism. Following the photograph of the Supreme Court, the statement "there is no such thing as an exclusively Negro race" reinforces the liberal ideal that race does not matter. If blacks have white and Indian blood, then are we not all the same underneath?

Omi and Winant have contended that the dominant racial theory in the 1940s and 1950s was the ethnicity paradigm.[30] Postwar critics viewed race as a type of ethnicity, relying on a model of European immigration to claim that equal opportunity would eliminate racial distinctions and that individual achievement would enable blacks to overcome unfair barriers. While this vision proved to be problematic, dismantled by other theories of race in the 1960s, in the 1950s civil-rights activists used this argument to marshal radical and moderate forces in the fight against inequality in the South.[31] Evaluating blacks in terms of the degree of whiteness in their skin upheld (albeit crudely) this model of ethnicity. Therefore, *Life*'s gaze normalized an ideal of whiteness by which to judge the progress of African Americans.

The fourth installment, which concerns another African American family, demonstrates how this theory shaped the representation of race in this series.[32] Here, the photo-essay presented a narrative of economic progress from Mr. and Mrs. Albert Thornton (Figure 8.3), the sharecropper parents, to a schoolteacher daughter and her husband, a successful but illiterate businessman, to a son who is a university professor (Figure 8.4). *Life*'s writer, Robert Wallace, stated, however, that further progress had been halted because of "restraints." Using this euphemism for segregation, he explained that economic restraints against professor Thornton "are negligible, but social restraints remain strong . . . while some restraints are removed because he is an above-average citizen, remaining restraints are more wounding to him, for the same reason."[33]

Sequential photographs reinforced Wallace's claim of progress by moving from a picture of sharecroppers through pictures of individual families of varying economic status to the final spread of the professor and his wife, which included a photograph of them in formal attire at a university function. These images narrow the visual focus to an upwardly mobile black family working within the system but constrained by unfair barriers. The photo-essay's focus on individualism and the nuclear family offered a problematic and limiting representation of race that denied the politics of racial difference and the importance of community.

A theory of multiple gazes enables us to consider who is looking at whom and the racial consequences of that looking. What did it mean when white readers examined the faces of a black family to gauge their degrees of whiteness, or looked down on those small figures of the clergy? Did they associate the blacks in these photos with subordinate (smaller) status, or did they see them as ordinary citizens? Amid escalating postwar tensions over integration, *Life* supported the Supreme Court decision and advocated integration as the law. Yet, competing ideals appeared in the series because the magazine's address to its white readers often relied on a racial ideology at odds with its own critique of segregation.

Whiteness was not a stable category in this series (or

elsewhere for that matter). Instead, contradictions in these photo-essays spoke to social anxieties about race and conflicts over ideals of whiteness. *Life*'s recurring themes of normalcy and deviance depended on concepts of gender, sexuality, and domesticity that demonstrate the historically contested nature of racial ideologies. The magazine's promotion of color-blind and power-evasive rhetorics of race helped to shape the postwar national imagination about race and racial conflict, creating a visual construct that continues to dominate popular debates today. Contemporary debates over affirmative action, for instance, still revolve around concepts of progress, merit, and color blindness. Assessments of merit or progress in turn have their historical (and visual) antecedents in the postwar period.

Brown v. Board of Education was a cataclysmic decision that provoked violent responses from white segregationists who no longer felt they had other forms of legal redress. In news stories in the same issues as the special series, *Life* reported on Southern whites' opposition to integrating public schools.[34] The editorial tone condemned the lawlessness of white segregationists and praised those whites whose belief in the law took precedence over their antipathy to integration.

This viewpoint is most apparent in the third series installment, "The Voices of the White South," which featured five white segregationists who articulated their racist anxieties, especially fears about miscegenation.[35] In the magazine's attempt to be fair and objective, the essay gave voice to these segregationists without commentary. It featured white men from different classes (a mayor, a sharecropper, a mechanic, an office worker, and an owner of a plantation) who all supported segregation. While this strategy acknowledged economic differences, it undermined any potential for class solidarity between blacks and whites or any critique of capitalism by depicting different individuals who held the same beliefs about segregation. This portrayal normalized racism as beliefs shared by people from different walks of life.

The essay's photographs depicted a benevolent South where the two races lived in harmonious small towns. One spread featured the mayor of Greenville, South Carolina, who supported "equalization," not integration. In the spread there is a picture of a swimming pool full of African Americans having a good time, a pool that the mayor built "for them." These images imply a caring white paternalism, and, according to the mayor, there is "no race trouble here, and won't be, unless an agitator comes in and stirs things up."[36] The absence of photographs of the active and ongoing struggles against segregation within African American communities left unquestioned this claim that outsiders would disrupt otherwise harmonious relations. Moreover, this reference to outsiders who threaten social stability reminded readers of thier concurrent anticommunist fears.

The layout featuring the plantation owner offered the most stereotypical images of the Old South. One picture shows the owner and his wife walking down a grand staircase while dressed in formal clothing. Another photograph depicts the owner supervising his workers in the fields. The owner's back is to the camera in the foreground, so that the viewer looks with him into the background at the black field hands. Yet this picture raises questions about how the spectator perceives the politics of the image. In 1956, did viewers gaze sympathetically with the owner, seeing his economic prosperity and accepting the text's explanation of his benevolent concern for his workers' health? Or did they remember the earlier picture of the lynching and associate the workers picking cotton with slave practices? Clearly, we cannot answer this question, but just as we can envision multiple readings, so too would readers in 1956 bring various political perspectives to their viewing of this series. Since viewing practices do not isolate individual pictures or photo-essays, these competing images of Southern race relations provide ambiguous, and often contradictory, messages about race and segregation.

In general, the editorial agenda of the series appears critical of the inequalities of Southern segregation. Because the editors in this series relied on representational conventions popular in the magazine, many of the photographs depict scenes familiar to its readers. This familiarity at times legitimized a social politics at odds with the magazine's critique of Jim Crow. With the exception of the unmarried mayor, each story included a family picture. Domestic ideology pervaded postwar culture, including *Life* magazine, which routinely turned to white middle-class families to represent social and national concerns.[37] Pictures of families in the third installment placed white segregationists within a wider national ideal of family values. This, in conjunction with comments that described these men as "thoughtful, pious gentlefolk—who are still in favor of segregation," constructed racial conflicts as differences of opinion.[38] For instance, the layout about the sharecropper included several pictures of family members working on the tobacco farm. According to the text, the white family's hard work had paid off in the form of a recently purchased harvester, depicted in a full-page photograph. Even recreation was wholesome, as the farmer was shown relaxing in a country store and drinking a soda. Such images were familiar and accepted norms of social behavior. The narrative underscored the connections between these social norms and whiteness through the sharecropper's comparison of his family's hard work with blacks who did not work as hard and "just don't care."

Also reinforcing the normative whiteness of socially approved behavior is a two-page layout featuring pictures of African American deviance. Beginning with a picture of black couples dancing in a juke joint, the narrative proceeds to a street brawl broken up by white police, and a couple being charged with a domestic dispute. Such transgressive behavior and the presence of white policemen visually contrast with the white families on the previous pages. The final photograph in this two-page spread depicts a white girl with her back to the camera looking at a chain gang of black prisoners. The composition encourages the viewer to look with the female at the black male criminals.

The complex gazes here—the white girl looking at the chain gang, the camera looking at the girl, the viewer's gaze at the "transgressive behavior"—play out common notions about race and sexuality, notably myths about dangerous black men who threaten white women. Such images reinforced the concerns expressed by white segregationists about integration, namely the fear of miscegenation. As Wallace wrote, millions of Southerners feel that "the end of segregation will soon lead to intermarriage between white and Negro on a large scale." One of the men interviewed "calls it amalgamation and dreads it." Fear of miscegenation, in turn, connected anxieties about whiteness to nationhood. At the end of this essay, Wallace quoted Governor Herman Talmadge of Georgia: "Certainly history shows that nations composed of a mongrel race lose their strength and become weak, lazy and indifferent. They become easy prey to outside nations. And isn't that just exactly what the Communists want to happen to the United States?"[39] Talmadge's anti-Communist rhetoric vividly articulates the centrality of racial myths to postwar national ideologies. Moreover, the historical resonance of this rhetoric calls attention to the persistence of these mythologies about racial deviance. For instance, current debates about individual rights and government responsibility frequently blame black women on welfare for their financial predicaments.

Talmadge's fears of a mongrel race also articulate the presence of sexuality in discursive struggles around race and nation. Here we need to return to the genealogical chart and the photograph of African American men (see Figure 8.2) in the second installment. The editors used these photographs to discredit laws against miscegenation. Yet, the text perpetuates silences on the history of sexual violence against black women, as well as the history of intimate interracial relations, by never discussing how this blood became mixed. Instead, the writer voices these anxieties in terms of marriage. Domesticity, which was so much at the heart of *Life*'s representation of the nation, here links the sexual threat to family and ultimately national

Figure 8.5. Ondria
Tanner and grand-
mother window shop-
ping, from "The Editors
of *Life* Present a Series
on the Background of
Segregation," *Life,*
September 24, 1956.
(Courtesy Gordon
Parks/TimePix)

WINDOW-SHOPPING, Ondria Tanner and grand-mother, Ondria Thornton, look at fashions. They look long, buy carefully because of limited funds.

OUTSIDE LOOKING IN, the three young Tanners and three friends watch some children at a play-ground in a white neighborhood not far from theirs.

ideals. By implication, miscegenation threatened to taint or contaminate the whiteness at the heart of popular visions of middle-class domesticity. Such anxieties spoke to the interrelated ideals of whiteness, family, and nationhood.

Such images of domesticity demonstrate that race and gender are never isolated or distinct categories but rather always intersect each other. As Higginbotham has argued, "in societies where racial demarcation is endemic to their sociocultural fabric and heritage . . . gender identity is inextricably linked to and even determined by racial identity."[40] Given the historical

meanings of domesticity in the postwar period, it is significant that *Life*'s fourth installment turned to family imagery to represent African Americans' experiences of segregation.[41] Equally important, the photographer for this photo-essay, Gordon Parks, was the only photographer in the series to receive a byline. The appearance of a byline signaled Parks's recognized status in the 1950s and the privileging of his vision by the magazine. Although some of Parks's photographs conformed to domestic ideals prevalent throughout the magazine, in significant ways this photo-essay differed from others in the series. In our discussion, then, we also need to consider the photographer's gaze, which was, at least here, distinct from, if not a challenge to, *Life*'s vision of racial progress.

The essay opens with a full-page photograph of an elderly couple, Mrs. and Mrs. Albert Thornton, seated on a sofa staring directly at the camera (see Figure 8.3). Can we read resistance in their gaze back at the camera? By confronting the viewer, could this picture confront racist ideologies or did the other pictures in the series, as well as the dominant emphasis on white America in this magazine, overwhelm such challenges? While we cannot know what individual viewers thought, we can explore the significance of the Thorntons' gaze, and Parks's gaze at them, within the cultural and social politics of the time period.

Photographing the Thorntons as a nuclear family enables them to look like the families *Life*'s readers routinely saw in the magazine. Only one small photograph shows the large Thornton family, and even here no extended family beyond children and grandchildren appeared. Instead, in a series of two-page stories, the essay featured the Thorntons' children as individual nuclear families. Thus, the layout presents only a heterosexual, nuclear family norm for this African American family, at the expense of other family and community relationships. This includes the first picture of Mr. and Mrs. Thornton, which conforms to traditions of family portraiture and to that extent is contained by the genre, despite the potential resistance of their gaze.

Only two of the Thornton photographs signal the importance of community relations for African Americans. One picture depicts a girl being helped by a male passerby while she drinks at a water fountain, with two other women looking on as they walk past. Whether Parks only shot a few such photographs or the editors decided to use only the pictures of nuclear families, the published photo-essay includes just this photograph and a small picture of a church congregation to represent community. This is a significant omission since the Civil Rights movement depended so much on the

strengths of the community.[42] Instead of looking at community to tell the story of black responses to racism, *Life* turns to the family to legitimize its support for African Americans' struggles. In some ways, then, this photo-essay, like the series, depends on white models of domesticity to construct "who or what is a Negro." These family pictures demonstrate the benefits of a historical rather than a psychoanalytic analysis. The tendency in psychoanalytic theory toward universal claims runs the danger of imposing white middle-class family ideals onto other types of family arrangements.[43] Instead, this gaze at the Thorntons mobilized postwar ideals of (white) domesticity. Domesticity legitimized this African American family, but not in some kind of universalized notion of family; rather, meanings are activated within the context of a postwar hegemonic discourse that ignored cultural differences.

Even as the photo-essay conforms in some ways to *Life*'s conventions of focusing on individual families, however, another vision of race appears. As Stuart Hall has written, "It would be . . . wrong to read these portraits as exclusively the result of the imposition of codes of formal (white) portrait photography on an alien (black) subject, for that simplification would be precisely to collude, however, unconsciously, with the construction of [blacks] as objects, always 'outside time,' outside history."[44] The Thornton's unsmiling, stern faces, as well as their age and the poverty of their surroundings could challenge the ideals of domesticity they were meant to encode. There are also other pictures in this photo-essay that more overtly destabilize the social norms popularized in the magazine.

Like the white girl looking at the chain gang, two photographs in this photo-essay use a similar composition of a foreground figure whose back to the camera directs the viewer's gaze to the background. Parks's images, however, challenge assumptions about a monolithic gaze of power. In both pictures, the subjects of the camera's gaze, African Americans, look at signs of whiteness. The first depicts a black woman and her

Figure 8.6. Six young children, from "The Editors of *Life* Present a Series on the Background of Segregation," *Life*, September 24, 1956. (Courtesy Gordon Parks/TimePix)

young granddaughter window shopping (Figure 8.5). The granddaughter leans on the glass as she peers at the white female mannequins, which signify popular, commercial ideals of femininity. While the girl's leaning body suggests desire for the image and the products they are selling, her gaze and the window separating her from the mannequins emphatically underlines racial differences. Parks's photograph of exclusion turns this white ideal of femininity, protected so fiercely in Southern culture, into a symbol of Jim Crow. Parks relies on gender here to question social ideals of whiteness.

On the page opposite this picture, another photograph shows six African American children with their backs to the camera looking through a chain-link fence at a park with amusement rides (Figure 8.6). The caption reminds the viewer that these children can only watch the white children at the playground. These images of racial difference and exclusion encode a different gaze than the plantation owner or the white girl's gaze at a chain gang. While it is a gaze by the powerless at that from which they are excluded, Parks's gaze and the images themselves are not powerless. Parks challenges the seemingly stable ideology of domesticity by linking images of children playing or a grandmother and granddaughter to the hard truth of segregation. Again, a historical reading helps us to move beyond a generalized statement about the gaze of the powerless who confront oppressive institutions. In this photoessay, Parks draws on postwar domestic ideals, especially ideals of femininity and childhood innocence, to portray the effects of segregation. This strategy in turn demonstrates that domesticity is not monolithic or universal, but rather a historical construct subject to challenges and reappropriations.

Although Parks's photographs directly confront racial barriers, neither here nor elsewhere in the series does *Life* include specific images of African American activism. This absence is equally apparent in the fifth and final installment. The series ends not with more photographs, but with a lengthy roundtable discussion between white Christian ministers debating whether the church should participate actively in integration efforts.[45] By concluding with ministers, not civil-rights activists, *Life* avoided a discussion of political and legal solutions, and instead framed the problem of segregation as a moral issue. The ministers agree that nowhere does the Bible condone segregation. Instead, they debate whether or not the church has a moral obligation to participate in efforts to change race relations. Some ministers emphatically insist that this is their moral duty, while others argue that Southerners are making changes, and that any efforts to hurry along the process will damage these developments. Like the rest of the series, this roundtable presented blacks as the problem, but these ministers made it a moral dilemma. By giving equal weight to both sides, as in earlier photo-essays, the roundtable legitimized segregation as a debatable issue.

Life's special series on postwar race relations illustrates important theoretical issues about acts of looking. How the camera visualizes the problem, who the viewer gazes at, and the varied meanings of those gazes affect how we explore the politics of representation. When scholars discuss a racial gaze, they should consider that this gaze is also always about sexuality, gender, national ideals, class, and other forms of power. Gazes convey multiple meanings with varied, unstable, and often unpredictable effects. Rather than conclude that photographs are open to infinite interpretations,

however, a historical perspective reveals that gazes hold particular meanings within their specific social, cultural, and political contexts.

Life's series on segregation was just as much about liberalism, nationalism, and democracy, as it was about family, sexuality, and whiteness. Whiteness was implicated not only through what whites bestow on or do to blacks, but also through the family, gender, and sexual norms promoted throughout the magazine. *Life*'s representation of race relations encoded social and political ideals that legitimated blacks within a national ideal in problematic ways and also limited readers' knowledge about African American families, communities, and activism. As Parks's photographs demonstrate, however, this was not a monolithic, stable, or uniform message but one open to critique and revision through alternative ways of seeing race. These varied ways of seeing were tremendously influential in shaping *Life*'s readers' knowledge about African Americans, race relations, segregation, and the struggle for civil rights during the postwar period.

Life's complex visual statements about race depended not only on silences about African American activism and past instances of sexual violence, but also on the presence of certain legitimizing discourses such as domesticity. The magazine's series on segregation in turn had important social and political consequences for later understandings of race relations. *Life*'s implication that nuclear families were at the heart of civil rights produced ways of seeing that ultimately condemned the worst practices of Jim Crow. However, this visual legacy has also severely circumscribed racial discourses. Most notably, devaluations of African American families that fail to resemble this progressive ideal have maintained a persistent presence in political discourse from the 1965 Moynihan Report to recent caricatures of welfare queens. These racialized images of domestic deviance owe much to visual codifications of race relations such as those in *Life*'s series on the segregated South of the 1950s.

I wish to thank A. G. Miller, Paula Richman, and Sandy Zagarell for a most productive and fun brainstorming session. Wendy Hesford, Christin Mamiya, Andrea Volpe, and Steven Wojtal all gave valuable support and insightful criticisms. I am most grateful to Erika Doss, both for her comments on this chapter and for her energies and commitment to developing critical perspectives on *Life* magazine.

1. Robert Wallace, "Freedom to Jim Crow," *Life,* 10 September 1956, 106–7. The other photo-essays in the series appeared on September 3, 17, 24, and October 1, 1956.

2. See *N. W. Ayer and Son's Directory: Newspapers and Periodicals* (Philadelphia: N. W. Ayer and Son, annual volumes) for circulation rates. Throughout the magazine's history, *Life* commissioned demographic and marketing studies to determine the composition and consumption habits of its readership. These studies clearly profile the racial and class status of its readers. See, for example, Life *Study of Consumer Expenditures,* conducted for *Life* by Alfred Politz Research (New York: Time, 1957).

3. See, for example, Linda Williams, "Something Else Besides a Mother: *Stella Dallas* and the Maternal Melodrama," *Cinema Journal* 24, no. 1 (Fall 1984): 2–27; Stuart Hall, "Reconstruction Work: Images of Post-War Black Settlement," in *Family Snaps: The Meanings of Domestic Photography,* ed. Jo Spence and Patricia Holland (London: Virago, 1991), 152–64; and Catherine A. Lutz and Jane L. Collins, *Reading* National Geographic (Chicago: University of Chicago Press, 1993), 192.

4. *Life* typically reserved bylines for lengthy photo-essays by famous photographers. Even then, photographers had difficulties with the magazine about credit. For a discussion of this issue, see Vicki Goldberg, *Margaret Bourke-White: A Biography* (New York: Harper and Row, 1986), 194–95.

5. See Roland Barthes, *Image—Music—Text,* trans. Stephen Heath (New York: Hill and Wang, 1977), 38–41, for his now-classic discussion of anchorage. Conflicts with the *Life* staff over editorial control led some photographers, like W. Eugene Smith, to resign from the magazine; see Loudon Wainwright, *The Great American Magazine: An Inside History of* Life (New York: Knopf, 1986), 149–50.

6. Lutz and Collins, *Reading* National Geographic, 216.

7. Evelyn Brooks Higginbotham, "African-American Women's History and the Metalanguage of Race," *Signs: Journal of Women in Culture and Society* 17, no. 2 (Winter 1992): 253.

8. See Laura Mulvey's landmark essay, "Visual Pleasure and Narrative Cinema," *Screen* 16, no. 3 (Autumn 1975): 6–18; reprinted in *Visual and Other Pleasures* (Bloomington: Indiana University Press, 1989). For other discussions of *Screen* theory, see, for example, Constance Penley, ed., *Feminism and Film Theory* (New York: Routledge, 1988).

9. See, for example, Teresa De Lauretis, *Technologies of Gender: Essays on Theory, Film, and Fiction* (Bloomington: Indiana University Press, 1987); Jane Gaines, "White Privilege and Looking Relations: Race and Gender in Feminist Film Theory," *Screen* 29, no. 4 (1988): 12–27; bell hooks, "The Oppositional Gaze: Black Female Spectators," *Black Looks: Race and Representation* (Boston: South End Press, 1992): 115–31. See also E. Deidre Pribram, ed., *Female Spectators: Looking at Film and Television* (London: Verso, 1988), and Lutz and Collins, *Reading* National Geographic, 187–92, for other recent examinations of theories of the gaze.

10. Linda Williams, "Corporealized Observers: Visual Pornographies and the 'Carnal Density of Vision,'" in *Fugitive Images: From Photograph to Video,* ed. Patrice Petro (Bloomington: Indiana University Press, 1995), 6.

11. Linda Williams, "Feminist Film Theory: *Mildred Pierce* and the Second World War," in Pribram, *Female Spectators,* 12–30.

12. Gaines, "White Privilege and Looking Relations," 24–25.

13. See Brian Wallis, "Black Bodies, White Science: Louis Agassiz's Slave Daguerreotypes," *American Art* 9, no. 2 (Summer 1995): 39–61, for an analysis of how Agassiz used photographs of slaves to naturalize arguments about race and biology.

14. Consider, for instance, the 1955 lynching case of Emmett Till, in which Till's alleged sexual action toward a white woman was the source of provocation for this violence. For an in-depth discussion of this case, see Stephen Whitfield, *A Death in the Delta: The Story of Emmett Till* (New York: Free Press, 1988).

15. Williams, "Feminist Film Theory," 19, similarly cautions film studies against relying on sociological perspectives that read texts as reflecting isolated political and historical referents. She argues that film analyses need "to account for the complex ways in which a text mediates, rather than simply reflects, history."

16. See John Tagg, *The Burden of Representation: Essays on Photographies and Histories* (Amherst: University of Massachusetts Press, 1988); Allan Sekula, "The Body and the Archive," in *The Contest of Meaning: Critical Histories of Photography,* ed. Richard Bolton (Cambridge, Mass.: MIT Press, 1989), 342–88; and Lutz and Collins, *Reading* National Geographic. For a discussion of photography and colonization, see, for example, Malek Alloula, *The Colonial Harem* (Minneapolis: University of Minnesota Press, 1986); David Green, "Classified Subjects," *Ten/8* 14: 30–37; and Sarah Graham-Brown, *Images of Women: The Portrayal of Women in Photography of the Middle East, 1860–1950* (London: Quartet Books, 1988).

17. Lutz and Collins, *Reading* National Geographic, 192.

18. *Life* used this format from the first issue, 23 November 1936, in a photo-essay about Franklin D. Roosevelt.

19. See Todd Gitlin, *The Whole World Is Watching: Mass Media in the*

Making and Unmaking of the New Left (Berkeley: University of California Press, 1980).

20. Michael Omi and Howard Winant, *Racial Formation in the United States* (New York: Routledge and Kegan Paul, 1986), 89.

21. Robert Wallace, "How the Negro Came to Slavery in America," *Life,* 3 September 1956, 44–64, especially 44–54.

22. Wallace, "Freedom to Jim Crow," 96–108.

23. Ibid., 102.

24. "The Editors of *Life* Present a Series on the Background of Segregation," *Life,* 3 September 1956, 43.

25. I thank Andrea Volpe for this insight.

26. Wallace, "Freedom to Jim Crow," 104–5.

27. Wendy Kozol, Life's *America: Family and Nation in Postwar Photojournalism* (Philadelphia: Temple University Press, 1994), 143–56.

28. Wallace, "Freedom to Jim Crow," 108.

29. Ibid., 106.

30. Omi and Winant, *Racial Formation in the United States,* chap. 1.

31. Ibid., 90.

32. Wallace, "The Restraints: Open and Hidden," *Life,* 24 September 1956, 98–112.

33. Ibid., 108.

34. See, for example, "The Halting and Fitful Battle for Integration," *Life,* 17 September 1956, 34–41; and "The Lonely Hostages of a South in Strife," *Life,* 24 September 1956, 46–49.

35. Robert Wallace, "The Voices of the White South," *Life,* 17 September 1956, 104–20.

36. Ibid., 109.

37. For discussions of postwar domestic ideology, see Elaine Tyler May, *Homeward Bound: American Families in the Cold War Era* (New York: Basic Books, 1988); Lynn Spigel, *Make Room for TV: Television and the Family Ideal in Postwar America* (Chicago: University of Chicago Press, 1992); and Kozol, Life's *America.*

38. Wallace, "The Voices of the White South," 104.

39. Ibid., 119.

40. Higginbotham, "African-American Women's History and the Metalanguage of Race," 254.

41. Wallace, "The Restraints: Open and Hidden," 98–112.

42. For instance, a year before *Life*'s special series, African Americans in Montgomery, Alabama, worked together as a community, car pooling, walking in groups to work, and resisting coercive pressure in order to sustain the boycott. See Aldon D. Morris, *The Origins of the Civil Rights Movement: Black Communities Organizing for Change* (New York: Free Press, 1984), especially 40–63.

43. Gaines, "White Privilege and Looking Relations," 12–13.

44. Hall, "Reconstruction Work," 156.

45. "A Round Table Has Debate on Christians' Moral Duty," *Life,* 1 October 1956, 140–62.

PART FOUR   TO SEE THINGS THOUSANDS
OF MILES AWAY, THINGS
HIDDEN BEHIND WALLS AND
WITHIN ROOMS, THINGS
DANGEROUS TO COME TO;
THE WOMEN THAT MEN LOVE

JOHN IBSON

MASCULINITY UNDER FIRE

Life's Presentation of Camaraderie and Homoeroticism before, during, and after the Second World War

In Allen Drury's 1959 best-seller *Advise and Consent,* a World War II veteran recalls to his wife his wartime love affair with another man. "People go off the track sometimes, under pressures like the war," Senator Brigham Anderson explained. "That's what happened to me. I went off the track." Despite his characterization of the affair as a singular deviation, the senator refuses to accept his wife's description of it as "a horrible thing." "It didn't seem horrible at the time," Anderson insists, "and I am not going to say now that it did, even to you." Portrayed by Drury as a Mormon model of rectitude in the 1950s, Anderson sees his postwar posture as an attempt to atone for his warmly if guiltily recalled time "off the track" during the war. "I have lived all of my life since being as good a man as I could, to make up for it," he says.[1] The novel's depiction of Anderson is one of the most appealing, elaborate, and complex portraits of a character with a homosexual dimension in American fiction up to its time. Drury, nonetheless, eventually has Anderson, a man whose sexuality and whose very person could not survive in the years immediately following the Second World War, die by his own hand.[2]

The various dislocations wrought by World War II subverted traditional gender prescriptions, among them the strictures regarding American males' relationships with one another.[3] Once the war ended,

Figure 9.1. Advertisement for Four Roses Whiskey, *Life*, January 15, 1940. (Courtesy Four Roses)

though, attachments allowed or even promoted in wartime were discouraged or rendered sinister. In its photographs, news stories, and especially its abundant advertisements, *Life* magazine was elaborately and interestingly involved in this process of sexual reorientation. On an unprecedented scale, the war seriously challenged America's tidy dichotomizing of erotic expression into heterosexual and homosexual realms.

Similarly, reviewing the history of wartime masculinity, focusing especially on *Life*'s iconography of maleness, calls into question a simple binary view of male sexuality. Further, *Life*'s men during the war, especially in contrast to those represented immediately before and after it, make it difficult to draw with certainty a fixed line (if any line at all) between erotic and platonic attachments. What follows, then, is a study of American maleness in general, not of American men in allegedly immutable categories.[4]

A recognition of male ubiquity in World War II is not the equivalent of understanding the fate of masculinity during the conflict; a history of men is not necessarily men's history.[5] The fact that there is no twentieth-century equivalent of E. Anthony Rotundo's splendid survey of nineteenth-century masculinity, *American Manhood,* suggests how little is known of the inner workings of modern maleness.[6] We do know enough to understand that the intimacy with each other that was apparently common for Victorian males was missing for American men by the eve of the Second World War.[7] To be deeply intimate with another man, especially if that intimacy were romantic, had become culturally sinister in ways that it clearly had not been in the nineteenth century. Though there may well have been different emotional boundaries for men in the working class and in certain ethnic groups, for white middle-class men the pressures to inhibit intimacy with each other had grown intense. Men too cozy with each other were suspiciously like women. They were sissies, probably homosexuals, words that had not even existed for most Victorians.[8]

In the pages of *Life* magazine, American men were hardly cozy before the war.[9] The nature of this male-to-male interaction before the attack on Pearl Harbor is easily summarized: men were involved together in work, commerce, smoking, playing sports, drinking liquor, and talking about tires. They almost never touched one another, and, except for a few underwear ads featuring men in locker rooms, they were usually clothed from neck to toe.[10] Greatest intimacy came when men were involved in sports or, more often, when they were drinking liquor (Figure 9.1).[11]

In October 1940 *Life* produced a special issue devoted entirely to the U.S. Navy. Part of an elaborate effort to make the navy look more attractive on the eve of a potentially costly battle was a distinctive portrayal of the sailor, for *Life* an unprecedented focus on the individual American male. A portrait of a single sailor

adorned the cover of this navy issue, and the photographs inside included another close-up of a naked sailor "off to the showers with his duffel."[12] Such close and direct concentration on images of men would shortly abound in *Life,* in news stories and especially in advertisements, but before the war the individual male was seldom an object of such attention.[13]

Interestingly, near the end of that special prewar issue appeared an article on Admiral Alfred Thayer Mahan, often called the father of the modern navy and the author, as schoolchildren commonly learned, of an influential book in 1890 on the importance of sea power.[14] Like the schoolchildren's lessons, though, that *Life* article was oblivious to the extensive and highly romantic correspondence that Admiral Mahan carried on with a fellow officer, Samuel Ashe, about a relationship of forty years that had begun when both were Annapolis midshipmen before the Civil War. In one letter, Mahan wrote, "I lay in bed last night, dear Sam, thinking of the gradual rise and growth of our friendship. My first visit even to your room is vividly before me, and how as I went up there night after night I could feel my attachment to you growing and see your own love for me showing itself more and more every night." "When you come to a simple question of sex," wrote Mahan on another occasion, "on the whole commend me to men."[15] Mahan and Ashe had been involved at a time when a relationship like theirs had different connotations and consequences than such romance between men would acquire later on. The fact that male-to-male affection of many sorts eventually attracted a mainstream cultural stigma, however, hardly means that men utterly lost the capacity for such intimacy.[16] The mainstream culture and social structure of prewar America nonetheless provided little opportunity, viability, and inducement for strong bonds between men. The war changed that situation, and *Life* charted and promoted the change.

Much has been written about *situational homosexuality,* a term that often seems to be an excuse for regrettable behavior.[17] Perhaps, one should simply note

American flyers and ground crew "Somewhere in England"

...and during these precious moments, their camp on foreign soil really seems to become *America* ... *Home* ...

Snapshots can be that important – can be like a visit with old friends, in the old familiar surroundings. For a time, the little changes and happenings around home become more important than some world-shaking event ... On the word of our boys overseas, snapshots from home are the remembrance they "can use" and never tire of.

Don't let the film shortage (most film goes for military purposes) discourage you. Keep on trying. And when you get a roll, snap the home faces and home scenes you'd long to see yourself, if you were away from home. Make your letters "snapshot visits from home". ... Eastman Kodak Company, Rochester, N. Y.

REMEMBER THE U. S. RANGERS ON THE NORMANDY COAST—how, scaling a 200 ft. cliff, they silenced German guns menacing the allied landings?... how, under withering fire, they conquered the precipice and wiped out Nazi gun crews, "saving countless lives and tons of shipping and matériel" at a grim cost to themselves?... A stern example to us at home.
BUY MORE WAR BONDS.

Visit your man in the service with SNAPSHOTS

Kodak

Figure 9.2. Advertisement for Kodak, *Life,* **October 30, 1944. (Courtesy Kodak)**

that all of sexuality, indeed all of human expression itself, is substantially a matter of place and time. The situational alterations brought about by the Second World War were monumental; that they had profound consequences for how people expressed themselves should come as no surprise. To argue for the war's enormous impact is not to deny the obvious import of other situational changes in modern experience, nor is it to deny that war has analogies in, say, its charac-

teristic of extensive same-sex living environments. But an army barracks or a battleship was not the same as, for instance, an immigrant boarding house.[18] Writing at the war's end, psychologist and veteran Irving L. Janis did not exaggerate when he observed that "a man entering the army undergoes as profound a change in his way of life as he is likely to experience in his entire adult lifetime."[19]

Among the many distinctive features of military life

Figure 9.3. Advertisement for Camel cigarettes, *Life,* June 28, 1943. (Courtesy R. J. Reynolds Tobacco)

to which one had to adapt during the war, perhaps paramount was the utter exclusivity of gender boundaries, a segregation of the American population by gender of unprecedented proportion and duration. Civilian America before the war was far from well integrated by gender, but the war was something else again. Historians Beth Bailey and David Farber have written of the "very specific gulf between men and women" created by World War II. "The war brought the differences between men's and women's

lives into sharp contrast," wrote Bailey and Farber. "Men fought. Women didn't."[20]

Fighting, actual or potential, marked men's situation and gave to men's wartime relationships a peculiar intensity, a tenderness between men that was no doubt as common in the war as it was rare in civilian life.[21] No wonder, then, that popular singer Kate Smith reported that one of the most requested songs during her many visits to troops overseas was "My Buddy."[22] "Nights are

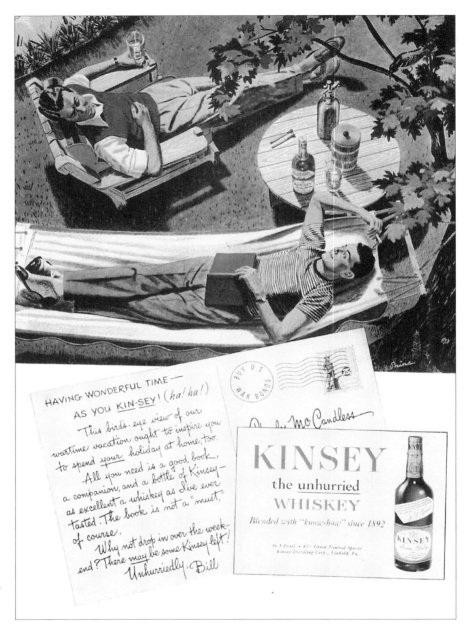

Figure 9.4. Advertisement for Kinsey Whiskey, *Life,* **August 13, 1945. (Courtesy Kinsey)**

long since you went away / I think about you all through the day," goes this mournful song to an absent love. "Miss your voice, the touch of your hand / I long to know that you'll understand / My buddy, my buddy / Your buddy misses you."[23] Has there been anything in American popular music quite like "My Buddy" since the war, any other mainstream song primarily imagined

as being sung man-to-man—other than son to father or vice versa—that so directly expresses affection?

It is not necessary, of course, to hear erotic longing in "My Buddy," but neither is it necessary not to hear such desire. Erotic potential was surely there, however, and the song's considerable popularity clearly reflects widespread feelings of affection. Like the song, many wartime photographs suggest strong bonds of affection and at least the potential of erotic attachments. Edward Steichen and the other talented photographers that assembled in the Naval Aviation Unit, for example, left an extraordinary visual record of wartime closeness between men.[24] In the "Pictures to the Editor" section that *Life* had in those years, the magazine published a photograph that seems uniquely a part of its time: two soldiers sleeping on a Washington, D.C., park bench, intricately and intimately wrapped in each other's arms.[25]

Men in such intimate poses became common in *Life* during the war. Not simply more frequent, male interaction in *Life*'s wartime ads was considerably more varied than what had appeared before Pearl Harbor. Often touching each other, men now ate, sang, listened to music, and read mail together, a far cry from just talking about tires (Figure 9.2).[26] The most intimate scenes were of the male couple, an especially common motif of wartime ads. Before the war, a 1940 *Life* cover had captured a prominent feature of twentieth-century American male coupling—two basketball players facing off. In illuminating contrast, the cover of a 1944 issue showed two weary GIs arm in arm.[27]

The wartime pairings presented what for *Life* was an unprecedented comfort with the spectacle of two men together—chatting and shaving, touching cigarettes, washing one another's hair, sleeping side-by-side (Figure 9.3).[28] Though most pictures were of men in the service, two males who clearly found some sort of pleasure in being together were also occasionally shown in civilian clothes during the war years, standing closer and more often touching than had their prewar brothers.[29] At the war's end there even appeared a civilian couple that unambiguously seemed to invite a homoerotic interpretation. Reclining inversely side-by-side while drinking (a whiskey named Kinsey, no less), the men are described in the ad as being companions on a wartime vacation (Figure 9.4).[30]

Also in stark contrast to *Life*'s ads before the war, men shown during the conflict wore considerably less clothing, frequently in each other's company. Shirtless soldiers and sailors were ubiquitous in wartime advertising, at a time when it was still a crime for men to so appear in public in some American localities, when men's popular swimming attire had only recently gone topless, and just a few years after Clark Gable had created a fuss by not wearing an undershirt in Frank Capra's *It Happened One Night*.[31] The widespread shirtlessness in these ads portrayed what had become a common custom of the Pacific War, of course, but men without their shirts was nonetheless an image (and a reality) of men in public with which Americans had been largely unfamiliar before World War II.[32]

Shirtless men were one thing in *Life,* men without their pants quite another. Cannon towels had an extensive series of advertisements in the middle of the war that went the shirtless soldier one better. Under the cover of war, these extraordinary ads managed to uncover American men and show them in intimate play to an extent quite unknown in mainstream advertising both before and well after the early 1940s. In August 1943, and on five more occasions over the year following, *Life*'s inside cover was devoted to color illustrations of "True Towel Tales," stories involving wartime bathing said to have been helpfully supplied to American servicemen by Cannon. In the first towel tale, soldiers were shown joyously bathing in a South Pacific Island stream, in poses of utter relaxation and pleasure, with only their crotches unexposed. Alaska, with hot water at a premium, was the scene of the next tale, in which a flier surprises his naked comrade with a dousing. In the next, marines on the Solomon Islands have rigged a shower from what look to be empty fuel drums; three watch appreciatively as a fourth prepares to scrub. Shifting theaters of war, the next tale depicts soldiers in Europe, tank corpsmen in the remains of an ancient Roman bath; as some soldiers lounge naked at poolside, one crowns another with a wreath of laurel. The fifth tale takes place in Ceylon, where sailors bathe in a river. Uncharacteristically for the "True Towel Tales," these sailors all wear shorts, but there is the typical merrymaking nonethe-

Right: Figure 9.5. Advertisement for Cannon Towels, *Life*, June 26, 1944. (Courtesy Cannon) *Opposite:* Figure 9.6. "California War Worker," *Life*, October 12, 1942. (Courtesy J.R. Eyerman/ TimePix)

less, the source of fun a squirt of water from an accommodating elephant's trunk. The sixth tale is perhaps the most extraordinary. In a "Buna village," as natives look on impassively, naked soldiers wash one another while sitting close together in a water-filled canoe. Out of the water, one of their comrades dances provocatively, a palm frond teasingly held over his genitals, to the evident pleasure of his buddies (Figure 9.5).[33] Cannon's "True Towel Tales" are unimaginable apart from the setting of the war. Only after military service at high stakes did American advertising portray men with those sorts of smiles, in those sorts of poses.[34] Interestingly, *Life*'s "Picture of the Week" for February 8, 1943, was an actual photograph, by Frank Scherschel, of dozens of American soldiers happily swimming naked together on Guadacanal.[35]

If the male-to-male intimacy of the war ads was unprecedented, so was the period's focus on the individual male, sometimes quite clearly as an erotic object, a concentration prefigured by the special 1940 issue on the navy. Throughout the war, on *Life*'s covers and in the ads, handsome men as the subject became commonplace. It is perhaps no more than ironic that one *Life* cover was of an Ensign Gay and that one ad depicted a "fagged flyer," but whether or not there was any homoerotic intent to these portrayals, it seems likely that a heightened homoeroticism was one of their effects (Figures 9.6 and 9.7).[36] There was even an occasional civilian male who got such rapt attention in wartime ads.[37] And near the end of the war there appeared an elaborate *Life* cover story on the American teenage boy that might not have occurred had it not been for the extraordinary focus on young men that World War II had brought about.[38]

When the war ended just two months after that cover story, the American male by himself as well as the male couple virtually disappeared from the pages of *Life*. Quite revealingly, the man alone as a focal point of advertising was replaced by the bride, a figure who became common in the magazine after August 1945.[39] The bride in her lacy gown was a suggestive contrast to another wife who had appeared in *Life* during the war in an ad for the Pennsylvania Railroad, a robust Mrs. Casey Jones, decked out in overalls.[40] Not surprisingly, the new couple in *Life*'s postwar advertising became the bride and groom, who were reminded didactically by one silverware promotion that their relationship was to be "for keeps." That ad appeared prominently, on the inside cover that *Life* had once devoted to the "True Towel Tales."[41]

Males did still interact in the ads of 1946, but not often. It was essentially back to drinking, fishing, and selling—rarely touching and almost always fully clothed. If a tent is pitched these days, as in a Schlitz beer ad, a woman is now along, maybe for the pleasure of her company, but perhaps also for a sort of newly needed reassurance.[42] Underwear advertisements, common during the war and one of the oldest sorts of ads to feature men, now had to present a contest, such as the tug-of-war

waged over a pair of boxer shorts by two men in a Reliance Ensenada depiction.[43] And any men shaving together now, oddly, wear shirts; they too must be competitors, sober participants in a "shavathon."[44]

By the 1950s the silence was striking when it came to male interaction in *Life* ads. On the rare occasions when men were depicted together at all, a drink nearly always had to be at hand (Figure 9.8).[45] *Life*'s men of the 1950s were a comparatively lonely, joyless lot. It was a long way from the "True Towel Tales" only a decade earlier.[46]

The war years, then, had witnessed a sudden and dramatic change in the appearance of men in *Life* magazine, while the postwar period saw another shift that was even more abrupt and striking. Men in various postures of intimacy had begun to appear in *Life* advertisements with remarkable frequency once the war was under way. While just before the conflict, in 1940, there had been several issues of the magazine with no adult men depicted virtually alone together, without women, by 1943 and 1944 there was but one issue with

no such male-to-male interaction in advertising. The number of depictions of men together per issue also increased markedly during the war. The pattern changed radically, however, once the fighting stopped. Several 1946 issues had no men alone together in ads, and by 1954 there were many more such issues. Depictions per issue were by far the fewest in 1954, a much smaller degree of interaction than had been shown be-

fore the war. Something drastic had occurred in *Life*'s pages and in the culture at large. That which had been affirmed and promoted during the war was denied and vilified in the war's aftermath.

An intricate consideration of the authorship and audience of *Life*'s masculine iconography is probably needed. My purpose in this study, however, is description and tentative interpretation, certainly not a full explanation. We do know, from Roland Marchand's outstanding study, that most mid-century advertising was devised by men.[47] Similarly, a review of the photo credits in *Life* reveals that the magazine's photographers during the 1940s and 1950s were also usually males. While women were, of course, often the consumers primarily targeted by advertisers, that hardly means that men did not see the images of themselves in *Life*, a magazine with a huge readership that during the war was widely distributed among servicemen.[48]

The exact impact of *Life*'s pictures may well be impossible to determine, but is nonetheless worth contemplation. In his valuable study of censorship in World War II, George Roeder Jr. said, "to write of the power of wartime visual imagery is not to assume that it had a precisely measurable or predictable effect."[49] One imprecise yet plausible and provocative suggestion of the effect of certain wartime images comes from a novel of the time, Charles Jackson's *Fall of Valor*, the story of a middle-aged man whose hibernating homosexuality is aroused during World War II. The primary source of this awakening is no mere image, but rather a live marine. Imagery has played its part, nonetheless:

> The war photographs which had been drawing his melancholy attention for so many months—what were they but nostalgia for youth? He envied the solidarity, fraternity and fellowship of servicemen (which they themselves would scarcely be aware of till it was a thing of the past) and felt keenly his forty-four years. The thousand pictures of GIS at chow, the young fliers strapping on their parachutes as they ran for the bombers tuning up in the gray dawn, the helmeted half-naked leathernecks grinning for the camera at the wheel of bulldozers, the packed waving soldiers crowding the rail of the transport and all of them smiling as if they were setting forth on some wonderful holiday, the marines holding their guns aloft as they jumped down the landing platforms or sprawled or crouched on the furious beach—these were today's tokens of romance, pored over by millions, vicariously experienced by men and women alike. His desire to be part of it was not diminished one whit by reminding himself that the aim of it all was death.[50]

The many "thousand pictures" of men together that appeared during the war, as well as those representations of men that appeared immediately before and after it, constitute a largely overlooked chapter in the history of twentieth-century sexuality. More importantly, perhaps, they form a chapter in the little-understood history of men's relationships with each other, unions that may have been erotic more often than realized though less often than feared.

Many of *Life*'s war images could serve as illustrations for one of the most moving evocations of World War II, Douglas Allanbrook's memoir, *See Naples*. Allanbrook, who after the war became a renowned composer and harpsichord player, spent most of the war as an infantryman on hazardous duty in Italy. His memoir captures the war years with stunning detail, grace, and power, yet it is curiously shapeless and out of sorts in dealing with his life as a civilian, despite his consid-

erable postwar accomplishments, wives, and sons who came along after he left the army. "In the middle years," Allanbrook wrote, "there is no drama, death is not imminent, and there's work to be done: children to be raised, music to be written, money to be earned."[51] The war was apparently a hard act to follow.

Among other things, *See Naples* is a testimony to profound friendships formed during or in anticipation of battle. Writing of men who had "what some of us called, without malice, a second marriage," Allanbrook reminds us without saying so that it is just as inhibiting to believe that intimacy must involve sex as it is to insist that it dare not, an implicit point in some of *Life*'s wartime pictures.[52] Allanbrook's own most memorable friendship was with Leonard, a soldier who was killed "so soon after our arrival at Naples." Leonard had been a tobacco farmer before joining the army; nearly fifty years after Leonard's death, smoking a cigar could remind Allanbrook of his friend's voice.[53] Indeed, Leonard's voice reverberates throughout Allanbrook's memoir, especially his unanswered beckoning to Allanbrook to join him as they slept outdoors on a December night in Italy. "He was cold; he wanted me. Together we would be warm," Allanbrook recalls a half century later.[54] While their association clearly had other moments of closeness, regret over his failure to accept this particular offer of intimacy seems paradigmatic, the essential controlling emotion of the rest of Allanbrook's life: "I had not answered then and never would or could. Was that voice, calling out my name, to be forever the guarantor of my loneliness, the only permanence granted or even possible, even though it had no substance and no existence except as a source of infinite regret? Was love to be forever linked to what was no longer and perhaps had never been?"[55] A sense of unrealized possibility permeates Allanbrook's memoir, as it surrounds many of *Life*'s images from the war.

The changes in *Life*'s characterization of men bear an interesting resemblance to some contemporaneous shifts in representations of males in American film. The wisecracking camaraderie of the five Bob

Hope–Bing Crosby "road pictures" of the 1940s had not yet waned in *The Road to Bali* in 1952, for example, but that was the pair's only movie together in that decade. In their final joint effort, *The Road to Hong Kong* in 1962, the chemistry of the war years was long gone.[56] Intriguingly, one relationship between men in American popular culture that was able to span the forties and the fifties was the one between Jack Benny and Eddie "Rochester" Anderson, a union whose genuine intimacy was perhaps shrouded from audiences by the distractions of race and class.[57]

Revealingly enough, in the movies of the 1950s the descendants of Hope and Crosby became Dean Martin and Jerry Lewis, a duo more remembered for their parting than for their coupling. Their characters in *The Caddy* in 1953 seldom interact intimately, with their friendship usually rendered ridiculous by Lewis's shrill, juvenile excess. Genuine affection is suggested when together they sing "What Would You Do without Me?" a song that includes the lines "We will be just like lovers, you and I." This was the fifties; the song had to end with the men pummeling each other to the point of demolishing their straw hats.

A decade earlier, a fight had not been the obligatory end to a lighthearted suggestion of romance between men. In *The Road to Utopia* in 1945, for instance, Hope and Crosby managed to get through a duet of "I Don't Care Where I'm Goin' Just as Long as I'm with You" without having to hurt each other. In a memorable scene from *Anchors Aweigh* in 1945, Gene Kelly and Frank Sinatra flirt with homoeroticism as Kelly's character acts like a woman to help his sailor buddy learn how to attract the opposite sex. Similarly, audiences were teased by a scene in *Up in Arms* in 1944; the women sitting next to sailors played by Dana Andrews and Danny Kaye are obscured from view, giving the impression that a romantic interchange is between the men alone, not between them and their girlfriends.[58]

There were scenes between men in American films of the 1940s that were much more complex and intimate than those played for laughs by Kelly and Sinatra and Andrews and Kaye. Countless war movies actually made during the conflict convey an unfettered intensity.[59] In the war's immediate aftermath, closeness between men could be seen in a Western, Howard Hawks's magnificent *Red River* in 1948. Despite the presence of Joanne Dru's character, the film ends with the symbolic marriage (as ranch partners) between characters played by John Wayne and Montgomery Clift. Profound as is the attachment between these cowboys, it is much more reserved than the affection displayed by servicemen in the war movies, men sometimes played by Wayne himself. His character and Clift's have to be admonished to stop feuding at the conclusion of *Red River*, as Dru's character reminds them, "You two know you love each other." With the emergence of actors like Marlon Brando, James Dean, Paul Newman, and Kirk Douglas in the 1950s, the man alone dominated American movies, replacing the ensembled buddies of the 1940s war movies or couplings like Wayne and Clift's in *Red River*. Wayne, for example, is all alone and wants it that way in his towering portrayal of the rancorous Indian hunter Ethan Edwards in John Ford's masterpiece, *The Searchers*, in 1956.

Some films made right after the war had also featured lonely males, usually veterans returning to civilian life or men mourning the death of a wartime buddy. Film noir, the pessimistic, starkly brooding genre that emerged in the 1940s, was more, of course, than a response to losses suffered during the war or losses sensed upon returning home. Nonetheless, it is suggestive that noir films are largely a *post*war phenomenon; at least some of the genre's hopeless melancholy may have been animated by the severing of bonds that had been so common during the war.[60] In the dichotomized sexuality of an America at peace, loving women usually meant having not to love other men, sometimes undoubtedly promoting resentment against women at various levels of consciousness. Scarce roles for women and unflattering depictions of them are hardly exclusive to film noir, but the genre's unqualified characterization of females as a threaten-

ing, often deadly, lot is nonetheless striking. That women were an inappropriate target for male frustration should not discredit the frustration itself or distract us from examining the dynamics of thwarted male affection in postwar America.

Dislike and distrust of women pervade *Dead Reckoning*, a 1947 film directed by John Cromwell. Humphrey Bogart's Rip Murdock expresses his contempt for women with tedious frequency, making his purported affection for Lizabeth Scott's Coral Chandler seem forced and thoroughly unconvincing, without the slightest foundation apart from animal attraction. "I don't trust anybody. Especially women," says Murdock. "All females are the same, with their faces washed," he opines on another occasion, recalling another time that he had "heard of a girl once [who] kissed a guy and stabbed him in the back at the same time." As women usually are in noir films, Scott's character is unredeemably evil, the ultimate source of the considerable violence in the movie. The only believable affection expressed by Bogart's character is for Johnny, his dead buddy, a man not actually killed in the war but after it, as the result of his foolhardy fondness for a woman, Scott's amoral Coral Chandler. "I knew him like my own birthmark," Rip Murdock sullenly recalls. Comparing his own ill-fated attraction to Coral Chandler to his deep affection for Johnny, Murdock flatly declares, "I loved him more." Murdock had even given Coral a male nickname, "Mike," but it was just not the same. Authentic affection had been for another man, and there was no place for that sort of feeling after the war.[61]

Surely at no time before the Second World War had so many American men consciously felt deep affection for other males, and not since the previous century had romantic attachments between men been so widespread and little scorned. Further, perhaps at no time since the war has affection between men been as culturally unencumbered as it was from 1941 to 1945. The feelings unleashed and fostered during the war were threatening during peacetime, challenging as they did a cultural imperative that had had enormous power since the late nineteenth century; authentic men were to be strong above all else, doing manly work that was to be the antithesis of womanly endeavor.

The cult of toughness and the particular cultural reinforcements associated with it eventually gave open affection between men such a bad name—literally—in America. Weakness and loving other men is not an inevitable equation, of course, but it was the one that took root in nineteenth-century America, at a time when it was becoming especially important to many men to use any means available to differentiate themselves from women. The stereotypical homosexual male, his limp wrists symbolizing his lack of maleness, epitomized weakness, but he performed a vital cultural function in marking the boundaries of masculinity. The truly bothersome male was the one who seemed to violate some of these boundaries, the one who did not fit into the rigid dichotomies of modern notions of sexuality, the man who indeed openly loved other men yet who otherwise met the job requirements of maleness and did not appear stereotypically homosexual.[62]

The affectionate warriors of the early 1940s eventually became such bothers, to others and sometimes even—or maybe especially—to themselves when the war was over.[63] There was a mighty postwar effort to resolve the dissonance that they promoted and to revitalize rigid gender roles and the various stereotypes that those roles nurtured. As women were widely reminded after the war that home was their proper place, so too were men expected to return to a world of competition and emotional restraint.[64] And, like guards in a prison watchtower, negative characterizations of same-sex love were given dramatically new power in the Cold War era as a means of keeping men and women alike in their place.[65] The essential issue, then, was not sexuality as such, but gender roles and their postwar reconstruction, with freshly demonized same-sex affection the bugaboo charged with keeping everyone in conformity with convention.

The war had hardly ended, for example, when Therese Benedek, a psychiatrist at the Institute for Psychoanalysis, looked back with disdain, writing of how military service interrupted the "normal . . . psychosocial development of the young man." The all-male environment of the military "is insidious, and is slowly and unconsciously effective," wrote Benedek. "Living only with men in such close quarters is a threat to the not yet well-entrenched heterosexuality of the late adolescent."[66]

Even anthropologist Margaret Mead chimed in about men who did not fit into predictable categories of gender:

> Sometimes one has the opportunity to observe two men of comparable physique and behavior, . . . one of whom has placed himself as fully male, and with brightly shining hair and gleaming eye can make a roomful of women feel more feminine because he has entered the room. The other has identified himself as a lover of men, and his eye contains no gleam and his step no sureness, but instead an apologetic adaptation when he enters a group of women. And yet in physical measurement, in tastes, in quality of mind the two men may be almost interchangeable.[67]

If the prospect of a male "lover of men" was enough to unsettle Margaret Mead in 1949, little wonder that others were alarmed.

The first widely heralded novel about World War II, John Horne Burns's 1947 work *The Gallery*, warmly evoked the world of soldiers who openly loved each other. When he wrote about same-sex love in two subsequent novels, however, Burns's star fell as rapidly as it had risen. Voted the best war novel of 1947 by the editors of the *Saturday Review*, *The Gallery* was set in Naples, where Burns himself had been stationed for a year and a half. A meditation on love, suffering, responsibility, worldliness, and world-weariness, the novel focuses on several settings in the Galleria Umberto section of Naples. One of the places is Momma's, a gay bar frequented by Allied soldiers. The several men who patronize Momma's defy easy generalizations and are neither scorned nor pitied, perhaps the essence of Burns's departure from previous treatments of homosexuality in American writing. The war had profoundly altered these men's sense of themselves and of their particular yearnings for each other. "How can we speak of sin," wonders one of Burns's soldiers, "when thousands are cremated in German furnaces, when it isn't wrong to make a million pounds, but a crime to steal a loaf of bread? Perhaps some new code may come out of all this. . . . I hope so."[68]

There was a new code after the war, but not of the sort that Burns's character hoped. With critical acclaim for *The Gallery* still fresh, Burns turned his candid attention to American men in domestic settings. His 1949 novel, *Lucifer with a Book,* examined the inner workings and exceptional conceits of a private boys' school, an environment Burns knew as both student and teacher.[69] In *A Cry of Children* in 1952, he observed Boston's Irish Catholicism, a culture not unlike that of his own Andover, Massachusetts, boyhood.[70] Both novels were excoriated by critics, and while neither is perhaps the equal of *The Gallery,* the venomous criticism seems curiously out of proportion to Burns's offense. No fan of Burns's later work, Gore Vidal nonetheless wrote that *Lucifer with a Book* "was perhaps the most savagely and unjustly attacked book of its day."[71] The attackers were part of the postwar mood in American literary criticism that flatly refused to tolerate all eroticized love between men. Alfred Kazin, for example, railed against "apologies for abnormality, designed to make us sympathize with the twig as it is bent the wrong way."[72] Similarly, Malcolm Cowley denounced stories about "the sensitive and so artistic young man" that appeared in "the fairy Freudian novel."[73] Burns's work was buried in an avalanche of this criticism, which seemed less concerned with the merits of a particular novel than with keeping out of circulation any even remotely affirmative treatment of unsublimated affection between men.[74]

The reputation of John Horne Burns is at best obscure today, while much better remembered is Burns's contemporary, another veteran, Norman Mailer, author of *The Naked and the Dead.*[75] Though he came to fancy himself quite the iconoclast, it was Mailer, much more than Burns, whose work was compatible with convention. Like Burns's work, Mailer's too had a homoerotic dimension, but what Burns savored Mailer scorned. Mailer's General Cummings is a posturing, effeminate, father-fearing, fascism-admiring sadist who is attracted to one Lieutenant Hearn, a man whom the general sends to his death when he cannot possess him. Later on Mailer became virtually a parody of chest-thumping heterosexuality, managing every now and then to remind us of his contempt for the homosexual, his purported antithesis.[76] The fact that Mailer would later appropriately title an apologia *The Prisoner of Sex* is a good reminder that those who speak the loudest about a matter are often the least free of its yoke.

If there is an overdone quality to some of Mailer's rantings, so is there an element of the postwar experience at large that suggests cultural overcompensation. The widespread "sex crime panic," an obsession with goings-on in men's rooms, and various schemes to entrap sexual outlaws all seem to bespeak a personal agenda on the part of those who said they spoke for conventional morality in the 1950s.[77] According to Martin Duberman, there was, revealingly enough, an "outpouring of glossy popular magazines published during the 1950s that prided themselves on catering to the interests of Real Men."[78] One of these magazines, *Rave,* regaled its readers in 1956 with the adventures of New York detective Ray Schinder, "The Master De-Queerer" famous for ridding the St. Regis Hotel bar of gay men, people the magazine called "an unusually revolting species of pest[,] . . . that breed of humanity variously referred to as queers, fags, fairies, pansies, and so on and on and on."[79] Schinder was a minor player, to say the least; self-styled upholders of righteousness were all over the place in 1950s America. It is at least intriguing that the decade's three principal symbols of overripe

Americanism—Senator Joseph McCarthy, Francis Cardinal Spellman, and J. Edgar Hoover—have themselves all been the subject of considerable speculation and innuendo about unconventional sexuality. Of McCarthy's deputy, Roy Cohn, there can be no doubt. He was a pathetically repressed gay man, the sort who could rail with a special passion in public against precisely what he was doing in private.[80]

While Tony Kushner's provocative 1993 play *Angels in America* presents Roy Cohn and his repressions as broadly representative of postwar America's cultural conceits, that may be too severe an indictment, too grave a diagnosis.[81] Still, one might at least suggest the relevance of the dusty psychoanalytic concept of reaction formation, the lashing out against behavior that one secretly finds appealing, but which, in one's current circumstances, is unpopular or in some other way ill-advised.[82] Shakespeare, of course, had it right long before Freud, writing of the suspiciously strong protest. Perhaps for many Americans the postwar period was the morning after, a time for expressing regrets over indiscretions of the night before.

For some, there had never been such a night. In his 1995 memoir of the war, poet Robert Peters said that "freneticisms engendered in sensitive young male minds by the dislocations, threats of maimings and death, and fevered patriotism of war intensify testosterone levels to a degree seldom seen in civilian lives."[83] Peters recalls a series of erotic encounters, mostly with other men, during his years in the army. While a Lutheran upbringing in Wisconsin had not prepared him to welcome such experiences, memories of them remained vivid. Though he eventually married and became the father of five, Peters notes that he had sexual fantasies of both men and women after the war, and when he "dreamed of love as tenderness, males were the object."[84]

Just after the war's end, as Robert Peters was having those dreams, political theorist Sebastian deGrazia wrote of war as the "Great Association," an utterly singular time that provided the rootedness and cooperative spirit missing in mass society.[85] Half a century later, a devoted and gifted chronicler of the conflict would tell an interviewer on Veterans Day what impressed him the most about American infantrymen in World War II. "Above all else," Stephen Ambrose insisted, "their own comradeship, the way in which they love each other. . . . It's just the most wonderful, in its own way, of human relationships, brought on by this worst situation human beings can ever find themselves in, and that's to be a combat infantryman. There is nothing to compare to it."[86] Studs Terkel's gathering of veterans' memories leaves no doubt why, despite the horrors recounted, he chose to call his volume *The Good War*.[87] To Mario Puzo, the war was a deliverance, an escape from the ghetto of his boyhood, a place where he had set his sights no higher than being a railroad clerk. "I must have been one of millions," Puzo recalled, "sons, husbands, fathers, lovers, making their innocent getaway from baffled loved ones. And what an escape it was. The war made all my dreams come true."[88] For veteran Ted Allenby, the escape had been from Dubuque, Iowa, where he knew simply that his sexual yearnings made him different; he only named and acted on those desires for other men after he joined the marines in 1942. According to him, real opposition to his romantic relationships did not come until after the war ended. During the conflict, "officialdom made no big thing about it," Allenby told Studs Terkel. "There was a war on," said Allenby. "Who in the hell is going to worry about this shit?"[89]

Especially in light of its aftermath, it is no wonder that many Americans actually missed certain features of the war. As Sebastian deGrazia wrote, "once returned to civilian life, [veterans would] look back with longing to the fellowship of the barracks."[90] Some of the longings felt during and after World War II came to be shrouded in guilt and regret; much of the shroud is still there. In peering under that shroud, we might do well to recall that reportedly one of the most popular pieces of writing among servicemen was James Thurber's 1939 story "The Secret Life of Walter Mitty," a tale if ever there was one of a man who falls short of his culture's prescriptions for manly toughness and daydreams of glorious pursuits. There were Mitty Clubs in the Pacific and in Europe, while bombers bore the names of story characters, and terms from the story became wartime passwords.[91] A superficial reading of Thurber's work might focus largely on its unbecoming portrait of Mitty's overbearing wife, a characteristic Thurber woman. At heart "The Secret Life of Walter Mitty" is a story of the tyranny of roles, not females. Mitty's powerful (and unnamed) wife is as miscast in life as he is. Perhaps in appreciating the story so much, some of Thurber's wartime readers simply honored the little man who could not measure up, with honoring Walter Mitty being a means of criticizing the gender role to which he was so ill suited.

In spite of the war's horrors some American men indulged a Mitty-like fantasy of escape from domestic convention during World War II. In his magnificent memoir, Douglas Allanbrook, for example, recalled a "riverine idyll" that occurred before he was shipped overseas. On maneuvers along the Sabine River in Louisiana, Allanbrook and his buddies spent three days naked, much of the time swimming in the Sabine's warm waters. "[W]e were more naked than any civilian ever was," Allanbrook maintained, noting that "[i]n later years painters' pictures of bathers would recall to me those innocent days we spent together in that unlikely Eden, the Sabine River. We were so young, none of us over twenty-three." Allanbrook even managed to have a similar respite in Italy, on leave at a Tuscan spa. "Sporting in the warm waters were naked soldiers," he remembered, "both black and white. There were no officers present; they were segregated in their own establishment. . . . Fifty years later the army is worried once again, concerned about men naked together in barracks, showers, and baths."[92]

Apparently more than the war itself ended in 1945. Quite appropriately, in their various representations of maleness, *Life*'s wartime pages bore little resemblance to the pages that appeared before and after the conflict. *Life*'s wartime rendering of masculinity existed, like wartime maleness itself, as a thing apart—more tender, more cooperative, more frolicsome, more colorful, and much more affectionate. The pity was that this hiatus from the cold confinements of modern masculinity could not continue in times of peace.

NOTES

1. Allen Drury, *Advise and Consent* (New York: Doubleday, 1959), 432–33.

2. For descriptions of earlier American literary treatments of homosexuality, see for example, Roger Austen, *Playing the Game: The Homosexual Novel in America* (Indianapolis: Bobbs-Merrill, 1977).

3. Most accounts of World War II feature men, of course, yet few directly analyze maleness. As a chapter in gender history, the war is usually seen in its effect upon women. For more wide-ranging treatments, see Beth Bailey and David Farber, *The First Strange Place: Race and Sex in World War II Hawaii* (Baltimore: Johns Hopkins University Press, 1994); Allan Bérubé, *Coming Out under Fire: The History of Gay Men and Women in World War Two* (New York: Free Press, 1990); John Costello, *Virtue under Fire: How World War II Changed Our Social and Sexual Attitudes* (Boston: Little, Brown, 1985).

4. There is a growing recognition in scholarship of sexuality's cultural construction, an awareness in particular of the fairly recent vintage of the categories "homosexual" and "heterosexual." Of towering significance is Michel Foucault, *The History of Sexuality*, 3 vols. (New York: Random House, 1990). See also, George Chauncey, *Gay New York: Gender, Urban Culture, and the Making of the Gay Male World,*

1890–1940 (New York: Basic Books, 1994); John D'Emilio and Estelle B. Freedman, *Intimate Matters: A History of Sexuality in America* (New York: Harper and Row, 1988); Jonathan Ned Katz, *The Invention of Heterosexuality* (New York: Dutton, 1995); Kevin White, *The First Sexual Revolution: The Emergence of Male Heterosexuality in Modern America* (New York: New York University Press, 1993). For an attempt to collapse most distinctions, see Marjorie Garber, *Vice Versa: Bisexuality and the Eroticism of Everyday Life* (New York: Simon and Schuster, 1995).

5. William L. O'Neill, *A Democracy at War: America's Fight at Home and Abroad in World War II* (Cambridge, Mass.: Harvard University Press, 1993). In this fresh scholarly overview of the war, the entry for "women" in the index is followed by several references, but there is no entry at all for "men."

6. E. Anthony Rotundo, *American Manhood: Transformations in Masculinity from the Revolution to the Modern Era* (New York: Basic Books, 1993). For an overview of twentieth-century masculinity, see Michael Kimmel, *Manhood in America: A Cultural History* (New York, Free Press, 1996), 81–335.

7. On male-to-male intimacy in the nineteenth century, see especially Rotundo, "Youth and Male Intimacy," chap. 4 in *American Manhood*, 75–91, and D'Emilio and Freedman, *Intimate Matters,* 127–30.

8. Rotundo charts the emergence of this cultural shift toward an emphasis on toughness and the consequent inhibition of intimacy in "Passionate Manhood: A Changing Standard of Masculinity," chap. 10, "Roots of Change: The Women Without and the Woman Within," chap. 11, and "Epilogue: Manhood in the Twentieth Century," in *American Manhood,* 222–93. On linguistic innovations, see Chauncey, *Gay New York,* 114–15, and D'Emilio and Freedman, *Intimate Matters,* 226.

9. For this study, I have reviewed every wartime issue of *Life.* For gauging the prewar period, I have read every issue from 1940, the year before American entry into the fighting. For assessing postwar patterns, I read every issue from both 1946 and 1954.

10. See, for example, ads in the following issues of *Life* from 1940: 15 January, 1; 12 February, 80; 19 February, 3; 4 March, 84; 6 May, 101; 29 July, 52; 7 October, 99.

11. Advertisement, *Life,* 15 January 1940, 30.

12. Photographs, *Life,* 28 October 1940, cover and 89.

13. Also see ibid., 32.

14. "Mahan Foretold Modern Navies," *Life,* 28 October 1940, 95. Mahan's book was *The Influence of Sea Power upon History* (Boston: 1890).

15. Mahan to Ashe, 29 October 1858, and 10 October 1868, in Ronald T. Takaki, *Iron Cages: Race and Culture in Nineteenth-Century America* (New York: Oxford University Press, 1993), 273.

16. It is crucial to distinguish here between intimacy and mere sexual activity between men. Prewar prevalence of the latter is brilliantly documented in Chauncey's *Gay New York*. The extensive sexual activity

between men during the war is documented throughout Bérubé's *Coming Out under Fire.* See, also, Costello's "Comrades in Arms," chap. 7 in *Virtue under Fire,* 101–19.

17. Prisons are the principal "situation" described. See, for example, Wayne S. Wooden and Jay Parker, *Men behind Bars: Sexual Exploitation in Prison* (New York: Plenum Press, 1982).

18. George Chauncey instructively reminds us that the war was far from the first disruptive force in American life. See his *Gay New York,* 11. In its scale and intensity, however, the war was singular.

19. Irving L. Janis, "Psychodynamic Aspects of Adjustment to Army Life," *Psychiatry,* May 1945, 159–76.

20. Bailey and Farber, *The First Strange Place,* 21.

21. See, for example, Victor Jorgensen's 1945 photograph in which "Pvt. J. B. Slagle receives his daily dressing of wounds on board the USS *Solace* en route from Okinawa to Guam" in Christopher Phillips, *Steichen at War* (New York: Harry N. Abrams, 1981), 227.

22. Will Friedwald, liner notes for *Kate Smith: Sixteen Most Requested Songs* (Columbia, CT 46097). Bérubé alludes to the song's popularity and briefly discusses the "buddy system" in *Coming Out under Fire,* 37–40, 187–90.

23. "My Buddy," Walter Donaldson, Gus Kahn, and Eric Lane, 1922. (Lane was also the author of "Goodbye G.I. Joe" and the intriguingly titled "Pansies Everywhere.") Though "My Buddy" was written well before World War II and Al Jolson had had some success with it, it was the war that made the song famous. Along with Kate Smith and others, Bing Crosby and Frank Sinatra recorded it, and it was even a frequent theme song for wartime Warner Brothers cartoons. Bérubé, *Coming Out under Fire,* 38; Friedwald, liner notes.

24. For a sizable sample of Steichen's work, see Phillips, *Steichen at War.* The Still Picture Branch of the National Archives houses a vast number of photographs of American men in war. A sample of these is contained in Jonathan Heller, ed., *War and Conflict: Selected Images from the National Archives, 1765–1970* (Washington, D.C.: National Archives and Records, 1990). On World War II, see pages 176–307.

25. "Pictures to the Editor," *Life,* 13 September 1943, 130.

26. Advertisement, *Life,* 30 October 1944, 3. See also, for example, advertisements in the following issues: *Life,* 8 February 1943, 45; *Life,* 16 August 1943, 35, 104.

27. See the covers of *Life,* 15 January 1940, and *Life,* 3 July 1944.

28. Advertisement, *Life,* 28 June 1943, 39, and advertisement, *Life,* 24 May 1943, 1. See also advertisement, *Life,* 6 September 1943, 45; advertisement, *Life,* 11 June 1945, back cover; advertisement, *Life,* 21 December 1942, 21.

29. See, for example, advertisement, *Life,* 8 February 1943, 9; advertisement, *Life,* 12 October 1942, back cover; advertisement, *Life,* 26 June 1944, 82.

30. Advertisement, *Life,* 13 August 1945, 69.

31. On conventions of male attire, see Paul Fussell, *Wartime: Understanding and Behavior in the Second World War* (New York: Oxford

University Press, 1989), 106. On the attention given Gable's lack of an undershirt, see, for example, Frank Capra, *The Name above the Title: An Autobiography* (New York: Macmillan, 1971), 177.

32. See, for example, advertisement, *Life,* 13 September 1943, 21, and advertisement, *Life,* 17 July 1944, 37, 43.

33. Advertisement, *Life,* 26 June 1944, inside cover.

34. See also the inside covers of *Life* for the 16 August 1943, 4 October 1943, 20 December 1943, 3 January 1944, and 20 March 1944 issues.

35. "Picture of the Week," *Life,* 8 February 1943, 25.

36. Photograph, *Life,* 12 October 1942, cover; advertisement, *Life,* 26 February 1945, 5. Ensign Gay is on the cover of *Life* for August 31, 1942; the "fagged flyer" is depicted in the July 17, 1944, 62, issue. For a few examples of the numerous depictions of individual men, often provocatively posed, see *Life,* 31 August 1942, 60; *Life,* 13 September 1943, 3; *Life,* 11 June 1945, 68.

37. See, for example, advertisement, *Life,* 11 June 1945, 84.

38. "Teen-Age Boys," *Life,* 11 June 1945, cover and 91–97. Kevin White instructively examines the culture's attention to male appearance early in the twentieth century in his *First Sexual Revolution,* 27–35. On the male body in film, see Peter Lehman, *Running Scared: Masculinity and the Presentation of the Male Body* (Philadelphia: Temple University Press, 1993).

39. See, for example, advertisement, *Life,* 28 January 1946, 22; advertisement, *Life,* 25 February 1946, 12; advertisement, *Life,* 13 May 1946, 109.

40. Advertisement, *Life,* 6 September 1943, 19.

41. Advertisement, *Life,* 6 May 1946, inside cover.

42. Advertisement, *Life,* 17 June 1946, 93.

43. Advertisement, *Life,* 23 September 1946, 24.

44. Advertisement, *Life,* 28 September 1946, 136.

45. Advertisement, *Life,* 22 November 1954, 101.

46. See also the following advertisements, *Life*, 15 February 1954, 88; *Life,* 22 February 1954, 109; and *Life,* 4 October 1954, 40. By the end of the 1950s and into the early 1960s, before the Vietnam War began receiving extensive coverage, *Life*'s most commonly featured servicemen probably were the astronauts, men who not only had their shirts and pants on, but were often seen armored in their cumbersome spacesuits.

47. Roland Marchand, *Advertising the American Dream: Making Way for Modernity, 1920–1940* (Berkeley: University of California Press, 1985), 33–35. For another instructive examination of advertising in cultural context, see William M. O'Barr, *Culture and the Ad: Exploring Otherness in the World of Advertising* (Boulder, Colo.: Westview Press, 1994).

48. On *Life*'s readership, see Wendy Kozol, *Life's America: Family and Nation in Postwar Photojournalism* (Philadelphia: Temple University Press, 1994), 5.

49. George Roeder Jr., *The Censored War: American Visual Experience during World War Two* (New Haven: Yale University press, 1993), 5.

Roland Marchand sensibly hesitates to make claims regarding the impact of the advertising that he so elaborately describes in *Advertising the American Dream,* especially xviii.

50. Charles Jackson, *The Fall of Valor* (New York: Rinehart, 1946), 170–71.

51. Douglas Allanbrook, *See Naples: A Memoir* (Boston: Houghton Mifflin, 1995), 268.

52. See ibid., 79, regarding "second marriages." Regarding men who clearly had erotic involvements, see pages 196 and 251.

53. Ibid., 80.

54. Ibid., 103.

55. Ibid., 265.

56. Bob Hope and Bing Crosby made the following films together: *The Road to Singapore* (1940); *The Road to Zanzibar* (1941); *The Road to Morocco* (1942); *The Road to Utopia* (1945); *The Road to Rio* (1947); *The Road to Bali* (1952); *The Road to Hong Kong* (1962).

57. Joseph Boskin instructively explores this relationship that was "extraordinary in its depth and sensitivity," noting its homoerotic overtones, in his *Sambo: The Rise and Demise of an American Jester* (New York: Oxford University Press, 1986), 175–97. See also Margaret T. McFadden, "'America's Boy Friend Who Can't Get a Date': Gender, Race, and the Cultural Work of the Jack Benny Program, 1932–1946," *Journal of American History* (June 1993): 113–34. Though remembered mostly for Benny's radio program, the pair made two movies together: *Buck Benny Rides Again* (1940) and *The Meanest Man in the World* (1943).

58. Concentrating solely on the disdain shown by passersby, Vito Russo interpreted the scenes in both *Anchors Aweigh* and *Up in Arms* as reinforcements of homophobia. See his *The Celluloid Closet: Homosexuality in the Movies* (New York: Harper and Row, 1981), 66, 68.

59. The better war movies had an ethnographic eye for men's relationships; significantly, they also had no women in prominent roles. They include John Farrow's *Wake Island* (1942); Howard Hawks's *Air Force* (1943); Tay Garnett's *Bataan* (1943); Louis Seller's *Guadalcanal Diary* (1943); and John Ford's *They Were Expendable* (1945).

60. I am indebted to Lary May for the suggestion that film noir, as well as the early "buddy movies" of Hope and Crosby and Martin and Lewis, were pertinent to my interests. On film noir, see, for example, R. Barton Palmer, *Hollywood's Dark Cinema: The American Film Noir* (New York: Twayne Publishers, 1994), and Robert Ottoson, *A Reference Guide to the American Film Noir* (Metuchen, N.J.: Scarecrow Press, 1981).

61. Other noir films that feature a returning veteran mourning a buddy's loss include Lewis Milestone's *The Strange Love of Martha Ivers* (1946); Robert Montgomery's *Ride the Pink Horse* (1947); and John Huston's *Key Largo* (1948). The returning veteran's role in postwar popular culture is meticulously examined in Timothy Shuker-Haines, "Home Is the Hunter: World War II Veterans and the Reconstruction of Masculinity, 1944–1951," (Ph.D. diss., University of Michigan, 1994).

62. On the special scorn for "perverts" in contrast to "inverts" when American medicine began to take up this matter, see Chauncey, *Gay New York*, 121–27.

63. Paul Fussell has argued that "compared with passionate writing in the Great War, the convention in the Second is that love is strenuously heteroerotic." To Fussell, homoerotic expression seemed "largely limited to POW camps, with their extreme circumstances of deprivation." Fussell, *Wartime*, 109. Fussell's mistake may have been an anachronistic expectation that affection would be expressed in the same ways—poems, for example—in wars a generation apart. Fussell's generalization is unsustainable in the face of Bérubé's *Coming Out under Fire*, yet even Bérubé's book is limited by his firm reliance on conventional gay/straight categories.

64. Elaine Tyler May, among others, has documented the inhibiting quality of postwar mainstream culture, but she underestimates the severity of this problem for men. See her *Homeward Bound: American Families in the Cold War Era* (New York: Basic Books, 1988).

65. Historians are beginning to appreciate the compatibility of overly fervent postwar anticommunism and the period's vehement homophobia. See Chauncey, "The Postwar Sex Crime Panic," in *True Stories from the American Past,* ed. William Graebner (New York: McGraw-Hill, 1992), 160–78; D'Emilio and Freedman, *Intimate Matters*, 292–95; John D'Emilio, "The Homosexual Menace: The Politics of Sexuality in Cold War America," in John D'Emilio, *Making Trouble: Essays on Gay History, Politics, and the University* (New York: Routledge, 1992), 57–73; and Stephen J. Whitfield, *The Culture of the Cold War* (Baltimore: Johns Hopkins University Press, 1991), 43–45.

66. Therese Benedek, *Insight and Personality Adjustment: A Study of the Psychological Effects of War* (New York: Ronald Press, 1946), 67.

67. Margaret Mead, *Male and Female: A Study of the Sexes in a Changing World* (New York: William Morrow, 1967 [originally published in 1949]), 138.

68. John Horne Burns, *The Gallery* (New York: Harper and Brothers, 1947), 149–50.

69. Burns, *Lucifer with a Book* (New York: Harper and Brothers, 1949).

70. Burns, *A Cry of Children* (New York: Harper and Brothers, 1952). There is only one brief biography of Burns: John Mitzel, *John Horne Burns: An Appreciative Biography* (Dorchester, Mass.: Manifest Destiny Books, 1974).

71. Gore Vidal, "John Horne Burns," in *United States: Essays, 1952–1992* (New York: Random House, 1993), 343–46.

72. Alfred Kazin, "The Alone Generation," in *Recent American Fiction: Some Critical Views*, ed. Joseph J. Waldmeir (Boston: Houghton Mifflin, 1963), 18–26, 19; Kazin's remarks first appeared in 1959.

73. Malcolm Cowley, *The Literary Situation* (New York: Viking, 1955), 60.

74. Among the most vigorous and influential critics was John W. Aldridge. See his *After the Lost Generation: A Critical Study of the Writers of Two Wars* (New York: McGraw-Hill, 1951).

75. Norman Mailer, *The Naked and the Dead* (New York: Holt, Rinehart, and Winston, 1948).

76. For some of Mailer's comments on homosexuality, see *The Presidential Papers of Norman Mailer* (New York: Bantam, 1964), 125, 144, 210.

77. See Chauncey, "The Postwar Sex Crime Panic"; Lee Edelman, "Tearooms and Sympathy, or, The Epistemology of the Water Closet," in *Nationalisms and Sexualities,* ed. Andrew Parker et al. (New York: Routledge, 1992), 263–84; Lloyd Wendt, "The Vilest of Rackets," *Esquire,* April 1950, reprinted in Martin Duberman, ed., *About Time: Exploring the Gay Past* (New York: Penguin Books, 1991), 173–76.

78. Martin Duberman, headnotes to "How the King Cole Bar at the St. Regis Got De-Fagged," in Duberman, *About Time*, 224–27.

79. Ibid., 225.

80. On Cohn, see Nicholas Von Hoffman, *Citizen Cohn* (New York: Doubleday, 1988), passim. On the alleged homosexuality of McCarthy, Spellman, and Hoover, see David M. Oshinsky, *A Conspiracy So Immense: The World of Joe McCarthy* (New York: Free Press, 1983), 310–11; John Cooney, *The American Pope: The Life and Times of Francis Cardinal Spellman* (New York: Times Books, 1984), 109; Richard Gid Powers, *Secrecy and Power: The Life of J. Edgar Hoover* (New York: Free Press, 1987), 171–72, 185; and Athan G. Theoharis and John Stuart Cox, *J. Edgar Hoover and the Great American Inquisition* (Philadelphia: Temple University Press, 1988), 107–8, 208–12, 288–92, 331–32, 409.

81. Tony Kushner, *Angels in America: A Gay Fantasia on National Themes* (New York: Theatre Communications Group, 1993).

82. David F. Greenberg dusts off Freud's concept and gives it cultural significance in *The Construction of Homosexuality* (Chicago: University of Chicago Press, 1988), 13–14.

83. Robert Peters, *For You, Lili Marlene: A Memoir of World War II* (Madison: University of Wisconsin Press, 1995), xiv.

84. Ibid., 105. See also 21, 38–39, 41, 59–60, 81–83, 89, 93–96.

85. Sebastian deGrazia, *The Political Community: A Study of Anomie* (Chicago: University of Chicago Press, 1948), 159.

86. Stephen E. Ambrose on *The Today Show,* NBC, 11 November 1997. See especially Ambrose, *Citizen Soldiers: The U.S. Army from the Normandy Beaches to the Bulge to the Surrender of Germany, June 7, 1944–May 7, 1945* (New York: Simon and Schuster, 1997). On comradeship, see also Gerald F. Linderman, "The Appeals of Battle: Comradeship," chap. 7 in *The World within War: America's Combat Experience in World War II* (New York: Free Press, 1997), 263–99.

87. Studs Terkel, *The "Good War": An Oral History of World War Two* (New York: Ballantine, 1984). For a critique of the "legend of the Good War," see Michael C. C. Adams, *The Best War Ever: America and World War II* (Baltimore: Johns Hopkins University Press, 1994).

88. Mario Puzo, "Italians in Hell's Kitchen" in *The Immigrant Experience: The Anguish of Becoming American,* ed. Thomas C. Wheeler (Baltimore: Penguin, 1971), 35–49.

89. "Ted Allenby," in Terkel, *The "Good War,"* 176–82. Allan Bérubé's *Coming Out under Fire* makes it clear that Allenby's sense of unfettered homosexuality during the war was by no means universal, but Bérubé does show as well how the situation worsened greatly after the war.

90. DeGrazia, *Political Community,* 159.

91. Walter Blair and Hamlin Hill, *America's Humor: From Poor Richard to Doonesbury* (New York: Oxford University Press, 1978), 448.

92. Allanbrook, *See Naples,* 84–85, 213.

10

RICKIE SOLINGER

THE SMUTTY SIDE OF *LIFE*

Picturing Babes as Icons of Gender Difference in the Early 1950s

For a researcher like me at the University of Colorado's Norlin Library interested in the pictures, the flavor, and the narratives that captured American women in *Life* magazine in the early 1950s, a question that must come up right at the beginning is, what do Marilyn Monroe, Dorothy Dandridge, Anita Ekberg, Gina Lollobrigida, Elizabeth Taylor, Mickey Mantle, Sir Edmund Hillary, and a Renoir nude have in common with each other but not with Conrad Adenauer, Dwight Eisenhower, Christian Herter, and Richard Nixon?

They were on *Life* covers in the early 1950s. In 1995, however, each cover in the first group had long ago been ripped out of the Norlin collection while the second group of covers was fully intact. At first I was open-minded about who ripped the covers off. I thought I ought to be wary of presuming that furtive, horny guys were the library miscreants; after all, more than 17 million women between the ages of twenty and forty-four read *Life* in the early fifties, and more than a few of them in Boulder might have wanted to take one of these gals home to admire and study the star after whom they wished to model their own style. But Mickey and Sir Edmund Hillary and Roy Campanella, to boot, all missing from Norlin, along with the beauty queens. No, I concluded, the ripper was a guy (likely a series of guys over the years) who treasured and thus tore up *Life* magazine for its steady supply of babes and other paeans to mid-century heteromasculinity.

I am going to look at the interesting role of the babes in *Life* and elsewhere in the United States between about 1950 and 1956. In the years after World War II it became much more difficult than it ever had been in this country to construct and market a compelling, convincing, and symbolically resonant image of model American womanhood, and much more difficult to answer simply the question, "Who is the American woman?" During the Depression and the war, cultural arbiters like *Life* promulgated unified, iconic images of female identity (Figure 10.1).[1] It did not matter if some substantial part of the audience could not identify personally with these images. The point was that the audience could *recognize* the American woman.

As Susan Douglas has pointed out regarding changing but unified ideas about female roles at mid-century, "In the ten year period from 1940 to 1950, our mothers had been told, first, that they shouldn't work outside the home . . . then that there was no job they couldn't do . . . and finally that their real job was to wash diapers . . . and obey their husbands."[2] Despite the potentially disorienting injunctions that mandated that American women wear an apron in one era and overalls in the next, the flourishing postwar mass media produced these serial, unified images indefensibly and with a confidence that they reflected a shared belief in the qualities of ideal American womanhood.

After World War II, American women may have been fiercely enjoined to wash diapers and obey their husbands, but, as many social historians have recently argued, the 1950s was a deeply complex and not a quiescent, conservative era, especially for millions of women.[3] Wendy Kozol has argued brilliantly that *Life*, in particular, responded to this complexity in a way that aimed to tame gender-related disruption: "In the midst of so many social changes in American society, *Life*'s special gift was to make change seem traditional by locating the tensions of an unfamiliar world within the seemingly familiar and non-threatening orbit of the 'happy' nuclear family."[4]

In reading *Life* from the 1950s, however, I find a decidedly nonfamilial context that surrounded and challenged Kozol's "non-threatening orbit of the 'happy' nuclear family." The woman-in-the-family-frame occurred within a field of large, highly sexualized, sometimes pin-up style images of women, images of what I call "babes." They appeared two each month on the cover in the fifties, like clockwork—Conrad Adenauer, a babe; Adlai Stevenson, a babe.

In the 1940s *Life* had used the babe less often (and in the 1960s, too, although by the end of that decade the babes who appeared were often likely to be almost naked). There is no question that the babe on *Life*'s cover, and inside, in the early 1950s was a marketing strategy. Babes addressed the concern that increasingly predictable material about other women—the housewife, the worker, the community achiever, the socialite—innovative though a lot of this material was, did not satisfy the need for national, female icons. The women's pages did not answer the big, increasingly pressing postwar questions: "Who and what is the American woman?" The eighty-hour-a-week housewife, the woman politician, the Wellesley coed, the young African American woman integrating a southern school, did not answer these questions coherently or reassuringly enough, or this material began to answer the questions in confusing or unacceptable terms.

In the early 1950s *Life*'s pictures of American women yielded a fractured set of images, a development potentially disturbing for readers of either sex. Who was the recognizable, ideal American woman after World War II? Who could be the ideal American woman in a cultural field crowded with moms, momism, Marilyn, Mamie, Mrs. Career Woman, the specter of Mammy's daughters—educated African American women—and, oh God—the Butch.[5] In this context, the babe in *Life* became a symbol of resistance against the fractured concept of the American woman and against the various alternative contenders for that title.

Figure 10.1. "FSO Victory Belle," *Life*, June 29, 1942. (Courtesy Johnny Florea/TimePix)

The question "Who is the American woman?" was so pressing in the early 1950s and so hard to answer satisfactorily because the war years and early postwar era together were times of substantial social and economic changes for women. Despite reconversion policies that aimed to eliminate huge numbers of women from the workplace, 16.5 million were employed out-side their homes in 1950, and that number was increasing by hundreds of thousands each year. Social commentators regularly reported that, the postwar domestic imperative notwithstanding, lives of American women were increasingly characterized by behaviors that had not been associated with femininity in the twentieth century. The catalog of these behaviors cast an ironic gloss across mid-century diagnoses of female sexual frigidity. They included, besides paid employment, declining female premarital chastity, increasing frequency of illegitimate pregnancy, declining concern about the sexual double standard, and a steadily rising rate of divorce. Some observers calculated that American women more frequently recognized themselves as sexual beings and pursued opportunities within and outside marriage to enhance their erotic lives. In the interests of this pursuit, women completed the disassociation of sex and procreation via the widespread use of what Jonathan Katz called "pleasure enhancers," that is, birth control.[6]

Nelson Foote, a postwar commentator on gender matters, noted with equanimity and hope in the early 1950s that social and economic "equality of opportunity for women has tended to replace exploitation in society at large."[7] Many other social analysts were far from equanimity as they surveyed the new roles and behaviors of American women in the fifties. Swift, harsh, and even venomous censure of modern women was rife. Experts' attacks on women in the 1950s are well-known and are, for feminists today, discouragingly familiar: the equation of feminism with pathology, the crackdown on abortion practitioners, the targeting and punishment of so-called deviants, such as lesbians and unwed mothers, and the pervasive adaptations of Freudian theory as bases for attacks on working women, especially mothers.[8]

The handwringers and the writers who published jeremiads decrying the decline of "traditional femininity" and the rise of "the new spirit of female boldness" in the 1950s lamented most that American women were becoming more like—too much like—men, especially as money earners and as pursuers of sexual pleasure without fear of pregnancy.[9] American women, many claimed, were destroying the basis of heterosexual life as Americans had known it.[10] In mainstream culture, the masculinization of women was considered willful and destructive and perhaps remediable.[11]

Robert Coughlan, writing for *Life* in 1956, described the pervasive fallacy behind the growing postwar tragedy of gender relations. The idea that women were as good as men became transposed, he wrote, into the idea that women are really "the same as men, saving only for a few anatomical details." This was a claim supporting the unfortunate view that "what is good for one sex is equally good for the other."[12] Whether the rhetorical style was vituperative or cautionary, the laments lavished on the state of American womanhood shared the qualities Elizabeth Hartwick noticed all around her in the early 1950s as "a dismal sadism and regression in the contempt for American women."[13]

The question here is, what was *Life*'s response, as Kozol has written, to this "complex terrain of relations between men and women that occurred at the end of the war in both social and work arenas?"[14] Or, put another way, how did *Life*'s coverage of women reflect the breakdown of the possibilities for picturing a positive, national female identity? My reading of *Life* magazines from the early 1950s suggests that a central concern of the editors then was to resist the postwar fear that women were becoming more like men. *Life*'s pictures and texts regarding women regularly emphasized gender difference, primarily by means of the figure of the babe, but also, prominently, through images that placed women firmly within the family frame, in gender-regulated roles.

Focusing on the babe, one notes that *Life* struck a number of different attitudes toward her place in American society, while in all cases, underscoring her extreme gendered essence. Marilyn Monroe, of course, regularly carried her sexualized, gendered essence into *Life* in the early fifties (not one of the Monroe spreads remains intact in Norlin Library, except for pictures of the star in relatively demure poses "as she becomes Mrs. [Arthur] Miller in a simple religious ceremony with her husband's family").[15] A typical Monroe piece, "The Pin-Up Takes Shape," pictured her in 1954 "doing the shimmy" while 10,000 GIs in Korea "whistled, howled, and took their personal pin-up pictures."[16]

In a domesticated and slyly hypocritical treatment

of the gambit of the sexy babe, *Life*'s cover story in 1951 on TV chorus girls claimed that television had tamed these broads who high kicked from the smutty edges of show business: "The American chorus girl who used to be considered a fit companion only for playboys, is a good girl now. She is being invited, on TV-musical shows, into everybody's living room where she sashays before the entire family."[17] In "Boudoir Business" a few months later, Arlene Dahl, modeling her own line of lingerie, created what *Life* called a new (or was it newly mainstream) style of "tempest-tossed pin-up art" and demonstrated, at the same time, that when you bring a babe into your home, she may not be so tame after all. *Life* found "Arlene . . . flushed and disheveled—a tousled temptress" and made the point that these pictures were much more explicitly sexy than pictures of Rita Hayworth modeling similar clothing in the pages of *Life* ten years earlier.[18]

Arlene Dahl's drop-dead cheesecake poses, along with the generally rich and steady diet of babes in *Life* in the early fifties, are reminders, of course, that *Playboy* magazine—the great mainstreamer of babes and the great proponent of gender difference—was born at just this time, sporting the famous nude Marilyn pinup in the early 1950s. In *Playboy*'s first editorial, the mission statement, the editors specifically and emphatically distinguished their magazine and its readership from the *Life*-style publication: "We want to make clear from the start we aren't a 'family magazine.' If you're somebody's sister, wife, or mother-in-law, and picked us up by mistake, please pass us along to the man in your life."[19] *Life*'s managing editor in the same era, Edward Thompson, expressed, on the contrary, his periodical's innovatively inclusive and wholesome appeal: "*Life* to me, is a friendly neighbor, almost one of the family."[20] Clearly the packagers of *Playboy* and *Life* aimed to construct distinct identities for their products. In the context of the market, the magazines shared an understanding of the financially remunerative potential of babes, and of their power as symbols of sex difference. Not least of all, both magazines recognized the power of babes as symbols of resistance against the modern woman alienated from her feminine self.

The exposure of female flesh that defined *Playboy* and played an important role in *Life*'s postwar presentation of women was related to another media form that also flourished in national and local mainstream publications of every stripe in the early 1950s: the exposé. Both the mass production and marketing of sexually exposed female bodies and the tabloid-style exposé depended on the existence, first of all, of a mass, mainstream readership that wanted to see smut, or what in today's parlance might be called sex-drenched and forbidden images. Further, the mainstreaming of both exposé and exposure depended on a middle-class, consumerist public that believed it had the right to see, even the need to see, these images and took pleasure in seeing what was ordinarily denied, hidden, invisible, but common knowledge. Publishers of mass media began to depend on the purchasing power of a large public more eager than ever to look at large photographs that pictured the dark, juicy underside of ordinary life.

The postwar public consisted of men and women willing, even eager, to behave voyeuristically without feeling guilty. They could gaze at raunchy material without imagining that their own status as upright citizens of the most vigilant democracy on earth was threatened. In fact, for most adults seeing smut could strengthen their claim to citizenship, because exposure and exposé, as they were packaged and sold, claimed to reinforce fraying national standards of masculinity and femininity on the one hand and national standards of virtue and decency on the other.[21]

The mainstreaming of the smut genres that underwrote the exposure of female flesh and the exposé both drew appeal from and reproduced in the soft spots of what Kozol has called, "the complex gender terrain." Both forms invited media treatments that engaged, clarified, and resolved interlocking questions of power, questions of the relationship between power and pleasure, questions of sex and gender differences, and questions that dealt with a particularly recurrent 1950s preoccupation, the relationship between appearance and reality.

Exposés and exposure at mid-century fed on each other, then incorporated and displayed each other's features. Together they promoted a market-oriented, mainstream mutualism between *porno* (the packaged display of sexualized, usually female bodies, for the purpose of selling erotic gratification) and what I have called elsewhere *cryptoporno* (a public event in which, in the name of the law and public morality, men invoke women's naked bodies, their sex, and their vulnerability in a style that is both contemptuous and erotic). The cryptoporno exposé, which conditioned the public to sanction and enjoy sensational revelations about prostitution and abortion rings and sex crimes, for example, nurtured and underwrote the regular appearance of porno exposure in the mass media. Conversely, the increasing frequency and normalization of porno exposure in the mass media sanctioned the ratchetting-up of erotica content in exposés created and sold by mainstream media. In this hot context, with gender roles blurring, with heterosexuality itself on the defensive, and with porno and cryptoporno profitable for an eagerly cooperative mainstream media, *Life*'s babe covers became a twice-a-month event, apparently aimed as deterrence weapons against disturbing gender instabilities.[22]

Sometimes *Life* explicitly acknowledged the difficult adjustments required to maintain gender difference and harmonious gender relations. In early 1952, a piece called "The Wife Problem" reported on wives as potential liabilities since, if they lacked the skills, abilities, and cachet required of a corporate helpmeet, they could block rather than facilitate their husbands' success. This article and "Working Wives" in 1953 both stressed the adjustments women needed to make in order to sustain their femininity while meeting the demands of modern society.[23] In "Soap Opera Wails and Woes," *Life* responded harshly to aspects of the culture that appeared to interfere with the clarity of gender distinctions. The magazine expressed its contempt for daytime dramas

this way: "In most soap operas, men are relegated to shadowy roles as spineless foils of [the] heroines."[24]

The babe in *Life*—Marilyn Monroe and her clones—were drop-dead foils to the bitch heroines of daytime TV, and *Life* often published citizen appreciations of the type. For example, in 1954 *Life* printed a letter from Lt. Joseph Orlay of the Second U.S. Infantry Division in Korea who wrote about the impact on the guys at the front of Marilyn Monroe's shimmy performance and the photos of the event in *Life*. The soldier wrote that Monroe was "the World Series, the 4th of July, the Mardi Gras rolled into one," and, most significantly, he wrote, she "made us feel like men again."[25] In the same vein, "The Siren Look" touted in the September 8, 1952, issue of *Life* was characterized by sleek hair falling loose and "naked sandals" that would please "male America" because "the new fashion's whole point is to make the wearer look like a woman" (Figure 10.2).[26] Reassuring reconfirmations of gender identity were in order, and *Life* participated as a champion of gender difference. It is worth noting that neither the soldier's letter nor *Life*'s article guaranteed that gender was fixed and knowable, only that one could *feel like* a man or *look like* a woman.[27]

Life's interest in shoring up patterns of sexuality and sex roles, frayed by more than twenty years of Depression and war, was shared by cultural arbiters playing the role that Katz called the "sex-norm police": medical doctors, psychologists, clergy, teachers, and marriage counselors who adopted a stance of "narrow, loutish genderism" in pursuing their project.[28] The sex-norm police generally mounted a good cop–bad cop strategy as they sought to hold the line on sex difference. The bad cop harshly exhorted women to sustain traditionally feminine styles. They chastised transgressors or those who might consider resisting. They shamed, blamed, and spewed out censorious judgment and threats of punishment. A particularly representative and flavorful example of the bad cop's warrant was issued in the early 1950s by Arthur J. Mandy, a gynecologist and psychiatrist, who asserted, "There is no rea-

BEADED SHEATH slit to the knee (Ceil Chapman, $175) is worn here with bare Julianelli sandals.

THE
SIREN
LOOK

It is not always ladylike
but few men will protest

To the surprised pleasure of male America, the long-vanished siren look is finally returning to fashion and will be available this fall in a wide variety of sleek and slinky styles. The new collections of America's top designers show that last year's popular, crinoline-padded skirts are giving way to sexy, sheathlike coverings for night-blooming sophisticates (*left*). Glittering with sequins or dripping with long-haired fur, these exotic trappings take on added dazzle this year through unexpected touches of white: plain white collars, long white kid gloves and the newly popular white fox which appears most extravagantly in a full-length coat from Paris (*p. 102*). From hairdo (sleek on top, falling loose at one side) to shoes ("naked" sandals or plain, high-heeled pumps), the new fashion's whole point is to make the wearer look like a woman. If she also manages to look like a lady, that is simply a dividend.

Figure 10.2. "The Siren Look," *Life,* **September 8, 1952. (Courtesy Milton Greene)**

son to expect that a woman who cannot get up to prepare her husbands' breakfast will serve him any better as a bed partner the previous night."[29] Here and elsewhere, women were pressed to cease the kinds of blurred sex-role behaviors that were wrecking contemporary society. They were exhorted to stop resisting femininity and their own female destiny.[30]

On the other hand, men were urged to marshal their natural masculine defenses and fight back against female encroachments onto man's rightful terrain. As the editorial director of *True Magazine* put it, men must "fight back against women's efforts to usurp [their] traditional roles as head of the family."[31] The "devastated male ego," many of the good-cop experts counseled, could be repaired by bolstering and emphasizing gender differences.[32] As for masculinity or masculine prerogatives, good cops argued implicitly and explicitly, these could be recaptured on the field of pleasure, not shame. One way that men who were suffering and confused in the midst of a sex role–blurred world could reestablish a healthy relationship with their masculinity was through the pleasure of buying and viewing women's exposed bodies, in the new mainstream venues. As Barbara Ehrenreich has pointed out, "In every [*Playboy*] issue, every month, there was a Playmate to prove that a playboy didn't have to be a [henpecked] husband to be a man."[33]

When *Life* provided men with this opportunity, its editors published the results. In a 1952 response to a spread called "Italian Film Invasions" that featured a slew of "provocative beauties," including a prominent picture of Rossana Podesta as a "half-naked girl" who summed up the "sex and naturalism" of contemporary Italian films, a Rhode Islander wrote in, "Today I walked into my place of employment and saw a group of men talking in loud and excited voices. I walked over to find out what was the cause of this excitement, and I found out soon enough. There in the center of this group was *Life* with its story, 'Italian Film Invasions.' These men were actually drooling, and who could blame them."[34]

A few months later, Frank Walton, imagining himself the spokesman for the fraternity of postmen, wrote in a particularly evocative style from Glendale, California, about the satisfactions of having looked at "sexy tomboy" Terry Moore. "The weather was hot and humid, but your cover picture of Terry Moore made the day easier for us mail carriers. I had a pleasant feeling of lying on the cool sand with the surf gently washing over me every time I yanked a copy of *Life* out of my satchel—which was often."[35]

Kozol's convincing treatment of the ways *Life* used powerful visual tropes of domesticity—to contain desires threatening to the social order, to contain gender conflicts threatening to the family, and to contain femininity itself, which, unleashed, threatened the body politic—does not consider the role of women in *Life* who were not contained within the frame of domestic imagery. Since these women were frequently present in *Life* and so often posted up front as come-ons, one can consider these "uncontained" babes as the opposite of women contained in domestic images.

To begin to consider the cognitive—and somatic— male response to these sexy women in a family magazine, one can start by seeing these images as both contained, by their two-dimensional, packaged, and commodified aspects, and uncontained, because the images picture females on the market, variously unwrapped and unconstrained by conventional definitions of feminine propriety. The women in the pictures are domesticated in a sense because they showed up on the front-hall table, on the coffee table, or in the bathroom. They were consumed at home. They were, at the same time, detached from domesticity. These women were unleashed and unattached, apparently disassociated from proprietary and protective men, and they exuded a brazen essence that was not wifelike. Babes, even flat images of them, suggested danger because they stimulated longing and because their direct gazes pressed the viewer to acknowledge the feral power of female sexuality. Nevertheless, they were traditional because they rendered women as objects of male pleasure. These images in *Life* acknowledged that sexualized women were one important source of male power.

The babe reassured those who were not comfortable with the postwar-era woman. She provided an alternative, a symbol of resistance against both domestically contained, less sexually forthright women and masculinized female competitors. The babe, however, was a disruptive presence in a family magazine. On the one hand she carried conservative and reassuring messages about distinctive sex differences and women's bodies as pleasure sources for men. On the other hand, she was dangerous and exciting and raised the possibility that female bodies and their sexuality could probably be exposed anywhere now, if a self-avowed family magazine were featuring such spreads.

At the same time that highly sexualized women were coming on strong in *Life,* other current affairs that explicitly grappled with female sexuality and gender identity were getting hot media attention. In 1953, in particular, three explosive media sensations—the Kinsey Report on female sexual behavior, the Christine Jorgensen phenomenon, and the Mickey Jelke vice trial—stormed public attention, and the presence or absence of these events in *Life* provides further guidance to the kind of problem *Life* faced defining the postwar American woman.

Two of the most intensely covered and deeply exciting media events of the early 1950s, arguably of the decade, were the publication of *Sexual Behavior in the Human Female,* usually known in the media as "The Kinsey Report on Women" or *K2,* and the public presentation of Christine Jorgensen.[36] The second Kinsey Report and Jorgensen were, to use the lingo of the day, bombshell events, even in a twelve-month period that witnessed several explosive exposures of women's bodies and women's sexuality, including Marilyn Monroe's calendar picture in *Playboy,* the advent of *Playboy* itself, and the splashy publication of Polly Adler's memoir, *A House Is Not a Home* (1953), about her life as a whorehouse madam.[37] Soon after *K2*'s publication, a prominent sexologist described the effect of the report as "the

source of an overnight sexual revolution, a veritable atomic bomb blasting to bits the forces which have kept women submerged."[38] Others referred to its "tremendous impact" on an "hysterically curious" public and compared the secrecy and drama surrounding its publication to "Oak Ridge and the explosion on Nevada Flats."[39]

Christine Jorgensen was not charged with fomenting a revolution. The daily headlines that chronicled her transformation and debut as a blond beauty, just lately George Jorgensen, an obscure private in the U.S. Army, were bombshell caliber, indeed. In the first week of December 1952 various New York newspapers and others all over the country carried front-page banners that read "Bronx Veteran's Own Story of How He Became a Girl," "Most Happy at Change, Hopes Some Day to Wed," "Ex-GI becomes Blond Beauty," "Folks Are Proud of Their Gal," "The Girl Who Used to be a Boy Isn't Quite Ready for Dates," "Family Sending Girly Yule Gifts," and finally, the cautionary, "Sex Conversation Not a Simple Matter," a subject that the whole country, even six-year-olds in Cincinnati like me, were uneasily considering that week.[40]

Life responded to the publication of *Sexual Behavior in the Human Female* with a lengthy, though just about strictly gray, print spread. Five small black-and-white photos accompany the voluminous text: a picture of the book, a portrait of each of the three commentators *Life* engaged to pronounce upon the report's significance, and a prophetic picture of thousands of eager students at Berkeley gathered to hear Alfred Kinsey deliver a sex lecture on campus.[41]

The main thrust of *K2* was the recognition of women as subjects whose behaviors and identities were frequently sexual, even erotic, on their own terms. Absolutely central to this recognition was that women are just as entitled to sexual experience and gratification as men. These ideas were deeply radical in the early 1950s, and *Life* magazine was nowhere near prepared to embrace or showcase the radicalism at the heart of *K2*.[42] Instead, the editors assembled a group of three white,

Figure 10.3. Christine
Jorgensen, from *Time*,
December 15, 1952.

THE PRESS

Headline of the Week
In the Rome *Daily American*, over a review praising a new Italian production of *Hamlet*: GOOD PRINCE, SWEET NIGHT.

Trouble for the *Workers*
Manhattan's Communist *Daily Worker* has been in financial trouble for so long that even its most devoted readers yawn at the cries for help. But last week the cry of "wolf" had a convincing ring to it. Said a boldface box covering Page One: "We are at the end of all resources. Our printers' bill has piled up, and he cannot go without payment . . . We must receive at least $5,000 in the next few days if we are to be able to continue, and $10,000 by the end of next week. We ask that every reader—and we mean every reader—immediately send from five to ten dollars." The *Worker* could expect no help from its blood brother across the Atlantic, the London *Daily Worker*. For months it, too, has been appealing for money on Page One, may have to slim down to a single page, or fold altogether.

The Great Transformation
The New York *Daily News*, which covers sexy, sensational stories with a flair that no other tabloid can match, last week broke a story that surprised even hardened *News* readers. Splashed across Page One was a banner headline: EX-G.I. BECOMES BLONDE BEAUTY. Said the story: "A Bronx youth, who served two years in the Army during the war and was honorably discharged, has been transformed by the wizardry of medical science into a beautiful woman." Under the banner were pictures of George W. Jorgensen, 26, the George who "is no more," and Christine, "the new woman" he became after "five major operations, a minor operation and almost 2,000 [hormone] injections" in a Copenhagen hospital.

The paper was tipped to its exclusive by a letter that *News* Reporter Ben White received from a friend who is a laboratory technician in Copenhagen. White tracked down the parents of George and/or Christine in New York City, talked them into giving him the full story, together with pictures of Christine in a low-cut dress and a letter from her breaking the news to the folks at home. Wrote she: "I am still the same old Brud, but my dears, nature made a mistake, which I have had corrected and now I am your daughter." Wire services and other papers pounced on the *News* exclusive, phoned Copenhagen directly and sent dozens of correspondents converging on Christine's room in the hospital, where she is awaiting a final operation.

Needlework or Ball Games.
"Lying in a hospital bed," said an A.P. dispatch from Copenhagen, "her long yellow hair curling on a pillow, [she] widened her grey-blue eyes and lifted her hands in a surprised, frightened gesture." One newsman got into her hospital room using a

bouquet of flowers as a pass key. Others bombarded her with such questions as "Do you sleep in a nightgown or pajamas?" "Will you ever be a mother?" "Do you still have to shave?" "Are your interests male or female? I mean are you interested in, say, needlework, rather than a ball game?"

The *News* added its own fillip from its correspondent in Copenhagen who cabled: "Chris now is a girl I could have fallen in love with had I met her under different circumstances." At Bentwaters Air Force Base in England, reporters found a U.S. Air Force sergeant who said he had dated

GEORGE JORGENSEN
Pop said "he" . . .

CHRISTINE
. . . when he meant "she."

TIME, DECEMBER 15, 1952

---

middle-aged experts—Ernest Havemann, a journalist with a special interest in psychology, and two lady novelists, Kathleen Norris and Fanny Hurst—who were set to the task not of critiquing the volume, exactly, but of bringing their own strongly defined perspectives and prejudices to bear on the issue of female sexuality in the modern world. Only Havemann seemed to have actually read *K2*. Norris said straight out that she had not, and Hurst gave no evidence in her essay of having done so. The debate that ensued is a good reflection of *Life*'s larger effort to come to terms with the essence of the postwar, modern American woman: Who is she? Who is she *now*?

Ernest Havemann's emphatically delivered position was steeped in Freudian language and concepts. He pooh-poohed implications that women have a strong relation on their own to sexuality or sexual experiences. Most sexual encounters, including the abundant encounters reflected in Kinsey's statistics on women, were male-initiated, he assured *Life*'s readers. This must be so, Havemann argued, because of what we know about the profound sex differences that make men "leering goats" and women "passive and frigid." Nothing in *K2*, he said, challenged his belief in these difficult verities that, unfortunately, made good sex between men and women just about miraculous. Havemann found, and counseled the public to find, *K2* "bleak and old hat" altogether. He did take the occasion, however, to justify, on the basis of the aforementioned deep differences between the sexes, man's interest in—in fact his craving need for—images of exposed female flesh. This was, he said, something that women must understand and accept. Havemann was writing in terms that *Life*'s editors could credit and in terms that reflected *Life*'s position in the early 1950s. Havemann's essay, given the lead position in the dis-

cussion of the Kinsey Report, is approximately three times longer than the pieces by the lady authors, and thus creates the baseline of authority.

Kathleen Norris could not have been less interested in either Kinsey or Freud.[43] She simply and literally dismissed Kinsey's respondents as liars; no truth-telling woman had ever had such quantities and varieties of sexual experiences as Havemann wrote about finding in *K2*. Obviously, she argued, Kinsey and his researchers had missed all the "genuine women," the ones who were at home and well-behaved, "naturally assuming the proud estate of being wife, homemaker, Mother." In the context of *Life*, Norris was essentially correct, but a little bit kooky and old-fashioned, holding as she did so fiercely to a definition of the American woman that was steadily becoming an endangered species in real life.[44] But her insistence surely had its appeal to many *Life* readers.

Finally, Fanny Hurst, a feminist compared to Norris, and a lady novelist associated with sexual themes, made her case that *K2* was "nourishing and healthy."[45] Hurst slighted the importance of Freud in relation to Kinsey, stating "the Kinsey bombshell will shake the psychiatric couches of the atomic age." She also refuted the idea of natural sex roles, and used the report as a springboard for imagining a future "when women achieve economic independence" and will no longer "need to chase men for security." As a feminist, Hurst believed that social and economic structures were relevant to women's experience, though here she expressed herself in cautiously elliptical terms.

It is likely that Hurst was an acceptable commentator because the editors of *Life* appreciated her name recognition and her American sense of progress, and they knew that in the summer of 1953, eight years after the war ended, Hurst's vision of female independence resonated with some proportion of its enormous female readership. At the same time, Hurst's image of the independent woman of the future appeared as a distant chimera, barely discernible in the fog of her rich prose, and faintly ridiculous, even less concrete an entity than Kathleen Norris's apparitional "genuine woman." Neither Hurst nor Norris produced a vision of the American woman that competed—in terms of specificity or recognizability—with Havemann's evocation of the modern woman struggling against contemporary norms of sex difference but destined to obey them.

Christine Jorgensen did not get this kind of scrutiny in *Life*. In fact, she was the missing member, the place where *Life*'s editors drew the cut-off line for family fodder. Other mass media venues, including *Time* (Figure 10.3), and especially the tabloids and Hearst papers gave Jorgensen wildly generous coverage.[46] The huge number of pictures appearing daily in late 1952 and the spring of 1953 (when Jorgensen arrived in New York from Denmark), made her the pictorial subject of the year, challenged only by the Queen's coronation. And yet, she did not appear in America's "favorite" picture magazine.

Newspapers across the county created the Christine Jorgensen story by publishing image after outrageous image of the "former American GI who became a beautiful blond with silken hair," and by giving her public space as the first to raise an issue that she claimed concerned "millions of other people" like herself "who have a system imbalance."[47] Jorgensen's story, of course, engaged and challenged fundamental mid-century verities such as "boys will be boys," "biology is destiny," and other expressions of the stark drama of sex difference stressed in *Life* and elsewhere. According to the science reporter for the *New York Journal-American*, Jorgensen's transformation was enough to "startle the whole world. People," he wrote, "are wondering about how certain and changeable any person's sex can be."[48]

To underscore what Jorgensen's story revealed about the mutability of sex, the papers began to quote experts like Dr. Charles Hocks, associate professor of urology at the University of Texas School of Medicine, who counseled, "If you want to change your sex, you should do it before you reach school age." According to other doctors, sex was not only mutable, it was a far subtler, more indeterminate characteristic than the American public had ever imagined. One newspaper reported that wrong-sex diagnosis was made in one out of one thousand newborns in the United States, "even today." Readers were cautioned that to deal with such a gravely high rate of inaccurate diagnosis, "parents and physicians on regular medical checkups should maintain year after year vigilance regarding the development of the child. Both physical and psychological patterns must be judiciously observed."[49]

Jorgensen plastered on the cover of newspapers,

like babe pictures on the covers of *Life,* sold the product and also provided an occasion, albeit in Jorgensen's a very odd one, to catalog what it took to be a woman in the early 1950s. The earliest reports of Jorgensen focus on her "long blond hair," her "very nice legs," and the "sensitive dignity in her voice." The *New York Journal-American* ran hundreds of pictures, including a group of four with this text: "These close-ups vividly point out the feminine loveliness that is Christine. Her gestures are truly girlish and she has a peaches-and-cream complexion, heightened by judicious application of makeup. There is nothing to indicate she ever had used a razor."[50]

Reporters asked Jorgensen, "Do you consider yourself to be a beautiful woman?" "Do you want to get married?" (*The New York Daily Mirror* reported that when asked if she wanted to get married, she "quickly identified herself with her new sex [when she answered,] 'Every woman wants to get married, doesn't she?'"[51]), and "What about children?" As Jorgensen gamely fielded these questions for America, she became, in the style of Jean Genet's characters, a key to the "constitution and beliefs" of 1950s heterosexual femininity on the one hand and a mockery of these structures on the other.[52] If Jorgensen demonstrated what it took to be a woman (hair, legs, voice, certain hopes, and dreams), she also raised questions for a transfixed public about the sufficiency of a set of mandated attributes in determining sex.

These questions sprung from a shocking aspect of the snippets of interviews that kept appearing in the papers: over and over, reporters asked Jorgensen how she saw herself, how she defined herself, and who she was. Reporters asked her these questions, and they allowed her to answer. The process, as it was published all over the country, implicitly made the case for the dumbfounding proposition that *self-definition*—or choice—in the case of sex was possible, relevant, printable, even an interesting idea, and highly marketable. If George Jorgensen could become the woman, Christine, then opting in or opting out of a

sex could be part of the definition of what it meant to be a man or a woman. Clearly this was a perspective that did not fit into *Life*'s bounded tripartite discussion of the identity of the American woman as revealed by the Kinsey Report.

In a culture that yielded the Kinsey Report and Christine Jorgensen in the same year, and in a culture beset by burgeoning and unprecedented numbers of women entering the paid labor force, the question, "Who is the American woman?" was becoming more perplexing than ever. Throughout this period, *Life* brought out the babes, but it drew the line at Jorgensen. It did, however, feature crime stories that underscored the sensationalistic potential of everyday life and the wages of gender violation. Despite the deadly, domestic violence that was often at the center of these stories, these tales (unlike Jorgensen's story) found a home in *Life,* the friendly, family magazine. In stories such as "The Not Quite Perfect Crime" and "The Case of the Beat-Up Blond," *Life* offered stories of spousal murder with a deeply pointed and cautionary moral: being a real woman meant living vigilantly within the sharply defined bounds of femininity.[53] Crossing boundaries could be deathly dangerous.

When the wife of osteopath Sam Sheppard was murdered in 1953, the media across the country capitalized wildly on the trial of the doctor. *Life,* however, covered the event only once in the early 1950s, perhaps because Sheppard's wife appeared to have been blameless and this story lacked the necessary ingredient of a role-violating female.[54] In contrast, *Life* ran four stories in 1952 and 1953 about another crime trial that did provide support for the campaign in favor of extreme gender difference that *Life* was waging at this time, and specifically in favor of the proposition that the essential quality of the American woman was her visible, sexualized femininity in a context that underscored her subordination to men.[55] In this hotly publicized trial that incorporated exposé *and* exposure, a rich young man was accused of "compulsory prostitution." Mickey Jelke, the twenty-three-year-old defendant, was,

Figure 10.4. "Models for Reginald Marsh," *Life*, March 2, 1953.

as *Life* put it, "the somewhat rancid heir to three million of his family's margarine fortune."[56] Jelke was also a "café society" punk who hung out with petty gangsters and fringy show-business types. While he was waiting to collect his inheritance, he trained a stable of beautiful young women to turn tricks for his benefit, or as the papers said, for "his pin money."[57]

The New York newspapers promised readers that this most publicized vice trial of its generation would dish out "the most lurid court testimony since Charles 'Lucky' Luciano's conviction as a vice-master on a much lower social scale in the 1930s."[58] *Life* dittoed the comparison with Luciano's trial and explained the excitement surrounding the 1953 trial this way, "For most Americans the Jelke vice trial was a rare opportunity to peep into doings of the sinful set."[59]

People were eager to see what sin looked like à la Jelke. Regarding the men massed outside the Criminal

Courts Building, one New York paper quipped, "What's the attraction? World Series tickets? . . . $25,000 job open? You've guessed wrong. It's an all-male line up for seats at the Mickey Jelke trial. . . . They're expecting some interesting testimony at the trial—and they didn't bring their wives along."[60] The presiding judge announced in court that the heated newspaper coverage of the trial, including a description of how smutty pictures of one of Jelke's girls, in sexual poses with another woman, were passed among the "blue-ribbon all-male jury"—caused him "revolting nausea." The papers, he said, were creating "mushrooming public anticipation of lurid and salacious details, to the point where [in the second week of the trial] we find it competing with the President's message on the State of the Union."[61]

The sexy V-girls captured center stage in the courtroom, but ordinary citizens were also excited about the promises that "wealthy patrons of Cafe Society V-beauties" were to be named. Dorothy Kilgallen, covering the trial for the Hearst newspapers, made the point that the average man in the street was pretty apathetic about the moral questions raised by prostitution, but he loved looking at prostitutes and considering the identity (and vulnerability) of "a good-looking Wall Street broker who haunts model agency waiting rooms," the name of a "bachelor whose work aids the defense of the nation," and the other gents listed in the "dynamite-laden address books" frequently referred to in the courtroom.[62]

Judge Francis L. Valente was not, it turned out, willing to pander to the public's desire to view sin. Just after Pat Ward, "the raven-haired star witness," announced she would tell all, including the names of her prominent clients ("reportedly a kiss-and-tell Who's Who of high-flying Government officials, business men, and night club hangers-on who could afford up to $500 a night for a fling with a good-looking doxy"), and the defense "promised to tear the wraps off Pat's . . . tarnished past," the judge barred the press from the trial. This was an unprecedented decision since the judiciary law specifically allowed a judge to close his courtroom to the press, if necessary, in cases of seduction, assault, bastardy, rape, and abortion, but not in the case of a prostitution prosecution. Judge Valente claimed his action was "in the interests of common decency and good morals," though others maintained that the judge was responding to intense "political pressure" from johns who had a lot to lose if their names were exposed in open court.[63]

Whatever the judge's motivation, press coverage intensified after his order. Leaks from the courtroom could not be stopped, the photos of the V-girls on page one got larger and sexier, and the mob scene in the corridors beyond the courtroom got wilder and more circuslike. *Life* described the consequences of the judge's order this way: "What resulted outside the court was one of the most unjudicial circuses ever witnessed in New York's Criminal Courts Building. At every recess, photographers and reporters surrounded emerging lawyers and Pat Ward. Seeking crumbs of information, they got cake."[64]

Life covered the trial four times between Jelke's arrest in late 1952 and the summer of 1953. Two of the stories were built around drawings by Reginald Marsh (Figure 10.4) who was, according to *Life*, the perfect artist to chronicle these salacious goings-on: "One of the most distinguished of contemporary U.S. painters, Marsh has spent more than thirty years gustily painting the sleazy side of life . . . fallen ladies, Bowery bums, and bedraggled burlesque queens."[65]

Life's decision to use Marsh's drawings instead of photographs to capture the trial's titillating sleaze was a calculated move. Media photos of the prostitutes, the lawyers, other witnesses, and the "oleomargarine heir" taken in the courthouse corridors were a dime a dozen. So *Life* went with the form that made its trial coverage look more authentic than anyone else's—and also smuttier. One print journalist noted in a New York daily, under the headline "Portrait of a Fancy Lady Painted at a Vice Trial/Demurest Girls Are Naughty, Too," that "[w]ithout a scorecard, as they say at the ballparks, you would never have known that these girls were not the models or actresses they once claimed to be."[66] Another remarked that one of the call girls came into court "looking more like a Park Avenue debutante than a girl in the racket," and she "drew admiring gasps from spectators as she marched head high, down the corridor to Valente's courtroom."[67]

Marsh was not constrained by either the confusingly ordinary or anomalously classy looks of the V-girls or by the camera's eye as he "set down a series of portraits of the most raffish and expensively dressed collection of trollops the big city had ever gotten a chance to see."[68] He sketched them as "one after another the prostitutes wriggled seductively to the stand to testify . . . [and] as they paraded in and out of the courtroom, most of them unembarrassed by their sudden public exposure."[69] It was impossible to see the artist's renderings of the call girls and require a scorecard to identify the subject matter.

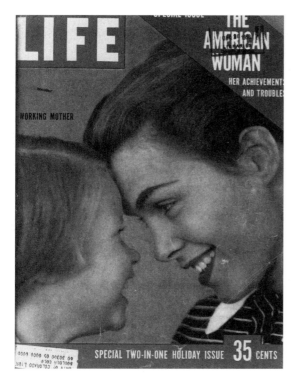

Figure 10.5. "The American Woman:
Her Achievements and Troubles,"
Life, December 24, 1956. (Courtesy
Grey Villet/TimePix)

highlighting the distinctive sexual, subordinate essence of women. These images of resistance—the babe, the whore, and the showgirl—positioned against the housewife, the lady mayor, and the coed, appeared week after week in *Life* and made the magazine an excellent venue for viewing the tortured process of redefining the American woman after World War II, and for gauging just how fractured and contested the American woman had become at mid-century. The ecstatic sexual display of women's bodies in *Life* is a clue to the depth of cultural and political resistance to female dignity and to full citizenship status for women, even in a family magazine that is often thought of as a publication where the postwar domestic imperative prevailed unimpeded and uncontested.

The consistent presence of these images of resistance in *Life* illustrate, once again, that the early 1950s was an era in which the questions "Who and what is the American woman?" were major preoccupations and increasingly difficult or impossible to answer. To some extent, *Life,* itself, contributed to the problem by picturing so many varieties of women week after week, while still believing in its ability to disseminate iconic representations that captured those nationally resonant types, even into the last half of the decade when, for the first time, explosive social changes were beginning to ruin the public's belief in such a figure.

Just on the other side of the period covered in this essay, *Life* made its most concerted and explicit effort to assert the magazine's capacity to define and picture the American woman. Its 1956 Christmas issue was called just that, "The American Woman" (Figure 10.5).[72] The result was a pretty depressing spectacle for a celebration. It was a thirteenth-hour effort to mask the variety and complexity of female life in the United States at just the moment when the lives of millions of

In a trial where the judge, lawyers, jury, and spectators were all male (one reporter noted that on the second day of the proceedings, "as usual Mrs. Ralph Teal [Jelke's socialite mother] was the only woman in the courtroom"[70]), and the defendant was a rich young man, the females brought into court were what *Life* called "the major attraction of the trial."[71] As prostitutes, these women were completely sexualized in court and in the magazine. Their presence in both venues confirmed *Life*'s postwar position that a woman's identity was derived from her sexualized body as a source of pleasure for men. The prostitutes' presence and the stories they told in this madly public context also affirmed that an important source of male power and identity sprung from physical, fiscal, legal, and journalistic authority over the sexualized bodies of women.

Life's repeated exposure of prostitutes throughout 1953 suggests an intention to provide America with pictures and texts of resistance, material that challenged the boring housewife and the masculinized female achiever as sufficient models of womanhood while real women were beginning to be profoundly shaped by paid employment as well as labor-union activities, peace activism, school integration, the availability of legal birth control and illegal abortion, the flourishing of lesbian culture, and other innovative aspects of postwar life. The impact of all of these seem irrelevant to *Life*'s 1956 American woman. Instead, she is pictured as a white, heterosexual, daughter, student, woman, wife, mother, homemaker, volunteer, and widow, almost all roles that derived legitimacy from legally sanctioned relations to men. Only fleetingly she appears as a worker, despite the fact that in 1956 22 million women in the United States had paying jobs outside their homes.[73] A number of essayists writing in this special issue lambasted the American woman—surprisingly harshly in this context of appreciation and celebration—for lacking "staying power and inner resources," for her materialism, restiveness, lack of imagination, for depending too much, or alternately, not enough, on her marriage, for her "pattern of living," for flaunting her accomplishments, for her expensive obsession with holding on to her looks, and for competing with men.

There, finally, was the crux of the problem, according to my reading of *Life:* the blurring of sex roles, the most dangerous of modern maladies, unhealthy for individual men and women, disastrous for modern marriage, and ultimately destructive to the American way of life, that is, democracy itself. The central essay in the 1956 Christmas issue, called "Changing Roles in Modern Marriage," laid out the chief cultural dilemma in postwar America: "Spottily and sporadically but increasingly, the sexes in this country are losing their identities. . . . They are suffering from what psychiatrists call sexual ambiguity." The author was depressed about the possibility of staving off further erosion of gender identity, but he was certain about what it would take to hold the line. Men must represent and exercise authority in our society, the author said, and in the process, well-adjusted men should admire women "for their miraculous, God-given, sensationally unique ability to wear skirts."[74] That was a genteel way of affirming that real men like to look at babes and that real American women had better cultivate and display their physical attractiveness.

Less than a decade after the American woman issue appeared, *Life* published a photo-essay on crime in the city that dramatically illustrated the futility of its attempts throughout the 1950s to dig in its heels on these issues. One part of this photo-essay, a two-page spread titled "Lesbians Try to Peddle Each Other," was also in a sense, one of a number of harbingers of *Life*'s demise. The text accompanying gritty demimonde shots of New York's Forty-second Street at night lamented in terms reminiscent of the Jelke trial, "Telling the players without a program can be all but impossible in Times Square. The four people in the three pictures are all women. Two are drug addicts, and one is a pusher. Two are prostitutes, the other two are pimps. All are Lesbians."[75]

The fact is, *Life* was not comfortable in an America where you needed a program to tell the players, to know the men from the women, the respectable beauties from the prostitutes, the straight women from the dykes. *Life*'s heart was in a world where, as one essayist in the 1956 issue put it, "men are men and women are women and [both] are quietly, pleasantly, securely confident about which they are." Lesbians in Times Square reflected back on the magnitude of the threat Christine Jorgensen represented to the consensus woman back in 1953. After all, how would it have looked then, in the midst of babes, Kinsey's revelations of the sexualized American woman, and Jelke's deluxe call girls, if *Life* had shown pictures of Christine Jorgensen too, the only real lady among them? How would it have looked, indeed, if the only lady was a man?

NOTES

1. In the early years of *Life,* certainly till the beginning of World War II, the magazine did not regularly feature sexy dames on its cover. In its first year of publication, 1937, cover photos typically depicted wholesome Americana: puppies, a cow in a winter pasture, a white leghorn rooster, saddle shoes, Harpo Marx, a one-hundred-year-old woman. The first "babe" cover, I suppose, was Jean Harlow, May 3, 1937, though the actress is *fully* clothed and seen from the back. From mid-1938, when girls, dames, and movie stars—potential "babes"—began appearing on *Life* covers with some frequency, the character of these images seems today pretty thoroughly unsexualized. Exposed skin was almost nil, and the eyes of subjects never engaged with the camera. By the early fifties, cover babes were more often than not decidedly undomesticated, variously unwrapped she-wolves, suggesting, with boldly direct come-hither eyes, that they were positioned for male pleasure.

2. Susan Douglas, *Where the Girls Are: Growing Up Female with the Mass Media* (New York: Times Books, 1995), 54.

3. See, for example, Joanne Meyerowitz, ed., *Not June Cleaver: Women and Gender in Postwar America, 1945–1960* (Philadelphia: Temple University Press, 1994).

4. Wendy Kozol, *Life's America: Family and Nation in Postwar Photojournalism* (Philadelphia: Temple University Press, 1994), 56.

5. See, for example, "The Feminine Butch," *Life,* 19 July 1954, 68–70, an article that stimulated letters printed in the 9 August 1954 issue of *Life,* like this one from John E. Stanko of Athens, Ohio: "First we lost our pants, then shirts, along with cuff links, tie bars and ties. Now women are invading the realm of the male haircut. It is high time we males put our foot down in an effort to keep our females looking feminine."

6. Jonathan Ned Katz, *The Invention of Heterosexuality* (New York: Dutton, 1995), 184.

7. Nelson Foote, "Sex as Play," *Social Problems* 1 (Autumn 1954): 154–63.

8. See, for example, John D'Emilio, "The Homosexual Menace: The Politics of Sexuality in Cold War America," in John D'Emilio, *Making Trouble: Essays on Gay History, Politics, and the University* (New York: Routledge, 1992), 57–73.

9. "Illegitimacy Rise Alarms Agencies," *New York Times,* 9 August 1959, 62.

10. As Katz has recently put it, "Disposing of their bodies on the labor market, [American] women asserted their right to dispose of their bodies' eroticism, earlier the sole prerogative of men" (*The Invention of Heterosexuality,* 183).

11. See, for example, Donna Penn, "The Sexualized Woman: The Lesbian, the Prostitute, and the Containment of Female Sexuality in Postwar America," in Meyerowitz, *Not June Cleaver;* and Geoffrey Gorer, "Nature, Science, and Dr. Kinsey," in *Sexual Behavior in American Society: An Appraisal of the First Two Kinsey Reports,* ed. Jerome Himmelhoch and Sylvia Fleis Fava (New York: W. W. Norton, 1955), 50–58.

12. Robert Coughlan, "Changing Roles of Modern Marriage," *Life,* 24 December 1956, 109–18.

13. Elizabeth Hartwick, "The American Woman as Snow Queen," in *The Scene Before You: A New Approach to American Culture,* ed. Chandler Brossard (New York: Rinehart, 1955), 109.

14. Kozol, *Life's America,* 22.

15. "Monroe Weds Arthur Miller," *Life,* 16 July 1956, 13ff.

16. "The Pin-Up Takes Shape," *Life,* 1 March 1954, 28–29.

17. "T.V. Chorus Girls," *Life,* 17 September 1951, 146–51.

18. "Boudoir Business," *Life,* 7 July 1952, 40–41.

19. Quoted in Barbara Ehrenreich, *The Hearts of Men: American Dreams and the Flight from Commitment* (New York: Anchor, 1983), 43.

20. Quoted in Kozol, *Life's America,* 39.

21. For a discussion of exposés and exposure in the media and the courtroom around abortion prosecutions in the postwar era, see Rickie Solinger, *The Abortionist: A Woman against the Law* (New York: Free Press, 1994), chaps. 7 and 8.

22. John D'Emilio has written, "The anti-homosexual campaigns of the 1950s represented but one front in a widespread effort to reconstruct patterns of sexuality and gender relations shaken by depression and war. The targeting of homosexuals and lesbians itself testified to the depth of the changes that had occurred in the 1940s. . . . The attempt to suppress sexual deviance paralleled and reinforced the effort to quash political dissent" ("The Homosexual Menace," 68).

23. "The Wife Problem," *Life,* 7 January 1952, 32; "Working Wives," *Life,* 5 January 1953, 74.

24. "Soap Opera Wails and Woes," *Life,* 5 April 1954, 125.

25. Letter to the editor, *Life,* 22 March 1954, 19.

26. "The Siren Look," *Life,* 8 September 1953, 98–99.

27. Ehrenreich notes that "Since a man couldn't actually become a woman (Christine Jorgensen was the only publicized exception throughout the fifties) heterosexual failures and overt homosexuals could only be understood as living in a state of constant deception. And this was perhaps the most despicable thing about them: they looked like men, but they weren't really men" (Ehrenreich, *The Hearts of Men,* 26).

28. Katz, *The Invention of Heterosexuality,* 179, 107.

29. Arthur J. Mandy, "Frigidity: As Seen by a Gynecologist and Psychiatrist," in *Sex Life of the American Woman and the Kinsey Report,* ed. Albert Ellis (New York: Greenberg, 1954), 97–109.

30. "If one can believe it is necessary to learn how to be a woman, there

is not much one will refuse to the authoritarian voice," notes Marion Nowak in "How to Be a Woman: Theories of Female Education in the 1950s," *Journal of Popular Culture* 9 (Summer 1975): 81.

31. Quoted in Ehrenreich, *The Hearts of Men*, 47.

32. See, for example, George Simpson, "Nonsense about Women," in Himmelhoch and Fava, *Sexual Behavior in American Society*, 59–67.

33. Ehrenreich, *The Hearts of Men*, 51.

34. Letter to the editor, *Life*, 20 October 1952; letter to the editor, *Life*, 10 November 1952.

35. Letter to the editor, *Life*, 27 July 1953.

36. Alfred Kinsey, Wardell B. Pomeroy, Clyde E. Martin, and Paul H. Gebhard, *Sexual Behavior in the Human Female* (Philadelphia: W. B. Saunders, 1953).

37. Polly Adler, *A House Is Not a Home* (New York: Rinehart 1953).

38. Edwin W. Hirsch, "Coital and Non-Coital Sex Techniques: As Seen by a Medical Sexologist," in Ellis, ed. *Sex Life of the American Woman and the Kinsey Report*, 161.

39. See, for example, Donald Porter Geddes, ed., *An Analysis of the Kinsey Reports on Sexual Behavior in the Human Male and Female* (New York: New American Library, 1954).

40. "Sex Conversation Not a Simple Matter," *New York Journal-American*, December 1, 1952–December 7, 1952. On December 11 the same daily printed a letter from a Brooklyn woman that was headlined, "$64 Question." It read, "I think that the press put the fathers and mothers of America on the spot with the stories of Christine Jorgensen. What are we going to tell our children when they ask us how they can change a man into a woman?"

41. "Kinsey Lecture," *Life*, 24 August 1953, 41–65.

42. Even Diana Trilling's husband expressed scorn for a book that seemed to assert that women could have sex without love, possibly without a male partner and the pleasures provided by a penis. As Lionel Trilling fastidiously put it in *The Liberal Imagination*, Kinsey seemed to be promoting "the desirability of a sexuality which used a minimum of sexual apparatus." Lionel Trilling, "Alfred Kinsey," in *The Liberal Imagination: Essays in Literature and Society* (Garden City: Doubleday, 1953).

43. Kathleen Thompson Norris (1880–1966) wrote eighty-one novels, mostly about women, including *Martie, the Unconquered* (1917), *Uneducated Mary* (1924), and *Lost Sunrise* (1939).

44. In *Life*'s 1956 issue on "The American Woman," the editorial was entitled "Woman, Love, and God." The writer defined "the most important role of women" in the United States as "the one symbolized by Mary as source of love," and concludes this way, "Only as women guard the art and guide the quest of love can mankind know all the kinds and heights of love of which they are capable. The art and the quest begin in the family and end at God's feet" (*Life*, 24 December 1956, 36).

45. Fannie Hurst (1889–1968) wrote novels, short stories, and plays. One of her most famous, *Backstreet* (1931), about clandestine and foolish love was made into movies three times between the 1930s and the 1960s.

46. See, for example, "The Case of Christine," *Time*, 20 April 1953; "Ex-GI becomes Blonde Beauty," *New York Daily News*, 1 December 1952, A1, 3, 10; "Christine," *Newsweek*, 15 December 1952, 64; "Folks Are Proud of Their Girl," *New York Daily Mirror*, 2 December 1952, 1, 3, 26.

47. *New York Daily News*, 1 December 1952, 4, 10. This article contains the letter Jorgensen wrote to her parents explaining why she chose to change her sex. A few days after the story broke, the *New York Journal-American* printed this letter from Patricia Olmstead of New York City: "The strange case of Christine Jorgensen has touched me deeply. I think this young person should be commended for her great faith and courage . . . for the sensitive and intelligent way in which she has handled her tragic problem. I think, too, the warmth and understanding her parents have given her show a true mother's and father's love" (10 December 1952, 34). All the coverage stressed her ordinary, loving, trusting relationship with her parents who were "thunderstruck" by her transformation, but nonetheless, never spoke a word against their daughter to reporters.

48. *New York Journal-American*, 7 December 1952, 18.

49. Ibid.

50. *New York Journal-American*, 1 December 1952, 1; *New York Journal-American*, 13 February 1953, 21.

51. *New York Daily Mirror*, 4 December 1952, 5.

52. This sentence is drawn from Jonathan Ned Katz's use of Kate Millet's observation: "Because of the perfection" with which Genet's male homosexuals "ape and exaggerate the 'masculine' and 'feminine' of heterosexual society, his characters represent the best contemporary insight into its constitution and beliefs" (*The Invention of Heterosexuality*, 129).

53. "The Not Quite Perfect Crime," *Life*, 15 September 1952, 60, and "The Case of the Beat-Up Blond," *Life*, 30 November 1953, 67.

54. "Cleveland Builds Murder Case," *Life*, 22 November 1954, 44.

55. "A Deluxe Vice Ring Is Exposed," *Life*, 25 August 1952, 38; "Vice Trial Courthouse Farce," *Life*, 23 February 1953, 29ff; "Girl Witnesses at Vice Trial," *Life*, 2 March 1953, 34–35; "Scrapbook of a Girl from Richmond, Indiana," *Life*, 1 August 1953, 18–19.

56. "Vice Trial Courthouse Farce," 29.

57. "Deluxe Vice Ring Exposed," 38.

58. *New York Journal-American*, 2 February 1953, 1, 4.

59. "Girl Witnesses at Vice Trial," 34.

60. "Charge Pat Ward Paid Jelke $15,000 from Her Earnings," *New York Journal-American*, 6 February 1953, 18.

61. "Press Barred While Vice Girls Testify," *New York Journal-American*, 9 February 1953, 6.

62. "V-Girl Patrons to be Named at Jelke Trial," *New York Journal-American*, 2 February 1953, 1,4; "Testified Jelke Boasted of Big Profits in Vice Dates," *New York Journal-American*, 18 February 1953, 1, 10, 13.

63. "Pat Wothug to Talk Openly, Judge May Forbid Secrecy," *New York Journal-American,* 7 February 1953, 1, 19.

64. "Vice Trial Courthouse Farce," 29ff.

65. "Girl Witnesses at Vice Trial," 34.

66. "Jelke Trial," *New York Journal-American,* 7 December 1953, 1, 9.

67. "Lawyer Reports Jelke Won't Take Stand," *New York Journal-American,* 20 February 1953, 1, 8.

68. "Girl Witnesses at Vice Trial," 34.

69. Ibid.

70. "V-Girl Patrons to be Named at Jelke Trial," 1, 4.

71. "Girl Witnesses at Vice Trial," 34.

72. "The American Woman," *Life,* 24 December 1956 (special issue).

73. Ibid., 31.

74. Ibid., 109–18.

75. "Lesbians Try to Peddle Each Other," *Life,* 3 December 1965, 98–99; quoted in Donna Penn, "The Sexualized Woman," 368.

11

ERIKA DOSS

VISUALIZING BLACK AMERICA

Gordon Parks at Life, *1948–1971*

In November 1948 *Life* published "Harlem Gang Leader," a photo-essay that focused on Leonard ("Red") Jackson, the seventeen-year-old leader of a New York gang called the Midtowners (Figure 11.1). Juxtaposing tense shots of neighborhood fights and funerals with more relaxed scenes of family and friends, the ten-page spread featured nineteen visually commanding photographs of black youth and inner city violence, many of them taken from acute angles, closely framed, and dramatically lit. The text highlighted Red Jackson's "shrewd and quick-thinking" gang leadership and the daily hardships of his life in the "crowded tenements" and "cluttered, dreary streets" of Harlem. Jackson did not want to be a gang leader, *Life* revealed, but "like other Harlem boys," he was unable to "get a job that amounts to much more than low-grade janitor or messenger work" because "employers or the unions are usually prejudiced against him." Worse, he had "no one to talk to about his doubts, fears and troubles before they boil over into mischief and violence." As the essay concluded, Red Jackson "could count the people—white or colored—who were seriously and practically interested in his troubles, on the fingers of one hand."[1]

"Harlem Gang Leader" was a postwar paean to social responsibility, a liberal call addressing the needs

Figure 11.1. Red Jackson, from "Harlem Gang Leader," *Life,* November 1, 1948. (Photograph by Gordon Parks)

of black urban poor and, especially, black male youth. *Life*'s readers responded in kind. Frank Carr of Waukesha, Wisconsin, heralded the photo-essay as "the best sociological study of your magazine's career." Thomas Robinson of Pittsburgh expressed his "hope that the people who are seriously and practically interested will get out and do something about it." And New Yorker Shirley Cohen wrote, "I for one have made up my mind to try to help boys like Red Jackson and members of his gang become somebodies. . . . I am further going to dedicate myself to this cause." Interestingly, *Life*'s earlier coverage of juvenile delinquency had not drawn these sorts of letters, which suggests that response to this 1948 article lay with its difference and, in particular, the compelling character of its photographs.[2] Indeed, "Harlem Gang Leader" was *Life*'s first photo-essay to feature the pictures of Gordon Parks, hired a year later as the magazine's first African American photographer.[3]

Twenty-two years later, in February 1970, *Life* published Parks's last major work for the magazine, a ten-page spread on "militant black rage" titled "Black Panthers: The Hard Edge of Confrontation."[4] Focused on the "running guerrilla war of rooftop sniping, midnight ambush and mass shoot-outs that the Panthers and police have been waging in a number of cities," *Life*'s article featured more than thirty pictures, including Parks's dramatic full-page portrait of Black Panther Party leaders Eldridge and Kathleen Cleaver posed beneath a poster of Huey Newton (Figure 11.2). Other images (taken by newspaper reporters) included amateurish snapshots of nineteen dead Panthers and similar shots of four policemen who had "died in gunfights" with them; photos of the San Francisco riot police; pictures of staffers at the *Black Panther* (the party newspaper); and party chairman Bobby Seale conferring with his attorney. The final pages featured Parks's portrait of five Panthers staring straight at the camera (and thus at *Life*'s readers), caught in a moment of intense strategizing around a conference table littered with notes, coffee cups, and packs of Marlboros (Figure 11.3). The caption included this statement from Panther chief of staff David Hilliard: "After 400 years of struggle and death, revolution is the only thing left."[5]

Life's photo-essay sensationalized the Panthers as outlaw extremists and rebels, ever ready to take up arms because of their belief "that law officers are conducting a nationally coordinated campaign to exterminate them." Although the story opened with government statistics estimating the Black Panther Party at only about 1,200 members in 1969, the pictorial layout and narrative focus of the article stretched the threat of black power insurgency to seemingly implicate all of America's black men, especially those who proposed a radical political critique of racial injustice. Parks's humanizing pictures made the Panthers persuasive heroes, but contrasting shots of the police hardly cast the cops as convincing enemies: *Life* showed them doing their jobs, not leading a war of African American extermination. Laid out next to one another in the pages of a popular magazine where "photographs carried great weight in conveying a specific ideal as a transparent or unmediated visual truth about society," the Panthers came off as tropes of black male rage, while the white policemen they were embattled against—symbolic representatives of white America, or at least, law and order—were shown as victims, not tyrants. As one *Life* reader wrote, "How dare Gordon Parks depict Eldridge Cleaver (a man who has been in and out of jail since he was 16 for rape, robbery and assault) as the wronged instead of the wrongdoer? And then to insinuate that the Black Panther cause is just is the consummate insult."[6]

Admittedly different—the one a liberal portrait of racial difference and social responsibility, the other an angry and fearful report on racial violence and political dissent—both photo-essays visualized black America, and more specifically, black men in postwar America. Their comparison provides an opportunity to assess *Life*'s attention to issues of race and representation

from the late 1940s through the early 1970s, as well as to consider the nature of Gordon Parks's autonomy and authority at the magazine.

Perhaps best known today as the director of such films as *The Learning Tree* (1969), *Shaft* (1971), and *Leadbelly* (1976), Parks worked for *Life* from 1948 to 1971, producing some of the magazine's most memorable photo-essays: slum life in Rio de Janeiro (1961) and Harlem (1968), the Black Muslims (1963) and black power (1967), Muhammad Ali (1966) and Martin Luther King Jr. (1968). Born in Fort Scott, Kansas, in 1912, the youngest of fifteen children, Parks migrated to St. Paul and worked as a busboy, bellboy, piano player, lumberjack in the Civilian Conservation Corps, and semiprofessional basketball player. He first turned to photography in late 1937, inspired by a magazine layout of Farm Security Administration (FSA) photographs left on the North Coast Limited, the train where he was working at the time as a waiter. "Those FSA photos made me think really seriously about photography," Parks recalled decades later. "I became pictorially inclined by those magazine photos. They had a very strong impact on me."[7]

During layovers in Chicago, Parks began visiting the Art Institute. "I was intrigued by all those master painters," he later wrote, "the style and colors of their compositions—so visually and subconsciously I was pulled into doing something. I could have been a painter possibly, at first, but painting was such a long, long road. I had to make money instantly. It takes you a number of years to even master a style in painting. So photography came first." Over the next decade he was employed as a photographer at the FSA and as a war correspondent with the Office of War Information. He also worked with Roy Stryker's documentation project for the Standard Oil Company and as a fashion photographer for *Glamour* and *Vogue*, produced photos for *Ebony*, wrote two best-selling technical manuals on camera portraiture and flash photography, and collaborated with Ralph Ellison on a photo-essay that eventually led to *Life*'s publication of "Harlem Gang Leader."[8]

During his decades at *Life,* Parks took pictures for hundreds of stories ranging from crime, politics, and fashion to Babe Ruth, off-Broadway plays, and Spanish-style furniture. Not infrequently, he was also the photo staffer assigned to stories about race, racism, and black America: when *Life* wanted pictures of an African American family in Alabama for their five-part "Segregation in the South" series in 1956, they called on Parks (see Figures in Chapter 8); when the Reverend Martin Luther King Jr. was murdered in 1968, Parks was assigned coverage of the funeral in Atlanta; when *Life* turned its attention to black insurgency in 1970, Parks got the job. "If I could bring special significance to a story because I was black," he recalled in the late 1970s, "it was given to me."[9] Yet, *Life*'s assumptions about Parks's "special" racial sensitivity were a major source of anxiety for him, particularly as he often resisted limiting racialized categorizations of himself and his photography in favor of a more complex aesthetic hybrid. Parks's first and final *Life* photo-essays, and many others produced from 1948 to 1971, embody the complexities and contradictions of an artistic vision that blended political activism with the seeming objectivity of documentary photography, and further emphasized individuality and personal style.

Partially as a result of his interests and training in the FSA's photo-documentary style, Parks viewed his photography on social and political terms. If *Life*'s stories about African Americans were consistently "given" to him because he was black, Parks also avidly pursued them, pointedly using his camera "as a tool of social consciousness." The race hatred and discrimination he experienced in his life, from the lynchings he witnessed as a child in rural Kansas (recounted in his best-selling

Figure 11.2. Eldridge and Kathleen Cleaver, from "Eldridge Cleaver in Algiers, a Visit with Papa Rage," *Life,* February 6, 1970. (Photograph by Gordon Parks)

Figure 11.3. Black Panthers, *Life*, February 6, 1970. (Photograph by Gordon Parks)

1963 novel *The Learning Tree*), to the bigotry he en- countered in mainstream journalism (*Harper's Bazaar* refused him work in 1944 because the Hearst empire forbid hiring blacks, and *Life* picture editor Wilson Hicks had to be "cajoled" into accepting him), deeply influenced Parks's visualization of civil rights and black agency. Early in his career, Parks declared the camera his "weapon against evil" and his photographs his means of fighting and often extracting revenge against racial intolerance. As he remarked in 1983, photogra- phy helped him "expose the evils of racism, the evils of poverty, the discrimination and the bigotry, by show- ing the people who suffered most under it."[10]

Critic bell hooks writes that "the history of black lib- eration movements in the United States could be char- acterized as a struggle over images as much as it has also been a struggle for rights, for equal access." In Gor-

don Parks's hands, the camera became a powerful po- litical tool capable of creating a "counter-hegemonic world of images that would stand as visual resistance, challenging racist images."[11] That those images were often presented within the pages of a mainstream media institution such as *Life* suggests an editorial and institutional openness to alternative modes of racial representation, especially in the 1960s, and a keen in- terest in Parks's aesthetic and political vision.

Many of his *Life* photo-essays bore a moral agenda of reimaging black representation and rectifying the decades of oppression that he, and millions of other black Americans, experienced. To an extent, Parks's agenda fit with *Life*'s own moralizing tendencies to tell the truth in "a language of pictures" and by so doing, to shape and direct an overall vision of a progressive and democratic American society. *Life* has a reputation as the monolithic medium of a dominant white consensus; James Guimond wrote, for example, that the magazine's photo-essays "are notable for their homogeneity: virtually everyone in them is white, middle class, and a member of a small nuclear family." Yet in the post–World War II era the magazine published numerous stories condemning racial violence (such as their coverage of the trial of Emmett Till's murderers in 1955), generally supported civil rights, and printed images of black Americans that challenged a formerly denied or aberrant history of black representation. All the same, as Wendy Kozol argues, it is important to recognize that *Life*'s coverage of African American struggles for racial equality "supported social activism within a narrative that limited or masked critiques of systemic racism."[12] The magazine never championed more radical civil-rights demands, let alone political movements or racial images that might seriously disturb its liberal vision of an integrated, middle-class American democracy.

While Parks not infrequently pictured his personal causes within *Life*'s liberal pages, he also insisted he was a documentary photographer, an objective reporter who bore the responsibility of "unemotional detachment." In a 1946 *Ebony* interview he asserted that the "function" of a photographer was "just to report accurately the way we live—our social system, our moods, what we think is ugly, what beautiful. The photographer's job isn't to change these things; he just shows them up as they are, and the people take it from there." In 1948 he wrote that the "photographer's moral obligation is to report accurately the truth as he sees it." Decades later, when talking with an exiled Eldridge Cleaver in Algiers for his 1970 *Life* photo-essay on the Black Panthers, Parks reiterated his faith in journalistic "objectivity and credibility."[13]

Documentary photography, of course, is no more neutral than any other form of photography, or image making in general. Despite this, photographic documents have long been held as evidence of some sort of transparent or inherent truth. Parks's repeated affirmation of his own pictorial objectivity suggests that he linked the supposed truth of documentary photography with its seeming persuasiveness. He also linked it with his own political and social agenda, convinced his photographs of black America would gain most acceptance if *Life*'s editors and audiences saw them as the output of an impartial reporter, not a subjective black artist. That they were both were obvious points of tension; in later years, Parks recalled walking a "tightrope" at *Life* between picturing racial justice and reportorial objectivity.[14]

Most of all, and yet clearly attached to these hyperpoliticized and also depoliticized cultural perspectives, Parks embraced photography as a serious creative endeavor, as a way of making art.[15] Keenly interested in technical experimentation, in his predecessors in photography and modern art, in the perfection of his craft, and in developing a readily identifiable personal style, Parks consistently selected irregular angles, dramatic lighting, high tonal contrasts, and provocative subjects when he composed pictures. As fellow photographer Robert McNeill observed, Parks did things "that were different": "I remember seeing him covering a Howard University commencement, and even the other black photographers who were there were saying, 'Who is that crazy [guy]?' I mean, Gordon would use four flashbulbs for a single shot, outdoors where he could have gotten away without using any. He wasn't content just to stand up and take shots from a position that was comfortable for him—he lay on the ground, he shot up, he shot down. He was more like a movie director, trying to capture the whole academic atmosphere."[16]

Parks was not entirely a formalist, and he also absorbed the social protest aesthetics of Ben Shahn and Charles White, whose work he saw at the South Side Community Art Center in Chicago in the late 1930s. He adopted the reformist bent of FSA photographers such as Dorothea Lange and Russell Lee, with whom he worked in Washington, D.C., in the early 1940s. Some of his most powerful photographs were portraits, especially of other black Americans, some famous, some

Our outward guise still carries the old familiar aspect which three hundred years of oppression in America have given us, but beneath the garb of the black laborer, the black cook, and the black elevator operator lies an uneasily tied knot of pain and hope whose snarled strands converge from many points of time and space.

EACH DAY when you see us black folk upon the dusty land of the farms or upon the hard pavement of the city streets, you usually take us for granted and think you know us, but our history is far stranger than you suspect, and we are not what we seem.

10

Figure 11.4. Two photographs from Richard Wright and Edwin Rosskam, *12 Million Black Voices.* (Photographs by Farm Security Administration photographers)

not, with whom he sensed a shared dedication to individual will and talent. His 1942 FSA photo series on Ella Watson, for example, which produced his well-known picture of her posed, with broom and mop, in front of the American flag, clearly rendered the cleaning woman as a formidable working-class heroine. His 1948 book *Camera Portraits,* a sort of Who's Who of famous postwar Americans, featured several African American notables, including writer Ralph Ellison, politician and preacher Adam Clayton Powell Jr., and conductor Dean Dixon.[17] Parks's interest in strong black personalities and leaders, in black Americans who embodied power and conviction, often resulted in visually compelling images that had a profound impact on *Life*'s readers.

These facets of Parks's aesthetic and intellectual

style may seem paradoxical and even unfocused. Indeed, the general paucity of critical writing about Parks's long career of image making suggests that many have found it impossible to "see" his photography in terms of its composite tensions and convictions, preferring either to read race out of his pictures or to reduce them to politically overdetermined tracts.[18] A more substantive analysis of Parks's work for *Life* provides a way beyond these limited binary assessments of his visual imagery, suggesting how he, like other postwar black intellectuals and artists, negotiated these tensions within mainstream cultural institutions to sustain both creative autonomy and commitment to racial consciousness.

Importantly, Parks was completely self-conscious

about the contradictions implicit in using his camera as a weapon, swearing fidelity to visual objectivity, and being an artist. As he recalled in the late 1970s, "The problem was clearly defined from the beginning. It would be hard not to betray myself, to remain faithful to my emotions when facing the controversial issues of Black and White. I was a journalist first, but I would have to remain aware that being true to my own beliefs counted even more."[19] Taking advantage of *Life*'s primary interests in the power of pictures, Parks used his *Life* photo-essays to disrupt stereotypes about race in America, while simultaneously forging an autonomous creative path.

During its first decade, *Life*'s representation of African Americans was meager and abysmal, like most of mainstream media. When blacks were represented it was usually in the form of demeaning photographs and texts that signaled difference and hence, inferiority, in comparison with whites. An April 1937 article, for example, on Huddie Ledbetter, better known as Leadbelly, was subtitled "Bad Nigger Makes Good Minstrel" and featured a full-page photograph of the musician, barefoot and clad in overalls, strumming his guitar in a warehouse. The caption informed *Life* readers that Leadbelly "calls himself 'De King of De Twelve-String Guitar Players of De Worl.'" A year later, when *Life* addressed racial bigotry in the fourteen-page spread "Negroes: The U.S. Also Has a Minority Problem," it reified racist stereotypes by captioning one photograph of a group of African American stevedores with "Tote dat barge, lift dat bale" and by describing a shot of black crapshooters as "Baby needs new shoes." Claiming journalistic objectivity and ignoring its own role in framing the black subject, *Life* smugly wrote that the "Negro is probably the most social and gregarious person in America." Similarly, an August 1943 report on a Harlem riot that left five dead and hundreds injured, focused on photographs of black looters and provided little explanation of the complicity of white police in the uprising and violence.[20]

From its inception, as Kozol observes, "*Life*'s vision of American society as steadily progressing toward greater democracy included support for African American struggles for equality." During World War II, especially with the influx of blacks in the U.S. military and the increasing pressure of civil rights, that idea became ever more vocalized. In a 1944 editorial titled "Negro Rights," *Life* editor Henry Luce described the "Negro Problem" as "America's No. 1 social problem, its great, uncured, self-inflicted wound," adding that it was "aching violently, perhaps reaching a crisis." Impassioned rhetoric about black rights was one thing, of course; the fact that throughout the war the magazine continued to print pictures of blacks as lessers suggests its hesitancy about actually visualizing American racial justice, or its lack of knowledge about how to do so. After the war, *Life* tackled this head-on in its repeated attention to the American family, white and black, using idealized images of middle-class domesticity to suggest a larger narrative of national equality and cohesion.[21] But it also searched for other pictorial visions that might embody its liberal agenda. In June 1945 it provided readers with a four-page "picture-dramatization" of *Black Boy* by Richard Wright, which the magazine staged, scene by scene, in a respectful but cautious article.[22] In 1949 it hired Gordon Parks.

Despite its early history of racist representation, *Life* was where Parks wanted to work. "*Life* was *the* magazine as far as photographers were concerned," he recalled in 1995. "It was the goal of thousands to work there. *Life* had an edge on every other magazine—it was slicker, it was better known throughout the world."[23] When Parks was hired, *Life* had around forty photographers on staff, and another dozen or so on contract. More than a few, including Carl Mydans and Arthur Siegal, had worked on FSA photo-documentation projects. Likewise, other staffers had worked for mainstream magazines such as *Fortune*, *Time*, and *Vogue*. Shared knowledge and *Life*'s clubbiness (its "aristocracy of talent" former editor Loudon Wainwright called it) attracted Parks, but so, too, did the magazine's aesthetic, its sense of personal opportunity, and its audience. *Life* was a "prestigious base for me to work from," he wrote in 1990, which "reached millions of readers."[24]

Life treated its photo staff extremely well, often listing them higher on its masthead than its reporters. The money was not bad either; as Parks and numerous other *Life* staffers fondly reminisce, the magazine's "unlimited expense accounts" were hard to resist. If working for *Life* was the dream of many of the best postwar photographers, it was largely because the magazine took seriously Henry Luce's vow that *Life* would treat photographic pictures—"big pictures, beautiful pictures, exciting pictures," he once wrote—with the sort of reverence and awe generally ascribed to fine art. As picture editor Wilson Hicks remarked in 1952, *Life* let photographers be "artists."[25] As an African American artist with a particular social and racial agenda, Parks was not only personally drawn to *Life*'s permissive art-making milieu but to the reformist possibilities the magazine afforded. Being a *Life* staffer was surely a sign of having made it in a white-dominated postwar America. Being able to reach the millions of white Americans who looked at *Life* each week, and to educate them with a pictorial message of racial equality, was equally appealing.

"Harlem Gang Leader," Parks's first *Life* photo-essay, may be seen as his first of many curricular efforts in this regard. Its genesis, and much of Parks's vision of social activism, documentary photography, and personal creativity, stemmed in large part from his relationships with other black intellectuals in the 1940s. In 1943, for example, he was commissioned to provide portraits for *13 against the Odds,* a compilation of short biographies about America's "top Negroes," including educator Mary McLeod Bethune, poet Langston Hughes, and author Richard Wright.[26]

Parks considered *12 Million Black Voices* (1941), a collaborative photo book about the history and migration of African Americans that featured an essay by Wright and FSA pictures selected and edited by Edwin Rosskam, "my bible, a big part of my learning, and the inspiration needed to keep my camera moving where it might do the most good." Wright's powerful narrative focused on "black folk" from slavery through the Great Depression, from Southern sharecropping to the Northern urban experience. It was paralleled by equally stunning photographs embedded within the book, which, Alan Trachtenberg writes, served as "illuminations, pictorial correlatives, parallel visual texts," not simply as illustrations or appendages (Figure 11.4).[27]

12 Million Black Voices provided the photo-essay model that Parks repeatedly pursued in his work for *Life,* combining seemingly autonomous pictures within a textual frame of reference and definition. It was not always successful: depending on whether Parks or another *Life* staffer controlled the narrative and whether or not that staffer shared Parks's point of view, the text either reinforced or worked against the tone and intentionality of his photographic documentation of black America. In "Harlem Gang Leader," for example, images and words easily correspond and, in fact, Parks seems to have written some of the narrative. In *Life*'s 1970 article on the Black Panthers, however, the two photo-essay components are visibly at odds.

Still, the aesthetic model of the 1941 Wright-FSA collaboration, as well as its moving and multilayered focus on the cultural and racial panorama of the African American diaspora, had a profound effect on Parks's own documentary style and his photo-essay future at *Life.* Years later, he fondly recalled his 1943 portrait session with Wright, the two talking at length "about the black man's problems in America," and Wright inscribing Parks's copy of *12 Million Black Voices* with, "To one who moves with the new tide." As Parks remembered: "So often I had read the inspiring passage in that book: 'We are with the new tide. We stand at the crossroads. We watch each new procession. The hot wires carry urgent appeals. Print compels us. Voices are speaking. Men are moving! And we shall be with them!'"[28] Ralph Ellison was equally enthusiastic about *12 Million Black Voices,* exclaiming in a November 1941 letter to Wright that the photo book called for "exaltation—and direct action." He added, "After reading it and experiencing the pictures, the concrete images, I was convinced that we people of emotion shall land the most telling strokes, the destructive-creative blows in the struggle. And we shall do it with books like this!"[29]

Seven years later, Ellison himself took a stab at a socially reformist photo-essay, joining forces with Parks to produce an article on Harlem's Lafargue Psychiatric Clinic for the short-lived postwar literary journal, *Magazine of the Year '48.* While the photo-essay was never published, the project was instrumental in terms of shaping Parks's postwar understanding of race and representation. Ellison's essay, titled "Harlem Is Nowhere," centered on the "confused" and alienated character of the "Negro personality," in particular Northern urban blacks damaged economically and psychologically by pervasive American racism. Harlem was a world, he wrote, "in which the major energy of the imagination goes not into creating works of art, but to overcome the frustrations of social discrimination." The stock response to "How are you?" in Harlem was, "Oh man, I'm *nowhere*"; the reaction to racism was often "free-form hostility" and "spontaneous outbreaks" like the Harlem riot of 1943. Ellison praised the clinic, the only New York center where both whites and blacks could receive psychiatric treatment, for giving each patient "an insight into the relation between his problems and the environment, and out of this understanding to reforge the will to endure in a hostile world." Challenging the "sickness of the social order" by restoring psychological balance to Harlem's residents, the Larfargue Clinic was "an underground extension of democracy."[30]

"Harlem Is Nowhere" was a rare sort of polemic for Ellison, perhaps his "Northern Negro" rejoinder to Wright's focus on Southern migration in *12 Million Black Voices.* While seizing on "damage imagery" to show the destruction of racism, to encourage an empathetic response from postwar Americans, and to thereby promote racial rehabilitation and inclusion, Ellison also spoke to black agency, arguing that African Americans must reject general assumptions of black

pathology, and their characterization as victims, and reimage themselves as American citizens. Further, if Ellison found the origins of black suffering in a racially oppressive American society, his understanding of racial justice, the "direct action" he had praised in Wright's 1941 photo book, was keyed more toward individual behavior than social policy.[31]

It was this complex model of the black personality, progressive social change, and the emphasis on self that Parks embraced in the photos for Ellison's essay, and in much of his future work for *Life. Street Scene,* for example, one of the few surviving pictures from his collaboration with Ellison, pictured a dejected man sitting on a Harlem curb; another photograph, titled *Neighbors,* showed a sullen group of four women, isolated and nonspeaking, in front of a Harlem storefront.[32] A few months later, after Parks began freelancing for *Life,* he took hundreds of other pictures of the streets and citizens of New York's black ghetto, veering between evocations of urban alienation and images that revealed the strength and resilience of black youth. His brief apprenticeship with Ellison helped Parks hone a narrative strategy he often employed at *Life:* producing powerful photographs that existed in tandem with provocative socially conscious texts about black America, which held a tense position between pity and agency, and that spoke especially to an eminent individuality—his own, and that of other African Americans.

Given his interest in imaging black America, it is interesting that Parks pursued a career at *Life* rather than *Ebony,* which first appeared in 1945. In fact, Parks produced several photo-essays for *Ebony* during its first years of publication, including a November 1946 spread on Sugar Hill, an upscale section of Harlem inhabited by America's "best-known" black elites, including Langston Hughes, Joe Louis, Duke Ellington, and Roy Wilkins. The article typified *Ebony*'s general focus on black success stories; as editor and publisher John Harold Johnson announced in the magazine's first editorial, *Ebony* aimed to "mirror the happier sides of Negro life—the positive, everyday achievements from

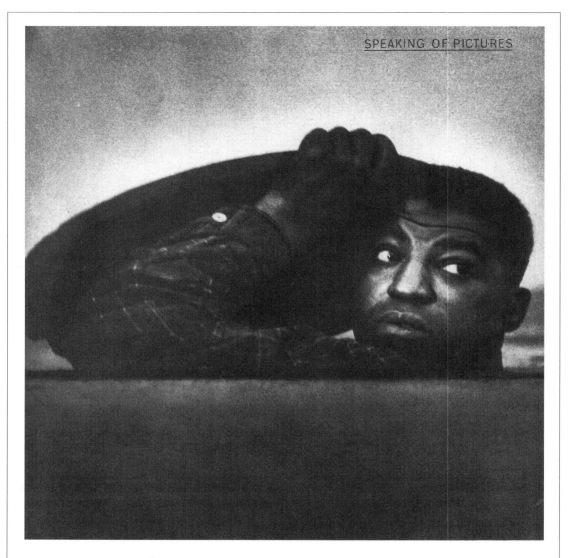

A MAN BECOMES INVISIBLE

Photographer re-creates the emotional crises of a powerful new novel

The wide-eyed man peering cautiously from beneath the manhole cover is "invisible" to the rest of the world. He is the unnamed hero of *Invisible Man* (Random House, $3.50), a sometimes confusing but powerful first novel by Ralph Ellison. Born a southern Negro, as was the author, the hero comes to New York City, hoping to find a meaning and purpose for his life. Instead, he finds the Brotherhood,

a Communistlike organization which uses his eloquence to arouse Harlem to action. Too late he realizes that the Brotherhood is indifferent to Negroes and is ruthlessly using him for its own purposes. The disillusioned hero loses all hope as he learns that other men see him not as an individual but as "just another Negro"—an invisible man. He temporarily withdraws from society, symbolically

going underground, until he can learn to live with his tragic truth.

LIFE Photographer Gordon Parks, a friend of Author Ellison, was so moved by this story that he translated it into pictures. With Ellison's help he re-created from the novel the scenes on these pages to show the loneliness, the horror and the disillusionment of a man who has lost faith in himself and his world.

CONTINUED ON NEXT PAGE   9

Figure 11.5. "A Man Becomes Invisible," *Life,* August 25, 1952. (Courtesy Gordon Parks/TimePix)

Harlem to Hollywood," rather than getting "all hot and bothered about the race question." *Ebony*'s primarily middle-class black audience apparently preferred this too: after the magazine published a 1946 editorial on urban poverty, which was accompanied by a powerful photograph Parks had taken of a disabled African American child, one reader wrote, "Your magazine is nice but for God's sake, lay off this mess about Negroes living in a ghetto and the horrible conditions that the Negro lives under. . . . You cannot help a person that is too lazy to help himself. They are nothing but poor black trash and we cannot help them any more than the white person can help poor white trash."[33]

Ebony played a major role in disrupting longstanding racist representations of black Americans. But its primary attention to black celebrities and consumerism, its general disinterest in civil rights (until the 1960s), and, perhaps most importantly, its vision of itself as a magazine specifically for and about middle-class and upwardly mobile African Americans was largely antithetical to Parks's postwar interests and aims. *Life* was also, of course, smitten with stars, shopping, and the American middle-class but, different from *Ebony*, saw itself also as a news magazine that, because of this purview, was often obligated to tackle controversial issues. Further, while Parks and *Ebony* were both concerned with African American subjects, Parks's interest in black individuality was predicated less on success than on effort, on conviction and fervor rather than adaptability.

There was also the issue of aesthetics. Longtime *Ebony* editor Ben Burns credits *Life* as *Ebony*'s main media model: "I had copies of *Life* constantly in front of me to emulate, and I did so religiously, replicating entire page layouts and seeking to match title types and writing styles as much as possible. The *Ebony* logo in a bold gothic typeface was a copycat of the logo of *Life*." Yet *Ebony*, compared to *Life*, was simply a second-rate product. Criticized by *Newsweek* (not exactly an exemplar itself of a tony magazine) for its "lax editing, loose writing and inaccuracies," *Ebony* consistently featured

dreadful production qualities and a text-heavy emphasis that belittled the often outstanding photographs it published.[34] *Life*, as Parks observed, "was slicker."

Working at *Life*, however, at least during his first years with the magazine, was tense and alienating, and Parks often felt that he was being "tested." Seeing *Life*'s other staffers as "a blur of silent white," Parks saw himself as a "pepper seed in a mountain of white salt" and "an island" of isolated blackness, often walking a "tightrope" between expectations of objectivity and his own agenda of raising racial consciousness, between succeeding as a photojournalist and succeeding as a black man. He worked constantly, and like *Life*'s other staff photographers, his assignments were plentiful and diverse. During the late 1940s and throughout the 1950s, his photographs for *Life* included pictures of spring hats and fashion models, movie stars, high school proms, tennis games, and New York artists. And, like other *Life* staffers, not everything he did wound up being published. "The rejection bin on *Life*'s thirtieth floor was overflowing with good stories that failed to make it into print," Parks recalled, disappointed when photo-essays such as a 1949 piece he did on his hometown, Fort Scott, Kansas, were nixed by the "capricious nature of news."[35] Given the numbers of times that Parks's visualization of black America did appear in the pages of *Life*, however, it was evident that news about race held a heightened degree of interest at the magazine and with *Life*'s postwar audiences.

In 1950 Parks was assigned a two-year stint with *Life*'s Paris bureau, where he provided photos for stories ranging from haute couture and European royals to Sugar Ray Robinson and Philippe Pétain's funeral.[36] Living in France, Parks came to understand "why other black artists had chosen expatriation over the evils of their native land." Still, he sustained his faith in the promise of American democracy, and in creating his own style of American art, "I could never bring myself to say I hated America. I acknowledged her as a great country, but without trembling at her greatness. I damned her at times, but without allowing her to consume me with bitterness. The ironic thing about all this is that no country in the world offers a black the opportunities America does. The sad thing is that America makes it so difficult for blacks to take advantage of those opportunities."[37]

By January 1952 Parks was back in New York. While *Life* was devoting increasing pages to segregation and civil rights (the index listings under "Negroes" steadily multiplied as the decade progressed), Parks, always considered a photographer—not a reporter—at the magazine, was assigned less straight-news coverage than particular stories that his visual imagery and personal aesthetic might enhance. In 1952, for example, he visually "re-enacted" scenes from Ralph Ellison's *Invisible Man* (portions of which were written in Parks's house in New York) in four fairly avant-garde photographs, including one of Ellison's unnamed protagonist emerging from his underground lair through a manhole cover (Figure 11.5). While *Life*'s writers called *Invisible Man* a "powerful yet also confusing first novel," the essay was a complete aesthetic jump from the magazine's earlier "picture-dramatization" of Wright's *Black Boy* in 1945, indicative of both a postwar shift toward more experimental forms of modern art and the magazine's increasing forays into African American life and experience.[38]

Those forays took Parks to Mobile and Shady Grove, Alabama, in the summer of 1956, where he was assigned coverage of an African American family in the segregated South. As Wendy Kozol discusses in this book (see Chapter 8), Parks was the only photographer given a byline in *Life*'s five-part series on segregation, indicative of both his "recognized status in the 1950s and the privileging of his vision by the magazine."[39] Contrasting shots of COLORED ONLY drinking fountains, WHITE ONLY playgrounds, and dilapidated black schools with images of hardworking black farmers, loggers, barbers, and well-dressed professors, Parks's photographs clearly pictured the inequities of a Jim Crow society and made the case for the full restoration of African American citizenship. Yet, there is a tentative

character in the photo-essay, one leaning to the psychological damage caused by segregation and ignorant of the ongoing fight for civil rights on Southern turf. The Reverend Martin Luther King Jr. went unmentioned in the photo-essay, as did Rosa Parks and the nearby Montgomery, Alabama, bus boycott—despite the fact that *Life* had covered it earlier that year. The word *integration* appeared only a few times in the text.[40]

In the 1960s Parks struggled with such ambivalence in a series of *Life* photo-essays that spoke directly to African American assertiveness. "Black Muslim's Cry Grows Louder" (1963), a fourteen-page piece subtitled "The White Devil's Day Is Almost Over," and "The Redemption of the Champion" (1966), a long article on boxing champion Muhammad Ali, both imaged black power and racial pride. They included some of Parks's strongest *Life* photographs, from spellbinding portraits of Elijah Muhammad, Malcolm X, and Ali to revelatory shots of the "closed world" of the Black Muslims—in prayer, in school, and in tough physical training "for defense against unprovoked white attacks." "The Cycle of Despair: The Negro and the City" (1968), an agonizing photo-essay on Norman and Bessie Fontenelle and their ten children, featured harrowing images of hungry and cold children, desperate adults, and horrifying Harlem living conditions.[41] Photographing Bessie Fontenelle and four of the children at a New York antipoverty office (Figure 11.6), Parks updated Dorothea Lange's famous photograph *Migrant Mother* (1936) for *Life*'s contemporary audiences. The powerful spread revealed his constancy to the humanism of the FSA photo-documentary tradition and to the circumstances of black urban poverty that he had first imaged for *Life* two decades earlier in 1948.

Despite their gripping visual power and steadfast assertion of African American humanity, however, many of these 1960s photo-essays were couched—both by Parks and by *Life*—as the style and voice of an individual black American. A 1963 article titled "How It Feels to Be Black," for example, featured excerpts from *The Learning Tree*, moody photographs of Parks's Mid-

Figure 11.6. Bessie Fontenelle and family at the Poverty Board, from "The Cycle of Despair: The Negro and the City," *Life,* March 8, 1968. (Photograph by Gordon Parks)

western hometown, and this introductory statement: "Gordon Parks, a Negro born in the border state of Kansas—neither north nor Deep South—spent a large part of his life fighting for a place in the white world. He won that place and became a famous photographer, a member of *Life*'s staff. Now he has turned to writing and has produced his first novel, a violent and perceptive fictional autobiography."[42] There is no doubt of *Life*'s keen interest in Parks's social and aesthetic vision. By focusing primarily on his personal struggle, and ignoring *why* he had to fight "for a place in the white world," *Life* avoided the larger critique of individual and institutional racism, and thereby significantly reduced the authority of his visual style and voice.

Parks's own ambivalence played a role in this. In

"What Their Cry Means to Me—A Negro's Own Evaluation," written for *Life*'s 1963 article on the Black Muslims, Parks noted that his interview with Malcolm X had a "corrosive" effect and forced him to reexamine his own "moral convictions" and "faith in America." Malcolm X "is right," he wrote, "because for all the civil rights laws and the absence of Jim Crow signs in the North, the black man is still living the last-hired, first-fired, ghetto existence of a second-class citizen." While admitting that "the circumstance of common struggle has willed us brothers," Parks did not want to join the Muslims: "I've worked too hard for a place in this present society. Furthermore, such a hostile frontier would only bristle even more with hatred and potential violence. Nor will I condemn all whites for the violent acts of their brothers against the Negro people. Not just yet, anyway."[43] It was an extraordinary report, a personal warning to *Life*'s readers about the strong appeal of black nationalism if integration failed. It also revealed Parks's primary commitment to the terms of his own individual creativity, to his personal fight to gain access and support at an institution—*Life*—that facilitated his ability to make art.

Some *Life* readers denounced this sympathetic portrait of Malcolm X—"Mr. Parks's compassionate report undeservedly dignifies the Black Muslims," wrote J. M. Lengyel of Atlanta. Others praised the photo-essay for its seeming display of objectivity and its representation of black pride, and they lauded Parks's manifest individuality. "I salute a fellow American and obviously superior human being, Gordon Parks, for his impartial classic, 'What Their Cry Means to Me,'" wrote Marguerite S. Peterson of Salt Lake City. "Gordon Parks's photographs of the Black Muslims have for the first time revealed to me a new and different Negro, men and women alive, self-controlled and self-respecting," wrote Ruth Stein of Albertson, New York. Mrs. Robert Draving of Fort Washington, Pennsylvania, wrote, "The Black Muslims won't frighten me as long as there are Negroes like Gordon Parks."[44]

Plainly, Parks's photographic agenda was keyed to humanizing black America for *Life*'s primarily white readers, and such letters suggest his success. They also suggest that Parks himself came to represent an ideal model of the contemporary African American: a liberal voice of reason and compassion, a talented black artist. Whether or not Parks actually intended to pacify *Life*'s audiences in this manner is unknown. What is clear is the degree to which his ambivalence about social and political activism segued with that of *Life* magazine. While visualizing and speaking on behalf of black America, Parks sidestepped direct political engagement in black nationalism and the black power movement—claiming the seemingly disengaged turf of documentary photography and artmaking. Similarly, while *Life* covered the Black Muslims and the Black Panthers in

the 1960s, it did so as news rather than an affirmation of radical social change and racial justice. Likewise, Parks's celebration of black heroism, including his own, certainly provided an important model of individual African American achievement. It also permitted *Life*'s mostly white audience to ignore the social and structural realities of racism in America and to assume that talent is "naturally and inevitably recognized."[45]

On the other hand, by captivating many *Life* readers with his image and voice, Parks was also able to persuade them of the social and psychological damage of racial oppression, and to convince them of his liberal vision of a racially just America. More than one *Life* reader praised his "intentness on brotherhood" and his efforts to dignify the black subject. Heading his 1968 article on urban poverty, and facing a plaintive photograph of Norman Fontenelle looking through a broken window into the camera, Parks wrote:

> I am you, staring back from a mirror of poverty and despair, of revolt and freedom. Look at me and know that to destroy me is to destroy yourself. . . . We are not so far apart as it might seem. There is something about both of us that goes deeper than blood or black and white. It is our common search for a better life, a better world. . . . I too am America. America is me. It gave me the only life I know—so I must share in its survival. Look at me. Listen to me. Try to understand my struggle against your racism. There is yet a chance for us to live in peace beneath these restless skies.

Parks's sympathetic prose and pictures drew hundreds of letters from *Life* readers asking "What, in the name of God, can I do to help?" and offering money, housing, adoption, and jobs. Their contributions, and money Parks asked for from *Life,* helped the Fontenelle family buy a small house in Long Island, and "a new chance."[46]

Parks's attempts to humanize the Black Panthers, however, prompted quite a different response. When *Life* asked him to do the story, he readily agreed, first interviewing Eldridge Cleaver in Algiers and then Panthers in San Francisco and Oakland. Parks was now fifty-seven years old, described by *Life* as "a man respected in both the black and white communities." As he later wrote, "This was a tough one to do. I had the feeling we were out of the same mold. I had to be a journalist, try to get across accurately what they were saying. At the same time I was caught up in this fierce new sense of pride—pride of heritage, pride of color—that has stiffened the young ones to fight back against the kind of persecution that I knew." Opening his *Life* essay with a personal tale of that persecution, Parks described how the night before he flew to Algiers he had been harassed by two policemen as he walked from his East Village apartment to the theater. When asked for identification, ostensibly because "robbers" were in the neighborhood, Parks pulled out his *Life* ID. "I have always tuned out at the term *pig,*" he wrote. "But when those two fat faces reddened at the sight of that card, I too got the image—very clearly." In the rest of his photo-essay, Parks elevated the Panthers' fight for "social justice" and "racial solidarity," completely rejecting the damage imagery he had employed in his portrait of the Fontenelle family. He revisualized the black subject in terms of racial pride and, importantly, recounted the patently evident institutional racism, especially that of the police, which the Panthers had chosen as their "political target."[47] It was not exactly *Life*'s point of view.

The sheer scale and pictorial authority of Parks's portrait of Eldridge and Kathleen Cleaver in Algiers and his photographs of an organized black brotherhood strategizing revolution in Oakland cast the Black Panthers as appealing and credible figures. "To understand these kids," Parks told *Life*'s readers, "you have to understand racism as a black man knows it. Their enemy *is* the police. And if you are part of that silent majority that wants the police to wipe them out, then you are their enemy too." Less attracted by the Panthers' choice of weapons than their fight against racism, Parks downplayed their militant reputation and quoted Eldridge Cleaver's promise "to replace racism with racial solidarity" and Bobby Seale's remark that "our goals are the same ones the white man fights for. A decent education for our children, good jobs, good housing." He also re-

peatedly referenced incidents of police brutality, remarking that he, "like many other black people, experience this type of harassment constantly."[48]

Life's editors were not entirely unsympathetic with Parks's position. Snapshots, for example, of the nineteen dead black men that the Panthers said had been killed in skirmishes with police alluded to a journalistic technique employed eight months earlier in *Life*, in a June 1969 cover article that consisted of snapshots of the 217 American soldiers who had died in a single week during the Vietnam War (see Figure 13.5). If that essay, claimed by some as "the single most powerful piece of journalism on the war," signaled *Life*'s "unequivocal confrontation with governmental policy," the repeated use of that snapshot style in *Life*'s story on the Panthers may have been used for similar reasons.[49] *Life*'s article also featured the snapshots of the four policemen who had "died in gunfights with the Panthers." The general tenor of the piece suggests that the magazine's editors were more attracted, and repelled, by the Panthers' embodiment of political anarchy, undercutting Parks's photographs and his comments about racism with captions and a general layout that presented them not as kids ("young ones") but as violent and dangerous black men. The result was an ambiguous and skewed photo-essay that partially bore Parks's affirmation of black power and his anger about racial oppression, but mostly conveyed *Life*'s fears that the Black Panthers were a menace to their vision of America.

Life, of course, certainly knew what it was getting when it hired Parks to cover the Panthers; his forceful pictures of the Black Muslims in 1963 and revelatory comments about the powerful appeal of black nationalism were not that distant a memory. More recently, in 1968, the magazine had juxtaposed photographs taken at Martin Luther King Jr.'s funeral with Parks's anguished and angry words: "White racists warned Dr. King that they would kill him. They kept their word. . . . He had protested the way American whites preferred that he protest—nonviolently. He spent the last dozen years of his life preaching love to men of all colors. And for all this, a man, white like you, blasted a bullet through his neck. And in doing so the madman has just about eliminated the last symbol of peace between us."[50] But if *Life* permitted Parks the personal voice of black outrage in 1968, they may have felt that his powerful views of the Black Panthers in 1970, and his validation of their critique of institutional racism and racial injustice in America, were tantamount to *Life*'s own validation of this critique, and even their embrace of revolutionary politics.

Parks, too, certainly knew what he was in for when he accepted this *Life* assignment; he had, after all, visualized black America for the magazine for over two decades and had both shaped and directed *Life*'s liberal vision of an integrated American society. He knew his own ambivalence, too, and how his goals of consciousness raising, documentation, and creativity both segued with and worked against *Life*'s own liberal vision of America. "Honored" when Eldridge Cleaver asked him to join the Panthers and become the party's minister of information ("A lot of young cats would be glad to follow you in"), Parks said he worried about losing his journalistic "objectivity" and added, "I have things I want to report to as big an audience as possible." Later, he wrote, "I should have said: Both of us are caught up in the truth of the black man's ordeal. Both of us are possessed by that truth which we define through separate experience. How we choose to act it out is the only difference." However much he recognized their differences, Parks's final words about the Black Panthers betrayed pessimism about social activism: "That night I left Cleaver on a wet, wind-swept street. It was strange that his last words were about social justice, the kind that is irrespective of a man's color. I thought about other brilliant young black men like Stokely Carmichael, Malcolm X, and Martin Luther King, one self-exiled, two long since gunned down. I couldn't help but feel that Cleaver's promise, like their dreams, would go unfulfilled. Social justice, it seems, is much more difficult to come by than martyrdom."

Years later, in a follow-up article for the monthly *Life* titled "What Became of the Prophets of Rage?" (1988), Parks retraced his photo-essay exploration of 1960s black nationalism, which he now described as "a mighty ship wrecked, lying abandoned."[51]

Parks's article on the Black Panthers was his last major piece for *Life*. In the spring of 1970 he helped launch *Essence*, a monthly magazine marketed toward black women; in 1971 he directed *Shaft*, the first in a series of blaxploitation movies. In 1989 he scored the music for *Martin*, a ballet about the life of Martin Luther King Jr.; in 1992 he wrote the introduction for *Songs of My People*, a book of photographs by and about African Americans that he called "a revelatory window to a world of pulsing Blackness."[52] Parks never abandoned his creative efforts to critique and recast the representation of black America, but transferred them to other media and institutions. Still, as he recalled in 1995, the photo-essays of black America he produced for *Life* were among the most important of his long career: "I still get letters from people all over the world telling me how much I got to them with my photos and stories in *Life*. I couldn't say I loved it, but I had a tremendous respect for the magazine. I'm enormously thankful to *Life* magazine. It was a great institution."[53]

Such comments suggest the ambivalent nature of Parks's relationship with the magazine. During his tenure at *Life*, Parks helped shape a far more humanist representation of African American lives and experiences and guided the magazine's liberal vision of racial and social justice in America. At the same time, *Life* nurtured his complex pictorial aesthetic, although not without generating considerable tensions and occasionally disrupting Parks's dual commitments to picturing racial equality and forging his creative autonomy with its own, more hesitant, liberal agenda. Recognition of these nuances and ambiguities reveals the complexities inherent in representing race in America, and in the pages of *Life*.

NOTES

1. "Harlem Gang Leader," *Life,* 1 November 1948, 96–106.

2. Letters to the editor, *Life,* 22 November 1948, 19–20. For one earlier article on inner city youth, see "Juvenile Delinquency: War's Insecurity Lifts Youthful Crime 100%," *Life,* 8 April 1946, 83–93.

3. Parks freelanced for *Life* from 1948 to 1949, first appearing on the magazine's masthead on August 22, 1949.

4. "Black Panthers: The Hard Edge of Confrontation," *Life,* 6 February 1970, 18–27. Parks's photographs appeared in a few subsequent issues of *Life,* but the only photo-essay he did was a short piece on boxer Luis Miquel Dominguin; see "An Old Master Back in the Ring," *Life,* 5 November 1971, 74–79.

5. "Black Panthers," *Life,* 18–27. Parks did not take all of the photos for the story; Gordon Stone, Ken Hamblin, Robert Stinnett, Stephen Shames, Howard Bingham, and various U.P.I., A.P., and Liberation News Service photographers took the shots of police and those of murdered Panthers.

6. Wendy Kozol, *Life's America: Family and Nation in Postwar Photojournalism* (Philadelphia: Temple University Press, 1994), viii; letter to the editor, *Life,* 27 February 1970, 20A.

7. Parks quoted in interview with author, New York, December 15, 1995.

8. Parks quoted in Mary Jane Hewitt, "The Eye Music of Gordon Parks," *The International Review of African American Art* 8, no. 4 (1989): 50. Parks was a member of *Life's* photographic staff from 1949 to the mid-1960s, and worked under contract, accepting special assignments for the magazine, until 1971. For further information on his life, see his various autobiographies, including *The Learning Tree* (New York: Harper and Row, 1963), *A Choice of Weapons* (New York: Harper and Row, 1966), *To Smile in Autumn: A Memoir* (New York: Norton, 1979), and *Voices in the Mirror: An Autobiography* (New York: Doubleday, 1990). For specific information on his work with the FSA, see Carl Fleischhauer and Beverly W. Brannan, eds., *Documenting America, 1935–1943* (Berkeley: University of California Press, 1988), 226–29, Nicholas Natanson, *The Black Image in the New Deal: The Politics of FSA Photography* (Knoxville: University of Tennessee Press, 1992), and Deborah Willis, "Flashback: Gordon Parks and the Images of the Capital City," in Willis and Jane Lusaka, eds., *Visual Journal: Harlem and D.C. in the Thirties and Forties* (Washington, D.C.: Center for African American History and Culture and the Smithsonian Institution Press, 1996), 173–205. The texts and some of the pictures from some of Parks's *Life* photo-essays are reproduced in his book *Born Black* (New York: J. B. Lippincott Company, 1971); see also Gordon Parks, *Moments without Proper Names* (New York: Viking, 1975), and Parks, *Half Past Autumn: A Retrospective* (Boston: Little, Brown, 1997), an exhibition catalogue with text by Parks and an essay by Philip Brookman. In 1995 Parks donated his photographic archives to the Library of Congress.

9. Parks, *To Smile in Autumn,* 93.

10. Ibid., 149; Parks, *Voices in the Mirror,* 93, 103; Martin H. Bush, "A Conversation with Gordon Parks," in Bush, *The Photographs of Gordon Parks* (Wichita, Kans.: Wichita State University, 1983), 38, 42.

11. bell hooks, "In Our Glory: Photographs and Black Life," in *Picturing Us: African American Identity in Photography,* ed. Deborah Willis (New York: New Press, 1994), 46.

12. Robert T. Elson, in *Time, Inc.: The Intimate History of a Publishing Enterprise, 1923–1941,* vol. 1 (New York: Atheneum, 1968), 284, comments that an early dummy for *Life* posited the magazine's important role "in articulating a language of pictures." James Guimond, *American Photography and the American Dream* (Chapel Hill: University of North Carolina Press, 1991), 170–71; Kozol, *Life's America,* 149.

13. Parks, *To Smile in Autumn,* 149; "Reporter with a Camera," *Ebony,* July 1946, 25; Gordon Parks, *Camera Portraits: The Techniques and Principles of Documentary Photography* (New York: Franklin Watts, Inc., 1948), 7; Parks, *Voices in the Mirror,* 298.

14. For various writings on documentary photography, see, for example, William Stott, *Documentary Expression and Thirties America* (New York: Oxford University Press, 1973); Richard Bolton, ed., *The Contest of Meaning: Critical Histories of Photography* (Cambridge: MIT Press, 1989); and Paula Rabinowitz, *They Must Be Represented: The Politics of Documentary* (New York: Verso, 1994). Parks, *To Smile in Autumn,* 54, 93.

15. On hyperpoliticized and depoliticized analytic tendencies in African American cultural studies, see Jerry Gafio Watts, *Heroism and the Black Intellectual: Ralph Ellison, Politics, and Afro-American Intellectual Life* (Chapel Hill: University of North Carolina Press, 1994), 11 and passim.

16. McNeill quoted in Natanson, *The Black Image in the New Deal,* 266.

17. Parks discusses the influence of other artists and photographers in *A Choice of Weapons,* 194, 232. On the Watson series, see Fleischhauer and Brannan, *Documenting America,* 226–39; for information on *Camera Portraits,* see note 13 above.

18. This problem is exacerbated by the degree to which Parks has carefully controlled his image through his own voluminous body of writing, including his multiple autobiographies, which seem to stymie the need for other assessments of his life and work. It is furthered by his often elusive response to questions of race, telling one critic, for example, "When I make a film I don't think of that film as a black film," and telling another, "I try to do things that will help my race. I have a race consciousness as I create." See Walter Dean Myers, "Gordon Parks: John Henry with a Camera," *The Black Scholar* 7, no. 5 (January–February 1976): 26–30, and Hewitt, "The Eye Music of Gordon Parks."

19. Parks, *To Smile in Autumn,* 149.

20. "Lead Belly," *Life,* 19 April 1937, 38–39; "Negroes: The U.S. Also Has a Minority Problem," *Life,* 3 October 1938, 48–59; "Harlem Riot," *Life,* 16 August 1943, 32–33. Thanks to Joyce Henri Robinson, who discussed *Life*'s 1938 photo-essay in her paper "Marching to the Beat of a Different (Voodoo) Drummer: *Life* and African American Art, 1936–1950," presented at the "Looking at *Life*" conference, University of Colorado, Boulder, September 14–17, 1995.

21. Kozol, *Life's America,* 149; "Negro Rights," *Life,* 24 April 1944, 32.

22. "Black Boy," *Life,* 4 June 1945, 87–89.

23. Parks quoted in interview with author, New York, December 15, 1995.

24. Parks, *Voices in the Mirror,* 102; Loudon Wainwright, *The Great American Magazine: An Inside History of* Life (New York: Knopf, 1986), 110.

25. On *Life* expense accounts, see Dora Jean Hamblin, *That Was the* Life (New York: Norton, 1977), 175–88; Luce quoted in Wainwright, *The Great American Magazine,* 21; Wilson Hicks, *Words and Pictures: An Introduction to Photojournalism* (New York: Harper and Row, 1952), 147 and passim.

26. Edwin R. Embree, *13 against the Odds* (New York: Viking, 1944). See also *Midway: Portrait of a Daytona Beach Neighborhood* (Daytona Beach, Fla.: Southeast Museum of Photography at Daytona Beach Community College, 1999), which features photographs Parks took while working on this project for Embree's book.

27. Richard Wright and Edwin Rosskam, *12 Million Black Voices* (New York: Viking, 1941); Parks, *Voices in the Mirror,* 85; Alan Trachtenberg, "From Image to Story: Reading the File," in *Documenting America, 1935–1943,* 66.

28. Parks, *Half Past Autumn,* 56.

29. Ellison quoted in Michel Fabre, "From *Native Son* to *Invisible Man:* Some Notes on Ralph Ellison's Evolution in the 1950s," in *Speaking for You: The Vision of Ralph Ellison,* ed. Kimberly W. Benston (Washington, D.C.: Howard University Press, 1987), 210.

30. Ralph Ellison, letter to Richard Wright, November 3, 1941, as noted in Fabre, "From *Native Son* to *Invisible Man,*" 210; Ellison, "Harlem Is Nowhere," in *Shadow and Act* (New York: Random House, 1964), 294–302. The Ellison-Parks photo-essay for *Magazine of the Year '48* was never published, as the journal (a literature and arts review that ran from March 1947 through May 1948 and was published by the Associated Magazine Contributors, Inc.) folded in spring 1948.

31. On "damage imagery," see Daryl Michael Scott, *Contempt and Pity: Social Policy and the Image of the Damaged Black Psyche, 1880–1996* (Chapel Hill: University of North Carolina Press, 1997); Ellison is discussed on pages 168–70.

32. For photographs taken for the 1948 photo-essay collaboration with Ellison, see Parks, *Half Past Autumn,* 62, 64.

33. *Ebony*'s first editorial is quoted in John Harold Johnson, with Lerone Bennett Jr., *Succeeding against the Odds* (New York: Warner Books, 1989), 160; "Sugar Hill: All Harlem Looks Up to 'Folks on the Hill,'" *Ebony,* November 1946, 5–11; "*Ebony* Photo-Editorial," *Ebony,* April 1946, 40–41; letters to the editor, *Ebony,* May 1946, 50. For more on *Ebony*'s attention to issues of race and representation, see Walter Goodman, "*Ebony:* Biggest Negro Magazine," *Dissent* (September–October 1968): 403–9; and Tom Pendergast, "Consuming Men: Masculinity, Race, and American Magazines, 1900–1950" (Ph.D. diss., Purdue University, 1998), 237–55.

34. Ben Burns, *Nitty Gritty: A White Editor in Black Journalism* (Jackson: University Press of Mississippi, 1996), 85–86. Parks's disinterest in *Ebony* may also have been the result of a personality conflict between himself and publisher Johnson; see Parks, *To Smile in Autumn,* 221–23, 232–34.

35. Parks, *To Smile in Autumn,* 54; Parks, *Voices in the Mirror,* 193; Parks, *Half Past Autumn,* 104.

36. On *Life*'s attention to postwar fashion, see Richard Martin, "Style from Paris, Reality from America: Fashion in *Life* Magazine, 1947–1963," *Journal of American Culture* 19, no. 4 (Winter 1996): 51–55.

37. Parks, *To Smile in Autumn,* 65–66.

38. "Invisible Man Enacted," *Life,* 25 August 1952, 9–11. On the postwar shift in art style, see Erika Doss, *Benton, Pollock, and the Politics of Modernism: From Regionalism to Abstract Expressionism* (Chicago: University Press of Chicago, 1991).

39. Robert Wallace and Gordon Parks, "The Restraints: Open and Hidden," *Life,* 24 September 1956, 98–112; Wendy Kozol, "Gazing at Race in the Pages of *Life:* Picturing Segregation through Theory and History," Chapter 8 in this book.

40. "A Bold Boycott Goes On: Montgomery Negroes Keep Up Bus Protest as Leaders Are Arrested," *Life,* 5 March 1956, 40–43.

41. "Black Muslim's Cry Grows Louder," *Life,* 31 May 1963, 22–33; "The Redemption of the Champion," *Life,* 9 September 1966, 76–86; "The Cycle of Despair: The Negro and the City," *Life,* 8 March 1968, 48–54. Parks's story on the Fontenelles was utilized as the basis for the 1968 TV documentary *Diary of a Harlem Family,* which won an Emmy Award.

42. "How It Feels to Be Black," *Life,* 16 August 1963, 72–88.

43. "Black Muslim's Cry Grows Louder," 33.

44. Letters to the editors, *Life,* 21 June 1963, 17.

45. Watts, *Heroism and the Black Intellectual,* 116.

46. Letters to the editors, *Life,* 26 March 1965, 25; Parks, "The Cycle of Despair," 48; letters to the editors, *Life,* 29 March 1968, 23. The Fontenelle story ended in tragedy, however, leading Parks to wonder "about the serious problem of altering human lives." See Parks, *Voices in the Mirror,* 269–72; and George P. Hunt, "Editor's Note: Tragedy in a House That Friends Built," *Life,* 2 May 1969, 3.

47. Parks quoted in Ralph Graves, "Editor's Note: Knowing Too Much Can Be a Problem," *Life,* 6 February 1970, 1, and described in "Black Panthers," 18. Parks described his harassment by New York police in "Eldridge Cleaver in Algiers: A Visit with Papa Rage," *Life,* 6 February 1970, 20. See also Erika Doss, "Imaging the Panthers: Representing

Black Power and Masculinity, 1960s–1990s," *Prospects: An Annual of American Studies* (1998): 470–93.

48. Parks, "Eldridge Cleaver in Algiers," 23; Seale quoted in "Black Panthers," 25.

49. "The Faces of the American Dead in Vietnam: One Week's Toll," *Life,* 27 June 1969, 20; Susan D. Moeller, *Shooting War: Photography and the American Experience of Combat* (New York: Basic Books, 1989), 397–98.

50. Parks, "A Man Who Tried to Love Somebody," *Life,* 19 April 1968, 30.

51. Parks, "Eldridge Cleaver in Algiers," 22–23; Parks, "What Became of the Prophets of Rage?" *Life,* Spring 1988, 32.

52. Parks was editorial director for the first few issues of *Essence;* on the magazine, see Roland E. Wolseley, *The Black Press, U.S.A.,* 2d ed. (Ames: Iowa State University Press, 1990), 149–51. Parks's portraits of various African American women, including Rosa Parks and Kathleen Cleaver, accompanied Gilbert Moore's article "Five Shades of Militancy," *Essence,* May 1970, 16–23. Gordon Parks, Introduction to *Songs of My People: African-Americans: A Self-Portrait,* ed. Eric Easter, D. Michael Cheers, and Dudley M. Brooks (Boston: Little, Brown, 1992), xi.

53. Parks quoted in interview with author, New York, December 15, 1995.

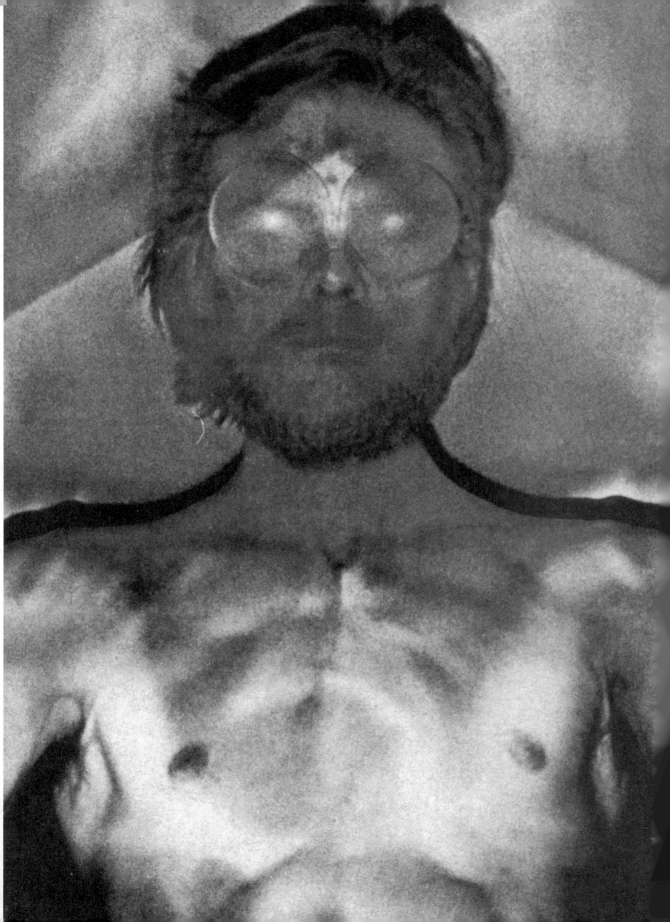

PART FIVE **TO SEE AND TO TAKE PLEASURE IN SEEING . . . TO SEE, AND TO BE SHOWN**

12

NEIL HARRIS

THE *LIFE* OF THE PARTY

Few subjects generate more unashamed curiosity
than other people's entertaining. There is much to
be curious about. Dinners, dances, housewarmings,
weddings, cocktail parties, holiday feasts, anniver-
saries, barbecues, birthdays, showers, masquerades,
excursions, initiations, picnics, conventions, home-
comings, reunions—the social calendar is long and
varied as well as powerfully stimulating. For we are,
most of us anyway, deeply interested in our social
reputations. The character of our entertainments,
our successes as hosts or guests, and our reputed
sociability, these remain for many of us vital components of ego identity.

While the history of the party in America remains
to be written, it is difficult to gainsay its significance.
Few activities with so large an investment of time,
money, and interests have received so little serious
analysis. The ritual practices that lie beneath the simple label of partying—the shifting occasions for providing diversion, the growing appeal of informality, the
transformed status and appearance of menus, an-
nouncements, entertainments, and invitations, the
roles of flowers, caterers, servants, cooking, dancing,
drinking, and food serving, the seasonal rhythms, the
gender, age, race, and ethnic segregations and subdi-
visions—have been in continual motion. To talk about

parties is to invite ethnological commentary about human behavior itself.

That may be why the party became a compelling subject for *Life* from its first issue. *Life*'s editors and some of its best photographers devoted themselves to social engagements. The camera brought to readers, many of whom enjoyed only a limited repertory of fancy entertainments, the chance to observe elaborate social rituals; *Life* carried invitations that would otherwise never have come in the mail. The opportunity to depict partying must have seemed, to its advocates, like a pioneering act of social exploration.

In *Life*'s hands the party was certainly a capacious category. In the course of its twenty-five-year history this feature allowed vicarious attendance on a stunningly broad array of events, some of them involving small groups of people. Most of them shared an element of celebration or festivity, although calling certain expeditions parties stretched the most liberal definitions.

The party feature granted *Life* far more than the satisfaction of curiosity. It permitted, through inclusions and exclusions, juxtapositions and parallels, thematic recurrences and reaffirmations, construction of a clarifying paradigm. It revealed in brief compass just how the editors defined the larger social world. Whose pleasures were deemed noteworthy? What kind of notice would they receive? And how could narratives be constructed from an apparently arbitrary sampling of snapshots? Strategic solutions to such questions were built around prevailing assumptions that stressed unity in pluralism, the universality of human emotions and life stages, and, by comparison, the marginal character of ritualized divergencies. Despite its apparent love of triviality and more than occasional silliness, "*Life* Goes to a Party" exposed, with telescoped precision, the vision of the world that animated the magazine's very existence. For that reason satirists, early and late, seized upon it as a juicy emblem of the magazine's larger stylistic essence.[1]

In form "*Life* Goes to a Party" stood somewhere between the photo-essay and the news story, the two large poles that bounded the magazine's identity. Smaller in scale (and far less expensive) than those classic photo-essays created by noted photographers like W. Eugene Smith, Margaret Bourke-White, Edward Steichen, and Alfred Eisenstaedt, the "Party" feature offered the editorial staff an opportunity to flavor an issue without depending on breaking-news stories. Spread over three to five pages, it incorporated, even in its early days, as many as twelve to fifteen photographs. Although sometimes the photographs were provided by agencies, they were usually the work of staff photographers, giving the editors broad powers of thematic selection. While many "*Life* Goes to a Party" entries were built around specific photographic assignments, the sequencing and arrangement of photographs, the length and character of the accompanying text, the captions, and the choice of subject to be included reflected the ideas of the managing editor and the department heads.

To a remarkable extent, the formal durability of this twenty-five-year feature revealed just how deep and immutable were the management's basic values about their editorial charge. Despite some recollections of change on the part of participants, the "Party" subjects sustained uncommonly consistent patterns. Their values, not surprisingly but with impressive repetition, were deeply conservative, emphasizing the ideals of community, continuity, family, and hierarchy, as well as the importance played by education and imitation when dealing with younger generations.[2]

Covering the doings of society, fashionable society in particular, was not an invention of *Life*. It had been a preoccupation for European and American newspapers since they began to circulate in the eighteenth century, and of course a subject of interest for much longer than that. As readership broadened and American newspapers multiplied before the Civil War, the preoccupation occasionally became an obsession. The penny press organs of Jacksonian America like the New York

Figure 12.1. The Comte de Fels (left) and friends waiting before the hunt, from "*Life* Goes to a Party with French Aristrocrats and Sir George Clerk," *Life,* November 23, 1936. (Courtesy Pictures Inc./TimePix)

Herald reported exhaustively (and sometimes satirically) on expensive parties, using them to symbolize either the dangers or the rewards of wealth, and demonstrating through them the stubborn survival of class loyalties in an egalitarian community. And, as one historian of journalism put it, fashionable society itself proved "at first aghast, then amused, then complacent, and finally hungry" for such news about itself.[3]

By the late nineteenth century society columnists were taking up extensive space on the pages of metropolitan newspapers. In fact, coverage of specific social events had become, during the Gilded Age, an activity with significant political consequences. The opulence of extravagant weddings, dinners, and masquerade balls, publicized through the photographic coverage that half-tone reproduction and new, more mobile cameras made possible, provoked indignant comparisons of conspicuous consumption with mass destitution. The ignominious fate of James Hazen Hyde of the New York Life Insurance Company, host for a costume ball at Sherry's in New York reputed to have cost more than $200,000 (and his job), or the Bradley Martins, forced to leave the country after angry responses to their immoderate entertaining, were warnings about the dangers of graphic coverage.[4]

Party cartoonists as well as photographers managed to provoke extensive debates that rivaled political campaigns. Although some of this publicity was self-consciously induced, it also rested on the hostility of embittered employees or social critics, aware that photographs and detailed descriptions could make life unpleasant for ambitious hosts and hostesses. The public appetite for such events, however, seemed limitless, and investigators happily covered everything from menus and costumes to flower costs and guest lists. The multiplying institutions of this period, from art museums and opera houses to country clubs and prestigious dog shows, enhanced the opportunities for—as well as the varieties of—social display. Crowds thronged the streets right up to the church doors to catch sight of guests at fashionable weddings, and they devoured descriptions of dress and behavior at stylish entertainments.[5]

Monthly and weekly magazines were natural sites for such depictions. By the early twentieth century *Harper's Weekly, Century,* and *Country Life,* once de-

pendent on woodcuts or lithographs for pictorial expression, now featured glossy pictures showing the rich at play, attending one another's weddings and christenings, going to opening nights, weekending on elaborately landscaped estates, making their debuts, and similar events. These photographs, normally not more than a couple for any single occurrence, had captions that did little more than identify the various players. As captors of a specific moment in time they were generally posed and static in quality. They served principally as records of being seen, not so different from the classic poses of celebrities standing at the rail of a transatlantic liner or about to board the Twentieth Century Limited.

The dream of moving beyond set pieces, penetrating private life with the camera, and presenting candid, unposed scenes and meetings constituted, according to some historians of *Life,* a primary motive for its establishment. In the early 1930s the "mildest sort of photographic invasion of privacy seemed a considerable accomplishment," wrote Loudon Wainwright. The former *Life* staffer offered as evidence one article in a pre-*Life* dummy titled "Candid Weekend in Connecticut," which featured photographs taken at the home of the well-known journalist Heywood Broun, entertaining some equally well-known friends. John Stewart Martin, one of those proposing the new picture magazine, described this rather mild effort as experimenting where "no ordinary camera would go."[6] There was little truly scandalous or even titillating about such a piece, but to devote six to twelve photographs to some ordinary incidents of domestic life seemed daring and novel. That, it was suggested, may have provided the impetus to establish "*Life* Goes to a Party" as a regular feature.

Yet the first entries into the genre do not quite bear this interpretation out. While the initial November 23, 1936, issue did include "*Life* Goes to a Party," the editors remarked that it almost did not, "because just this week it couldn't find anything interesting enough to invite itself to," until "it sighted Sir George Clerk and some dead rabbits."[7] It was interest rather than intimacy that seemed to be calling the tune. A reader might, presumably, have paused at this point. Why would a titled Englishman and some dead rabbits provoke such curiosity? Sir George Russell Clerk, the British ambassador to France, was among twenty guests attending a hunt given by the Comte de Fels at the Château de Voisins, near Rambouillet, about thirty miles southwest of Paris. Other participants included the Marquis de Paris, François de Wendel ("the greatest munitions maker in France"), the Comte de Beaumont, the Comte de Maille ("900 years of aristocracy behind him, wants no democratic foolishness when he guns"), and the Duc d'Ayen. Photographs, large and small, featured noblemen lounging around waiting for beaters to drive up the game, butlers uncorking bottles of wine in the fields, and hundreds of dead partridges, hares, and pheasants (Figure 12.1).[8]

Why, in the heart of the Great Depression, were the readers of *Life* exposed, in their first issue, to an exten-sive (and not unsympathetic) pictorial spread of the titled aristocracy of Europe depopulating the French countryside of its smaller animal population? Was this the intimate invasion of daily life that the magazine's planners had in mind, the secret wish of hundreds of thousands of American readers, to know what it was like to shoot game on a French estate? Apparently someone at *Life* must have thought so, for the following week the Duke of Rutland's pack was photographed at Belvoir Hunt, at Croxton Park near Melton Mowbray in England.[9] Only one photograph, but two issues had brought two hunts.

In its third issue, however, "*Life* Goes to a Party" chose an American setting, although again it was one that seemed an improbable contender. This was the convention of the American Petroleum Institute at Chicago's Hotel Stevens (today's Conrad Hilton), an annual extravaganza undertaken for the organizations's three thousand members. Here oil producers, lobbyists, lawyers, tax specialists, and their spouses gathered for several days of lectures, rallies, meetings, and collations, climaxed by a five-dollar-a-head banquet.[10] This last, the clearest basis, perhaps, for the article itself, was diverted by a program of "clean" entertainment. Again, it was not clear why *Life* readers would have found compelling the restrained antics of middle-aged businessmen, shown consuming food, getting dressed for dinner, and holding discussions in smoke-filled hotel rooms. "Well behaved," *Life* called it; prosaic or mundane might be a more appropriate description.

There was nothing mundane or prosaic about the third party excursion the magazine made, this one coming in early December 1936: the elaborate birthday party honoring the Sultan of Surakarta in Central Java (Figure 12.2).[11] Here, on the arm of "Elder Brother" (the resident Dutch Governor), *Life*, through the first European photographer ever to "crash" such a party, entered on a scene of exotic splendor, with thousands of relatives (the Sultan had fifteen wives and eighty-eight grandchildren), officials, servants, soldiers, and guests

For lonely black boys Harlem's Savoy Ballroom provides these dusky hostesses, chosen for their looks, dancing ability and sense of decorum.

Life Goes to a Party

At the Savoy with the boys and girls of Harlem.

MOST densely populated section of New York City is Negro Harlem. Most densely populated square block in Harlem—nearly 4,000 residents—is at 142nd Street and Lenox Avenue. A block and a half south is the Savoy Ballroom, Harlem's most densely populated dance hall. It attracts some 500,000 paying guests a year, grosses $275,000 annually, has 150 people on its payroll, pays its two orchestras $1,200 a week, its black manager $100 a week, provides over $100,000 a year for its white owners. Opened in 1926, the Savoy is noted for its barbaric dancing, its absence of brawls, its 15% white clientele. Harlem calls it "the home of happy feet."

Current favorite at the Savoy is the Lindy Hop, a complicated affair which gives the couple above a chance to do practically everything from solo steps to an Apache twosome. Like many another trick dance, including Trucking and the Susie-Q, the Lindy Hop originated at the Savoy, was named, for no good reason, after Charles Augustus Lindbergh.

The Lindy Hop in a stomping phase. Savoyites often turn professional, become cabaret dancers.

Figure 12.3. "*Life* Goes to a Party at the Savoy with the Boys and Girls of Harlem," *Life*, December 14, 1936. (Courtesy George Varger/TimePix)

in attendance. The palace had the requisite crystal chandeliers, silken canopies, thrones, and other evidence of royal splendor, and the scenes of guests at table, army reviews, princes dancing and kneeling in homage before their father, fulfilled the most elaborate, Hollywood-induced expectations of romantic opulence. The dozen photographs accompanied a text that introduced readers to some of the court's most distinctive features, including the barefoot, batik-shirted advisers who could not stand in the presence of their ruler and had to crawl about on all fours and the Sultan's liking for bridge, cars, and foreign decorations (he had not yet received one from the United States). While hardly an intimate examination, the photographs did admit readers to an event they would hardly have witnessed, or even known about, without its intervention.

The same thing could be said about *Life*'s fourth party visit the following week, although it was set on home soil (Figure 12.3). This was a trip to Harlem's Savoy dance hall on Lenox Avenue and 142nd Street, the area's "most densely populated" hall.[12] Established in 1926 and noted for "its barbaric dancing, its absence of brawls, its 15% white clientele," the Savoy was open until 3 A.M. and served only wine and beer rather than hard liquor. The standard twelve or thirteen photographs included a few individualistic poses, but for the most part the pictures simply caught what the magazine called "the black boys and girls" in arresting postures on the dance floor.

There was little in the photographs that an ordinary patron of the Savoy would not have seen, but then "*Life* Goes to a Party" was beginning to reveal one of its thematic thrusts: site inclusiveness rather than penetration of the private sphere. For those outside New York City, the character of a Harlem dance hall may well have been as exotic as the birthday party of a Javanese sultan. Both, however, served to reinforce stereotypes about otherness, fulfilling expectations of different lifestyles. The Sultan's blend of authoritarian rule and love of modern gadgets fit the prevailing image of oriental despotism: self-indulgent, less cruel than indifferent to social need, courted by colonial governments, barbaric in domestic life, but good for a laugh. Similarly, the Harlem dance-hall essay contained pictures that fed existing beliefs about the "primitive" energy of black Americans, their pleasure in a good time, the coexistence of lawlessness and respectability, and the carefree habits of porters, domestic servants, and elevator operators on their time off. Emphasizing the "white owned" character of the dance hall, as the article did, it went still further, suggesting black business incapacity even within its own community. The larger tone—Harlem's "social set looks down its black nose at the Savoy"—reinforced, through simple insinuation, a patronizing sense of black life as an odd though ultimately unsuccessful imitation of white culture, a burlesque and caricature. Such stories hinted at a *National Geographic*–inspired

excursion to distant shores, even while they appeared to meet literally the need for democratic inclusiveness in the general coverage of social events.[13]

French aristocrats and American oilmen were treated with occasional touches of sarcasm themselves, although there was apparent respect for the discipline and power on display. The occasional put-down of a big businessmen or peer—dozing during a meeting or proving to be a bad shot—was the entry ticket to spend time with the rich at play. Suggesting that such occasions could occasionally be tedious, uncomfortable, or repetitive, invited sympathy for the principal actors. It fit the technique employed by celebrities—in politics or entertainment—to engage the empathy of a general public by allowing them glimpses into their private lives. This had been going on systematically since the days of William McKinley. The rise of film stars, perhaps the most conspicuous arena of celebrity culture in the two decades preceding the founding of *Life*, had engendered a rash of fan magazines, like *Silver Screen, Photoplay, Modern Screen, Screen Book,* and *Motion Picture,* devoted to exposing the heartaches, foibles, hobbyhorses, and indiscretions of screen royalty. The stars, said one student of the fan magazines, wanted their fans to know they had heart, needed privacy, worked hard, and shared ordinary needs and hardships.[14]

Was *Life*'s "Party" series turning into an apologist for celebrity lifestyles? The answer is yes, but only for certain kinds of celebrities. To a remarkable degree the hosts for *Life*'s parties, in these first years and for some time to come, were the traditional lions of society whose goings on had for so long excited newspaper readers. It was not the shock of intimacy, the exploration of ordinary domesticity, or the penetration of private lives that absorbed *Life*'s partying. Instead, there was an immersion in elegance, costliness, and scale that betrayed either highly traditional values by the editors or a sense that, even in a Hollywood age, social elites retained the power to charm and fascinate.

There were continuing bows to middle-class values

and settled commercial ways. In its fifth party visit *Life* reemphasized interest in the lives of business leaders by attending a golden wedding anniversary; the male celebrant was president of the Union Pacific Railroad in Omaha, and his guests from out of town arrived in special trains provided by sympathetic railroad executives.[15] Fourteen hundred diners consumed 2,500 pounds of steak and half as many pounds of mushrooms. This was industrial-scale entertaining.

It was also highly respectable fun. Mrs. Gray, the executive's wife and a deeply religious woman according to *Life,* entertained a group of wives at a table shaped like a cross; the waiters were National Guardsmen. Power and business were amply represented—businessman and future diplomat Averell Harriman was among those in attendance—and received generally good marks for their taste and restraint. Here was no orgy of extravagant spending or senseless pursuit of social rituals. It was just good, clean fun by a class of industrial leaders whose reputations had gone into eclipse since the autumn of 1929.

With five straight partying episodes, *Life* was entitled to a break, and it took one for two issues. Doubters might have wondered whether the feature would actually be continued. In January 1937 it reappeared in full flower, this time devoted to the Philadelphia debut of Joan Peabody, Mrs. Peter A. B. Widener's daughter (Figure 12.4).[16] The text took a mildly critical stance toward the propriety of this $55,000 extravaganza at the Bellevue-Stratford, attended by Wanamakers, Stotesbureys, and Dorrances. Months of planning for one thousand guests required "the expenditure of twenty average working people's annual incomes for an evening of fun." However, *Life* went on in palliation of this impressive investment, "if your grandfather, like Mr. Widener's, left $50,000,000, you can't rent an ordinary ballroom and hire an ordinary band for a daughter's debut."[17]

A sense of social obligation provided the spur for renting out three hotel floors and hiring Meyer Davis and his seventy-five-piece orchestra for the event, to say nothing of constructing a miniature version of the Hialeah Race Track and erecting a fence to keep out would-be gate crashers. The society photographer, Jerome Zerbe, who would work for *Life*'s parties on many future occasions, took the photographs of formally clad diners and dancers; somewhat larger than had been customary in the previous features, they assumed a high-gloss glamour that belied the slightly sardonic tone of the commentary. If satire had been the objective, Zerbe was the wrong choice of photographer. If anything his shots flattered his well-dressed subjects, carrying out an ancient familial ritual that had somehow survived the collapse of so many other things. "*Life* Goes to a Party" seemed particularly fond of family occasions; they were statements of solidarity and reassurances of continuity, and some might argue that this recovery of domestic linkage seemed to undergird the journals' larger enterprise of social exploration.

As if to acknowledge that less-traditional celebrity deserved attention along with old-line families, *Life* next visited an event dominated by café society, a barnyard dance hosted at New York's Waldorf Astoria by Elsa Maxwell, one of the doyennes of this set.[18] *Life* emphasized what many others found intriguing about café society: its arresting blend of many social types, "as catholic as it is sophisticated," and its cross section of Manhattan's most colorful residents, "a good sprinkling of Hollywood and Broadway topnotchers, a handful of foreign titles, a smattering of esthetes and wits." To meet their hostess' demands, guests turned up in combinations of calico, gingham, diamonds, and pearls, mingling as well with chickens, geese, sheep, and donkeys. Champagne emerged from a papier-mâché cow, and decorations were provided by underclothes hanging from a clothesline. It is not clear whether rural readers of *Life* found the juxtapositions amusing, but the editors seemed convinced that this kind of frivolity was significant, even when it played with cherished symbols of national identity.

Life made still more explicit its concern with café

Figure 12.4. Hostess Joan Peabody, from "*Life* Goes to a Party in Philadelphia with the Stotesburys, Wanamakers, and Dorrances at the Launching of a Widener Debutante," *Life,* January 18, 1937.

society a few months later when it once again covered Elsa Maxwell, here as an honoree rather than a hostess.[19] This time, apparently, it felt constrained to offer a more elaborate explanation of new metropolitan rituals. While Mrs. Astor and Mrs. Fish would "turn in their graves" were they to suspect it, "Society in New York today is based primarily not on Connections or even Wealth," *Life* said. Instead its foundation was built upon "people of varied antecedents and occupations who like to have a good time and who know how to have it." This, said *Life,* was café society, ostensibly a classless democracy despite the fact that this second Waldorf Astoria party entertained its guests in fancy dress.

The real point of the article was the guest list. No

"stuffed shirts" or "heavyweight intellectuals." Society was certainly represented: Auchincloss, Livingston, and Frelinghuysen, along with foreign nobility, mingled with actresses Bea Lillie and Ina Claire, financiers and businessmen Myron Taylor and John Mortimer Schiff. "Talent ogled ancestry, ancestry ogled industry," all apparently in search of nothing more than a good time. "Smiling through" was one of *Life*'s solutions to Depression-era miseries— "Whoever, wherever, whatever, however, people were having fun."

"'All work and no play' is no motto of Americans," was how *Life* titled a two-page self-advertisement in the same issue that featured Elsa Maxwell and café society.[20] When the nation had "thrown up its day's quota of gigantic dams, bridges and skyscrapers, wrangled through long hours of politics and strike situations, made its movies," it "goes forth to relax. This nation likes to play. . . ." *Life* did not confine itself to politics, bridge building, and moviemaking; "since *Life* 'came out' it's been to a party or a dance or a picnic or a carnival every week." The photographs the advertisement included showed *Life* attending its parties. The hayride, church fair, and bridge tournament had not yet been covered, the promotion admitted, but their time would come. *Life* would go on showing readers the way "all kinds of people have fun (or don't) at all kinds of parties. White tie, black tie, or no tie— *Life* will go—and tell."

This was one of a series of *Life* advertisements that each focused on a different aspect of the magazine's coverage. In highlighting, after eighteen issues, this particular feature, *Life* was emphasizing the inclusiveness of its social scrutiny, asserting its democratic embrace of all kinds of human diversion, and, by implication, giving all of them equal dignity. The following week *Life* further emphasized its party commitment by printing a reader's complaint that it had not attended a party in the April 26 issue.[21] The editors explained that "Sometimes *Life* goes to a party, does not have a very good time, hesitates to bore its readers." Then *Life* invited reader suggestions for interesting festivities to visit. Three weeks later it published a series of such invitations.[22]

In fact, the first few months show distinct trends in party selection. First, there was fascination with high society—on Park Avenue, Philadelphia's Main Line, Boston's Beacon Hill, Chicago's Lake Shore Drive, or wherever the wealthy and wellborn gathered. Second, there was an interest in the world of media, entertainment, high living—Elsa Maxwell's social sphere. Third, there was absorption with the unusual, the exotic, the surprising—Asian court dances, Harlem dance halls, and Woolworth sit-in strikes. And fourth, a subject extending far beyond "*Life* Goes to a Party," there was a preoccupation, some might argue an intense fixation,

with American youth culture, the pastimes, hobbies, diversions, institutions, sports, and fads that color their lives. Colleges and high schools were favorite sites for *Life* stories, which generally focused, in those years at least, on the wholesome, carefree, and high-spirited qualities of the young.

The first expression of this interest in youngsters came in February 1937, when *Life* visited the Dartmouth Winter Carnival.[23] With some eighteen pictures by Peter Stackpole, a pillar of the staff photographers at the magazine, the emphasis was on the "breathless" character of the entertainments in this "weekend of sport and pleasure" for several thousand "boys and girls." The many small pictures served to evoke the rapid pace depicted. College students were on skis, in tails and dinner jackets, disporting themselves at fraternity house parties, creating snow sculpture, greeting trains, skating, all working together in the interests of athletic young America exploiting the New England winter.

Three weeks later, after a couple of excursions to Mobile, Alabama, and Philadelphia, along with some unconventional high-society scenes, "*Life* Goes to a Party" returned to the young at play, visiting the annual dance at Rosemary Hall, a "topnotch" female boarding school in Connecticut, whose fifth and sixth formers had invited dates from Harvard, Princeton, Exeter, and Yale.[24] The young men were dressed either in dinner jackets or white ties. The behavior depicted was decorous and highly ritualized: chaperones, formal checking in of guests, polite cutting in while dancing, etc. Less exuberant than Dartmouth's Winter Carnival, Rosemary Hall revealed adults in training, privileged, wealthy, carefully brought up youngsters going through a rite of passage.

Sprinkled through these early issues were other articles highlighting youth culture. The week following its Rosemary Hall piece, *Life* ran an essay entitled "A Day in the Life of a Coed," a humorous piece set at Drake University. The week after that came two separate entries, one on swimmers at Harvard and Yale, the other, a more extensive essay on a Smith College weekend.[25] In June 1937 *Life* actually devoted an entire issue to colleges and universities.[26] Its party feature involved a Williams College Sunday picnic, which followed students and their dates hiking, swimming, and ball playing; there were also articles on university libraries, observatories, campus buildings, college customs, and academic dress. The whole issue had the feel of an anthropological investigation into the goings-on of some recently discovered civilization, its costumes and ceremonies unveiled by squads of intrepid field-workers.

Behind 1930s youth culture lay a hidden world of exuberance and privilege for the small minority who could afford a college education. In 1937 little more than 13 percent of the nation's eighteen to twenty-one year olds were enrolled in colleges and universities, a percentage that had doubled since World War I, and would triple in the next twenty years. To judge by the coverage given college life by Hollywood and Tin Pan Alley, the diversions of youth had achieved a firm hold on national attention.

Life's emphasis was still notable and its focus on the elite did not escape reader observation. In May 1937, weeks after its visits to Rosemary Hall, Harvard, and Yale, *Life* covered the annual prom at a Wisconsin high school.[27] This was in response to a written invitation by a member of the Junior Decorating Committee, who clearly had caught *Life* on a sore point. "Perhaps you say, 'But, such an obscure school, we've never heard of it, and anyway, we only select parties at Princeton, Harvard, or the Ritz.' I'm sure," she continued, "your readers would like to see a party of the more informal type, and not at a Ritz but at our High School Gym, transformed into a setting for any King to be crowned."

Life, apparently eager for some populist legitimacy, swallowed the bait. Using the photographs of Elmer Staub of the *Milwaukee Journal,* the editors created a reassuring narrative of small town America, following the teenagers as they prepared for the dance, visited the local beauty parlor, got dressed, left with their dates, arrived, crowned their king and queen, and ended the evening with hamburgers and soft drinks at the U-Needa Eat Shop. This kind of narrative had already become a standard procedure for the "Party" series: following the event through a time frame, doing something that newspapers had never been able to manage—describing just how these affairs were directed, contrasting guests and hosts at various moments of their encounter, and setting the galas within the life of the community.

By talking constantly and insistently about the occupational and social backgrounds of parents, *Life* was able to be optimistic about the upward mobility of society and, by implication, about its cohesiveness. In a Wisconsin high school the children of railroad workers, wealthy businessmen, teachers, and farmers were shown relaxed, affable, and moving easily together. That the students chose a coronation ball (the crowning of George VI, following closely upon the abdication crisis, was the news event of the season and a favorite subject for *Life*) posed no problems. The prom, theme aside, exemplified democracy at work, and, by covering it, *Life* reassured those anxious about its apparent concentration on elite institutions and the activities of the rich. The same issue contained a piece on Kent School rowing and high-society doings at the Memphis Cotton Carnival. This last essay allowed *Life* once again to emphasize the universality of social rituals, this time by covering both the white and black carnivals in Memphis, and portraying the separate reality of each set of parades, balls, and social maneuverings.

In the following weeks, through the end of June 1937, *Life* visited a Polish wedding in Cicero, Illinois, a Connecticut picnic with some young bicyclists, and a spring dance in Deerfield, Massachusetts, where the "children behaved with adult discretion."[28] The emphasis on the young and the ethnic balanced the previous month's excursion with Chicago society at an elite athletic club and a visit to some elegant supper parties

NEWLY CHOSEN ATLANTA DEBUTANTES SMILE FOR THEIR FIRST FORMAL PICTURE IN THE ENTRANCE TO THE BALLROOM OF THE PIEDMONT DRIVING CLUB

A Stately Welcome to Society

In the South where old traditions linger and it means a lot to be a debutante, no debutantes have to pass a tougher admission test than those in Atlanta, Ga. For in Atlanta the social arbiters are the debutantes themselves. They have organized a debutante club and each June the outgoing debs select the girls that will succeed them.

The girls lucky enough to pass this careful screening make their first public bow at a ball in Atlanta's exclusive Piedmont Driving Club. This

month, dressed in her whitest gloves and dress, each of this year's 30 new girls walked the length of the ballroom on the arm of her proud father and officially became a 1956 deb. This formal ceremony was followed by a sedate evening of dinner and dancing under the watchful eye of Atlanta society. But after the ball was over the newly recognized young ladies went to breakfast parties where they kicked off their dancing shoes and played party games just like young girls everywhere (next page).

IN HER PRESENTATION TO SOCIETY MARY ANN CAMPBELL IS ESCORTED BY FATHER ACROSS BALLROOM TO JOIN OTHER NEWLY INTRODUCED DEBUTANTES

Figure 12.5. "A Stately Welcome to Society," *Life,* **November 19, 1956. (Courtesy Robert W. Kelley/TimePix)**

in Louisville preceding the running of the Kentucky Derby, this last photographed by Alfred Eisenstaedt. "New York Society may have submerged into Cafe Society led by Elsa Maxwell," *Life* insisted, two weeks after attending another Maxwell gala, but despite the Depression, "Chicago Society is once again actively led by the McCormicks, Swifts, Armours, Wendells, Palmers, Ryersons, and Meekers."[29] Conservatives could breathe easier. Social standards, at least west of New York and east of Los Angeles, were being maintained.

The values being deployed in "*Life* Goes to a Party" may, of course, have been a function of the first few months of the magazine's existence, reflecting the taste of the editorial staff and the diffuse and sometimes variant purposes that were surfacing in those early moments. To provide a check on their durability, the same months, from November to June, twenty years later, were analyzed to see how things had changed. Those were years of extraordinary events and experiences: World War II, the birth of the atomic age, television, the Cold War, school desegregation, decolonization, creation of the United Nations, and Elvis Presley. The economic, geographic, and social bases of American society had undergone a transformation.

Life's parties had certainly acknowledged some of these events. During World War II, *Life* had partied with soldiers and war workers, it had visited makeshift galas held in bombed-out European cities, and it had exposed the social delights of training-camp towns and recruiting stations.[30] But, a reader in 1956 or 1957 could be forgiven for thinking that *Life*'s partying had remained frozen in a time warp, resembling nothing more than the ritual forms displayed twenty years earlier in the heart of the Great Depression. The pace of three or four parties a month was basically unchanged. And, if anything, the profoundly conservative bias of its coverage had been intensified. While café society seemed to have largely disappeared, high society, and to a lesser extent youth culture and exoticism, remained focal points.

November 1956 featured the last fling of an Indian maharajah, whose elephants, Rolls-Royces, and bagpipers gathered before him on the eve of his assuming an appointed office in the new republic; a formal dance in Providence, preceded by dinner parties in the "city's finest old homes," to support the Rhode Island School of Design; Atlanta debutantes at the Piedmont Driving Club, "where old traditions linger" (Figure 12.5); and a banjo jam at Yale.[31] December and January brought more of the same: a royal wedding in Europe; Bostonians whirling at one of their famous waltz nights; the nuptials of Attorney General Herbert Brownell's daughter; a stately ball in Montreal; swank New Year's Eve parties; a pheasant shoot in communist Czecho-

slovakia with a party of West European aristocrats; and the wedding of New Jersey's governor with a cousin of Adlai Stevenson. Later in the year came Irenee Du Pont's eightieth birthday party, a champagne supper with the Weyerhausers in Minnesota, the Canadian governor general's annual ball in Ottawa, a Paris society party, and a Baghdad gala bringing together the kings of Saudia Arabia and Iraq. The lifestyles of the rich and famous, luxurious settings, great families, prominent politicians, successful businessmen, and, more occasionally, glimpses of the young or ordinary folk continued to preoccupy the editors. By recovering the early planning of such events, catching informal moments and postparty moments, above all by highlighting the experiences of individual participants, *Life* humanized hosts and guests, using photographs less as instruments to probe into intimate details than to establish links between the readers and the subjects.

Life kept the "Party" series until May 1961, when it finally disappeared as part of a larger redesign. The last in the series, titled "Stars Swing Out at Children's Hop," focused on a children's dancing school in California and showed celebrity parents dropping in. It shared the issue with articles covering a John F. Kennedy state visit to Canada and Queen Elizabeth's visit to Italy. *Life*'s June 2, 1961, issue showed its new design, accompanied by the statement "What We Like We Hope You Will Like."[32]

Loudon Wainwright said that the 1950s coverage of "couth" parties and an avoidance of once-popular madcap events was part of a broader editorial concern with social responsibility, as well as the result of anxious hosts and hostesses barring the magazine from events it wanted to cover.[33] This view is not entirely persuasive. *Life* had always been absorbed by staid society affairs, and why would the hosts and hostesses of madcap parties, presumably less concerned than their more retrained counterparts about public opinion, have feared the intrusion of photographers and journalists? *The Philadelphia Story* (1940), perhaps one of the best-known dramatic recreations of reluctant party givers encountering aggressive journalists, was a high society affair, after all.

Life's partying, then, serviced unambiguously traditional modes and long-established popular appetites. Forty years before *Life* existed, Edward S. Martin of *Harper's Weekly*, reproving public fascination with fashionable weddings and balls, concluded, with some resignation, that Americans "like to read of the doings of people whose manner of life is strong contrast to our own, and are entertained, idly perhaps, but with neither envy nor caviling, by the workings of the highly elaborate and artificial apparatuses by means of which they carry on the highly interesting and important

business of having fun."[34] Despite some expectations of radical novelty and populist redemption that marked the magazine's first years, *Life*'s coverage of parties did little more than meet the taste that publishers, editors, and journalists had carefully isolated half a century earlier. Except, *Life* was able to provide hosts and guests with a far more persuasive validation than the society pages of newspapers ever could. In so doing, it reaffirmed the hierarchical values of the larger social establishment, even while trumpeting the virtues of everyday, ordinary life. Having one's cake and eating it too, a perfect party activity, might serve as an appropriate epitaph for this sector of *Life*'s work.

NOTES

1. See, for example, "*Life* Goes to the Collapse of Western Civilization," *New Yorker*, 25 October 1941, 20–22, a spoof of the "Party" feature wherein some New York career girls lightheartedly observe the Axis invasion and bombing of Manhattan.

2. In this, it seems to me, the magazine had parallels with a number of other popular journals, before and since. See, in particular, the analysis offered in the opening pages of Catherine A. Lutz and Jane L. Collins, *Reading* National Geographic (Chicago: University of Chicago Press, 1993), a highly suggestive and significant interpretation.

3. Frank Luther Mott, *American Journalism: A History, 1690–1960* (New York: Macmillan, 1962), 233.

4. These goings-on are detailed in a number of popular descriptions, among them Cleveland Amory, *Who Killed Society?* (New York: Harper, 1960), and Dixon Wecter, *The Saga of American Society: A Record of Social Aspiration, 1607–1937* (New York: Scribners, 1937).

5. The changing technology of handheld cameras was obviously a significant element in such coverage. For such technology, on the British side of the Atlantic, see Ken Baynes et al., *Scoop, Scandal, and Strife: A Study of Photography in Newspapers* (London: Lund Humphreys, 1971). For parallel American developments, see John Szarkowski, *From the Picture Press* (New York: Museum of Modern Art, 1973).

6. Loudon Wainwright, *The Great American Magazine: An Inside History of* Life (New York: Knopf, 1986), 10–11.

7. Editorial, *Life*, 23 November 1936, 3.

8. "*Life* Goes to a Party with French Aristocrats and Sir George Clark," *Life*, 23 November 1936, 90–94.

9. "Belvior Hunt," *Life*, 30 November 1936, 40.

10. "*Life* Goes to a Party with the American Petroleum Institute," *Life*, 30 November 1936, 70–72.

11. "*Life* Goes to a Party," *Life*, 7 December 1936, 70–72.

12. "*Life* Goes to a Party," *Life*, 14 December 1936, 64–68.

13. Again, see the analysis offered in Lutz and Collins, *Reading* National Geographic.

14. Martin Levin, ed., *Hollywood and the Great Fan Magazines* (New York: Arbor House, 1970).

15. "*Life* Goes to a Party," *Life*, 21 December 1936, 68–72.

16. "*Life* Goes to a Party," *Life*, 18 January 1937, 61–65.

17. Ibid., 62.

18. "*Life* Goes to a Party," *Life*, 1 February 1937, 62–64.

19. "*Life* Goes to a Party in Honor of Elsa Maxwell," *Life,* 3 May 1937, 80.

20. Advertisement, *Life,* 3 May 1937, 60–61.

21. Letters to the editor, *Life*, 10 May 1937, 6.

22. Letters to the editor, *Life*, 31 May 1937, 6.

23. "*Life* Goes to a Party," *Life*, 22 February 1937, 62–65.

24. "*Life* Goes to a Party," *Life*, 15 March 1937, 72–75.

25. "A Day in the Life of a Coed," *Life*, 22 March 1937, 44; "Yale Swim-

mers," *Life,* 29 March 1937, 30–32; "Smith College Week-End," *Life,* 29 March 1937, 38–43.

26. *Life,* 7 June 1937, see entire issue.

27. "*Life* Goes to a Party," *Life,* 31 May 1937, 82–84. In this same issue, on page 6, the magazine printed a series of letters of invitation in response to a printed request made several weeks earlier.

28. These were covered respectively, in "*Life* Goes to a Party," *Life,* 21 June 1937, 88–91; "*Life* Goes to a Party," *Life,* 14 June 1937, 84–88; "*Life* Goes to a Party," *Life,* 28 June 1937, 92–96.

29. "*Life* Goes to a Party," *Life,* 17 May 1937, 82–84.

30. See, among others, "*Life* Goes to a Party in Savannah," *Life,* 21 Sep-tember 1941, 100–3; "*Life* Dances," *Life,* 13 October 1941, 140–43; "*Life* Goes to a Navy Party at Fort Schuyler," *Life,* 20 October 1941, 126–29.

31. These were "A Maharaja's Last Fling," *Life,* 5 November 1956, 177–78; "A Gay Gathering in a Gallery," *Life,* 12 November 1956, 209–10; "A Stately Welcome to Society," *Life,* 19 November 1956, 193–94; and "Banjo Jam at Yale," *Life,* 26 November 1956, 193–94.

32. "Stars Swing Out at Children's Hop," *Life,* 26 May 1961, 109–10.

33. Wainwright, *The Great American Magazine,* 249.

34. E. S. Martin, "This Busy World," *Harper's Weekly,* 20 February 1897, 175.

13

JOHN GENNARI

BRIDGING THE TWO AMERICAS

Life *Looks at the 1960s*

"The great thing about *Life* in the 1960s," a friend recently told me, "was that even if you were growing up in a suburban Republican household, your coffee table still had these big, juicy pictures of nude people frolicking in the woods." I too remember those *Life* nudes (Figure 13.1), as well as other hormone-stirring pictures—not, in my case, on the living room coffee table (mine being a working-class household in which the only reading matter was the local newspaper), but in the town library. There, where my fourth-grade buddies and I combed *National Geographic* in search of aboriginal full frontals, one of our crew happened upon the *Life* special edition on Woodstock. Under the galvanizing captions "See Me, Feel Me, Touch Me, Heal Me," "Lay Back and Groove on a Rainy Day," and "With a Little Help from My Friends," we saw what our older siblings and cousins were up to in the name of peace and love, and we liked it (Figure 13.2). My friend's father did not like it. *Life*, as he saw it, had abandoned its loyal, patriotic middle-class readers and, with the country itself, gone careening down a slippery slope toward godless socialism. Before it got there, he canceled his subscription.

Who knows how many other Republicans, or even traditional New Deal Democrats, canceled their subscriptions for similar reasons? Who knows, for that

GALLERY

Above: Figure 13.1. "Gallery," *Life,* December 25, 1969. *Opposite:* Figure 13.2. A young couple kissing, from "See Me, Feel Me, Touch Me, Heal Me," *Life,* August 24, 1969. (Courtesy Bill Eppridge/TimePix)

matter, how many school children, like another friend, figured out how to roll a joint from the October 1969 *Life* photo-essay on marijuana (Figure 13.3)? Or, like another friend, a musician, had their lives changed by a *Life* photo of the Jefferson Airplane? How many, like a Vietnam veteran acquaintance, remember *Life*'s "Faces of the Dead" (Figures 13.4 and 13.5) and its coverage of the My Lai massacre as decisive influences that turned the country against the war?[1] Conversely, how many, like an academic colleague who participated in antiwar protests, remember *Life* as an establishment organ that served as an apologist for the Johnson and Nixon administrations? How many of my fellow late baby boomers, who in the 1960s and early 1970s only looked at *Life*'s pictures, would be as surprised as I was, looking back at the magazine now, to discover how much interesting editorial material the magazine contained?

The July 1960 week I was born, the *Life* magazine that sat in the hospital waiting room was a special issue devoted entirely to that summer's Democratic Party and Republican Party national conventions. The *People* issue I perused at the barbershop recently led with a cover article on "How the Stars Lose Weight." Just what is the relationship between today's widely noted political apathy and Time-Life, Inc.'s, shift—in the death of the weekly *Life* in 1972 followed by the birth of *People* in 1974—from serious political coverage to celebrity tabloidism?

Absent a thorough reader-response survey, such questions must linger in the realm of the anecdotal and the speculative. One thing is clear: the weekly *Life,* in the years leading to its demise in 1972, was an influential magazine that served a diversity of audiences and several ideological, cultural, and generational subcultures within its predominantly white middle-class readership. Indeed, *Life* in the 1960s was speaking to different audiences, and being heard differently, within the same American households. This fracturing of the American popular center posed an acute challenge to *Life*, which, as Wendy Kozol and other scholars have argued, both reflected and shaped the dominant consensus values of the 1950s.[2] Consistent with its founder Henry Luce's missionary worldview, *Life* had always projected a confident optimism and foursquare adherence to the myth of the American Dream. But one had to look no further than the pages of *Life* itself in the 1960s to see the collapse of the consensual values and unitary, imperial national visions that had been cultivated and nurtured by *Life* for three decades.

Life's story on the trial of the Chicago Eight elicited one observer to write that the episode was "an ap-

peasement of America's vast middle class." One reader responded, "we appease the Yippies, the Black Panthers, the s.d.s., the war protesters, the Communists and about every other wild-eyed minority group. So what's so wrong about appeasing America's vast middle class for a change?" Another reader characterized the conspiracy charge against the Chicago protesters as "frighteningly alien to the basic concepts of American law and to any concept of justice."[3] In such high-profile cases, nothing less than the meaning of America was at stake, and *Life*, as sentinel of Henry Luce's "American Century" and as self-anointed public institution, undertook the task of mediating the convulsive national debate over the direction of its politics, its culture, and its social relations. But *Life*, as a large-scale corporate venture, was also in the business of "appeasing America's vast middle class." This was the American middle class that saw its children, as a *Life* editorial put it, take to new drugs the way suburban housewives took to new detergents.[4] It was also the middle class that elected Richard Nixon. Appeasing a class that included both law-and-order hardliners and Los Angeles dinner-party hostesses who, *Life* reported, "have been known to lay out reefers alongside the bread-and-butter plates," was no easy task.[5]

Life tried, and the results, from a quarter-century's distance, make for a fascinating portrait of a country in flux, an entire culture seemingly stretched out on a psychoanalyst's couch trying to locate its true identity and its real desires. *Life* failed to find this identity, and in retrospect its failure may be taken as a foreshadowing of the conflictual public discourse we today experience in the age of the culture wars. *Life*, boasted managing editor Ralph Graves in a parting note in the magazine's 1972 farewell issue, refused to pigeonhole its readers as "skiers, or teen-agers, or car-owners, or TV-watchers, or single women, or suburbanites, or inhabitants of New York City, or blacks, or whites." The magazine aimed to speak "across all barriers and special interests" to "people . . . who share the common experience of humanity."[6] It takes no great critical acumen

Figure 13.3. "Marijuana," *Life,* **October 31, 1969. (Courtesy Co Rentmeester/TimePix)**

to see that *Life* rarely ventured very far beyond the common experiences of Americans who lived in houses with two-car garages, and those who wished that they did. As limiting as *Life*'s ideological centrism was, however, it was flexible enough in the 1960s to permit coverage of the Black Panthers, the Berkeley Free Speech Movement, Woodstock, youth communes, pop art, underground cinema, and Swedish free-form marriages.

Life treated these stories as news, as important developments that informed readers ought to know about. The "new journalism" of Tom Wolfe, Norman Mailer, and others, with its emphasis on the subjective perspective and idiosyncratic voice of the writer, influenced *Life*'s tone (and *Life* turned to Mailer for coverage of Apollo 11), but the real breakthroughs in this style came in *New York, Esquire,* and *Rolling Stone.* Hunter S.

LIFE

**The Faces of
The American Dead
in Vietnam**
ONE WEEK'S TOLL

JUNE 27 · 1969 · 40¢

Figure 13.4. "The Faces
of the American Dead in
Vietnam: One Week's
Toll," *Life,* June 27, 1969.
(Courtesy TimePix)

Thompson, writing in *Rolling Stone,* compared Nixon
to Hitler and described Hubert Humphrey as a "brain-
damaged old vulture" who "should be castrated."[7] Such
"gonzo journalism" never found a home in *Life,* where
Hugh Sidey, in his column "The Presidency," couched
his criticisms in a genteel, archy tone studiously defer-
ential to the assumed aura of its subject. *Life* was not,
to be sure, an organ of the 1960s counterculture: it cov-

ered the era's voices of protest and the visions of alternative lifestyles, worldviews, and cultural sensibilities;
it was not—as *Rolling Stone* claimed to be—the bible of
peace and revolution. Nevertheless, looking at *Life*'s
farewell issue from December 1972, I can understand
my friend's father's sense of betrayal. The last political
word of that issue was given to Democratic Party insider Pierre Salinger. "[In] a time where there are really

VIETNAM ONE WEEK'S DEAD

The faces shown on the next pages are the faces of American men killed—in the words of the official announcement of their deaths—"in connection with the conflict in Vietnam." The names, 242 of them, were released by the Pentagon during the week of May 28 through June 3, a span of no special significance except that it includes Memorial Day. The numbers of the dead are average for any seven-day period during this stage of the war.

It is not the intention of this article to speak for the dead. We cannot tell with any precision what they thought of the political currents which drew them across the world. From the letters of some, it is possible to tell they felt strongly that they should be in Vietnam, that they had great sympathy for the Vietnamese people and were appalled at their enormous suffering. Some had voluntarily extended their tours of combat duty; some were desperate to come home. Their families provided most of these photographs, and many expressed their own feelings that their sons and husbands died in a necessary cause. Yet in a time when the numbers of Americans killed in this war—36,000—though far less than the Vietnamese losses, have exceeded the dead in the Korean War, when the nation continues week after week to be numbed by a three-digit statistic which is translated to direct anguish in hundreds of homes all over the country, we must pause to look into the faces. More than we must know *how many,* we must know *who.* The faces of one week's dead, unknown but to families and friends, are suddenly recognized by all in this gallery of young American eyes.

May 28 - June 3, 1969

Figure 13.5. "Vietnam: One Week's Dead," *Life,* June 27, 1269.

two Americas," Salinger wrote, "I still believe George McGovern could have brought them together."[8]

In the years leading up to *Life*'s folding, it too tried to bring the "two Americas" together. In retrospect, it seems clear that this notion that there were *only* two Americas helped to seal the magazine's fate. In today's niche-oriented media environment, the "common experience of humanity" *is* the pursuit of one's special interest: hence the proliferation of magazines and Internet sites aimed at skiers, teenagers, single women, African Americans. As *Life* reeled toward its doom in the early 1970s, only one editor seemed to foresee this future, and he only in broad outline. According to Loudon Wainwright's account in *The Great American Magazine: An Inside History of* Life (1986), Time-Life veteran Tom Griffith ventured a sinking-ship proposal calling for *Life* to narrow its audience focus to those

under thirty-five. The proposal fell on deaf ears.[9] Griffith, in hindsight, intuited one of the most important legacies of the 1960s: an intensification of America's historic celebration of youth. Today even youth is a highly differentiated media category. American teenage culture is a messy stew of subcultures: pity the poor high school teacher who does not grasp the distinction between Goth and grunge.

"'You're young and therefore hip,' shouts *Details;* 'you're hip and therefore young,' wheezes *Rolling Stone*"—so runs Tom Carson's argument that "successful magazines have always stayed that way by flattering their audience."[10] By 1972 *Life* no longer knew who it was trying to flatter. "The great American magazine had outlived its own strength, was dead on its feet, and its fatal weakness was apparent in every issue," Wainwright wrote: "That weakness was clear in

Life's pitifully skimpy contents, in its obvious uncertainty about the temper and makeup of the audience it wanted to reach in an increasingly fragmented society, in the fact that the audience it did reach generally received it with a detachment far different that the impatient ardor with which subscribers in better days eagerly awaited the postman and buyers snatched it from the newsstands."[11]

When we think of journalism and the 1960s counterculture, we think first of the alternative and underground press: *Village Voice, Boston Phoenix, Ramparts, Berkeley Barb, Los Angeles Free Press*—in all, 350 or so rags serving an estimated 9 million readers.[12] With the exception of *Ramparts,* and later *Rolling Stone* (which before becoming the *Wall Street Journal* of rock and roll fancied itself "a little rock 'n' roll newspaper from San Francisco"), these were neighborhood newspapers defined by a brand of journalism organically linked to the hip ethos and participatory, experiential impulses of the readers they served. The *Barb*'s Dr. Hip Pocrates, for instance, in a widely imitated advice column, doled out information useful for dealing with the snags of the new lifestyle: what to do if your dog swallowed a few tabs of acid, where to get an abortion, how to induce a level of sickness serious enough to hoodwink the draft board in the morning (but not so serious that you could not make the scene at that night's Jefferson Airplane concert). In language ("make the scene"), look (typically a photo-offset typeface, fourfold format, and nonlinear layout), and flair for the outrageous (page 23 of issue no. 5 of *Rolling Stone* featured a photograph of a $4\frac{1}{2}$ inch roach clip, an "essential accessory" promised to new subscribers), the underground and alternative press was one of the places where the 60s generation defined itself *for* itself by communicating *with* itself.

Life represented, in some respects, the antithesis of these journalistic practices and cultural values. As an institution, *Life* functioned in much the same fashion as the political and social establishments it so assiduously covered. In the years after World War II, as Wendy Kozol has convincingly demonstrated, the magazine developed an especially powerful photojournalistic discourse in which the suburban, white, middle-class family served as the cornerstone of national cultural identity.[13] To those postwar baby boomers who ended up identifying with the counterculture, *Life* was seen as a dominant symbol of the culture. "Growing up," remarks photographer Nan Goldin, "I felt it was a challenge to my generation . . . to overthrow *Life* magazine and [its] whole system of communicating with America." In the documentary film *Don't Look Back* (1965), Bob Dylan dresses down a *Time* reporter with a sneering critique aimed at the entire Time-Life, Inc., corporate journalistic approach. "You don't *know* the people who read the magazine. . . . How can you, sitting in an office in New York? Do you really *care* about what you say? I know more about what you do than you'll ever know about me."[14]

Dylan's screed, delivered with the same visceral passion that made his music such a powerful symbol of the era's protest spirit, prophetically evoked the emphasis on the personal and the authentic that animated any number of 1960s assaults on the unfeeling, remote bureaucratic establishment. And yet, in a practical sense, Dylan and other counterculture icons were dependent on that same establishment to cultivate their audiences and to convey their messages. It was not just that the spectacle of Dylan jockeying some earnest, balding *Time* reporter, or Abbie Hoffman beseeching a squarish TV network correspondent to get off his power trip and join the love-in, or Angela Davis denouncing the murderous racism of "the system" were crucial authenticating moments by which the counterculture defined itself. It was also that the existence of this counterculture depended on, and was a product of, the social and material infrastructure constructed out of postwar American affluence. "The counterculture," Kenneth Keniston pointed out in the pages of *Life,* "is in fact a subculture of middle-class white youth, . . . [which] takes for granted the technology, the institutions and the economy necessary to provide its own

material base—a high standard of living, psycho-chemistry, cars, films, electronics, and an enormously prolonged education."[15]

When *Life*, in a long two-issue article in March 1963, first investigated the hallucinogenic "mind-changers" hitting the American scene, it treated the development as a scientific discovery and an expansion of the domains of knowledge and experience: LSD was a "valu-able laboratory tool" that was helping neurochemists better understand the nature of the brain.[16] Three years later, a cover story on LSD art ("A New Experience That Bombards the Senses") dwelled on the "complex integration" of high-tech electronics with avant-garde painting, sculpture, and photography (Figure 13.6). This "drugless trip" appeared in the same issue as a feature on a very different kind of trip, the air war in Vietnam. With its pictures of phosphorous explosives spreading out like tentacles on the burning Vietnamese landscape, this feature bore a noticeable resemblance to the hallucinatory visions photographed in the LSD article.[17]

"A radical conflict of styles can mask a deeper unity of drives and needs," Marshall Berman wrote in his brilliant 1974 essay, "Sympathy for the Devil: Faust, the 60s, and the Tragedy of Development." Faust, with his restless energy to change and grow, would see, Berman trenchantly observed, "how our official culture and our radical 'counter-culture' are animated by the same insatiable lust for development, the same heroic will and energy and largeness of vision and courage to move," and also "the same reckless insensitivity to the lives and needs of people in the way."[18] Dylan went electric around the same time that President Johnson started the bombing campaign in Vietnam—both events signifying impatience with things the way they were, an unquenchable thirst for something more. Antiwar protesters at the Pentagon shouted the words of a Door's song: "We want the world, and we want it now!" The unrecognized irony, Berman lamented, was that Johnson wanted it even more than they did.

In the common cultural coinage of the 1960s everybody wanted more, and the pages of *Life* teemed with evidence of better living through chemistry, electronics, optical physics, engineering, social reform, experimental education, travel, free love, fashion, music, and celebrity. Apollo astronauts shared space with television game-show hosts. Advertisements for enormous cars, appliances, frozen foods, alcohol, cigarettes, insurance, aluminum tennis rackets, and Wonderbread appeared opposite feature stories on communes, free-form weddings, and astrology. A series on the history of revolution, from France in 1789 to Russia in 1917 to Berkeley's Telegraph Avenue in 1969, ran up against a piece titled "The Happy Protest in High School Fashion."[19] *Life's* August 29, 1969, issue ran a ten-page spread on Woodstock (". . . less a musical festival than a total experience, a phenomenon, a happening. . . ."), followed by the first installment of Norman Mailer's "A Fire on the Moon," a piece whose astounding length and typically Mailerian largeness of ambition ("Are we," Mailer asked *Life's* readers, "poised for a philosophical launch?") constituted a journalistic happening in its own right.[20] More experiences, more styles, more sounds, more ideas—an ethos of more fairly courses its way through *Life's* pages in the 1960s. Teeming with images of abundance, *Life* was itself an image of abundance, an icon of American plenty.

Life's ideology of progress could not just accommodate the 1960s zeitgeist; it could appropriate it. *Life* was the nation's leading photo magazine, and the 1960s was the nation's most photogenic decade. Think of moon shots, assassinations, be-ins, protests, miniskirts, Nehru jackets, pop art, underground movies, *Laugh-In*, and the Merry Pranksters, and one senses the way events and experiences accrued significance merely by virtue of their susceptibility to photographic documentation. The singular art form of the period, rock and roll, is as much a visual experience as a musical one, its meanings communicated through costume, lighting, album-cover and poster art, and of course magazine photography. Rock literature, both written criticism and oral history, is so saturated in visual imagery as to take on the feel of a documentary film forever in the making, a kind of celluloid loop doubled back inside a time machine. Listen to Jerry Garcia describing the first Trips Festival in 1966: "People came in total drag—the parking lot was full of cars painted Day-Glo colors and all kinds of crazy things. Nobody had seen any of this stuff before, this was all *brand-new*."[21]

Albert Goldman, later to achieve notoriety as the tendentious biographer of Elvis Presley and John Lennon, was *Life's* rock critic in the late 1960s, and his writing exuded a distinctive pictorial sensibility. His case for Aretha Franklin's superiority, for instance, was made by juxtaposing her blues-rooted authenticity with the "artificial . . . sequin-spangled angst" of the Supremes.[22] Blind Faith's questionable turn to what he called "syncretism" was likened to "the weaving to-

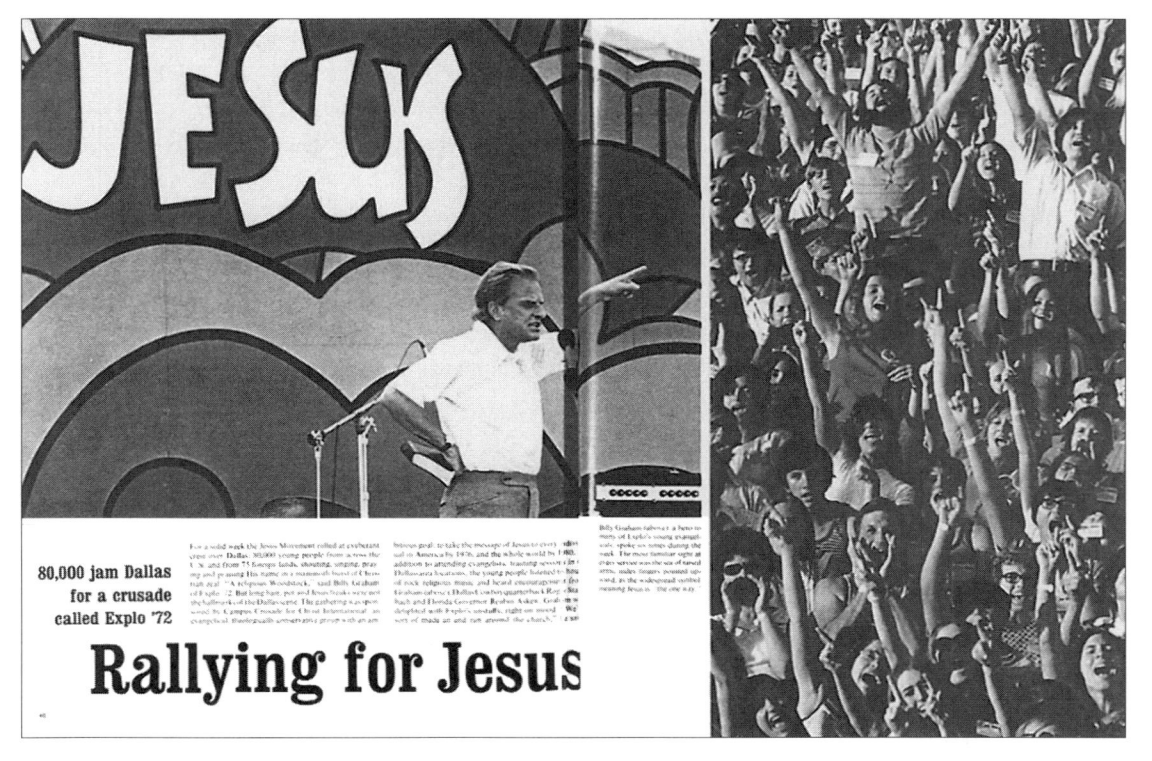

Figure 13.7. "Rallying for Jesus," *Life,* June 30, 1972. (Courtesy Heinz Kluetmeier/TimePix)

gether, like a hippies' costume, of the faded finery of other years."[23] The problem with casting Johnny Winter as the Great White Hope of the blues revival was that he was, well, too white—"a pure albino glowing eerily onstage like the pop-art ghost of some long gone black musician." When Goldman wrote a feature essay intended to help readers "experience the Age of Rock full-blast and to begin to grasp its weird complexities," he began with a description of a Saturday night at the Electric Circus, New York's most elaborate discotheque, where dancers faces are "marked with phosphorescent insignia" and where a "blinding white strobe light flashes across [a dancer's] body, chopping her absurd actions into the frames of an ancient flickering movie."[24]

In an essay often cited as the leading aesthetic manifesto of the 1960s, Susan Sontag called for a "new sensibility" that redeemed the body and the senses from an overly cerebral approach to culture. Calling for the displacement of literature, with its "heavy burden of content," by arts "with much less content and a much cooler mode of moral judgement—like music, films, dance, architecture, painting, sculpture," Sontag crafted what seems in retrospect a seminal postmodernist critique of institutionalized, academicized modernism. Endorsing camp, pop art, Motown, Marat/Sade, the cinema ("the most alive, the most exciting, the most important of the art forms right now"), and other artifacts and experiences now synonymous with the 1960s, Sontag advocated not only erasing the traditional elite-culture/popular-culture divide, but also changing the way we respond to art. "In place of a hermeneutics ['the effusions of interpretations of art' which 'poison our sensibilities . . . like the fumes of the automobile']," Sontag wrote, "we need an erotics of art."[25]

But if we follow Marshall McLuhan's dictum that

"the medium is the message"—as memorable a sixties soundbite as the eponymous "power to the people" or Jim Morrison's "break on through to the other side"—we come upon a hitch in Sontag's otherwise refreshing stance. Sontag's primary 1960s medium was *The New York Review of Books*, undeniably an important forum for the tumultuous intellectual politics of the period, but not by any stretch of the imagination a pioneer of the "new sensibility" that Sontag was advocating. Ask yourself to make up a list of adjectives to describe the look, feel, and general ambience of *The New York Review of Books*, and I dare say the word "erotic" does not make the list.

Life, though certainly not the standard bearer of the 1960s cultural sensibility, was not shy about new sensations, angles, and modes of consciousness and experience. A fascinating ten-page article by Gloria Steinem on "The Ins and Outs of Pop Culture" appeared in 1965, complete with a "A Vest-Pocket Guide to Camp" and a picture of Steinem in a Flash Gordon costume. The caption read, "As the author in Flash Gordon clothes demonstrates, there is only one thing that really counts: The Fun."[26]

A 1965 profile of Norman Mailer gave vent to his doctrines of sexual and pharmaceutical laissez-faire, took half-seriously his talk of an "existential" presidential candidacy, and approvingly described his famous all-night parties as "the boozy nightbloom of [Mailer's] own inexhaustible cool."[27] A 1967 cover story on "The Other Culture" introduced author Barry Farrell as "an explorer of the Underground of art [who] finds, behind its orgiastic Happenings and brutalities, a wild Utopian dream."[28]

That same year, *Life* gave its prized first-string film critic's slot to recent college grad Richard Schickel, who proceeded to focus almost entirely on underground films like *Putney Swope*, *The Wild Bunch*, and *Alice's Restaurant*. Films such as these, and others targeted at specialized adult audiences, represented Hollywood's retrenchment from a golden era in which films like *Gone with the Wind* and *The Philadelphia Story* were made

with the expectation of universal appeal. After Hollywood's production code office edited the frankest scenes of Michelangelo Antonioni's *Blow-Up* out of its American release, *Life* published stills of these scenes and unflinchingly discussed the movie's "naked rompings, casual sexuality, pot parties, [and] rock 'n' roll riots."[28]

Life's engagement with new cultural developments took place within the confines of a traditional ideology of journalistic professionalism. When a *Village Voice* reporter returned from a major antiwar protest in Washington, D.C., with no story because, as he told his editor, he had spent three days getting stoned, the editor took it in stride. One cannot easily imagine *Life* editors, who saw their publication as first and foremost a news magazine, abiding such a breach of professionalism in favor of a lifestyle priority. Like all major mainstream media institutions, *Life* hewed strongly to a professional code of objectivity, or at least the appearance of such. Out of an evident concern for "balanced coverage" of college student life, *Life* covered not just student rebellion at Columbia and Berkeley, but also student quiescence at Seton Hall and Indiana University.[30] An October 1969 photo-essay on Jimi Hendrix, featuring psychedelia-influenced photographs depicting "the scene of today in the colors of today," was paired with a series of time-lapse photos of a Jerome Robbins ballet, the effect being to balance rock music's avant-primitivism with ballet's mature classicism.[31] A 1969 update on trends in Hollywood carefully paired Dustin Hoffman in *The Graduate* with John Wayne in *True Grit*, implicitly applauding the film industry's (and *Life's* own) sensitivity to pluralist taste cultures and divergent political sensibilities. A June 1972 cover story on "The Great Jesus Rally in Dallas," a nine-hour rock festival dubbed a "religious Woodstock" by Billy Graham, showed a benign American youth culture safe from even paranoiac Nixon administration censure (Figure 13.7). According to the story, not one of the 150,000 participants called the Dallas police "pigs."[32]

The fracturing of America's popular center in the

1960s was no clearer than in *Life's* "Letters to the Editors" page. With the exception of the first Vietnam "Faces of the Dead" feature (in which twenty-six of the thirty respondents published staked out an antiwar position), on all the major social and cultural issues of the day *Life's* readers appeared to sort themselves into fairly neat "for" and "against" cohorts.[33] The impression created—and we must remember that magazine editors routinely filter and select reader mail for publication—is one of *Life* as a forum for vivid and healthy public debate and a catalyst of spirited national passions in which both sides of the story have their airing.

Response to an April 1965 photo-essay on student antiwar protests is illustrative. One letter praised college activists for "taking themselves and their world seriously," and offering "hope in a world too filled with despair." Another said that "the university is a place to learn about the world, not to change it," while yet another beseeched students, before they dismiss America's "two cars in the garage" civilization, to recognize that "this system has after all given them the leisurely opportunity to pursue the highest ideals of brotherhood and social welfare."[34] Likewise, one writer years later noted that *Life's* coverage on communes (Figure 13.8) appeared in the same issue as a story on Apollo 11, and the reader wondered "what those communal dropouts from life hope to prove or gain by turning their backs on . . . the ever-increasing development of human capabilities." Another reader, taking the opposite stance, reported that his "excitement for the moon shot was overshadowed by the beautiful [cover] picture [of a family living on a commune]," which "showed the real hope for mankind—people trying to harmonize with nature instead of conquering it."[35]

Life's coverage of Woodstock similarly elicited a split decision on the direction of American youth. "Maybe this will be our society's solution to the troubled young—electro-chemical pacification. Grass and circuses, as it were," read one curmudgeonly response. A mother, as if in direct response, stood up for her Wood-stock-attending son and nephew, "decent" American youth for whom three days in the rain on Max Yasgur's farm "was nothing new because the same thing happened one year at Boy Scout camp."[36]

Life's hope of speaking "across all barriers and special interests" to "the common experience of humanity" was a tall order given the cultural divisions evidenced in these kinds of letters. Clearly disquieted by mounting conflict in the culture at large, *Life* editors made an effort to bridge the generation gap. Introductions of young reporters and photographers in the "Editor's Note" column opposite the table of contents showed snapshots of long-haired recent college graduates ready and eager to offer *Life* readers their fresh perspectives—and to do so, the managing editor was happy to say, using time-honored journalistic techniques and the commitment to excellence and integrity enshrined in the *Life* tradition. Photographer John Dominis, who shot the feature on Dustin Hoffman and John Wayne, was himself featured in a Ralph Graves "Editor's Note" column titled "Bridging Two Worlds." "The two men [Wayne and Hoffman] are the best examples I know of the way America seems to be polarizing," Graves quoted Dominis. Claiming allegiance to Hoffman's worldview ("urban, young, liberal, intellectual, and basically pessimistic about the future"), Dominis reported nevertheless to have found common ground with Wayne, the "super Western conservative." Though "intellectually attracted more to Hoffman," the Duke was a real "man's man" who would make much better company "if I were getting up a poker game or a fishing trip to Canada."[37]

A young photographer who was hip and sensitive but also knew a Hemingwayesque male bonding opportunity when he saw it could certainly do well at *Life*, a magazine that in the 1960s published both Gloria Steinem and Norman Mailer; a magazine that in 1971 ran a cover photo of Germaine Greer with the caption, "Saucy Feminist That Even Men Like."[38] Feminism without gender warfare; youth commune dwellers honoring "a tradition of American utopianism going back to Brook Farm and Walden"; teenagers at rock concerts not calling police pigs—*Life* was more than happy to accommodate new social trends that appeared to pose no grave threat to the old order.[39] After running a story on how the American flag had become a lightning rod for cultural divisiveness—some Americans brandishing it in public displays of their support for the government, some (such as black baseball star–turned civil rights activist Jackie Robinson) refusing to honor it

until the country lived up to its ideals, and some (like antiwar activists) defacing it—*Life* received a letter from perhaps its ideal reader, a reader perfectly in sync with the values *Life* was trying to advance. "I have [an American flag] on my car window," wrote Cobey Dorf-man of Hollywood, California. "Right next to it I have a peace symbol and a sticker that says 'Love.' I believe it is possible to love your country, be a friend to Jackie

Figure 13.8. "The Youth Communes: New Way of Living Confronts the U.S.," *Life*, July 18, 1969. (Courtesy John Olson/ TimePix)

Robinson and be a fan of both John Wayne and Dustin Hoffman. Isn't that what this country is supposed to be about?"[40]

Life's management certainly thought so. In the magazine's farewell issue in 1972, managing editor Ralph Graves cited a "touching" letter from an eleven-year-old girl. "[*Life*] has always been my favorite magazine," wrote Marta Flanagan of Little Neck, New York. "It has articles which interest everybody in the family." In the hope that "my children will know about my childhood," the enterprising sixth grader resolved to make a scrapbook of all of her favorite *Life* articles. *Life* editor-in-chief Hedley Donovan took the occasion to scan his own mental scrapbook for memories of his initial contact with *Life* in the 1930s. For this worldly young man studying in England, the sweeping scope of *Life's* photographs—FDR's "expressive face" counterpoised with "a good-looking Kappa cheerleader at Northwestern," a showering Russian peasant juxtaposed with a strutting Mussolini and a Spanish militiawoman ready to do battle—was such as to quicken the pulse with a heady cosmopolitan excitement. The "common experience of humanity," the experience that connects children to parents and grandparents, Americans with the rest of the world, fans of John Wayne with fans of Dustin Hoffman, remained, Graves suggested, "important to our country."[41]

Unfortunately, *Life* would no longer be able to make that contribution to the American public. Since Graves's eulogy neglected to specify what made *Life's* last years "very difficult," the magazine's readers were left, as an explanation for *Life's* folding, with Donovan's plea of a fiscally suicidal but morally uncompromising commitment to quality in a time of skyrocketing production and distribution costs.

After turning a $10 million profit in 1966, the second most profitable year in the magazine's history, *Life* had lost over $40 million over its last four years. Advertising revenues had fallen off sharply as more and more firms shifted their marketing campaigns to television. An ill-conceived acquisition of the defunct *Saturday Evening*

Post subscription list had ratcheted circulation up to an artificially high level. With ad revenues running farther and farther behind increased printing and shipping costs, *Life* succumbed to the magazine world's version of anorexia: in its last year the magazine ran at roughly eighty pages an issue, half or one-third its size from the salad days of the 1950s and early 1960s.[42] The pioneering influence of what Donovan termed *Life's* "visual vitality" on print journalism, advertising, and television notwithstanding, it was now detrimental to the interests of "*Life's* readers and advertisers, our staff, and the stockholders of Time, Inc.," for *Life* to continue.[43]

In *Life's* death, we see the tropes of family, historical memory, an undifferentiated (and presumably unified) American populace, civic purpose, and corporate responsibility yoked together under the umbrella rubric of universal humanism. Given such a lofty purpose, *Life's* exit could not, properly, be *simply* a matter of the escalating price of paper or the creeping visual hegemony of television; it had to be emblematic of a full-scale cultural transformation, a shifting of the tectonic plates of national destiny. It is this self-important tone that permeates *Life's* final issue. *Life* at its last would not, it was clear, abandon its envied position in the lofty precincts of political officialdom. Its attention focused as ever on the trappings of power, the issue featured a three-page spread on President Nixon's diplomatic triumphs in China and the USSR. The largeness of *Life's* pages often lending grandeur and majesty to its photographic subjects, Nixon's elephantine jowls here appeared not as fodder for satire, but as signs of a kind of statesmanlike gravity. As if to underline the presidentialness of the president's achievements, the Nixon feature was preceded by a commemoration of Harry Truman and followed by a Hugh Sidey column praising the ailing LBJ for lending his magnanimous presence to a civil rights symposium at the Johnson Library.

Fittingly, however, the specter of Vietnam hung over this final issue. A pair of fold-out photo spreads at the front of the issue pointed out U.S. failure in Vietnam. In "The Peace That Soured," a picture of Henry Kissinger dining in the elegant U.S. ambassador's residence in Paris "before negotiations failed" was set against a picture of a U.S. military adviser ("one of 24,900 U.S. troops left in Vietnam") encamped in a Mekong Delta outpost. Turning the page, Life readers encountered "The Waste of War," two extra-wide–angle photographs showing the shattering effects of the U.S. bombing campaign in North Vietnam and the obliteration of the southern city of Quangtri.[44]

These disheartening images could have served as a metaphor for Life's own internal problems. In a mid-October 1972 editorial written by Donovan and his deputy Louis Banks, the magazine had gone on public record as supporting Richard Nixon for a second term. According to Loudon Wainwright, Graves had pushed for some language that upbraided Nixon for his failures in Vietnam, and a petition signed by 100 (of 145) of the editorial staff asked that the magazine publicly acknowledge the staff's support for McGovern. Their request for space was denied. Like the country itself, the magazine was rent by internal division; not unlike the Nixon White House, Life's management responded by lapsing into a sullen defensiveness. "For all of its techniques, skills, and good intentions," Wainwright later reflected:

the magazine seemed somehow out of sync with the tumultuous times, showing its middle age, truly aghast at hippies and dope and the counterculture, sensitive to attacks on the "establishment," shocked at the depth and violence at the protest against the root inequalities of the system, fighting off the enveloping possibility that the truth about the war was that we weren't going to win it, that we were, in fact, going to have to get out of Vietnam. Suddenly, it seemed, America had too many faces, and Life was having trouble keeping track of its own.[45]

Evident in the look of the magazine, Life's facial deformation was even more transparent than its political tensions. Wainwright was probably right in his speculation that "the readers themselves were just not finding the pleasure and punch they wanted in Life's shrinking issues."[46] The problem was not just one of size: just about any given page from an issue from 1971 or 1972 lacked the visual boldness, sumptuous texture, and sensual charge of a random page from an issue ten or fifteen years earlier. This was especially true of the advertisements. The ads in Life's late 1972 issue for 1973 Oldsmobiles look pretty fulsome—until you go back and look at the ads for the 1956 Fords. Back then, Ford and the other major car manufacturers bought multi-page over-the-fold spreads showing their entire fleet in bright Technicolor images, festooned with families engaged in recreational activity.[47] By the early 1970s the typical car ad was a single page (or less) featuring one model cast in a comparatively static vignette: the fuller auto sociodramas now ran on television, where images of cars and the people operating them actually moved.

Up to the mid-1960s Life was full of food advertisements, gaudy visual feasts that symbolized postwar middle-class affluence. Wesson Oil, to take one example of many, regularly took out two-page spreads picturing heaping platters of fried chicken, french-fried shrimp, and tuna-boat croquettes. Snow Crop filled whole pages with photographs of extra-plump lima beans and super-pulpy orange juice. But food advertisements had all but disappeared from Life by 1972. In an episode that perfectly captures the ideological muddle that Life had become, the magazine lost General Foods, one of its last big food accounts, when an ad for Birds Eye's turkey dinner appeared in the middle of a story about the dangers that the pesticide DDT posed to America's bird population.[48] In the end, there was no easy way to bridge the "Two Americas"—the new environmentally conscious America and the old America of the corporate bottom line—and the consequences for Life were fatal.

In his chronicle of America in the 1960s, Todd Gitlin wrote, "it seemed especially true that History with a capital H had come down to earth, either interfering with life or making it possible; and that within History, or threaded through it, people were living with a supercharged density: lives were bound up with one another, making claims on one another, drawing one another into the common project."[49] Gitlin is a histo-rian and a specialist in mass-media studies, but here he speaks as a participant in the events that defined the 1960s, notably the civil rights, free speech, and antiwar movements. When he speaks of "lives bound up . . . into the common project," he means a shared sense of purpose connecting those who experienced firsthand the freedom rides, the campus uprisings, the be-ins, the march on the Pentagon, and Woodstock. If Gitlin's no-tion of an apotheosis of history, of a people self-reflexively aware of their own involvement in events of significance, is true of the student radicals, hippies, and others who thought of themselves as "the 60s genera-tion," it is also true of those (such as Nixon's "silent ma-jority") who defined themselves *against* that genera-tion, of those (like myself) who were too young to participate in the 1960s modal events but old enough to experience them vicariously through media repre-sentations and hand-me-down folklore from older sib-lings and relatives, and even of those not yet born (today's college students) who have lately spearheaded a lively revival of 1960s music, clothing, language, and contraband chemicals. The decade functions for all of these groups as a touchstone, a turning point, a crucial reckoning with large cultural and political forces, and a time when important things happened that changed America forever.

In the movie *Forrest Gump* (1994), a leading example of Hollywood's 1990s historically amnesiac revision of post–World War II America, there is a hilarious se-quence in which Gump wanders *Zelig*-like in and out of

black-and-white television footage of Governor George Wallace standing up to black students who are trying to integrate the University of Alabama. We see Gump through a television set in a Southern barbershop. Three stereotyped rednecks stare at the screen in utter incredulity. The barber, in the middle, looks ready to lunge into the television screen to run his straight-edge razor across Gump's neck. He is flanked on either side by a pair of locals also overcome with apoplexy. Each holds in his hands—the detail I am interested in—a copy of *Life* magazine.

Since its inception in the 1930s, *Life* had arrogated to itself the role of defining an American common project. It had provided images and words for experi-ences, ideas, and desires that it presumed to capture a shared public imagination. By 1972, however, with America at war with itself, it became impossible for *Life* any longer to project a clear, unambiguous, and con-sensual vision of American life. As its prop placement in *Forrest Gump* suggests, *Life* had become associated with domestic conflict, discord, and disunity. To sug-gest harmony, tranquility, and common passions, di-rector Robert Zemeckis had to turn to another product of the Time-Life media empire. In the opening and closing scenes of the movie, Gump sits on a bus stop bench, telling his story to a black woman. Annoyed at first, by the end she hangs on Gump's every word, riv-eted by his poignant tale, emotionally bonded with this utter stranger. Throughout the narration, she holds a copy of *People*.

NOTES

1. In a personal interview with me, Vietnam veteran Michael Reade re-ports that in his duty as a training officer for the army's 73rd Infantry Battalion, unwilling draftees came with copies of *Life*'s "One Week's Dead" and My Lai massacre coverage to show their disdain for the war and the military.

2. Wendy Kozol, *Life's America: Family and Nation in Postwar Photo-journalism* (Philadelphia: Temple University Press, 1994).

3. Letters to the editor, *Life*, 8 August 1969, 16A.

4. "The Nixon Drug Law: A Crucial Fault," *Life*, 5 September 1969, 32.

5. Ibid.

6. Ralph Graves, "With Pride and Affection," *Life*, 29 December 1972, 96.

7. Robert Draper, *Rolling Stone Magazine: The Uncensored History* (New York: Doubleday, 1990), 186.

8. Pierre Salinger, "Four Blows That Crippled McGovern's Campaign," *Life*, 29 December 1972, 80.

9. Loudon Wainwright, *The Great American Magazine: An Inside Story of Life* (New York: Knopf, 1986), 417–18.

10. Tom Carson, "She, Tina," *Village Voice*, 21 July 1998, 47.

11. Wainwright, *The Great American Magazine*, 419.

12. Godfrey Hodgson, *America in Our Time* (New York: Doubleday, 1976), 342.

13. Kozol, *Life's America*, 11–15, and passim.

14. Bruce Hainley, "Nan Goldin at the Matthew Marks Gallery," *Artforum* 33 (May 1995): 97; *Don't Look Back* (film), dir. D. A. Pennebacker, USA, 1967.

15. Kenneth Keniston, "Young Radicals," *Life*, 27 May 1966, 75.

16. Robert Coughlan, "The Chemical Mind-Changers," *Life*, 15 March 1963, 81–94.

17. "Psychedelic Art" and "The Air War," *Life*, 9 September 1966, 60–69, 44–59.

18. Marshall Berman, "Sympathy for the Devil: Faust, the 60s, and the Tragedy of Development," *American Review* 19 (January 1974); reprinted in *The Sixties: Art, Politics, and Media of Our Most Explosive Decade*, ed. Gerald Howard (New York: Paragon, 1991), 495–504.

19. "The Happy Protest in High School Fashion," *Life*, 10 October 1969, 40–45.

20. "The Big Woodstock Rock Trip," and Norman Mailer, "A Fire on the Moon," *Life*, 29 August 1969, 14b–23, 24–41.

21. Hal Espen, "American Beauty: The Grateful Dead's Burly, Beatific Alchemist," *New Yorker*, 21 and 28 August 1995, 12.

22. Albert Goldman, "Detroit Retools Its Rock," *Life*, 25 July 1969, 12.

23. Albert Goldman, "The Blind Lead the Way-Out," *Life*, 26 September 1969, 28.

24. Albert Goldman, "The Emergence of Rock," *New American Review* 3 (April 1968); reprinted in *The Sixties*, 343–64.

25. Susan Sontag, "One Culture and the New Sensibility," in Susan Sontag, *Against Interpretation* (New York: Farrar, Strauss, 1966), 293–304.

26. Gloria Steinem, "The Ins and Outs of Pop Culture," *Life*, 20 August 1965, 72–89.

27. "A First-Rank Writer's Reckless Quest for—What?" *Life*, 24 September 1965, 94–117.

28. "The Other Culture," *Life*, 17 February 1967, 86–102.

29. "Antonioni's Hypnotic Eye on the Frantic World," *Life*, 27 January 1967, 62–67.

30. "The Campus That Kept Its Cool: Seton Hall's Quiet Revolution," *Life*, 7 November 1969, 80–90. "Who Says College Kids Have Changed?" *Life*, 19 May 1967, 90–100.

31. "An Infinity of Jimis" and "Dance at a Gathering," *Life*, 3 October 1969, 72–76, 42–51.

32. "Rallying for Jesus," *Life*, 30 June 1972, 40–45.

33. Letters to the editors, *Life*, 18 July 1969, 16A. Devoted entirely to feedback on the June 27 story, these letters serve as a poignant document of American grief over the war. "No peace demonstrations, no dovish editorial, no antiwar speech could approach the mute eloquence of those young faces," wrote R. W. Wadsworth of Columbus, Indiana. "My cousin was one of the faces of American men killed in Vietnam," wrote Geraldine Barrett of Saratoga, California. "The 'faces' show us that these young men are all our cousins, brothers, husbands, and sons." "My husband is presently serving his year there and each face in that article is his face," wrote Mrs. John Weyland of Wyandotte, Michigan. "I cried for those 18 to 20 Southern black soldiers," wrote Carol Kryd of Avon Lake, Ohio. "What did they die for? Tar paper shacks, malnutrition, unemployment, and degradation?" Resigned Marine Corps Capt. G. L. Guenther wrote, "Certainly these tragic young men were far superior to the foreign policy they were called upon to defend." Of the thirty letters printed, only four criticized *Life*'s story. While most thought the spectacle of young American faces would be an effective and necessary tactic in forcing the government to end the war, one respondent took the opposite position. "Almost all of us know someone who has lost his life there and we were grieved by it," wrote Mary Scherman of Kansas City. "There is enough dissension and unrest about this war and in my opinion your article will do far more damage than good."

34. "Students in a Ferment Chew Out the Nation," *Life*, 30 April 1965, 24–33; letters to the editors, *Life*, 21 May 1965, 27. See also Lynn Schofield Clark, "Who Read the Berkeley Riot Coverage and What Did They Think of It? A Review of Responses to *Life*'s Coverage of a Controversial Event," seminar paper, University of Colorado, November 1995.

35. Letters to the editor, *Life*, 8 August 1969, 16A.

36. Letters to the editor, *Life*, 26 September 1969, 3A.

37. "Bridging Two Worlds," *Life*, 11 July 1969, 1.

38. *Life*, 7 May 1971, cover.

39. "A Divided Decade—The 60s," *Life*, 26 December 1969, special double issue.

40. Letters to the editor, *Life*, 8 August 1969, 16A.

41. Graves, "With Pride and Affection," 96; Hedley Donovan, "*Life*'s Last Issue: A Message to Our Readers," *Life*, 29 December 1972, 1.

42. Wainwright, *The Great American Magazine*, 336, 346–47, 419, 423.

43. Donovan, "*Life*'s Last Issue," 1.

44. "The Peace That Soured" and "The Waste of Ware," *Life*, 29 December 1972, 2–3, 4–5.

45. Wainwright, *The Great American Magazine*, 339.

46. Ibid., 412.

47. See, for instance, the Ford ad in *Life*, 12 March 1956, 138–39.

48. The Bird's Eye ad appears on page 51 of the issue of January 22, 1971. Wainwright reports on the General Foods decision to pull its advertising from *Life* in *The Great American Magazine*, 373.

49. Todd Gitlin, *The Sixties: Years of Hope, Days of Rage* (New York: Bantam, 1987), 7.

CONTRIBUTORS

JAMES L. BAUGHMAN is professor of journalism and mass communication at the University of Wisconsin, Madison. He is the author of *Republic of Mass Culture: Journalism, Filmmaking, and Broadcasting in America Since 1941*, 2d ed. (1997), and *Henry R. Luce and the Rise of the American News Media*, rev. ed. (2001).

ERIKA DOSS is professor of art history at the University of Colorado, Boulder, where she also directs the American Studies Program. She is the author of numerous articles and books including *Benton, Pollock, and the Politics of Modernism: From Regionalism to Abstract Expressionism* (1991), *Spirit Poles and Flying Pigs: Public Art and Cultural Democracy in American Communities* (1995), *Elvis Culture: Fans, Faith, and Image* (1999), and the forthcoming *Twentieth-Century American Art* (2002).

BRETT GARY is assistant professor in modern history and literature at Drew University. He is the author of *The Nervous Liberals: Propaganda Anxieties from World War I to the Cold War* (1999) and is currently researching the Commission on Freedom of the Press and post–World War II anxieties about media industry consolidation, press freedoms, and public competence.

JOHN GENNARI is assistant professor of English and ethnic studies at the University of Vermont. His book *Canonizing Jazz: An*

American Art and Its Critics is forthcoming from the University of Chicago Press. His essay, "Passing for Italian: Crooners and Gangsters in Crossover Culture," appeared in *Transition* (1997).

PETER BACON HALES is a professor and university scholar in the Art History Department of the University of Illinois, Chicago, where he is also director of the American Studies Institute. His books include *Silver Cities: The Photography of American Urbanization (1984), William Henry Jackson and the Transformation of the American Landscape* (1988), and *Atomic Spaces: Living on the Manhattan Project* (1998). He is currently completing two books: a study of postwar American cultural landscapes, and an investigation of global cultural spaces, virtual and physical, at the turn of the millennium.

NEIL HARRIS is Preston and Sterling Morton Professor of American History at the University of Chicago. A cultural historian, his most recent book is *Building Lives: Constructing Rites and Passages* (1999).

JOHN IBSON is professor of American studies at California State University, Fullerton. He is the author of *Will the World Break Your Heart? Dimensions and Consequences of Irish-American Assimilation* (1990) and *Picturing Men Together: The Lost Variety of Male Relationships in a Century of American Photography* (forthcoming).

WENDY KOZOL is associate professor of women's studies at Oberlin College. She is the author of Life*'s America: Family and Nation in Postwar Photojournalism* (1994) and *Haunting Violations: Feminist Criticism and the Crisis of the "Real,"* edited with Wendy Hesford (2001). She has also published articles on television news, documentary photography, and news coverage of domestic violence in anthologies and journals such as *Genders* and *Signs*. She is currently working on a book about government agencies' reliance on visual media to represent violence and trauma experienced by its own populations.

KELLY ANN LONG is assistant professor in the Department of History at Colorado State University. She serves as a reviewer and contributor for *Education about Asia Magazine,* has published articles about the contributions of Helen Foster Snow (aka Nym Wales) to U.S.-China relations, and is featured as Snow's biographer in the documentary film *Witness to Revolution.*

The late ROLAND MARCHAND was a professor in the Department of History, University of California, Davis, and author of numerous important articles and books including *Advertising the American Dream: Making Way for Modernity, 1920–1940* (1985) and *Creating the Corporate Soul: The Rise of Public Relations and Corporate Imagery in American Big Business* (1998).

DAVID MORGAN holds the Duesenberg Chair in Christianity and the Arts at Valparaiso University. He is the author of *Visual Piety: A History and Theory of Popular Religious Images* (1998) and *Protestants and Pictures: Religion, Visual Culture, and the Age of American Mass Production* (1999). He is coeditor, with Sally M. Promey, of *The Visual Culture of American Religions* (2001).

TERRY SMITH is Power Professor of Contemporary Art and director of the Power Institute, Foundation for Art and Visual Culture, University of Sydney. He is the author of a number of books, most recently *Figuring the Ground: Landscape, Colony, and Nation in Nineteenth-Century Australian Art* (2001) and *Transformations: Modernism and Aboriginality in Twentieth-Century Australian Art* (2001), and editor of *In Visible Touch: Modernism and Masculinity* (1997) and *Impossible Presence: Surface and Screen in the Photogenic Era* (2001).

RICKIE SOLINGER is a historian and author of *Beggars and Choosers: How the Politics of Choice Shapes Abortion, Adoption, and Welfare in the United States* (2001), *Wake Up Little Susie: Single Pregnancy and Race before Roe v. Wade* (1992, 2000), and *The Abortionist: A Woman against the Law* (1994). She is an independent scholar.

INDEX

Page numbers in italics refer to illustrations.